1000
Wonders of the World

1000
Wonders of
the World

NGV

© Naumann & Göbel Verlagsgesellschaft mbH,
a subsidiary of VEMAG Verlags- und Medien Aktiengesellschaft, Cologne
www.vemag-medien.de

Author: Friedemann Bedürftig
Translated from German: Maureen Millington-Brodie p. 1–185,
Marian Cairns p. 186–297, John Kinory p. 298–375

Complete production: Naumann & Göbel Verlagsgesellschaft mbH, Cologne
Printed in China

Foreword

The Ancients were quite modest in terms of the number of their World Wonders: they knew just seven. Among them, for example, the Hanging Gardens of Babylon, the Colossus of Rhodes and the Lighthouse of Alexandria, on the former island of Pharos. Most of these masterpieces have long fallen into ruins and been forgotten, with the exception of the Egyptian pyramids which still remain today, maintaining the link between ancient and modern times.

Over the centuries, more and more riches have gathered, in addition to the old treasures of mankind. The new science of archaeology, which came into being in the 18th century, in the wake of the Enlightenment, brought to light new evidence of ancient cultures long thought lost – and these included not only ancient civilisations such as the Valley of the Kings in Egypt or the magnificent buildings of the Incas and Aztecs in South America, but also considerably older finds such as the prehistoric rock and cave paintings, which were gradually discovered on all continents.

Since the industrial revolution, these and other sites of cultural and natural heritage have been under threat from progressive destruction of the environment. Therefore, in 1972, UNESCO passed the Convention for the Protection of the World Cultural and Natural Heritage and has so far listed about 812 buildings, structures, monuments and Nature Parks as World Heritage Sites. Thus we can now easily name thousands of impressive monuments, prehistoric finds, breathtaking architectural masterpieces of the modern age and unique natural landscapes that deserve the title 'Wonder of the World'. This book brings together 1000 of them and as such presents as diverse a picture as possible of the treasures of the Earth.

The Wonders of the World are listed roughly in order of their geographical location from North to South. Extensive sites such as, for example, landscapes or rivers are shown either with just one dot representing their centre or with two dots marking their beginning and end. It should be noted that islands such as, for example, Madeira, Greenland or Hawaii have been allocated to the continent they are nearest to from a geographical point of view, rather than the country they belong to politically.

Of course, we cannot claim that our selection contains all the Wonders of the World. Instead, the sites described and illustrated in this book may serve as an incentive to discover the world's beautiful and precious sites for yourself. But first of all, this book invites you on a journey around the globe – to the Wonders of the World.

The Publisher and Editorial Team

Contents

Europe   8   Asia   186   Africa   262

North and Central America 298

South America 338

Australia and Oceania 360

Index 376

Europe

The Beauty and the Bull

Our brothers and sisters across the big pond are not usually known to suffer from an inferiority complex. And yet, they can't help being overcome by a feeling of envy when standing in front of buildings in 'good old Europe' that are several times older than their nation as a whole.

Of course there is no merit in age alone, but the more there is of the past the fuller is the treasure chest. This is combined with a richness of natural wonders scarcely to be found in such variety anywhere else. Climatically, the zones involved range from the polar North as far as the sub-tropical South; from

the tundras to the olive groves where long ago the beautiful nymph Europa met Zeus disguised as a bull — the old world, a child of divine love.

Iceland

Geysers *(right)*

65 million years ago, the earth's crust tore open between Greenland and Scandinavia, magma burst forth and rose higher and higher. A little over 50 million years later, the now cooled mountain rose above sea level, thus giving birth to iceland. The new island found no rest, as tremors went on close to the surface, geysers shot up, a total of 30 in all, including Strokkur (butter barrel) in the Haukadalur thermal field. Choose the wrong moment to look at it and its basin seems like a millpond, but then, no more than 10 minutes later, the surface swells and a fountain of boiling hot water shoots up 25 metres into the air. Many places on Iceland pulsate like this, places where the visitor, unlike anywhere else, so clearly feels that the Earth is alive.

Vatnajökull, Hvannadalshnúkur *(below)*

Twelve per cent of the Icelandic island is covered by glaciers, and the lion's share is found on Vatnajökull, the 2,119 metre high mountain range in the south-east. In some places the ice sheet is up to 1,000 metres thick and the giant glacier covers a total area of 8,300 square kilometres. In addition, it covers several volcanoes which, when they erupt, melt whole areas of glacier causing floods of melt water to stream forth from under the ice sheet and threatening the infrastructure of the island: in 1996 such a flood washed away a large part of the road along the south coast.

Norway

North Cape *(top)*

71 degrees 10 minutes and 8 seconds latitude north – the northernmost point of the Norwegian island of Magerøy is generally understood to be also the northern end of Europe. Here you can watch the raging sea through the safety of the windows of the North Cape Experience Centre or squint into the midnight sun in summer. Hardened types can enjoy this in the open, on the Knivskjelodden rock, which juts out another 1.5 kilometres further north on the same island. In the past, hardly a soul would find their way to this bleak and remote island, but these days you can reach it via a 6.8 kilometre long road tunnel which descends over 200 metres and then rises up again.

Trondheim *(bottom left)*

In 997 AD the Viking chief and King, Olaf I Tryggvason, founded the town of Nidaros, present day Trondheim, situated on the fjord of the same name and capital of the Norwegian administrative district of Sør-Trøndelag. His successor, Olaf II Haraldsson (1015–1028 AD), christianised the country and was killed by the clan chiefs at Trondheim. The town became a place of pilgrimage in honour of the king who was declared a saint and whose remains were interred in the world's northernmost cathedral when the town was elevated to the status of archbishop's seat in 1152.

Rock Drawings, Alta *(bottom right)*

Only a few kilometres south of Europe's northernmost town, Hammerfest, Alta is situated on a fjord of the same name. The village-like town owes its fame to *Hjemmeluft,* the nearby area of Stone Age rock pictures, where 3,000 drawings are etched into the rock: animals, people, manned boats, weapons and equipment. The oldest date from around 5,000 years BC, the most recent are from the Bronze Age (circa 500 BC). The information they give about the history of early settlement in the far North and about the way of life and thought of the local stone age people earned them the status of a UNESCO World Heritage Site in 1985.

Geiranger Fjord (top)

Geiranger Fjord, the southernmost branch of the Storfjord in West Norway, is cut deep into the rock. The area is mountainous with roads that wind in hairpins laboriously onwards, pass by pass. Magnificent views reward the traveller who follows the *Trollstigen* (troll's staircase), as the winding road is known: snow-capped peaks, wild mountain streams, plunging waterfalls, lush green meadows and boldly scrambling woods.

Port City of Bergen (above left)

The Germans are not well-remembered in Norway for their occupation during the Second World War. However, in Bergen, the second largest city in Norway, an earlier German era is looked upon more favourably. The trading organisation known as the Hanseatic League created a branch here, in Tyskebryggen ('German Bridge', now just known as Bryggen), building warehouses, infrastructure and the St Mary's Church, where sermons were still being held in German as late as the 19th century. Rebuilt after several fires, the town of Bryggen, with its narrow alleyways and weather-boarded houses, has been a UNESCO World Heritage Site since 1979.

Stave Church, Borgund (above right)

The Norsemen were highly gifted carpenters and there was certainly no shortage of wood in their homeland Norway. So, the obvious choice of building material for places to worship their new god after converting to Christianity was, of course, timber. All throughout the country the so-called stave churches emerged, although today only 29 of them remain. Borgund on Sogne Fjord, north of Bergen, has one of the most significant: a stave construction erected around 1150 on load-bearing posts and planks driven into the ground, with a roof of several storeys giving the building an almost pagoda-like air.

Stave Church, Heddal (top left)

The amount of colour originally used in historic buildings is often underestimated. For example, ancient Greek temples were not at all as white as the ruins that have been preserved and, in medieval churches, grey probably did not set the tone at all. The custodians of the largest Norwegian stave church in Heddal (East Telemark) had this in mind when they chose blue as the colour for the multi-angled tiled roofs and towers. The red colour of the wooden walls was also touched up, and the wood carvings and wall paintings dating from the 13th century have been restored to their original spendour.

Stave Church, Urnes (top right)

One of Norway's most fascinating stave churches is situated in a breathtakingly beautiful location, on a narrow band of land in the Lustra Fjord, which cuts deeply into the country's interior. Taking in the tree-covered rockface across the blue-green water, the gaze returns to the peaceful cemetery and the peculiar church building mimicking in timber the stone columns of a triple-naved basillica — yet unable to disguise the homely quality of the material. Probably the oldest of this type of construction in Norway (early 12th century), the church has a three-storey tiled roof. The spire has only crowned the church since the 18th century, though the rich carvings in- and outside are older. UNESCO World Heritage Site since 1979.

Sognefjord, West Norway (bottom)

Water above and below: the Sogne Fjord has eaten its way 1,308 metres deep into the subterranean rock of West Norway, and on its southern bank it rains more than anywhere else in Europe: the community of Brekke gets 1,200 millimetres every autumn month. With its length of 204 kilometres, it also holds the record of the longest of all fjords, forming several arms, or rather, a whole system of fjords. The walls of some valleys are so steep that sunlight only reaches the valley floor five months of the year.

Sweden

Gammelstad, Luleå *(top left)*

In in the remote areas of Northern Sweden, in bygone days when the only means of transport was to travel on foot or in horse-drawn carts, the Sunday trip to church was often too far to make the return journey on the same day. In addition, people liked to use the opportunity to do some shopping in town. More than 400 wooden houses are therefore huddled around the 15th century stone church, north-west of the present-day centre of Luleå – they used to serve as overnight accommodation for worshippers during their trips to town. The part of town now called *Gammelstad* (old town) is one of the best-preserved 'church villages' in the far north and has been a UNESCO World Heritage Site since 1996.

Skogskyrkogården, Stockholm
(top right)

Sweden was lucky enough to be able to keep out of both World Wars. So, whilst the rest of the world plunged into war, in the Swedish capital a woodland cemetery was created, which in peacefulness is hard to match: in an abandoned gravel pit in the south of Stockholm, a pine forest had grown. This tranquille and secluded setting inspired the landscape architects Asplund and Lewerentz to create their 'grove for the deceased' with a total area of 85 hectares. Between 1917 and 1940, they laid out burial plots among hills and on terraces, in clearings and under groups of trees, preserving the natural surroundings wherever possible. UNESCO deemed the harmonious accord between nature and culture worth honouring as a World Heritage Site in 1993.

Arctic Cultural Landscape, Lapland
(bottom)

Around one third of the approximately 60,000 Lapp or Saami people, live in the Arctic Circle region of northern Sweden. During the summer months, they traverse the land with their reindeer herds and live in traditional cone-shaped tents (kotes). The beauty of this landscape takes a while to grow on those not from here. The long winters allow for only sparse vegetation, yet the slower pace of life in the vast tundra slowly but surely has a beneficial effect on the visitor. In the large national parks many threatened animal and plant species are protected. Together with the seven Saami villages, they form a comprehensive natural and cultural monument with an area of almost 10,000 square kilometres, which has been a UNESCO World Heritage Site since 1996.

Drottningholm Palace (top)

'Queen's Island', *Drottningholm* in Swedish, is the name of the Swedish royal family's summer residence to the west of Stockholm, on the island of Lovö on Mälar Lake. Its location in an elegant French garden (from around 1700) together with its magnificent decor have earned the palace the title of 'Versailles of the North'. It was erected at the end of the 17th century in decorative Baroque style, had extensions and outbuildings added in Rococo style (e.g. two Chinese pavilions) and was completely refurbished several times over until 1974. As a model example of a Scandinavian royal residence of the 18th century, Drottningholm has enjoyed the title of UNESCO World Heritage Site since 1991.

Castle Gripsholm, Mariefred (bottom left)

There is no better preparation for a visit to this impressive palace than reading Tucholsky's summer novel of the same name. The stern and forbidding moated castle, flanked by mighty towers and erected by King Gustav Wasa from 1537 onwards, provided the contrasting backdrop for a romance of thrilling eroticism and inventive wit, yet also including reflective passages, such as the concluding question: "Actually, why don't we stay here forever?". Tucholsky did stay: in nearby Hindås, in 1935, the exiled author took his own life as a result of his persecution by the Nazis. He is buried at Mariefred cemetery.

Riddarholm Church, Stockholm (bottom right)

Since the death of Sweden's greatest King, Gustavus Adolphus II, at the battle of Lützen in 1632, this has been the final resting place of royalty: the Ridderholm church in the heart of Stockholm on the island of Ridderholmen in the Riddarfjärden (part of Mälar Lake). Admittedly, the cemetery's peace and tranquillity are somewhat impaired today, as there is now a railway line passing close-by and the endless flow of traffic on the Centralbron creates a backdrop of noise. The building was erected by Franciscan monks in the 13th century as a double-naved monastery church and it has been repeatedly expanded by adding on further chapels. It was deconsecrated in 1807 and has served secular purposes since then; it is now a museum.

Naval Port of Karlskrona *(top)*

King Charles XI (1655–1697) was looking for an ice-free harbour from which to monitor the movements of the Danish fleet, and the islands near today's Karlskrona in Blekinge were almost as though created for this purpose. So the king had a naval town planned and erected on this site from 1679 onwards, its well-considered arrangement still evident today. The Baroque town with its large market square and significant church buildings, including the Admiralty Church, the largest wooden church in the country, is an outstanding example of a late-17th-century European planned naval city and as such has been a UNESCO World Heritage Site since 1998.

Rock Carvings, Tanum *(bottom left)*

Perhaps they did not produce as magnificent artworks as their counterparts of previous millennia in the caves of Lascaux (France) or Altamira (Spain), yet they were at least as imaginative: more than 4,000 rock carvings by prehistoric Swedish artists from the Bronze Age have been discovered in 350 locations in and around Tanum in the Swedish province of Bohuslän. These consist of hunting and fighting scenes, numerous representations of boats, religious pictures such as the over 2 metres high 'Spear God'. The largest set depicts as many as 130 people involved in ritualistic activities and covers an area of 5 x 22 metres. It has been a UNESCO World Heritage Site since 1994.

Hanseatic Town of Visby *(bottom right)*

'Regina maris' – queen of the sea: there could not have been a better location for a medieval trading town than that of Visby, the main town on the Swedish island of Gotland. This is where the marine trading routes between Northern Germany, Poland and the Baltic on the one hand and Sweden, Denmark and the North Sea on the other converged. As a member of the Hanseatic League, the town prospered rapidly in the 13th and 14th centuries. Pirates and its rival Lübeck then caused Visby's star to fade. However, its former glory is still visible in the medieval ramparts, warehouses and wealthy merchants' dwellings as well as the white cathedral with its black turrets. UNESCO World Heritage Site since 1995.

Finland

Wooden Houses, Rauma *(top)*

About 600 wooden houses stand on the streets of Kauppakatu and Kuninkaankatu in the centre of the Finnish town of Rauma on the Gulf of Botnia, giving the town a colourful appearance. The first houses were built here by Franciscan monks around 1400; a few centuries later they organised the building of a stone church — something solid to offer support for the people and their lightly-built homes. During the Reformation the town was abandoned by royal decree and only resettled in the 18th century. Although ravaged by fire in the late 17th century, it has preserved its vernacular architectural heritage and has been a UNESCO World Heritage Site since 1991.

Fortress of Suomenlinna *(bottom)*

Only the bastion of Hyvä Omatunto and the Pikku Mustasaari military academy remind of its martial past. Otherwise, the grounds of the fortress of Suomenlinna in the south-east of the Finnish capital Helsinki are occupied by cultural institutions, shops, art galleries, theatres, refreshment facilities and parks. A happy bustle in front of a sombre backdrop, albeit one so impressively preserved that, as an especially interesting example of European military architecture, it was designated a UNESCO World Heritage Site in 1991.

Denmark

Nyborg-Korsør Bridge *(top)*

The challenge of connecting the Danish islands of Fünen and Seeland has excited generations of engineers. Yet the plan failed again and again because of the high cost involved and unresolved technical problems, such as how to provide sufficient span height for ships to pass. Finally, in 1997, a rail connection was built, followed, in 1999, by a motorway link. The small island of Sprogø had been the engineering solution. Now there is a 6.6 kilometre long flat bridge from Nyborg on Fünen to the island, and from there to Korsør on Seeland is a 6.8 kilometre long suspension bridge on two 260 metre high pylons, providing a clear height of 65 metres. It is hoped that the bridge will have paid for itself by 2035 through income from toll charges.

Jelling Mounds, Runic Stones and Church *(bottom)*

In Jelling, north-west of Velje in Jutland, the pagan Danish King, Gorm the Elder, had an unusual 'mausoleum' built for himself and his wife, Tyra Danebrod: a burial mound, over 60 metres long, fronted by a rune stone for Tyra. He was buried there after his death in 940 AD. His christian son Harald Blue Tooth had him re-interred in the church next to the burial mound, erecting a second burial mound with a rune stone for his parents on the other side of the church. Gorm's bones were found in 1978 in the remains of the original wooden church, which had been replaced by a stone building in the 19th century. The area has been a UNESCO World Heritage Site since 1994 as a monument to Denmark's conversion to Christianity.

Fredensborg Palace (top)

In the early and late summer it's 'off to the slot' for the Danish royal family. *Slot* is Danish for 'palace', and in this case it refers to the Fredensborg Palace on Lake Esrum in the north of the main Danish island of Seeland, some 30 kilometres north of Copenhagen. When the royal highnesses are in residence, only parts of the palace and park can be visited. Instead, the changing of the guard ceremony, then held in front of the gates, is an attraction in itself. The Baroque structure was restored in 1992 and has since been gleaming in all its former splendour.

Egeskov Palace, Kvaerndrup (bottom)

The word Renaissance may evoke many things for most people, but few will think of Denmark in this context. And yet, to the south-east of Odense, on the island of Fünen, one of the most beautiful renaissance palaces can be found, with stepped gables, oriel windows and a strictly symmetrical façade: Egeskov Palace rises up from amidst a lake, surrounded by the magnificence of its 15 hectare park, where a bamboo labyrinth adds an exotic flair. The outhouses have been turned into a museum where carriages and agricultural tools as well as veteran cars and old aeroplanes can be admired.

Bazaar in the Tivoli, Copenhagen *(top)*

Exoticism Danish-style: probably one of the most famous pleasure parks in the world are the Tivoli gardens in Copenhagen, just opposite the town hall. Fairground stalls, rides, cafés, bars and amusement arcades all add up to create the flair and bustle of an oriental bazaar. And it even looks like one: a brightly lit palace with pointed minaret-like towers, onion-shaped domes and oriental decoration looks down on the colourful goings-on, enclosing the courtyard with its two side wings and holding the visitor under the spell of an 'Arabian Nights' illusion.

Frederiksborg Castle, Hillerød
(bottom left)

"King Christian stood by the lofty mast…" – thus starts the Danish Royal anthem. However, King Christian IV, who in this song is mainly praised for his heroicism, also had an appreciation for the more peaceful aspects of life. This is manifested in the palace he had built from 1602–1620 in Hillerød, on the island of Seeland. Until 1840, this elegantly furnished palace was the residence of all Danish kings, and its chapel was the place of their coronations. The building now serves as the Danish National History Museum. Of particular interest is the great hall with its marble columns and the audience chamber with its gold decorations.

Chalk Cliffs, Møn *(bottom right)*

Chalk originated in the cretaceous period, an era of the Earth's middle age, about 100 million years ago. In walking along the steep eastern coast of the Danish island of Møn, south-east of the main island of Seeland, one can, if lucky, make closer acquaintance with prehistoric times. It is here that a mass of chalk rock breaks off into the Baltic Sea, forming cliffs up to 128 metres high, such as at *Dronningenstol* (the 'Queens' Chair'). Sometimes pieces break off, unveiling fossils which show the imprints of animals or plants.

Great Britain

Neolithic Monuments, Orkney Islands (top)

5,000 years ago, at a time when Northern Europe was still almost devoid of human inhabitants, stone age workers settled on the remote and difficult to reach Orkney islands far off the Northern Scottish coast. As if the struggle for physical survival alone was not sufficiently exhausting for them, they also practised a time-consuming cult, the heavy traces of which still survive today: the mighty stone grave of Maes Howe, the stone circles of Brodgar and Stennes, the settlement at Skara Brae, all of which are on the main island Mainland – a UNESCO World Heritage Site since 1999.

St. Kilda Island Group (bottom)

Inhabited for thousands of years, today the archipelago with its main island St. Kilda and further islands such as Hirta, Dun, Soay and Boreray are abandoned. The rugged rocky islands in the Scottish Outer Hebrides were barely managing to feed their inhabitants by 1930 and were thus evacuated. They are now owned by the National Trust for Scotland. Since then the already rich seabird population has increased further; the sparse vegetation too, up until then grazed by sheep, has been able to stabilise itself. The islands are now increasingly visited by scientists and tourists eager to experience their rugged wilderness and steep cliffs as well as research all manner of things: historical, meteorological, oceanographical, biological as well as geological. A UNESCO World Heritage Site since 1986.

Giant's Causeway *(top left)*

The 'remains of the causeway' really look as though created by giant hands jumbling building blocks into the sea. Off the Northern Irish coast the basalt columns – smoothly polished by millennia of waves – stand in a neatly arranged row, about 3 miles long. One can't help getting the impression they were placed here on purpose. Thus arose the legend that a Scottish giant had provoked an Irish counterpart for so long that the latter built the road out into the sea as a proof of his strength – and the Giant's Causeway is what remains. The geologically correct, though less poetic, version is that a volcanic eruption 60 million years ago was the master builder of the causeway. A UNESCO World Heritage Site since 1999.

Royal Mile, Edinburgh *(top right)*

Robinson Crusoe author Daniel Defoe described it as "Probably the largest, longest and finest street in the world" – the mile-long street in the Scottish city of Edinburgh, leading from the 11th century castle, on its rock, down to Holyrood Palace (from about 1500). A royal street with a turbulent history, and a street which cannot be separated from the tragic fate of Mary Stuart (1542–1587). However, the Royal Mile also draws visitors as a striking example of successful urban planning. In Mary's time 8,000 people lived here and 100 years later at least seven times as many inhabited the same narrow space. To accommodate them, the houses were built high, representing, effectively, an early version of modern high-rise appartment blocks.

Eilean Donan Castle, Scotland *(bottom)*

A delight for castle enthusiasts as much as it must have been for the future King Robert the Bruce (who reigned 1306–1329) when he saw this McKenzie stronghold. For Robert was on the run from the English, as was so often the case for Scottish heirs to the throne. Here he was safe and, after emerging victoriously from the battle of Bannockburn in 1314, he elevated his place of refuge by turning it into a royal stronghold. Situated on the A87 on the west coast of Scotland, close to the Isle of Skye, near Kyle of Lochalsh, the castle is looking out proudly over the blue waters of Loch Duich onto the green hills opposite, as it has done since 1220.

Craigievar Castle, near Aberdeen (top)

What a joy this castle is, its plain lower towers in perfect contrast with the playful turrets and cupolas embellishing the upper half. Unaltered since its erection in 1626, Craigievar Castle seems to appear in front of the traveller as if suddenly growing out of the ground. Gargoyles and over-hanging ledges decorate the building and from the top one can enjoy a spectacular view of the surrounding Aberdeen-shire hills. The tower with the many turrets is only one part of this L-shaped fairytale castle, and a large part of its 17th century furnishings are also well-preserved. There is only one entrance from which a number of staircases lead into the upper chambers, one of them forming part of a secret escape passage.

Dunottar Castle, near Stonehaven (bottom)

10 miles from Aberdeen, right on the eastern coast of Scot-land, where sheer cliffs drop almost vertically into the sea, Dunottar has been standing guard since the 12th century. In the picture only two angular defensive towers and some remnants of the building are visible, bearing witness to the former extent of the L-shaped complex — and to its turbu-lent history. For this location, like many others on the British Isles, was for centuries a bone of contention bet-ween the Scots and the English. Even Cromwell's mighty army took eight months before the Scottish occupants, only 70 strong, surrendered in 1652. After that Dunottar Castle fell into neglect and by 1720 only ruins were left. These appeal not only to tourists, but also pleased the film direc-tor Zefferelli so much that in 1990 he filmed his 'Hamlet' at Dunottar.

Hadrian's Wall *(top)*

Hadrian's Wall was started at the command of the famous Roman emperor Hadrian (117–138 AD) in the year 122 AD and completed after a period of construction lasting approximately 14 years. The five to six metre high double wall safeguarding the province of Britannia to the north, follows the Solway-Tyne line (Carlisle–Newcastle upon Tyne) for over 73 miles. It consisted partly of an earth embankment and partly of a stone wall, with forts at strategic intervals. Remains of the wall are left in the eastern section and outlines of the forts are still visible, showing the sophistication of Roman life: the legionnaires even had thermal baths. The wall, which was overrun by the Picts several times, was abandoned by the Romans in 383. A UNESCO World Heritage Site since 1987.

Edinburgh Castle *(bottom left)*

High above the Scottish capital Edinburgh, with its Baroque fountain in the gardens of Princes Street, the 11th century castle sits on its 130 metre high throne. It seems completely unassailable, and yet it changed hands several times during the battles between the Scots and the English, and much was destroyed in the process. For example, in the 14th century, when Robert the Bruce drove the English out and the castle was only repaired over 50 years later. The English pressure finally came to an end in the 19th century when the new fashion for romanticism made old Scottish castles and palaces, like this one, very popular, thus ensuring their preservation.

Durham *(bottom right)*

Two major buildings dominate the small town of Durham in North-East England: the cathedral which was built from 1092 until towards the end of the 13th century and the somewhat older castle, dating back to early Norman time. The cathedral was built to house the remains of the Venerable Bede (about 672–735 AD), the canonised Benedictine missionary of Northumberland. As the largest and finest example of Norman architecture in England, the cathedral (see picture) together with the impressive fortress was for a long time the residence of the Prince Bishop of Durham. A UNESCO World Heritage Site since 1986.

York Minster *(top left)*

With a cruciform layout, 158 metres long, 68 metres wide in the transept and over 30 metres high in the nave – the Cathedral of York is the largest in the UK. Its main tower is 65 metres high, the two front towers are 5 metres lower. Construction lasted from 1160 to 1470 and its architectural styles encompass the gamut of English Gothic, providing the visitor with a rich and varied architectural experience. This also applies to the chapterhouse, connected to the church through a passageway. It is in the shape of a regular octagon, 18 metres high and wide, with delicate columns and curved arches. The ceiling is supported by just one pillar and the windows are decorated in magnificent stained glass.

Roman and Medieval Buildings, Chester *(top right)*

In the first century BC, Julius Caesar expanded Roman power as far as Britain, and Deva became an important outpost. This is still evident in the name of the city of Chester (from the Latin *castra* = camp), which sports the largest remaining amphitheatre of the British Isles. Parts of the city wall date back to Roman times, although its extension is medieval. Also from medieval times are the Gothic cathedral and the many half-timbered houses, which were renovated in a romanticising style during the 19th century.

County of Gwynedd *(bottom)*

Venedotia is what the Romans called the coastal region of north-west Wales. This became Gwynedd in the language of the Welsh, who had to accept English rule after that of Rome. This rule was extremely precarious at the outset and several castles and fortresses built by King Edward I (1272–1307), the conqueror of Wales, bear witness to this. Be it Caernarfon Castle, where the heir to the British throne still makes his oath of allegiance to this day, Beaumaris Castle or Conwy Castle (picture) – a total of nine strongholds are memorials to Norman power and have been a UNESCO World Heritage Site since 1986.

Park and Fountains Abbey, Studley *(centre)*

Fountains Abbey in Yorkshire is a real treasure even as a ruin. Its unique setting made it a UNESCO World Heritage Site in 1988: in 1132, Cistercian monks moved into the area, which had been laid waste by the Normans, and founded Fountains Abbey, erecting the monastery church by 1147 whilst starting on healing the wounds of destruction caused by war in the area. Over time, the energetic men succeeded in this, but time also brought along the Reformation and with it the end of the monastery in 1539. The reason only ruins remain is that the building was used as a quarry for stone. Yet this also gives it its romantic appeal. In 1727, a royal park was created around it, and the combination of nature and culture provides its own particular charm.

Blenheim Palace *(top)*

Only a few miles from the university city of Oxford, in the middle of a romantic park, is this palace, which John Churchill, the first Duke of Marlborough (1650–1722) was given for his victory over the French and Bavarians at Höchstädt on the Danube in 1704. Known as the 'Battle of Blenheim' in English history (after the village of Blindheim near Hochstädt), this gave the palace its name. The Duke had the palace built from 1705 to 1722 and it rose to fame in the 20th century as the birthplace of the Duke's descendant, Winston Churchill, British prime minister during the Second World War and from 1950–1955. A UNESCO World Heritage Site since 1987.

Bodleian Library, Oxford *(bottom left)*

The unusual name for this most famous British library comes from its founder and benefactor, the scholar Sir Thomas Bodley (1545–1613, see statue in picture). Due to the amount of antiquarian, oriental and medieval manuscripts preserved here, it was given the Latinised form of his name: Bodleiana. Not only the intellectual content, in the form of the gigantic book collection, is awesome, but also the exquisite interior and the Late Gothic vaulting, which are very fine. The circular reading room, completed in 1748, can be regarded as a cathedral to intellectual thought and a temple of academic study.

Bath Abbey, *(bottom right)*

Like rows of seats in an amphitheatre, the English spa town climbs up the hills on both sides of the Avon estuary as it joins the Bristol Channel. It has been a spa town for an eternity, having already been used as a spa by the Romans in pre-Christian times. Their pious British heirs did the same and also used the waters to consecrate the Gothic abbey church built towards the end of the 15th century and a focal point in the centre of the valley. Although not very high at 52 metres, the exquisite structure of the tower and the front are captivating and are beautifully decorated with sculptures.

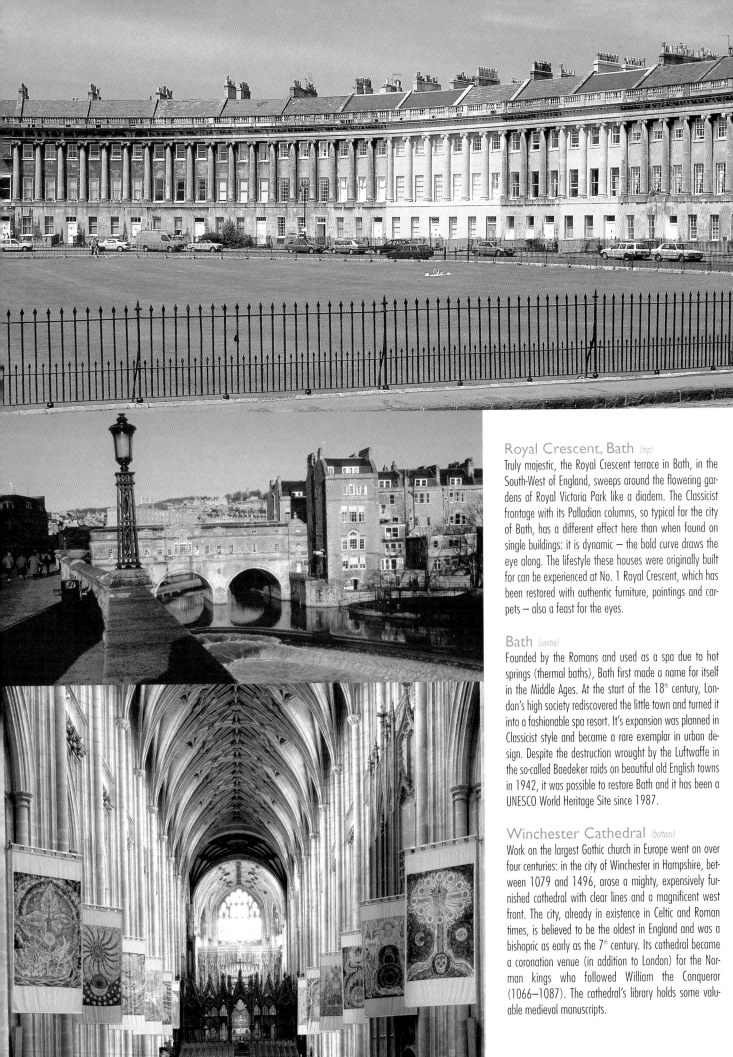

Royal Crescent, Bath *(top)*

Truly majestic, the Royal Crescent terrace in Bath, in the South-West of England, sweeps around the flowering gardens of Royal Victoria Park like a diadem. The Classicist frontage with its Palladian columns, so typical for the city of Bath, has a different effect here than when found on single buildings: it is dynamic — the bold curve draws the eye along. The lifestyle these houses were originally built for can be experienced at No. 1 Royal Crescent, which has been restored with authentic furniture, paintings and carpets — also a feast for the eyes.

Bath *(centre)*

Founded by the Romans and used as a spa due to hot springs (thermal baths), Bath first made a name for itself in the Middle Ages. At the start of the 18th century, London's high society rediscovered the little town and turned it into a fashionable spa resort. It's expansion was planned in Classicist style and became a rare exemplar in urban design. Despite the destruction wrought by the Luftwaffe in the so-called Baedeker raids on beautiful old English towns in 1942, it was possible to restore Bath and it has been a UNESCO World Heritage Site since 1987.

Winchester Cathedral *(bottom)*

Work on the largest Gothic church in Europe went on over four centuries: in the city of Winchester in Hampshire, between 1079 and 1496, arose a mighty, expensively furnished cathedral with clear lines and a magnificent west front. The city, already in existence in Celtic and Roman times, is believed to be the oldest in England and was a bishopric as early as the 7th century. Its cathedral became a coronation venue (in addition to London) for the Norman kings who followed William the Conqueror (1066–1087). The cathedral's library holds some valuable medieval manuscripts.

Greenwich Park and Observatory, London *(top)*

About 10 miles down the Thames from the centre of London, on the south bank of the river, is the borough of Greenwich, renowned for the meridian of zero degrees longitude, which runs through the observatory founded here in 1675 and is marked with a plaque. The observatory in Flamsteed House, which was built by Sir Christopher Wren (1632–1723), now houses both a planetarium and a museum for astronomical instruments. It is situated on top of a hill in the middle of the magnificent Greenwich Park, laid out in the 17th century as a royal park for Charles II by Louis IV's landscape gardener, André Le Nôtre (1623–1700). Building and park have been a UNESCO World Heritage Site since 1989.

Royal Naval College, London *(centre)*

Henry VIII and his daughter Elizabeth I were born here, although not in the present building, which was only completed at the end of the 17th century by master architect Christopher Wren and which represents one of the London Borough of Greenwich's architectural masterpieces. Later, the building served as a home and hospital for retired naval personnel and it now houses the Royal Navy's academy for officers. Especially worth seeing are the Painted Hall, so called for its ceiling paintings of King William of Orange and his wife Mary, as well as the chapel in the south-eastern building (Queen Mary building), which was also completed according to plans by Wren in 1752.

National Gallery, London *(bottom)*

On Trafalgar Square, in the heart of the British capital, stands the Classicist building, erected in 1838, which houses the National Gallery. It contains the largest collection of paintings in the world. The beginnings of this collection go back to 1824, when the British government purchased 38 paintings. Numerous extensions became necessary as more and more new purchases had to be accommodated. One of these extensions includes the famous dome of 1876. Visitors only get to see about 2,000 of the gallery's 4,500 pictures, the most prestigious being the collections of old Dutch masters and of the Italian schools of the 15th and 16th centuries but also, of course, of British artists such as Hogarth, Reynolds, Gainsborough, Constable and Turner.

Lloyd's Building, London *(right)*

For three hundred years, the London firm of Lloyd's regulated insurance losses and concluded deals in a coffee house in Tower Street, before it was able to move into a spectacular new building in 1986. Erected by Sir Richard Rogers (b. 1933), who designed the Pompidou Centre in Paris, it is turned inside out: lifts, staircases and pipes give the façade a futuristic look. The 14-floor high (76 metres) interior space has been conceived as an atrium and is clearly arranged as such. In the centre of the hall, under a canopy, is the famous bell — in earlier times it was rung once for bad news and twice for good news. Now it is only heard on official occasions. On the directors' floor is the original so-called Adams room, which has been reconstructed from the former coffee house.

Kensington Palace, London *(top)*

At the beginning of September 1997, it was surrounded by a sea of flowers and, for a few days, was the focus for all those who had Diana, the 'Princess of Hearts', in theirs: her death in Paris, on 31st August, had caused grief worldwide and had made Kensington Palace, her London home, a place of pilgrimage. The building was already prominent enough before this happened: after all, it bears the hallmarks of Sir Christopher Wren, the architect who rebuilt London after the great fire of 1666. Furthermore, it was in this majestic house in the middle of the park of the same name, that Queen Victoria was born on 24th May 1819.

Big Ben, London *(bottom left)*

At the north end of the Houses of Parliament stands the most famous English tower: the rectangular clock tower with the large clock face on all four sides. It strikes the hour or rather: the 13 tonne heavy bell of the clock tower called 'Big Ben' strikes the hour. Its name is also applied to the tower itself and its chimes go out daily as the time signal on the BBC World Service. The 97.5 metre high tower, slightly thicker in the clock area, is a London landmark and has become the symbol of the British capital, of the whole country even and also of the Commonwealth.

St. Paul's Cathedral *(bottom right)*

At 170 metres long and 75 metres wide in the transept, the Cathedral of St. Paul's is the largest house of worship in London. It stands on a site on which a previous, Gothic, cathedral rose into the sky before it fell victim to the Great Fire in 1666. The new construction in the form of a Latin cross was designed by Christopher Wren (1632–1723). The mighty Baroque building with two 67 metre high towers and the 111 metre soaring dome serves as the 'parish church of the British Commonwealth'. The best-known attraction is probably the Whispering Gallery which encircles the dome on the inside, 33 metres above ground. Each whispered word can be heard distinctly on the opposite side 35 metres away.

Buckingham Palace (top)

Royalty have always liked things at a slightly grander scale: in 1705, the Duke of Buckingham built a country house of such impressive size that King George III, a good half a century later, just had to have it – though he only used it as a refuge not as a residence. The chunky piece of architecture only became a proper royal residence in 1837, having been modified in Classicist style thus giving it a more prestigious appearance. The young Queen Victoria resided here, alone at first, and from 1840 onwards with her husband, Albert, the Prince Consort. Even then the official residence of the Queen in London attracted sightseers; and in today's world, where monarchs are an endangered species, it is a tourist magnet.

Houses of Parliament, London (bottom)

The complex of buildings housing the two Chambers of the British Parliament is actually called the 'Palace' of Westminster, as the King once ruled from here. Now the House of Commons (the lower house) alone determines policy, while the aristocratic House of Lords (upper house) has a less important role to play. The buildings set off the 19th century Gothic revival in architecture: Charles Barry, the architect who designed and built them from 1840 to 1888, was merely aiming to reflect the style of nearby Westminster Abbey. Yet in doing so, he not only made an impression on the British architectural world, but also inspired architects all over Europe (cf. the Budapest parliament).

The Tower and Tower Bridge, London (top left)

The best-known castle in England and, at the same time the oldest building in London, is the Tower, whose core, the White Tower (now a weapons museum), was built by William the Conqueror between 1066 and 1087. At times used as a royal residence, the fortress, which was continually added to, became a state prison in the 17th century (until 1820) and today serves as barracks and arsenal. Among its many towers, the Wakefield Tower has a special significance as the place where the British crown jewels are kept. Even more famous perhaps than the Tower, although considerably younger, is Tower Bridge (see picture), which was opened in 1894. The drawbridge with its two striking towers has become a symbol of London. A UNESCO World Heritage Site since 1988.

Westminster Abbey and St. Margaret's Church, London (top right)

The site of a monastery as early as the 7th century, this place in the heart of London has been occupied by the Gothic Westminster Abbey (see picture) since its foundations were laid in 1245. It is the place were coronations of British kings are held and where they are laid to grave. The choir was the first part to be built, followed by the completion of the nave and west front, as well as the King Henry VII Chapel with its fan vaulting – a famous example of the Perpendicular style. The two western towers were completed according to plans by Christopher Wren. The official church of the Houses of Parliament is the 12th century St. Margaret's Church, which was rebuilt by a Westminster Abbey masterbuilder from 1486–1543. Both churches have been a UNESCO World Heritage Site since 1987.

Stonehenge, Wiltshire (bottom)

The most impressive prehistoric monument in north-west Europe stands near Salisbury in the county of Wiltshire. The monument known as Stonehenge consists of five trilithons (pairs of tall standing stones with a horizontal lintel) set in a horseshoe shape which is surrounded by a ring of trilithons. The neatly worked sandstone blocks are up to 7 metres high and weigh as much as 50 tonnes. Within the two trilithon rings are circles of smaller 'bluestones' nearly 4 tonnes each. The arrangement of stones is aligned towards the summer solstice point. The entire site is 110 metres in diameter and surrounded by a ditch cut into the chalk subsoil. Stonehenge was erected over several centuries, reaching completion in 2100 BC. Together with Avebury and other monuments of the megalith culture in England, Stonehenge has been a UNESCO World Heritage Site since 1986.

Windsor Castle *(top)*

Only four years after his arrival in England, the new Norman King, William the Conqueror, began the construction of a stronghold in Windsor on the Thames. From that time, right up to the 19th century the building grew and grew, with every architectural style contributing another new part, until it had gained all the characteristics of a palace and was promoted to royal summer residence. The buildings are grouped around two large inner courtyards with the massive Round Tower in their centre. Green parkland surrounds the complex, which also houses a valuable collection of paintings. The damage from a major fire in 1992 has now been repaired.

Churchill's House, Kent *(bottom)*

Few people were surprised that the British statesman Winston Churchill, who steered his country to victory through the Second World War, received a Nobel Prize. However, the surprise was what he received the prize for: in 1953 he was awarded the prize for literature for his work as an author. The old war-horse a colleague of Shaw's? Yes, that's right, only Churchill did not write poetry but grand historical essays, and the one on the First World War, *World Crisis,* was so successful that the author was able to buy a house in the country, in Chartwell, Kent. Its appearance today is due in large parts to the master of the house himself, who in the 1930s was in the political wilderness and devoted his enormous energies to bricklaying. 'Powerful' would be the word to characterise his style.

Salisbury Cathedral *(opposite page)*

In the space of only 40 years (1220–1260) its builders set this early Gothic cathedral into the middle of a green meadow in the town of Salisbury in Wiltshire. The elegance of its lines, the construction soaring heavenwards and the cleverly simple external decoration come to full effect without distortion. Because of the slim 123-metre-high tower they probably had to economise on the other dimensions: the nave and both transepts are only 26 metres high.

Land's End *(top)*

The raw as well as the beautiful aspects of the coastal landscape of South-West England and the Cornwall peninsula have become well-known through the films of the Rosamund Pilcher novels. The extreme western tip of England lies between the end of the English Channel and the Irish Sea. Here on the cliffs of Land's End, at 5 degrees 44 minutes longitude west and 50 degrees 4 minutes latitude north, so many ships have been wrecked in earlier times that entire sections of the population were able to make a living from beach-combing. The lighthouse built on Wolf Rock in 1870 was not always successful in its warnings.

Royal Pavilion, Brighton *(bottom left)*

Originally it was a simple, solid country house in the seaside resort of Brighton, but the heir to the throne needed a love nest and it had to be decorated accordingly. Between 1815 and 1821, the Prince, who became King George IV in 1820, (1762–1830) had the Royal Pavilion built in historicising Mogul style. In the architect John Nash (1752–1835), the leader of the Picturesque School, he had found the right architect for this. The building has a mosque-like appearance with small minarets and oriental decoration.

Herstmonceux Castle, Sussex
(bottom right)

A better-preserved brick-built castle would be hard to find: Herstmonceux Castle in Sussex, north of Eastbourne, was built in 1415. To make it easier to defend in an otherwise flat landscape it was set on an island, though it never did come to a siege here or to any other armed conflict. One could espy possible attackers early enough from the towers to close the drawbridge in good time and to allow the archers to take up position at their embrasures. Today, a permanent bridge leads to the main gate, for nowadays only desired guests in the form of paying visitors approach.

Arundel Castle, West Sussex *(top left)*

It originates from the 11th century and has hardly changed since then: Arundel Castle in West Sussex belonged to the Howard family, the Dukes of Norfolk, for 850 years. They were always close to the throne, a fact which led some of them into danger. Thus the 3rd Duke of Norfolk, a cultured man and a courtier, had the bad luck to be the uncle of Anne Boleyn and Catherine Howard, who both married Henry VIII and were both executed for alleged adultery. Their uncle only escaped the same fate because the king himself died on the day before the Duke's scheduled execution. A happier man was the 14th Duke of Norfolk and a his pastime is now our pleasure: he had the nickname 'The Collector' and is responsible for a whole series of exhibits which make a visit to the castle so enchanting.

Leeds Castle, near Maidstone *(bottom left)*

Half a million visitors annually want to see the venerable Leeds Castle, near Maidstone in Kent. The charm of such buildings increases with age and the moated castle has had over a thousand years for its charms to unfold. The initial buildings date back to the 9th century, the main construction period was in the high and late Middle Ages. Leeds Castle has been host to many kings, including the notorious womaniser Henry VIII who was positively smitten by the location. After his death, royal interest waned and the castle came into private hands. In 1926 it came into those of the later Lady Baillie, a beauty with an eye for beautiful things. Her collection of chinoiserie and antique furniture forms one of the castle's main attractions.

Canterbury Cathedral *(top)*

The city of Canterbury lies in a very picturesque location in the green hilly landscape of the county of Kent on the river Stour. It is the seat of the primate of the Church of England, who holds the right to crown monarchs. In Canterbury he could choose between 11 churches for his appearances but he generally only uses the cathedral (see picture) with its late Gothic glory. After Roman beginnings (the crypt), the building was constructed from the 12th century on the outline of a bishop's double cross, and construction lasted until 1495. Built in Gothic style it is younger than the former Abbey of St Augustine and St Martin's Church whose baptismal font is said to hail from the time of King Ethelbert of Kent (d. 616). The three church buildings have been a UNESCO World Heritage Sites since 1988.

Chalk Cliffs, Dover *(bottom)*

They can even be seen from the other side of the channel: the walls of rock that gleam in the midday sun, connecting the estuary valley of the river Stour with the port of Dover. This is partly due to the height of the reflective steep chalk cliffs and partly to the fact that here the English Channel is at its narrowest, at 32 kilometres. As a result of this, even Julius Caesar undertook his first step on British soil here. Nearby is also the cliff known as Shakespeare Cliff, well known from the drama *King Lear*. The narrow straits were used by engineers as early as the 19th century for the first attempt to dig a tunnel under the channel. This only succeeded in 1994, from nearby Folkestone.

Ireland

Clonmacnoise (top)

If you wanted to balance the whole of Ireland on the point of a needle, the point would have to be where the ruins of the castle and monastery of Clonmacnoise are. They not only lie in the heart of Ireland but this place is also where its pulse was for several centuries at the time when the island was known as the 'Land of Saints and Scholars'. As early as 545 AD, St. Ciarán is supposed to have erected a chapel here, the monastery followed and drew monks from all over Europe, right up until the 13th century. Later on, the bishop's castle was constructed, but soon fell into ruins along with the cathedral and 13 other churches (8 can still be seen as ruins). 1552 saw Clonmacnoise's final demise when Cromwell's soldiers set fire to its remains.

Achilles Island (bottom)

The largest island off the north west coast of Ireland is named after the hero of antiquity. It is no longer a proper island, as it has now been linked to the mainland via a road bridge and connected to the town of Achilles. Visitors can now easily reach this rocky paradise, its sheer cliffs dropping off into the sea at a height of 650 metres in some places, but also offering sandy beaches, like those in the villages of Keel and Keem. From here, looking out over Clew Bay, one can see the pilgrimage mountain Croagh Patrick to the south, where in 441 AD the patron saint of Ireland is said to have fasted for 40 days and to have banished all reptiles from Ireland.

Trinity College and National Museum, Dublin *(top)*

The famous Trinity College harks back to the city's British history, both in its architectural style and in the multicultural throng of its students and lecturers: the old British Empire is reflected in the cosmopolitan mix to be found here. The mighty building complex houses the modern Trinity Library, which has preserved antiquarian jewels such as the 'Book of Durrow' gospels (circa 680 AD) and the 'Book of Kells' (circa 800 AD), the latter so richly decorated and with such fine detail that it is said to have been created by the hand of an angel. Cutting diagonally across the university campus to the south-east, one reaches the National Museum where Celtic metalworks are the main attraction.

The Burren *(bottom left)*

In County Clare, south of the Bay of Galway on the central west coast of Ireland stretches a barren plateau, its carboniferous limestone bedrock exposed in 'pavements' with sparse vegetation growing amongst the rocks. However, in early summer, when the Burren's unique alpine vegetation bursts into flower, this turns into a striking rock garden. The first settlers arrived here over 5,000 years ago and the countless generations who followed them have left a remarkable landscape where megalithic tombs, burial cairns, prehistoric farmsteads, early Christian hermitages, stone forts, medieval churches, castles, and even 19th century military fortifications all stand side-by-side.

Dingle Peninsula *(bottom right)*

Looking at a map of Ireland, the island's south-western coast looks rather frayed at the edges, and one particularly beautiful frazzle is the Dingle Peninsula, the tip of which is considered as Europe's most westerly point (ignoring some islands offshore). Both nature and culture show themselves at their best here: mountains (e.g. Beenoskee, 827 metres high) and fine sandy beaches such as the one at the village of Inch on the south coast, age-old strongholds such as Dunberg Fort, erected in the Iron Age and situated high above the sea. Only slightly younger are the remains of monasteries or the chapel Galarus Oratorium to the east of Ballyferriter: a pyramid-like structure built from field stones in the early Middle Ages.

Netherlands

End Dyke, Ijsselmeer (top)

Powerful storm flooding in the 13th century left deep traces on the North Sea coast, the most striking for centuries was the gigantic bay of the Zuidersee in the north-west of the Netherlands. In 1918, the government decided on a project to win back the lost area of land. After draining a trial polder, work began on the construction of a dyke to close off the bay directly across its mouth. It had to cross a 30-kilometre stretch and is 90 metres wide at the base; it was completed in 1932.

Wouda Steam Pumps (bottom)

Near the Dutch town of Lemmer in the province of Fries-land is an industrial monument which is still in operation: the Wouda steam pumping station. It was planned shortly before the First World War, built during the war, in which the Netherlands were one of the few European states not to be involved, and was inaugurated in 1920. It is the largest steam-driven pump system in the world and, as a symbol of the Dutch people's struggle against water, it has been a UNESCO World Heritage Site since 1998.

Costumes, Volendam *(top left)*

In most holiday resorts of Southern Europe, traditional dress is mainly worn for the sake of the tourists. However, in Volendam, a picturesque fishing village on the Ijsselmeer in the north of Holland, wearing the traditional costume on festival days is true tradition, and the pretty-looking girls pose for the photograph hunter with polite curiosity.

Schokland *(top right)*

Embankments from the height of the Middle Ages still bear witness today to the early settlement of the one-time peninsula of Schokland in the Dutch Zuidersee. How necessary these dwelling mounds were, was demonstrated in the 15th century when the sea washed away the land connecting them to the mainland and again in the middle of the 19th century when the buildings were evacuated due to heavy storm flooding. As a symbol of the age-old struggle against the encroachment of the sea, it has been a UNESCO World Heritage Site since 1995.

Beemster Polder, North Holland
(bottom)

For centuries the Dutch dyke-builders have fought a battle with the sea for every square kilometre of land and for centuries it was a losing one over and over again. The Beemster polder in North Holland was one of the first major successes where they managed to reclaim a fairly large piece of land for the first time. This 'droogmakerij de Beemster' (literally: dry-making of Beemster) has created a landscape with fields, dykes, canals and settlements and has been a UNESCO World Heritage Site since 1999.

Monnickendam (top left)

An ideal spot for hobby painters: the northern Dutch village of Monnickendam, with its colourfully pennanted yacht harbour, is enchantingly situated on the Ijsselmeer. On festival days the picture becomes even more animated, with fishermen and their wives in traditional dress striding to church or to the scales. Just outside the village one has the impression of stepping into a painting by one of the old Dutch masters: windmills, some still working, stretch their sails, pollarded willow trees grow alongside canals and cattle are grazing peacefully in the wide-open landscape.

Fortification Ring, Amsterdam (top right)

The ring of fortifications was started in 1880 and constructed at a 15 to 20 kilometre distance from the Dutch capital, consisting of forts, bunkers, trenches and locks. With this the Dutch were striving to protect the heart of their country against military attacks. If the fortification ring broke they could put the invading troops out of action within two days by flooding the countryside. The ring was more or less complete before the start of the First World War in 1914, but the Dutch were spared having to resort to this last defence. In the Second World War they refrained from flooding their own land in view of the overwhelming superiority of the German army. As the only fortification to deploy water as a weapon, the ring has been a UNESCO World Heritage Site since 1996.

Keukenhof, Lisse (bottom)

South-west of Haarlem in the Dutch province of South Holland lies the small town of Lisse. The 28-hectare garden at Keukenhof is really one big flower show with open beds and vast green houses. The flowers in the well-known song 'Tulips from Amsterdam' are much more likely to have come from here and at best to have taken a detour via the capital.

Windmills, Kinderdijk-Elshout (top left)

The contribution made by low-lying countries in coastal regions to the development and application of hydraulic technology cannot be overestimated. The Netherlands are typical of this and a particularly striking example is the region around Kinderdijk-Elshout. Here engineers have been at work for centuries on solutions for the drainage of land and on methods to exploit water and wind energy. Evidence from all eras can be seen here, bearing witness to these efforts: early dyke constructions, modern pumping stations, flood gates, dams, reservoirs, medieval sluices. In addition, numerous well-preserved windmills provide a charming backdrop to all this. The area has been a UNESCO World Heritage Site since 1997.

University Town of Leiden (top right)

One of the oldest and most beautiful Dutch towns lies in the province of South Holland on the Old Rhine: Leiden with its venerable – yet also highly modern – university, founded in 1575, is also an important cultural centre sporting an observatory and attractive botanic gardens, laid out as early as 1587. The town is traversed by canals and dates back to early Roman times. Monuments to its history are the Gothic *Sint-Pieter-Kerk*, the town hall (1577–1597), the weigh house and butter hall (1658), several old gates and town houses in Renaissance style, the cloth hall (*Laken-hus*) with the local history museum. Some gaps in the fabric of the town are attributable to the explosion of a gunpowder ship in 1807.

The Hague (bottom)

Today the seat of the Dutch government, The Hague has kept the character of a distinguished, even 'noble' town. Situated in an area of dunes, near the North Sea coast, between the Old Rhine (*Oude Rijn*) and the New Maas (*Nieuwe Maas*), it charms the visitor with villas, parks and modern administrative buildings on the one hand and on the other with its medieval centre around the Grafen Palace (1250), where the session chamber for the States General is located, and around the Gothic *Groote Kerk* (14th/15th centuries). This is also the area where the merchants' town with its gabled houses rose up just a century later. Royal palaces and the parliament building round off the townscape.

Belgium

Market and Bell Tower, Bruges *(bottom left)*

In the 19ᵗʰ century, the once flourishing Flemish port town of Bruges was considered 'dead', as the harbour had silted up long ago and the once pulsating life had given way to a quiet comfortableness. Yet today life has returned precisely because of this period of dormancy. For the town has kept its late medieval character and attracts tourists with its picturesque nooks and crannies, canals, atmospheric collections of beguines' houses, Gothic and Baroque town houses and cobbled alleyways. Everything is arranged round the large market square: the cloth halls and the 83-metre-high bell tower (*Belfried*), the brick-built Salvator Cathedral and the oldest Belgian town hall – all of this dating from the 13ᵗʰ century.

Beguines' Houses, Flanders and Brabant *(below right)*

In the 12ᵗʰ century, especially in Flanders and Brabant (Netherlands and Belgium), unmarried or widowed women formed convent-like communities led by a prioress and – albeit without taking a vow – devoted themselves to social and religious work. Members of such 'convents' were called 'beguines'. Often not without wealth, they built living quarters for themselves with ancillary buildings for work and prayer: the beguines' houses. Many of these cleverly-designed architectural ensembles have been preserved and are evidence of a kind of 'worldly' convent life, showing a closeness of community that was often regarded with suspicion by the church and secular authorities of the time. A collective UNESCO World Heritage Site since 1998.

Belfries, Flanders and Walloon *(far bottom right)*

They are features in the urban landscape of Belgian towns and are called *beffroi* in Walloon, *belfried* in Flanders: the 30 bell towers of the country (in the picture: Ghent) bear witness to the confidence of communities which had become independent in the Middle Ages and only recognised the superior authority of the Holy Roman Emperor. These were political and spiritual symbols at one and the same time, in that they could belong to either the church or the town hall. Their often artistic design also reflected the wealth of the communities which had broken away from their feudal ruler. The towers have been a collective UNESCO World Heritage Site since 1999.

Town Hall, Antwerp *(top left)*

With around 200,000 inhabitants, the Belgian port of Antwerp was the most important transhipment place on the continent in the 16th century. Up to 5,000 merchants a day carried out their business at the exchange, which came into being in 1460. There was a saying: "The world is a ring and Antwerp is the diamond in it." An important facet of its cut was and is the town hall (1561–1566), which shows the influence of French Renaissance architectural style and is evidence of the wealth of the city on the Schelde. The large windows are just as typical for this northern variation of the style as is the stepped shape of the façade and its ornamentation with colourful coats of arms, statues and marble columns.

Notre Dame Cathedral Antwerp *(top right)*

Aesthetically it can certainly measure up to the famous Cologne Cathedral, and even in size it is not far behind: the Gothic Notre Dame Cathedral (Cathedral of Our Lady), begun in 1322 and finished in the 15th century, in the North Belgian port city of Antwerp. The ground plan measures 117 metres by 65, the nave is 40 metres high and the main tower with its intricate stonework reaches a height of 123 metres (a second tower was planned but never completed). The tune of its 99 bells is well-known beyond the borders of Belgium. The main attraction however waits inside: three gloriously colourful altar paintings by Rubens show the elevation of the cross, the descent from the cross and the Assumption of Mary into heaven.

Ghent *(bottom)*

The town where Emperor Charles V (1500–1558, reigned 1519–1556) was born, and administrative capital of the Belgian province of East Flanders, presents its well-preserved old town *Kuip van Gent* on a peninsula at the confluence of the Schelde and Leie rivers. The centre is made up of the stronghold Gravensteen built from 1180 to 1200, together with a museum for sculpture and the Flemish University (1930 onwards), the cloth hall, the bell tower (1313–1321) with the famous Roland Bell, numerous gabled houses and the Gothic Cathedral of Saint Bavo. In this mighty house of worship, visitors stand in amazement in front of a triptych created 1420–1430 by the van Eyck brothers, Hubert and Jan, the first representatives of the Flemish Renaissance.

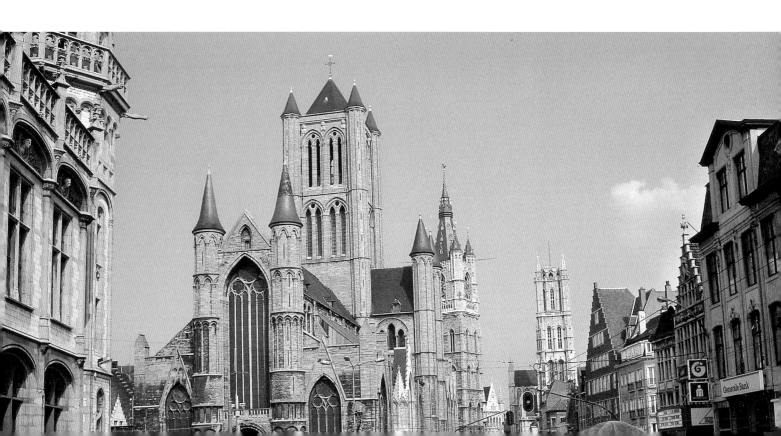

Grote Markt/Grande Place Brussels *(top)*

The present day EU capital and a modern trade and industrial centre, Brussels is over 1,000 years old, and this can be clearly felt, despite the modern streets and European Union buildings. In the lower town, around the *Grote Markt* (also called *Grande Place* in the bilingual Belgian capital), splendid merchants' and guild houses with their decorative façades, the *Maison du Roi* and the town hall stand witness to the city's significance as a clothmakers' town and a transhipment place for trade with the Rhineland and the sea ports during the Middle Ages. High above all this towers the Gothic cathedral, in former times dedicated to Saint Gudula and now to Saint Michael. A UNESCO World Heritage Site since 1998.

St. Michael's Cathedral, Brussels
(bottom right)

One person, even if a saint and fellow countrywoman, was not enough in the long term as the patron of the Cathedral in the Belgian capital city Brussels: out of Saint Gudula became Saint Michael – for with an archangel one is that bit nearer heaven. This was even more important at the time since the towers of the building, construction of which was begun in the 13th century, remained unfinished. The nave, which still has traces of the Romanesque, marks the transition to the Gothic, which then became the dominant style in the construction of the deep chapel-like side niches and in the design of the choir ambulatory. Damage from the war has long since been repaired.

Canal Lifts, Canal du Centre
(bottom left)

Eight hydraulic boat lifts were constructed for the Canal du Centre in Belgium between 1888 and 1917 (in the picture a more recent creation from the 1960s). They were particularly necessary south of Brussels where the terrain becomes hilly and a height difference of 67 metres has to be overcome. Four of the steel frame constructions, built in the style of Gustav Eiffel, are still in operation today – 100 years after their erection – thus bearing witness to the marvellous engineering skills of the 19th century. Their uniqueness within the Belgian industrial landscape won them the status of a UNESCO World Heritage Site in 1998.

Luxembourg Old Town

Today mainly a financial stronghold, Luxembourg, capital city of the grand duchy of the same name, was foremost a military base for several centuries. Evidence of the city's martial past are the remains of the medieval city wall, once nearly a kilometre long. The Ducal Palace from the 16th century was also built on older fortifications. Together with the cathedral of the same age, it stands in the Old Town on a high plateau looking down onto the lower city through which the Alzette flows. The Old Town of Luxembourg, as a fine example of military architecture spanning several centuries, has been a UNESCO World Heritage Site since 1994.

Luxembourg

Germany

Mudflats, North Sea Coast *(top)*

A unique habitat lines the German and Dutch North Sea coast: the mudflats which are up to 30 kilometres wide and which, in rhythm with the high and low tides, flood and then drain again; the German part is designated as a National Park. When the tide is out the blueish-black greasy-looking mud is exposed. The narrow channels and deep holes within this are home to a rich fauna of micro-organisms — at low tide this provides a feast for seabirds of all types. Along the coast thrive salt-loving plants such as glasswort, common sea lavender, wormwood, sea pink and many grass species. Providing a nursery for amphibians and stop-over point for various migratory birds, this wildlife haven also bears the stamp of human activity such as fishery and the building of dykes and polders to reclaim land from the sea. But first and foremost it is shaped through the elemental powers of nature.

Halligen, North Friesland *(bottom)*

In the mudflats off the North Sea coast, between the Eiderstedt peninsula and the island of Föhr to the north, are ten little islands, referred to in German as 'Halligen'. The name describes what are really remainders of the mainland, left after the old coast was lost in great storm floods. The larger islands now have a summer dyke, preventing the worst of the storm flooding which still regularly afflicts the other Halligen. There, the only protection lies in the small natural or man-made mounds on which the houses on these islands are built, keeping them above sea level, even in a flood. Many of these now also have extra protection by way of a ring dyke. The lonely houses in the vast sea are a vivid representation of man's struggle against the elements.

Haithabu, Schleswig *(below left)*

As early as the 8th century, a trading centre existed on a bay of the Baltic Sea, opposite Schleswig, where merchants traded goods with the north of Europe. Known as *Haithabu* ('settlement on the heath') in old Danish, the place was taken over by Swedish Vikings towards the end of the 9th century. A little later it was conquered by the German King Henry I and then became Danish again at the end of the 10th century. It finally perished in 1050. In the 18th and 19th centuries, stones with runic inscriptions in old Danish and old Swedish were found, providing valuable information about the history of Haithabu and guiding archaeological excavations which have been ongoing since 1900. A specially built Viking museum now displays many of the findings.

Old Town, Lübeck *(below right)*

Known as the 'Pearl of the Baltic Sea', the Hanseatic City of Lübeck was founded in 1143 and has been developed along the same basic outlines until today. Its Gothic architecture seems to have grown almost seamlessly from the Middle Ages right into the modern age. The old Town Hall buildings, the *Burgschloss*, the 13th century Koberg quarter with the *Jakobikirche* and the *Heiligen-Geist*-Hospital, the *Holstentor*, the patrician quarter from the 15th and 16th centuries, flanked by the cathedral and the *Petrikirche* – a more closely-knit fabric of pre-industrial buildings as in the heart of Lübeck will be hard to find. Lübeck's Old Town has been a UNESCO World Heritage Site since 1987.

Speicherstadt, Hamburg *(far bottom)*

Between 1885 and 1927, a town of brick-built warehouses (Speicher) rose up on Hamburg's harbour, between Kehrwiederspitze and Poggenmühle. With its turrets, niches and friezes, decorative ceramic elements, green copper roofs and glazed stonework, the Speicherstadt, which sits astride the river Elbe, appears uniform and vivid at the same time. The buildings are accessible from the street and via barges from the water. Originally they were intended for all kinds of goods, today mainly high-value commodities are stored here, and a switch to service industry companies is now apparent in its tenure. Yet this does not affect the picturesque appearance of this 'town', which has been designated as conservation area since 1991. It also houses a museum of spices and a museum devoted to customs and smuggling.

Chalk Cliffs, Rügen (top)
More than one million tourists annually visit Germany's largest island and Jasmund, the smallest National Park in the country, with its unique chalk coast. The 300 hectare National Park protects a natural landscape and haven for many rare plant species, with the aim to let it develop as undisturbed as possible. Its ancient stands of beech forest, wetlands and hillside woods are a living gene bank. The view from the chalk cliffs, which inspired many painters, including the great Caspar David Friedrich (1774–1840) to paint Romantic landscapes, is a feast for the eyes, whether viewed from the sea or from ashore: a unique wonder of nature.

Altstadtrathaus, Braunschweig (bottom)
One of Germany's most beautiful medieval buildings is found in Braunschweig's Old Town: the old town hall (*Altstadtrathaus*), built in the 13th century and in its present form dating back to the early 15th century. It consists of two wings arranged in an L-shape. Set into one of the columns of the cloister is the 'Braunschweig yard', used in the past as the official unit of measurement by the town's cloth merchants. On a rectangular balcony above, nine exquisite sculptures by Hans Hesse decorate the pillars, dating from the 15th century. They show Ottonic and Welfian rulers with their wives. Today the *Altstadtrathaus* holds an exhibition and serves as ceremonial building.

Cathedral and Castle Lion, Braunschweig *(top left)*

Henry the Lion had the collegiate parish church of St. Blasius, today a Lutheran cathedral, built as a triple-naved vaulted basilica from 1173 to 1195. The cathedral is the first fully vaulted building in Lower Saxony. With its central nave it accommodates the tomb, built in 1250, of the Duke and his English consort Mathilde, an important medieval sculpture. The same is said of the castle lion, a bronze cast of 1166, once covered in gold leaf, which Henry the Lion had erected as a symbol of his power and jurisdiction. The original can be seen in Dankwarderode Castle. A faithful copy can be seen in the castle square.

Herzog-August Library, Wolfenbüttel *(top right)*

Although the building in which the dramatist Gotthold Ephraim Lessing (1729–1781) worked as a librarian no longer exists, the new building of 1887 nevertheless captivates the visitor. From 1634–1666, under the reign of the scholarly book collector and peace-loving ruler Duke August, the Herzog-August Library in Wolfenbüttel, Lower Saxony, founded by Duke Julius in 1572, was the largest collection of books in Europe and as such was regarded as the eighth Wonder of the World. Today the library is a modern research institution of world renown. Since 1989, the Gospel book of Henry the Lion with illuminations from the 12th century (see picture), the most valuable book in the world (sold at Sotheby's for more than 8 million pounds in 1983), has found its permanent home here.

Palace and 'Little Venice', Wolfenbüttel *(bottom)*

Wolfenbüttel, in Lower Saxony, has, to a large extent, been able to preserve its old town with its Renaissance and Baroque buildings. The palace deserves particular mention, originally a moated castle, which was given a Renaissance tower in 1614 and then, 100 years later, a Baroque half-timbered façade with an impressive stone portal. The inner courtyard with its Palladian arcades dates from the 17th century. Even more picturesque is the 'Little Venice' area, with the last vestiges of the network of canals that used to service the town.

Bauhaus Locations, Weimar and Dessau *(top)*

"Between 1919 and 1933, the Bauhaus School, based first in Weimar and then in Dessau, revolutionised architectural and aesthetic concepts and practices. The buildings put up and decorated by the school's professors (Walter Gropius, Hannes Meyer, Laszlo Moholy-Nagy and Wassily Kandinsky) launched the Modern Movement, which shaped much of the architecture of the 20th century." With this explanation, the Bauhaus buildings in Weimar (*Haus am Horn*, 1923) and Dessau (*Hochschule für Gestaltung*, 1926 – see picture) were accepted onto the list of World Heritage Sites by UNESCO.

Herrenhausen Gardens, Hanover *(centre)*

The Herrenhausen Gardens, in Lower Saxony's capital Hanover, are a remarkable example of traditional garden design. With its trimmed trees and hedges, mazes and fountains, sculptures, cascades and grottos, an open air theatre and an orangery the *Grosse Garten* is the best-preserved early Baroque garden in the whole of Germany. The *Georgengarten* was created in the 19th century in the manner of English-style romantic gardens. Founded in 1666, the garden was taken over and restored by the town of Hannover in 1936. Its greenhouses are home to the largest orchid collection in Europe.

Parish Church and Old Town, Quedlinburg *(bottom left)*

Just a short broomstick ride from the Brocken, the mountain said to be the gathering place of witches, to the east of the Harz mountains, lies the town of Quedlinburg. Its medieval town centre is one of the best-preserved in the country. High above town on the castle hill, its 1,300 timber-framed houses look like a sea of pointed gables and turrets. Many of the houses have also had famous inhabitants, for example the Klopstock House, which commemorates to the poet Friedrich Gottlieb Klopstock (1724–1803) who was born here. The Collegiate Church of St Servatius from the 10th century is one of the masterpieces of Romanesque architecture and has been on the list of the UNESCO World Heritage Sites, along with the old town, since 1994.

Luther Memorials, Eisleben and Wittenberg *(bottom right)*

The hammer blows (whether real or metaphorical) shook the entire world: on 31st October 1517, when Martin Luther posted his famous '95 Theses' on the door of the castle church (picture) in Wittenberg, Saxony-Anhalt, it marked the end of the medieval universal church and launched the Reformation. The houses in Eisleben where Luther was born in 1483 and died in 1546, his room in Wittenberg, where he worked as a professor, and his colleague Melanchthon's house have been UNESCO World Heritage Sites since 1996 for "bearing testimony to the Protestant Reformation, one of the most significant events in the religious and political history of the world".

Brandenburg Gate, Berlin *(top)*

If there is one building symbolising Germany, it must be the Brandenburg Gate, finished in 1791. Originally the western gate to the city it soon became the setting for some of the most significant and symbolic processions. The Prussian kings paraded through it when returning to their residence in Berlin. Napoleon I rode through it as a symbol of his victory over Prussia and, whilst there, promptly took the Quadriga, which crowns the Gate, back to Paris. The victory over France in 1871 (and the return of the Quadriga) could only be celebrated properly by holding a parade here. Adolf Hitler also, as new Chancellor of the Reich in 1933, had himself honoured with a torchlight procession through the Gate. After the end of the Third Reich, the Gate marked the border between East and West and, after the building of the Berlin Wall in 1961, became a symbol of the Cold War. Open again since 1989, the Brandenburg Gate now stands for the regained German unity.

Kaiser Wilhelm Memorial Church, Berlin *(right)*

Commemoration is in its name. The Neo-Romanesque building, finished in 1895, was intended to be a religious monument for the old Kaiser Wilhelm – and only for 'the one with the beard'. The distinction from his nephew Wilhelm II was very important: as far as the Berliners were concerned, he was remembered sufficiently through the poverty and suffering after the First World War, a few decades later. Then, after the Second World War, only ruins were left. Demolish it? A compromise was found: the nave disappeared, the tower remained (gaining the nick name 'hollow tooth') as a warning against German arrogance. One might say that it has thus retained some of its original intention. Next to the monument, a new, modernist church (designed by the architect Egon Eiermann) was built by 1961.

Museum Island, Berlin (below left)

"The Berlin *Museumsinsel* is a unique ensemble of museum buildings which illustrates the evolution of modern museum design over more than a century." – this was the reason in 1999, for the Berlin Museum Island to be included on the list of the UNESCO World Heritage Sites. It comprises the Old Museum (built by Karl Friedrich Schinkel, opened 1830), the New Museum (1855), the National Gallery (1876), the Bode Museum (formerly the Kaiser Friedrich Museum 1904 – picture) and the Pergamon Museum (1930). A trip through all of them would be the equivalent of a journey through the history of Western art from antiquity right up to the 19th century and at the same time an excursion to the roots of the museum idea.

Hackesche Höfe, Berlin (below right)

The labyrinthine network of eight courtyards on the edge of the former *Scheunenviertel* in Berlin is Germany's largest mixed-use courtyard complex. This modern urban design concept has a long tradition here: in 1905 the buildings facing the street served as office blocks with a commercial façade, the first courtyard was used as a space for festivities, with various places for entertainment gathered around it. The façades of the blocks surrounding the second courtyard with their large windows still bear witness to the manufacturing industries once housed on each floor; and in the innermost blocks are 92 residential apartments. The strength of this concept is reflected in the fact that this mix of uses survived until reunification. After renovation, the *Hackesche Höfe* are once again a focal point within the cultural centre of Berlin.

Reichstag, Berlin (far bottom)

Created for the sham parliament of the Kaiser days (1884–1894) the imposing building now serves the German Bundestag as its 'plenary area'. The term is a compromise after much political song and dance over the discrepancy between the building's history and its present-day democratic use. However, the term is not likely to take hold, for the Reichstag remains the 'Reichstag', yet without holding on to its history. How this can be was shown by the Hungarian artist Christo in 1995, when he wrapped the giant block in silver foil until it seemed to float. Now with its feet back on the ground, the building has metamorphosed by means of a new glass dome replacing the one burnt down in 1933. The British architect Sir Norman Foster created the airy centrepiece, allowing bright daylight into the once gloomy interior.

Schloss Pfaueninsel, Berlin (top left)

On the so-called 'peacock island' (*Pfaueninsel*), an island in the Havel river south-west of Berlin, Friedrich Wilhelm II had a love nest built for himself and his mistress, Wilhelmine Encke. It was built by master carpenter Johann Gottlieb Brendel between 1794 and 1797 in the style of a Roman villa, and was designed to look like a ruin from the start. Two round towers connected via a curved bridge give the white building, which is entirely built from timber, its distinctive appearance. The rectangular blocks, which look just like granite, are merely painted on. The island, together with its stock of foreign and indigenous plants, some of them very rare, and its rich birdlife, is one of the Berliners' favourite and most attractive destinations.

Schloss Charlottenburg, Berlin
(top right)

One of Berlin's most beautiful and magnificent building is the Schloss Charlottenburg. The first Prussian king started work on it before his coronation in 1695 and completed it between 1701–1712. Under the king's successors, the central building with the 48-metre-high cupola tower acquired wings, a palace theatre and tea house. In 1943, the palace burnt out completely after an air raid, but was rebuilt and restored as a faithful copy of the original. Its rooms have been furnished in 18th century style and serve in part as a museum (for example the apartments belonging to Fredrick the Great on the upper floor) and as a gallery for art of the Romantic movement (on the ground floor).

Nikolaikirche and Town Hall, Potsdam (centre)

The site of the Nikolaikirche in Potsdam was home to a church as early as the 13th century. A Baroque building replaced it in the 18th century but burned down soon after, and so the present day cupola construction was designed by Berlin's most popular architect at the time, Karl Friedrich Schinkel (1781–1841), and completed by one of his students until 1850. Rebuilt after the damage caused by the war, it has dominated the Potsdam skyline ever since. The dominant building on the *Alte Markt*, however, is the old town hall (mid 18th century), built in Classicist style and crowned by the statue of Atlas carrying the globe. The former administrative building, which had become too small by 1885, now holds a theatre, galleries and cafés.

Sanssouci Palaces and Park, Potsdam (bottom)

After the two Silesian wars, Frederick the Great, King of Prussia (1712–1786) was clearly in search of peace and quiet. Hence the name of his summer residence *Sans Soucis* (meaning 'without worry') in Potsdam. Added to and improved repeatedly later on, initially (until 1747) there was just a single-storey palace atop the vineyard terraces with its central rotunda, built according to plans by Knobelsdorff (1699–1753), also the creator of the 290 hectare park. Here further buildings were erected: the picture gallery, the *Alte Orangerie*, a Chinese tea house, the *Neues Palais* in Rococo style and a plethora of temples, pavilions and grottos. Sanssouci, often called 'the Prussian Versailles', has been a UNESCO World Heritage Site since 1990.

Schwebebahn, Wuppertal (top)

In 1887, the towns of Elberfeld and Barmen decided on a revolutionary public transport system: in the narrow valley of the Wupper, giving the twin towns their new name of Wuppertal since 1930, space is at a premium. Therefore a unique transport system was developed: on a steel structure high above the valley runs a monorail train system with the train suspended below the rail rather than travelling on top. This hanging train, which travels over a distance of 13.3 kilometres, became operational in 1901 and has carried a total of 1.5 billion passengers in the 100 years of its existence.

Externsteine, Teutoburg Forest
(centre)

In the eastern part of the Teutoburg Forest at Horn-Bad Meinberg, near Detmold in North Rhine-Westphalia, a row of sandstone rocks tower high into the sky, the highest measuring 36 metres. According to an inscription, a chapel was hewn out of one of the rocks around the start of the second millennium, possibly in the intention to banish any spirits from the location's past use as a centre of pagan worship. Carved in one of the rocks is a relief, thought to date from 12th century, showing Christ's descent from the cross. Today these natural and cultural monuments lie amidst a nature reserve.

Castles of Augustusburg and Falkenlust, Brühl (bottom)

Originally, in 1288, Augustusburg Castle (picture) in Brühl in North Rhine-Westphalia was built as a moated castle. The home of the prince-elector (who was entitled to a vote in the election of the Holy Roman Emperor) was residence of the prince-archbishops of Cologne until the 16th century. It was then altered in Baroque style, at the behest of prince-elector Clemens August (1725–1770), and decorated in Rococo style. Artists from all over the world took part in its refurbishment, most notably the splendid staircase in the central wing based on the plans of Balthasar Neumann (1687–1753). The Falkenlust hunting lodge was built in the Augustusburg Park from 1729–1740. The ensemble in Brühl became the model for many other estates of German nobility. A UNESCO World Heritage Site since 1984.

Cologne Cathedral (right)

Its construction took 632 years, from 1248 to 1880: the cathedral in Cologne is, even in its newest parts, faithful to the Gothic style of its original plans. Upon its completion in the 19th century, it was the mightiest building in the world and the culmination of Gothic architecture. The largest of all church fronts, with 7,000 square metres, is flanked by two towers, which are 156 metres high. The church treasure inside this massive building includes the bones of the Three Wise Men in a medieval reliquary shrine. The processional cross on the altar from the time of Emperor Otto is the blueprint for all medieval triumphal crosses. The altar, created by Stefan Lochner in the 14th century, is considered to be one of the most beautiful altars in the world. A UNESCO World Heritage Site since 1990.

Speyer Cathedral (top)

The Church of St. Maria and St. Stefan, or Speyer Cathedral for short, is one of the most important Romanesque monuments in Germany. Construction started in 1030, it was consecrated in 1061, and then remodelled and given a vaulted ceiling from 1082–1106. The 134-metre-long triple-naved basilica has six towers and was the burial place of the German emperors for almost 300 years. The well-proportioned, symmetrical arrangement of its architectural elements give the structure a most formidable presence, further enhanced by the beautifully crafted stonework, created by stone masons from Lombardy. A UNESCO World Heritage Site since 1981.

Abbey and Altenmünster, Lorsch
(bottom left)

After a fire in 1621, the only parts remaining of this Carolingian Benedictine abbey in the Hessian town Lorsch are the gatehouse (presumably finished in 774 AD – see picture), parts of the church portal (from 1150) and a section of the outer wall. The abbey was founded during the reign of Pippin the Short (751–768 AD) and in the early Middle Ages the East Carolingian kings held their audiences here. Even the few buildings that remain give an impression of the extent of the former abbey, which was one of the most significant of its time. Incorporated into the archbishopric of Mainz in 1232, religious life in Lorsch was extinguished during the time of the Reformation. As rare architectural vestiges of the Carolingian era, the ruins have been a UNESCO World Heritage Site since 1991.

Aachen Cathedral (bottom right)

Built from 790–800, the Aachen Cathedral is one of the most impressive examples of religious architecture. Erected as chapel for Emperor Charlemagne (768–814 AD) on an octagonal plan with a side nave and galleries, the cathedral was further extended in the Middle Ages. In a deliberate gesture, linking him to the first Frankish Emperor, Otto I the Great held his coronation as King of Germany here, in 936 AD, thus establishing a tradition which was followed by 30 German kings until 1531. The cathedral treasure contains medieval works of art as well as archaeological and historical documents. A UNESCO World Heritage Site since 1978.

Roman Monuments, Trier *(top)*

Founded before the birth of Christ, Trier is the oldest town in Germany. Remains of major Roman buildings such as a Roman fort, the imperial palace, thermal baths, an amphitheatre and, above all, the monumental 'Porta Nigra' from the 2nd century AD are evidence of the city's former significance. A stone block construction with two prominent four-storey towers, the Porta Nigra's powerful appearance and skilful engineering is still impressive today. Together with the Cathedral of St Peter, which dates back to the 4th century, and the Gothic Church of Our Lady, it has been a UNESCO World Heritage Site since 1986.

Messel Pit, Darmstadt-Dieburg
(bottom left)

In 1886, while quarrying an oil shale deposit near the town of Messel, in the Hessian district of Darmstadt-Dieburg, a whole array of fossilized plants and animals were unearthed. They proved infinitely more valuable than the oil shale and very quickly scientists took charge of the excavations. Since then, more than 10,000 finds have been made, providing invaluable information about the climate, flora and fauna of the Earth's history, more particularly the Eocene period, 57 to 36 million years ago. Especially fascinating are the round 100 types of vertebrate from the early stages of the evolution of mammals, including exceptionally well-preserved mammal fossils, ranging from fully articulated skeletons to tissue outlines preserved in the slate. A UNESCO World Heritage Site since 1995.

Völklingen Ironworks *(bottom right)*

Sights do not have to be as old as the hills; some structures of the industrial age also deserve attention. The ironworks in the Saarland town of Völkingen were founded in 1873 and, for a long time, were Germany's biggest producer of iron girders, once employing 20,000 steelworkers, and enabling the village of Völklingen to grow into a medium-sized town. The well-preserved plant illustrates the main steps of the historic pig iron extraction process, from the ore bunker via the smelting pot to the furnaces and the roller presses. As a completely preserved and intact monument to the industrial age, the ironworks have been a UNESCO World Heritage Site since 1994.

Messeturm, Frankfurt am Main (top left)

The new symbol of the economic power of Germany's financial centre Frankfurt am Main was officially opened in 1988. Since then, the 256-metre-high *Messeturm* (exhibition tower) has dominated the city's skyline, together with other post-modernist skyscrapers of banks and multinationals. The tower also represents the confident image of the self-proclaimed 'Main Metropolis', which sees itself as a focal point of international trade. From such materialist commodities as cars to more intellectual ones, like books, the Frankfurt trade fairs are an important annual fixture for many different industries worldwide. With this in mind, this tower is actually quite modest – compared to its counterparts in places like Chicago or Kuala Lumpur.

Skyline, Frankfurt am Main (bottom left)

'Mainhattan' – the Frankfurters are just as proud of this nickname as the New Yorkers are of their skyscraper image. In terms of their number and size, the buildings on the Main cannot be compared with those on the Hudson River, but if measured relative to the cities' population figures, Frankfurt actually has far more skyscrapers per head and the ones in the Hessian metropolis are also many times higher in proportion. And, in addition to its skyline of steel and glass towers, Frankfurt can throw in a Gothic cathedral (far right in photograph) for effect. In the past, the German emperors were crowned here – eat your heart out, big sister New York!

Classical Weimar (right, top)

The homes of Goethe, Schiller and Herder, the *Wittumspalais*, the Herzogin-Anna-Amalia-Library, the National-theater, the park on the Ilm, Goethe's garden house, Belvedere Palace Park, the palaces and their parks in Tiefurt and Ettersburg, the *Fürstengruft* and the historical cemetery – all of these bear witness to the remarkable cultural flowering of the small Thuringian town of Weimar at the end of the 18th and the beginning of the 19th century. During those years literary works of extraordinary importance were written here, charcterised by open-mindedness, humanistic endeavour and striving for universal education. Weimar's classical era, which ended with Goethe's death in 1832, can still be felt in these places of intellectual poignancy. They have been a UNESCO World Heritage Site since 1998.

Wartburg Castle, Eisenach (right, bottom)

As an "outstanding monument of the feudal period in central Europe", the Wartburg Castle in Eisenach, Thuringia, came to be on the list of UNESCO World Heritage Sites in 1999. It is thought to have been founded in 1067 and was later extended in Romanesque style. Martin Luther translated the New Testament here while in exile, in 1521/22 and, 300 years later, students celebrated the Wartburg festival here. The troubadours competed with each other here, in the War of the Troubadours in the 13th century, and a few centuries before that, the 'Rose Miracle' of Saint Elisabeth of Thuringia occurred. After several restorations some of the buildings in the castle are now amongst the most beautiful secular building of their age north of the Alps. Their position in the heart of Germany also make them a symbol of German integration and unity.

Dresden Zwinger *(far top)*

The name *Zwinger* ('enclosure') for one of the most beautiful Baroque buildings in Germany stems from its original location between the outer and inner castle walls. Built 1709–1732 by Daniel Pöppelman and decorated by the sculptor Balthasar Permoser, the Dresden Zwinger was designed as a symbol of power for the ruler Augustus the Strong (1670–1733). It was used for festive occasions and to house valuable collections and several pavilions were added, linked via richly decorated gallery walks. Housed within are the 'Old Masters' art gallery, the Armoury, a porcelain collection, a natural history museum and the *Mathematisch-Physkalischer Salon* with its interesting collection of scientific instruments.

Elbe Sandstone Mountains and Königstein Castle, Saxony *(above left and right)*

The Elbe sandstone mountains in the region known as 'Saxon Switzerland', with their bizarre rocks, ridges and gorges are already a natural wonder, yet one of its summits also offers a cultural one: Königstein Castle, erected in the 16th century and then repeatedly expanded and added to, is situated high above the town of Königstein on a sandstone tabletop mountain about 300 metres above sea level. Anyone stationed here, whether soldier or prisoner, had the most amazing view far across the country. One of the castle's most famous inmates was the alchemist Johann Friedrich Böttger (1682–1719), the inventor of white porcelain. The castle now houses a museum.

Göltzschtal Viaduct, Vogtland *(top)*

Near Netzschkau, between Reichenbach and Plauen in the Vogtland, a masterpiece of engineering straddles the river Göltzsch. Renowned as the largest brick-built construction of its kind, the Göltzschtal Viaduct is 579 metres long at a height of 78 metres and carries the dual-track railway line from Leipzig to Hof. The eye-catching bridge spans the valley as a triple-tiered construction in 22 arches, with two larger, double-tiered arches, flanked by four double-pillars as an architectural feature in its centre. Construction work on the bridge lasted for just six years (1845–1851).

Veste Coburg *(bottom)*

Towering high above the town of Coburg in Franconia, the northern part of Bavaria, is one of the largest medieval fortresses in Germany. Known as *Veste* (pronounced 'feste') in German, its origins are said to date back to the 10th century. In 1530, Martin Luther — persecuted as a heretic at the time — found a safe haven here, from which he was able to watch and influence the Augsburg parliament. In the Thirty Years' War, the castle was still to play a military role, but was finally seized by the imperialists after a long siege in 1635. Restored and renovated in the 19th century, and then again at the beginning of the 20th, the extensive complex now houses art and natural history collections.

Cathedral, Bamberg *(top)*

Bamberg Cathedral came into being during the transitional period from the Romanesque to the Gothic style of architecture. It was built on the outline of the cathedral built by Emperor Henry II (reigned 1002–1024). In 1237 the double-naved construction with four towers and western transept was consecrated. Many works of art inside it are from the same era. The most famous stands next to the steps to the Georg Choir: the Bamberg Knight, a life-size figure of a slim, beardless, unarmed man on horseback. The lady altar by Veit Stoss is from the early 16th century. As a part of Bamberg's Old Town, the cathedral has been a UNESCO World Heritage Site since 1993.

Old Town, Bamberg *(bottom left)*

Cathedral, old court with the remains of the king's palace, Böttinger house, New Residence, the Roman Basilica of Saint James, the old Town Hall, the church of St. Michael, the Church of St. Stephen, the basilica of Saint Gangolf, the old parish church, the former Jesuit Church, the 'Little Venice' row of houses (see picture) — the medieval collection of buildings constituting the old town of the Upper Franconian town of Bamberg is of incomparable architectural authenticity. Here architecturally historic elements, which have had an influence on the whole of Europe, are alive and have been preserved in their original state. A UNESCO World Heritage Site since 1993.

Banz Monastery, Upper Franconia
(bottom right)

Originally a Benedictine abbey, then a prince's palace, Banz Monastery lies on a 440-metre-high prettily wooded ridge on the right bank of the river Main below Lichtenfels (Upper Franconia). Founded in the 11th century and after a turbulent fate in the Thirty Years' War, Banz received 1709–1719 one of the Baroque churches designed by the Dientzenhofer brothers with monastery and abbey buildings. This church today provides the real attraction of the complex. It is possible that it charmed the Wittelsbach ruling house, which acquired Banz in 1814. In 1920–1926 it became a monastery once again, this time of the silent Trappist order. Today the Hanns Seidel foundation runs the magnificent palace and uses it as a conference centre.

Residence, Würzburg (top)

It was possible to restore this pearl of German Baroque architecture after its destruction in World War II. This former residence of the prince bishops was designed by Balthasar Neumann (1687–1753). Its basic structure was completed in 1744. It is the result of European cooperation: Viennese and Parisian architects supplied designs, Flemish and Italian stucco artisans worked on the internal decorative features and the ceiling painting above the impressive staircase was created by the Venetian Tiepolo. A UNESCO World Heritage Site since 1981.

Valhalla, Regensburg (centre)

Eight kilometres south of Regensburg at Donaustauf, King Ludwig I of Bavaria (1786–1868, ruled from 1825 onwards) had a marble building erected on a hill. Its plans were drawn up by Leo von Klenze 1830–1841. 250 steps lead up to the building called Valhalla, which is reminiscent of a temple. It sits as if on a throne with terraces falling away below and has a length of 74 metres, a width of 35 metres and a height of 20 metres. 52 fluted Doric columns support it; the roof is decorated by figures. The interior of the hall of fame is illuminated from above through fanlights, and inscriptions and portrait busts remind one of famous Germans.

Stone Bridge, Regensburg (bottom)

A masterpiece of medieval civil engineering bridges the Danube in the German province of the Upper Palatinate: the stone bridge built 1135–1146. With its 16 arches it was once the only Danube crossing. Out of the original three towers on the bridge only the bridge gate has been preserved. On its north front there is a copy of a regal figure with a falcon, probably a representation of Emperor Frederick II.

German Museum, Munich *(top left)*

In 1903 the Munich engineer Oskar von Miller (1855–1934) founded the German Museum in his home city. In what is probably one of the most comprehensive exhibitions it shows the development of technology and industry as well as of the sciences using original apparatus, machines, reconstructions, models, classic installations, pictures and drawings. A new building was built in 1925 on the 'Museum Island' in the Isar, with an exhibition area of 50,000 square metres. In the library visitors have access to more than 700,000 volumes.

Old Town and Castle, Heidelberg *(top right)*

Like a jewel shines the red sandstone of the famous Heidelberg castle from upon a woody prominence of the Königstuhl Hill. It arose from a medieval fort and has been a ruin since being struck by lightening in 1764, which only increases the picturesque impression of the illuminated facade at night. The giant barrel (221,726 litres), which was built in 1751, was not damaged at the time. Below the palace is an imcomparable, extremely lively old town quarter with the late Gothic church of the Holy Spirit (15th century), the 'Zum Ritter' Renaissance period house, the Baroque town hall (1701–1705), the old university (1712) and the old bridge with the Neckar Gate (1786–1788). This idyll attracts visitors like a magnet, many of them have lost their hearts to Heidelberg.

Wieskirche, Steingaden *(bottom)*

The architect Dominikus Zimmerman was 60 years old when he laid the foundation stone for the pilgrimage Church of *Die Wies* ('the meadow') in the northern Bavarian town of Steingaden in 1745. It took nearly ten years until this lavishly furnished church was consecrated in 1754. Decorative detail was contributed by the architect himself and by his brother Johann Baptist Zimmermann. The result is an exuberant, colourful and joyful Rococo building in the beautiful setting of an Alpine valley. A UNESCO World Heritage Site since 1983.

Neuschwanstein, Allgäu *(top)*

With this building the Bavarian monarch Ludwig II (1845–1886) finally earned himself the title of a 'fairy-tale king'. Influenced by a visit to the Wartburg, Neuschwanstein was built from 1868 onwards, at a height of 964 metres, at Füssen, Allgäu, according to designs by the stage scenery painter Christian Jank (1833–1888). Its dramatic design really makes Neuschwanstein the ultimate fairy-tale castle, with its turrets and oriels, steep drops and battlements, all set against the perfect backdrop of the grandiose Bavarian landscape. All this, together with the enormously expensive interior decoration ensures that millions of tourists visit Neuschwanstein annually.

Hohenschwangau, Allgäu *(bottom left)*

Three kilometres south-east of Füssen in Bavaria stands the castle of Hohenschwangau at 800 metres above sea level, one of the 'fairy-tale king' Ludwig II's (1845–1886) favourite places to stay. A castle stood here as early as the 12th century, from which the last Staufer ruler, the very young Conradin, is said to have set out in 1267 on his last journey to Italy. From 1538–1547 this had to make way for a new building, and in 1567 the dukes, later electoral princes and kings of Bavaria, took over the castle, which then gradually fell into ruin. The ruins were restored from 1833 onwards and the magnificent rooms furnished with medieval and contemporary works of art.

Maulbronn Monastery *(bottom right)*

Only the Gothic porch, the south wing of the cloisters and the men's refectory – probably the most expensive 13th century dining room still in existence – remain of the beginnings of the Cistercian Monastery of Maulbronn, founded 1147 in the vicinity of Karlsruhe. Also preserved are the most important furnishings of the monastery church, which give a detailed insight into the daily life and work of the monks from the 12th to 16th centuries. Of particular interest is the water-management system built by the monks, consisting of an elaborate network of drains, irrigation canals and reservoirs. As the most complete and best-preserved medieval monastic complex north of the Alps it was admitted to the list of UNESCO World Heritage Sites in 1993.

Switzerland

Rhine Falls, Schaffhausen *(top)*

The German writer and poet Schiller always envied his wealthier colleague Goethe for his travels, but he also benefited from them: for his most famous work *Wilhelm Tell,* Schiller was keen to know more detail about how a waterfall looked and asked Goethe, on the occasion of the latter's journey to Switzerland in 1797, for a description of the famous Rhine Falls (20 metres drop, 150 metres wide), the largest waterfall in Europe. Goethe wrote: "From the large rock amid the torrent a rainbow seemed to cascade constantly, as it arose from the spray of the plunging river's foam. The setting sun colours part of the moving masses yellow, in deeper waters they seemed green, and all foam and spray appeared bright purple."

Convent of St Gall *(bottom left)*

The monastery ceased to operate nearly 200 years ago, its Baroque buildings, however, are evidence of its former glory. Soon after its founding in the year 602, Sankt Gallen Monastery, in the foothills of the Alps, was eagerly engaged in missionary and educational activities, which, in the Middle Ages, culminated in scientific work. Testimony to this are the more than 2,000 medieval manuscripts, which are preserved in the two-storey monastery library, one of the richest and oldest collections in the world. Most of the writing is the work of monks from the monastery itself. Early incunabula (books printed before 1501) are also here as the foundation stock of a library of over 100,000, mostly bibliophile, editions. Not only the contents fascinate, but also their accommodation with its ceiling paintings, pillars, balustrades and marquetry — the whole complex has been a UNESCO World Heritage Site since 1983.

Murten and Lake Murten, Canton of Freiburg *(bottom right)*

On 22 June 1476, the small capital of the district of See in the Canton of Freiburg (Fribourg) became famous because of a battle. At Murten (Morat in French) the members of the Swiss Federation were victorious over the powerful Charles the Clever of Burgundy. Since then nobody else has threatened the peace in the small town, which still has quite a medieval look to it. The narrow streets inside the town wall have been preserved, as have the ramparts, towers, gates, fountain and shaded walks. The castle from the 13th century on the shore of Lake Murten, which covers 23 square kilometres and is up to 46 metres deep, provides the finishing touch to the picturesque ensemble by the lake. The rich local history is presented by the Historical Museum housed within the old town mill, and the battle mentioned above is represented in a diorama of pewter figures.

Old City of Berne (top)

A lack of self-confidence is apparently something the residents of the Swiss capital Berne have never suffered from. For the saying "The world fades away, Berne remains" is still repeated with some self-satisfaction. The seat of the federal authorities since 1848, Berne has been able to preserve and care for its Old City, set on a hill site surrounded by the Aare river, thanks to centuries of peace combined with not inconsiderable wealth. Pergola walks, Renaissance fountains with statuary Baroque guild houses and those of well-to-do citizens, towers and churches from the early days of the modern era determine the magnificent picture of the historical centre which has been a UNESCO World Heritage Site since 1983.

Chapel Bridge and Water Tower, Lucerne (bottom)

This is where the cradle of the Swiss Federation stood: the Old Town of Lucerne, the capital of the canton of the same name, though not one of the original cantons, looks over the Vierwaldstätter Lake from which the Reuss flows out at this point and runs through the town. A fascinating bridge spanned the river until 1993 when the picturesque covered wooden chapel bridge, which was built around 1300 as part of the town defences, burnt down. Only eight months later it was standing again, though only a few remains and the design according to which it was re-built, are original. The pedestrian crossing leads from bank to bank at an angle and thus measures 200 metres in length. The construction is flanked by an octagonal water tower in the river, which is also of medieval origin and also belonged to the town's fortifications.

Glacier Express, Swiss Alps *(bottom left)*

This is where arriving is secondary – the journey itself is what it is all about: in the Glacier Express from Saint Moritz to Zermatt, one enjoys the achievements of Swiss engineering and above all the panorama of the peaks, in such a manner, in such comfort and luxury not to be experienced elsewhere. It is a switchback ride at high altitude, via artistic viaducts, through sudden tunnels, hugging precipitous cliff walls, high up over castles and monasteries, below soft alpine meadows and past towering four-thousand-metre-high mountains. In four hours the 'slowest express train in the world' travels 291 kilometres, unforgettable to anyone who experiences the journey, especially if they take the Comfort Express with the generous observation windows.

Sankt Gotthard, High Alps *(bottom right)*

On the border of the Swiss cantons of Wallis, Tessin and Graubünden, stands the Gotthard massif among the High Alps. A mountain pass leads across it, at a height of 2,108 metres, from Andermatt to Airolo. Today one can travel between the two using a 16.3 kilometre long motorway tunnel opened in 1980, but some people, who have the time and who like to experience the mountains, still prefer to use the slow and tedious, but scenically more rewarding route over the pass. After taking a rest at the top, enjoying the panoramic views you can test your driving skills on the incredibly convoluted hairpin bends on the way down.

Chillon Castle *(far bottom right)*

On a small rocky island at the far eastern point of Lake Geneva stands the many-towered Chillon Castle from the 13th century. It is not only picturesque but also has literary connections: Lord Byron (1788–1824), the great English Romantic poet wrote the ballad of the *Prisoner of Chillon*, telling the story of the protestant François Bonivard, who in 1530, at the command of the Duke of Savoy, was chained to a pillar in the castle and had to languish in this dungeon for six years, until the Bernese conquered Chillon and freed him. His tracks, allegedly worn into the stone floor by his walking around the pillar for years, are still shown to curious visitors today. The Knights' Hall, the Court Room and the Armoury are also worth seeing.

Tourbillon Fort and Valeria Castle, Sion *(top)*

Between vine terraces and high mountains in the Swiss Rhône valley, lies the capital of the Swiss canton of Wallis. Sion, the Romans called it Sedunum, the Germans Sitten, has preserved much from former times: on one side of a double-peak of rock stands a castle, Valeria (right), others say palace, where the bishops resided until their power was broken in 1798. Their parish church was Notre Dame de Valère, which came into existence in the 12th/13th centuries as a triple-naved basilica and with Romanesque features. There is also late Gothic decoration and wood carvings from the Renaissance. On the other, higher, rock sits enthroned the fort of Tourbillon (left in picture) with battlements from the 14th century. It burned down in 1788 and now keeps guard as a ruin.

Glacier World, Zermatt *(bottom)*

Today we experience the melting of the glaciers, perhaps because of global warming caused by the emission of so-called 'greenhouse gases'. However, shrinking glaciers, as well as an increase in glaciers, can also have natural causes, as demonstrated, for example, in Zermatt in the Swiss canton of Wallis: today one can get lost above the internationally popular spa town at the foot of the mighty Matterhorn (see picture), in a sheer infinite world of glaciers. Yet, 2,000 years ago this area in the high mountains on the border between France and Italy was completely ice-free. The Romans used the passes as trading routes to Ostratia, present-day Wallis. Today they lie under permanent ice, which only occasionally releases antiquities: coins, weapons and bridles.

Eiger North Face, Bernese Alps (top)

The picture is forever being shown in the press and on television – excited people with binoculars who are straining to stare up at an almost perpendicular rock wall upon which ant-like figures can be made out, whilst above the craggy 3,970-metre-high summit the clouds are gathering. The 1,800 metre towering north face of the Eiger was only climbed for the first time by mountaineers in 1938, after it had claimed innumerable victims who were either daring climbers or more mad than clever. And yet, this mountain side, so wrapped in tragedy, still draws adventurers as if under a magic spell, and the mountain rescue service often has its work cut out to prevent the worst.

Madonna del Sasso Pilgrimage Church, Locarno (bottom left)

On a rocky outcrop in the village of Orselina stands the most important sight of the Swiss spa of Locarno at the north end of Lake Maggiore: the Madonna del Sasso pilgrimage church. It takes its name and its attraction to pilgrims from a late Gothic picture of Mary, but this is certainly not all there is here for the visitor: for instance there are other important works of art – the panel depicting 'the Flight into Egypt' by Bramantino (1465–1530). There is also a charming view from the church terrace of the town of Locarno with its gardens resplendent in spring and of the colourful life of the lake and of the mountains round about.

Great Saint Bernard Pass, Valais Alps (bottom right)

One has been able to pass underneath since 1964, earlier though, you had to climb up to a height of 2,473 metres if you wanted to get to the Italian Aosta Valley from the Swiss Rhône Valley via the St. Bernard Pass. Anyone who manages to spare the time, even today, would prefer the route via the glorious mountain scenery to that through the dark pipe. The road, along the same route where the Romans had already built a road, now leads to the monastery which St. Bernard of Menthon founded in the 11th century and which was later taken over by the Augustinian Choristers. In their monastery church one can see magnificent choirstalls and a museum displaying antiquities found. Directly next door are the runs and kennels where the St. Bernards are trained to be rescue dogs.

Eiger-Mönch-Jungfrau Massif, Bernese Alps *(top)*

Massive steps lead up to the tourist resort of Grindelwald, in the Bernese Oberland, which is already above 1,000 metres above sea level. But the Eiger still towers above it with its 3,970 metres. Up there, on the summit, the succesful mountaineer has to look up again in a south-westerly direction to the Mönch, which is another 129 metres higher, but in turn must look up in the same direction to the Jungfrau, which is another 60 metres nearer to heaven. The latter is easier to reach though, than its colleagues: from the Kleine Scheidegg the Jungfrau rack railway, which was completed by 1912, brings visitors through a tunnel up to the 3,464-metre-high Jungfraujoch. 100 metres above the summit, an observatory looks into space while the tourists enjoy the view of this world.

Aletsch Glacier, Bernese Alps *(bottom left)*

In the Swiss canton of Wallis, the Alps reach out further than anywhere else: from the firn mass of the Finsteraarhorn group the Aletsch glacier pushes towards the valley. With a total length of 23 kilometres, it covers 87 square kilometres and, 1,800 metres wide, it flows past the Eggishorn (2,979 metres) and past the 300 hectare Aletsch forest reserve, the highest European wood; Swiss pine still thrive at 2,330 metres above sea level. The mountain station on the Eggishorn, only 60 metres under the summit, is reached from the Rhône valley side in Fiesch by cable car, the rest of the way can be covered in half an hour on the paved path. It is worthwhile as from the summit there is an unforgettable view of high mountain scenery.

St. John's Monastery, Müstair *(bottom right)*

As early as the time of Charlemagne, 1,200 years ago, the Benedictine Abbey of St. John in Müstair came into existence in the valley of the Rombach in the Swiss canton of Graubünden, which was run initially by monks and then later by nuns of the same order, and which was continually expanded throughout the Middle Ages. During the Gothic period, the monastery church, which dates back to the early days of the monastery, received fan vaulting, broken pediments and rows of columns. From the Carolingian time it has a fresco cycle with scenes from the life of Jesus and of the crucifixion of the apostle St. Andrew. In the monastery museum are further frescos and masonry sculptures from the early days. Beautifully furnished monastery rooms, including the princes' room with furniture from the 17th century, can be visited. A UNESCO World Heritage Site since 1983.

Austria

Old Town, Salzburg

A striking meeting point between Southern and Northern Europe was formed in the Austrian city of Salzburg over the course of the Middle Ages and right into the 19th century. For a long time a kind of city-state under the rule of an archbishop, the Old Town on the left bank of the Salzach on the slopes of the Mönch and fortress hill gained an unmistakable character. In the centre stands the cathedral from the early 17th century, added to this are the Residence from the same period, the Residence's fountain and the so-called New Building, further churches of different styles, the archbishop's palace, the riding school now converted into the festival theatre, the town hall, the old university and above all the house where Mozart was born. All these together have been a UNESCO World Heritage Site since 1997.

Fortress of Hohensalzburg, Salzburg *(bottom)*

From here you have Mozart's city at your feet: on the *Festungsberg* (fortress hill), overlooking Salzburg, stands the fortress of Hohensalzburg (in the background of the picture below), started in the 11th century and remodelled and extended several times since then. It is one of the few fortifications preserved intact in the town long ruled by the Prince Bishops. An ancient organ, richly decorated rooms, a castle museum — there is a lot to see in the fortress, and even more from it. The view reaches far over the roofs and cupolas to the Kapuziner Hill on the other side of the Salzach River. The fortress can be reached by a lift, but it is worth walking, for the sake of the splendid views.

Nonnberg Convent, Salzburg *(top)*

The German name (meaning nuns' hill) says it — that here is the counterpart to the Mönchberg (monks' hill) and the Festungsberg (fortress hill) of the city on the River Salzach. The convent has been occupied by Benedictines since 1463, making it the oldest convent of the German-speaking world. The convent building is of an even older date and the collegiate church is also considerably older. Frescos from the 12th century decorate the otherwise simple and stern interior.

Salzburg Cathedral *(bottom)*

The front is well known all over the world from films and TV broadcasts of Hofmannsthal's mystery play *Everyman*. It takes place annually in front of Salzburg Cathedral, and this is how it has been since the Salzburg Festival started in 1920. The Baroque church building (1614–1628, in the foreground in the picture, right) was erected on top of older churches from the Romanesque era the remains of which can be seen in the crypt. The Cathedral Museum too, with its paintings, sculptures and handicrafts, as well as the 'miracle chamber' with, not so much miraculous, but beautiful furniture, clocks and other valuables from the 17th and 18th centuries make a visit worthwhile.

Eisriesenwelt, Tennengebirge (below left)

South-east of the 'Mozart city' of Salzburg are the Tennen Mountains, which are neither very high nor memorable on account of their appearance. The attraction is underground: at a height of 1,664 metres, accessible by cable car and about 15 minutes uphill on foot, the earth opens up and allows the visitor to enter a bizarre cave system. With a length of 50 kilometres, the *Eisriesenwelt* ('World of Ice Giants') is the biggest ice cave in the world and despite busy streams of visitors has still not been fully explored into the last nook and cranny. The guided tour, without which one is not allowed to move through the cold and dark ice sculpture park, shows only a fraction of this underworld — but what an underworld: frozen waterfalls, ice towers, an ice gateway and many other frosty attractions.

Hallstatt-Dachstein Salzkammergut Cultural Landscape (below right)

The town of Hallstatt lies in the Salzkammergut region, at the feet of the mighty Dachstein range, which is up to 3,000 metres high. However, the place is not likely to be known from geography lessons, but instead the name might be familiar from history books: not just the picturesque lake nearby is named after it, but also an entire prehistoric era. A cemetery from the time between 800 and 400 BC was discovered here, with burial gifts in over 2,000 graves providing information about life in the late Bronze Age. They also tell of the technical skills required to exploit the valuable salt deposits in this area. The entire cultural landscape of the Hallstatt-Dachstein Salzkammergut has been a UNESCO World Heritage Site since 1997.

Benedictine Monastery, Melk (very bottom)

The Romans treasured the Danube landscape and erected a stronghold where the lower Austrian regional capital Melk is located. In the 10th century there was already a castle here and 100 years later the monks of the Benedictine order came and erected a monastery overlooking the town. In 1702, construction work began again in the location as the mighty building complex of a new seminary, designed by Jakob Prandtauer (1660–1726), was being erected. The architect did not live to see the seminary completed in 1736. However, he had established a permanent architectural memorial to himself with this complex, one of the most beautiful Baroque ensembles in Europe.

Karlskirche, Vienna *(top)*

The Karlskirche, the crowning jewel of the 4th district, is a must for visitors to the Austrian capital. It was built by the Fischer von Erlachs, father (1656–1723) and son (1693–1742) between 1716 and 1739 in Baroque style. At that time it lay outside the town on the banks of the River Wien. Together with the Schönbrunn Palace (see below), this monument of the Counter-Reformation is one of the most exquisite masterpieces of this famous father-and-son team.

Schönbrunn Palace and Park *(bottom)*

Schönbrunn was started in 1695 in accordance with plans by the architect Fischer von Erlach (1656–1723) in the vicinity of Vienna (now a part of Vienna), as a residence for the Habsburg emperor. Empress Maria Theresa and her husband, Emperor Franz I, were the ones who experienced the completion of the imposing construction in early Classicist style in 1744–1749. The interior was given a Rococo character in 1765–1780. In contrast, the extensive park was laid out as early as 1705/06 and runs up the Schönbrunn Hill whence one can enjoy a splendid panoramic view from the Gloriette erected in 1775. The zoo in the park, which was established as early as 1752, was the first of its kind in the world. A UNESCO World Heritage Site since 1997.

Hundertwasser House, Vienna *(top)*

There are almost no right angles on this building, straight lines are scarce and the eye starts to wallow pleasurably in the colourful swellings and waves on the façade: it is apparent that the creator of the colourful Viennese house was really a painter and graphic artist. Friedensreich Hundertwasser (1928–2000), whose real, slightly less poetic, name was Stowasser, was unwilling to put up with geometric architecture and box-like constructions. Initially, many of Vienna's citizens were rather bewildered by this appartment block, built in 1983–1986. By now they have all made friends with it — indeed are proud of this eye-catching edifice.

Belvedere Palace, Vienna *(centre)*

Not far from the Habsburg Schönbrunn Palace, the imperial Field Marshall Prince Eugen of Savoy (1663–1736) had the *Belvedere* ('Beautiful View') garden palace built between 1721 and 1723 by the court's architect Johann Lukas von Hildebrandt (1668–1745). In so doing, he presented the Austrian capital with a Baroque jewel that is one of the main attractions in the cityscape.

Hofburg, Vienna *(bottom left)*

"I'd rather live in the desert", emperor Leopold I (1658–1705) is reported to have said, than in his Hofburg, which in those days was not at all as elegantly furnished as it is today. These days, it has become a splendid mixture of different building styles and covers an area of 240,000 square metres. Originally a miserable defensive fortification from the 13th century, it had already become a magnificent palace by the time of the Vienna Congress in 1815. Today it is the official workplace of the Federal Chancellor and his 5,000 civil servants. The national library and some museums are also accommodated in the Hofburg.

Spanish Riding School, Vienna *(bottom right)*

A riding 'room' was founded in 1572 where the present day Josef Square is situated, this was the origin of the Spanish Riding School with its a rich tradition. It regards its duty to be the guardianship of the high school of equitation with Lippizaner stallions, the highest level of dressage. In 1735 it moved into the current building designed by Fischer von Erlach (1656–1723). This is where impeccably turned-out riders with cocked hat and brown tail-coat demonstrate piaffe and passage, flying changes and leaps on snow-white horses with gold-trimmed bridles.

St Stephen's Cathedral, Vienna *(top left)*

The symbol of the Austrian capital, Vienna, is the 137-metre-high main tower of the Gothic Cathedral of St. Stephen. The cathedral was first erected in a Romanesque style, but the building burned down and was replaced by a new building in the current form of a triple-naved hall church. It is 108 metres long, 27 metres high and 70 metres wide in the transept. It became the seat of a bishop and cathedral priest in 1469 and holds valuable treasures, including the grave of the troubadour Neidhart von Reuenthal (circa 1245) and the marble grave of Emperor Friedrich III (1415–1493). Also worth seeing is the bell in the main tower which weighs ten tonnes and was cast in 1711 from Turkish cannons.

St. Peter's, Vienna *(far top right)*

Along with the Belvedere Palace, the Baroque Church of St. Peter belongs to the masterful Viennese works of the Austrian court architect Johann Lukas von Hildebrand (1668–1745). Its sombre façade reveals the beauty of its proportions especially when illuminated at night. The light brings out the green dome with the small cupola above it, whilst the two short corner towers fade into the background slightly. Hildebrand set standards with his decoration of the portal and the internal decoration of the church.

Semmering Train, Eastern Alps
(above right)

In 1854, a remarkable railway was inaugurated: the 41-kilometre-long railway over the 985-metre-high Semmering Pass in the eastern Alps was completed after a construction period lasting 6 years, one of the most astonishing engineering feats in this pioneering age of the railway. Tunnels, viaducts and other construction work alongside the railway have proved to be solid enough to be still in use today. The trains travel through a unique mountain panorama in a landscape which only became accessible for most people through this rail link. As an outstanding example of solving extremely tricky engineering problems, the line has been a UNESCO World Heritage Site since 1998.

Stams Seminary *(top left)*

The stern walls of the Cistercian abbey in the Austrian town of Stams (Tyrol) seemed not to fit the strategies of the Counter-Reformation at the time. Furthermore, it was too narrow and too dark. The monks therefore had the monastery church remodelled in Baroque style between 1729–1732 and richly decorated with the stuccos of Franz Xaver Feuchtmayer (1705–1764). The seminary building, which now houses a boarding school, had already been remodelled earlier in line with the period.

Hohe Tauern National Park *(far top right)*

One of the most scenic mountain roads in Europe leads past Austria's highest mountain, the Grossglockner (3,797 metres, see picture), and through the Hohe Tauern National Park. The road through the high Alps, which was finished in 1935 and which at 2,505 metres reaches the highest pass at Hochtor, offers the most spectacular views. The summit of the Edelweissspitze (2,577 metres) allows an even better view across the breathtaking Alpine landscape. A side road from Fuscher Törl leads there, with 3,000-metre-high mountains towering all around it. On a clear day one can see as far as the Berchtesgarden area. The closest you can get to the gigantic Grossglockner is on the road to Franz-Joseph's Heights (2,362 metres).

Old Town, Graz *(above right)*

An extraordinary example of the successful integration of very different styles can be found in Graz, the capital of the Steiermark. In the Old Town is a collection of architectural monuments from a great variety of different eras, showing influences from as far apart as the Mediterranean as well as Northern Germany: the early Gothic Leech Church, which came into being at the end of the 13th century, and the late Gothic cathedral from the 15th century, the mausoleum of the Emperor Ferdinand II (1614) and the Renaissance building of the Landhaus, in which today the regional parliament meets, the castles of Eggenberg (completed in 1635) and Gösting (1728). A UNESCO World Heritage Site since 1999.

Italy

Milan Cathedral (top)

The Lombardy and its main city Milan lay under the influence of the German emperor for many centuries. As a result of this, and also its close proximity to Northern Europe, the second largest Italian city has a good number of Gothic buildings. The most important is the Santa Maria Nascente Cathedral, which was built, in its main parts, between 1387 and 1485, though it was only finished completely in the 19th century – in fact, some parts were only completed in the 20th century – without losing any of its medieval character. The mighty cathedral is 158 metres long, 93 metres wide, 108 metres high and is richly decorated with 2,300 sculptures and 135 turrets. Sculptures and heavy cluster columns also decorate the gloomy interior of the five-aisled nave.

Rock Drawings, Val Camonica (bottom)

Particularly industrious artists lived over 1,000 years ago along the river Oglio in the Camonica Valley in the Italian Alps, west of the rocky mass of the 3,554-metre-high Adamello. In 900 pictures, which they engraved in the rock of the 'Large Stone' or etched into the walls of caves, they captured everyday agricultural scenes, lengthy hunts or armed conflicts. The oldest pictures from the Neopalaeolithic era (New Stone Age) are only on the theme of hunting, but with the transition to the Mesolithic (Middle Stone Age) the artists outgrew their 'matchstick men' style of drawing, and in the Bronze Age they produced highly skilful compositions. A UNESCO World Heritage Site since 1979.

Santa Maria delle Grazie and The Last Supper, Milan *(top left and bottom)*

Painted 1495 to 1497, 'The Last Supper' by Leonardo da Vinci (1452–1519) covers the entire wall of a refectory used by the monks of the Monastery of Santa Maria delle Grazie in Milan (bottom left). Leonardo arranged it to appear like an extension to the monks' dining hall: a groundbreaking step, for never before had the sacred episode appeared so close and so life-like. The work captures the moment when Christ says "Verily I say unto you, that one of you shall betray me". Not only for its striking reality, but also for Leonardo's power of imagination that enabled him to put the scene before our eyes, it is one of the most important works of art in western culture. Today a carefully restored version of the 9 metre by 4.5 metre painting can be seen. A UNESCO World Heritage Site since 1980.

Galleria Vittorio Emanuele II, Milan *(top right)*

On 15 September 1867, Italy's king, Victor Emanuel, opened the new galleria, named after him, between the cathedral square and the Piazza della Scala in the northern city of Milan. A true temple of the bourgeois age, it is popularly known as the 'Milan Salon' (*Salotto di Milano*). The cruciform, five-storey shopping mall with two 196 and 105-metre-long arcades and a 47-metre-high dome, an exact replica of that of St. Peter's in Rome, has inlaid marble floors and an octagonal centre, 36 metres in diameter. Along the walls are pictures of famous Italians.

Residences of the House of Savoy, Turin and its surroundings

(top left, centre and right)

Not exactly off a production line like the cars made here to-day came the palaces of the Savoy dynasty in the North Italian town of Turin (Piemont) and its surroundings, but they did come into being in quick succession: Palazzo Reale (1646–1668, left), Palazzo Carignano (1679–1685), Palazzo Madama (1718, remodelling of a medieval castle, centre) and the hunting lodge Stupinigi (after 1720, right) which is situated to the south-west of the town. This is not all of them but the selection is sufficient to demonstrate the desire of the ruling house to build imposing monuments in the 17ᵗʰ/18ᵗʰ centuries, which brought the palaces the status of UNESCO World Heritage Site in 1997.

Verona *(bottom)*

Beautiful Verona lies on both banks of the river in the province of North Italy at the narrow exit of the Adige valley into the Po plain. Roman relics such as the amphitheatre (see picture) are amongst its beauties as well as the town gates, the Romanesque cathedral with its rich decoration of figures, the Piazza dei Signori with the Romanesque town hall (Palazzo del Comune) and many churches of various styles. Shakespeare fans and lovers are drawn above all to Juliet's house (Casa di Giulietta), with the famous balcony below which Romeo yearned.

The Shroud of Turin *(centre, top)*

Works of many volumes have been written about it and still clarification has not yet been obtained: since 1578 a 1.10 by 4.36 metres large linen cloth has been kept, which has been attested since the 14ᵗʰ century as the shroud of Christ and venerated as such. For some it is the most precious relic of Christendom, others doubt the authenticity of the cloth, which shows the impression of a victim of crucifixion. Facts, which people were hoping to obtain from an age analysis, remain ambiguous. In 1988 it was once again put on display, after it was saved at the last minute, the year before, from a fire.

Roman Remains and Basilica, Aquileia *(centre, below)*

Before the now small town of Aquileia, which lies in the Isonzo delta, was destroyed by Attila's Huns in 452 AD, it was the fourth largest town in Italy. From this golden age there are many remains: ruins of houses, port facilities, grave monuments, amphitheatre, forum; the town's museums display the smaller finds. As well as the testimonies to the town's Roman past there is the triple-nave basilica from the 11ᵗʰ century in which one can see a 645 square metre mosaic floor from early Christian times and a crypt from Carolingian times. A UNESCO World Heritage Site from 1997.

Venice and its Lagoon *(top and bottom)*

So well-known from many cultural references and yet, nevertheless, Venice never ceases to amaze at first sight. Northern Italy's pearl on the lagoon with the countless canals and bridges, does not leave its annual 1.5 million visitors indifferent. Its show side is imbued with art and culture from the Church of St. Mark's, begun in 1063, to the Doge's Palace (12th–15th century), the Renaissance building of the Sansovino library and the Church of San Giorgio Maggiore from the same time to the Baroque Church of Santa Maria della Salute and back to the arcaded piazza in front of St.Mark's — architectural gems at every step, which hide further masterpieces within. A UNESCO World Heritage Site since 1987.

Portovenere and Cinque Terre, Liguria (top)

Whole stretches of the Ligurian coast in the north-west of Italy drop off steeply into the Gulf of Spezia and some of the islands off the Riviera di Levante are steep too. It is only when you are close up that you see how nevertheless thickly settled these strips are and how cleverly the 'five places' (Cinque Terre) and Portovenere cling to the slopes. They rise up in rows and building by building, in so doing the churches seem almost to hover. At the first glance, the anchoring of the wholly medieval houses of God can be scarcely ascertained. And yet a railway snakes its way past in front of and behind the buildings along the coast. As a successful cultivation of a rich nature this stretch has been a UNESCO World Heritage Site since 1997.

Palladio's Villas, Vicenza (bottom left)

The buildings in Vicenza, the capital of the Italian province of Venetia on the Bacchiglione, originate from many centuries. Above all, the medieval churches bear witness to a significant past. Particularly impressive are the palatial buildings by Andrea Palladio (1508–1580), who shaped the appearance of the town with his architectural works in Renaissance style, which made it a UNESCO World Heritage Site in 1994. The Basilica of Palladio and the Villa Rotunda (1566/67), which is situated close to the town, should be mentioned in particular, as these were architectural precedents for generations to come.

Romanesque Churches, Genoa
(bottom right)

The Romanesque cathedral and the Church of San Matteo in the same style are representative of many treasured buildings in the North Italian port of Genoa. The archbishop's Church of San Lorenzo, which was consecrated in 1118, a columned basilica, although restored several times, its core and the spatial effect of the triple nave have however remained. The John the Baptist Chapel houses the relics of the saint, brought back by crusaders. On a smaller scale, the Church of San Matteo (see picture), founded seven years later, repeats the architectural experience. This is where the Genoese condottiere Andrea Doria (1466–1560) is buried.

Cathedral, Torre Ghirlandina, Piazza Grande, Modena *(top, left)*

The 'La Ghirlandina' bell tower towers above the city in the Italian province of Emilia-Romagna like an exclamation mark, pointing out a gem of the Italian Romanesque: the Cathedral of San Geminiano, consecrated in 1184, on the Piazza Grande in Modena. The triple-naved basilica with its decorative statues and both the small towers on the front captivates through refined simplicity and dignity. Together with the campanile, which takes its name from the stone garlands around the spire, and the square as the heart of the archbishop's town on the edge of the Po plain, the cathedral has been a UNESCO World Heritage Site since 1997.

Early Christian Buildings, Ravenna *(above left)*

The centre of power of the Romans' Western empire, Ravenna, in the Po delta was the capital of the Ostrogoth Empire and also in the Byzantine age. The buildings of both epochs are testimonies to early Christian art: the core of the cathedral, like the mausoleum of the Galla Pacidia, stems from the 5th century. The powerful grave of Theoderich the Great (circa 520 AD), which heralds the Romanesque style, the Sant'Apollinare Nuovo (507 AD), the Church of San Vitale, consecrated in 547 AD, and Sant' Apollinare in Classe (549 AD) with the round campanile are only slightly younger. Splendid mosaics in the houses of worship reflect the piety of this time of turmoil. A UNESCO World Heritage Site since 1996.

Old Town, Ferrara *(above right)*

During the 15th/16th centuries the northern Italian town of Ferrara flourished under the rule of the dukes from the house of Este. In those days, the poets Ariost and Tasso glorified the rulers, who at that time had their Castello Estense (see picture) completed. The castle, which was completed in 1570 in its current form, a building surrounded by a moat with its four towers dominates the Old Town with its holy counterpart being the Romanesque cathedral begun in 1135, whose campanile has remained incomplete. The palaces of the nobility in Renaissance style bear witness to the fact that a reflection of the glory of the ruling family also fell onto the aristocratic families. A UNESCO World Heritage Site since 1995.

Historical Centre, Florence (top)

The symbol of the capital of the province of Tuscany is the octagonal, 42-metre-wide dome of the Santa Maria del Fiore Cathedral (1296–1436) with which the architect Brunelleschi (1377–1446) crowned the building upon its completion. The octagonal baptistry (11th century) with the three later bronze doors and the campanile, which Giotto designed in 1334, also belong to the Florentine cathedral. Looking from here in the direction of the River Arno you can see the tower of the fortress-like Palazzo Vecchio (1298–1314), where the town council (*signoria*) met and the rooms of which are decorated with statues by Michelangelo, Donatello and Verrocchio amongst others. Directly next door one can visit the scarcely 200 years younger Uffizi, which today shelters one of the most important collections of paintings in the world. A few steps further on and you are standing on the oldest bridge of the city on the Arno, the Ponte Vecchio (1345), which has been built on and is lined with gold- and silversmiths shops. On the other side of the river is the Palazzo Pitti, which has been in its present-day monumental form since 1558. These and many other sights have been a UNESCO World Heritage Site since 1982.

Cathedral Square, Pisa (bottom left)

The first thing that comes to mind when one hears the word Pisa is, of course, the leaning tower, the symbol of the Tuscan town on the River Arno. However, the tower is part of an entire medieval building complex on the Piazza del Duomo (cathedral square), which has been a UNESCO World Heritage Site since 1987 due to its unique architecture. Here stands the Santa Maria Assunta Cathedral (1063–1118) on a cruciform outline with its galleried front over the three Romanesque portals and its crossing cupola. In front of the cathedral is the baptistry, the largest in the world, with the famous pulpit by Niccolò Pisano from the 13th century. The campanile for the complex is the leaning tower.

Historical Centre, Urbino (bottom right)

This is holy ground for fans of the Italian Renaissance: in the centre of Urbino, in the province of Marche, is the birthplace of the painter Raphael (1483–1520) and the buildings which thoroughly deserve to stand at the side of the greatest son of the town: Palazzo Ducale (1444–1472, national gallery since 1912), Data (stables for 300 noble steeds), cathedral (1474–1534) with campanile from the 18th century and the Church of Santo Domenico, consecrated in 1365 (remodelled in Baroque style). Urbino has been a UNESCO World Heritage Site since 1998.

Historical Centre, San Gimignano (top)

There is nowhere better to get an idea of what a medieval town in Italy looked like than in San Gimignano in Tuscany. Its strange silhouette alone, with the 13 towering clan towers, of which there are supposed to have been more than 70 originally, makes one curious upon approach. These were residential and defensive towers of the mostly estranged noble families within the settlement. Also preserved is the town wall as well as palace and church buildings. In the cathedral (12th century, remodelled 15th century) there are works of art from the Tuscan Renaissance, including frescos by Ghirlandaio (1449–1494). The Old Town is a UNESCO World Heritage Site since 1990.

Volterra, Tuscany (above left)

Barricaded behind the severe façades of medieval palaces the ancient heart of the Tuscan town of Volterra is hidden. It was founded in the 6th century BC by the Etruscans and was something of a metropolis for these pre-Roman people. Proof of this is the Porta all'Arco the six-metre-high town gate and the remains of the earlier protective wall. The rich ornamentation on hundreds of stone urns, which are on display in the museum of Volterra, give an idea of the Etruscans' beliefs. They cremated their dead and furnished them with rich burial gifts which referred to the things they liked when they were alive. Whole cities of the dead have been found as well as a large amphitheatre from the 3rd century BC, dating from before the Etruscans were defeated by the Romans.

Etruscan Town, Populonia (above right)

Above the small round bay of Porto Baratti, opposite the island of Elba in the Tyrrhenian Sea, a hill rises up and on it the tiny place of Populonia. It is the modern version of the Etruscan Pupluna, a town which ruled the surrounding countryside from 7th to 3rd centuries BC and which was famous as a place where iron was smelted. In the end they even covered an old cemetery with the slag from the ironworks. This was rediscovered in the 20th century and excavated: a real city of the dead. Imposing tumuli came to light, whole family fortresses, and the burial gifts which were found gave a good impression of Etruscan skills and customs: jewellery, equipment for the house, tools and weapons can be seen in the museum today.

Old Town, Pienza (facing, top left)

The centre of the town bears the name of the person who also gave the town his name: the trapezoid-shaped Piazza Pius II. Immediately upon being raised to the See of Rome, Pope Pius II had his birthplace, the village then known as Corsignano, over the valleys of Orcia and Asso in the province of Siena, turned into the town of Pienza. He entrusted the architect and sculptor Rossellino (1409–1464) with the task, who then created the first planned town of the Renaissance. The cathedral on the Piazza has a marble altar from Rossellino's workshop and he also created the Palazzo Piccolomini (the Pope's name at birth). A UNESCO World Heritage Site since 1996.

Etruscan Grave, Cerveteri (facing, top middle)

Their origins are in dispute. If one believes the legend and adds to this the similarity of some of the words in their language with some from the Hittite language, then the Etruscans were escaped Trojans. After the defeat of their city by the Greeks, they had settled in present day Etruria in Central Italy, which is named after them. Although they were successful in this, their superior technical skills were not enough when Rome began to subjugate the whole of Italy. The Etruscans also had to give way before them. In the first century BC, they became Roman citizens. The subsequent, almost complete Romanisation eclipsed their culture, of which today mainly the typical tombs bear witness: the so-called tumuli, round massive domed tombs, which protected the deceased like a fortress. A well-preserved example is to be found in Cerveteri, ancient Caere.

Castel del Monte, Apulia (facing, top right)

Like a walled crown on a 540-metre-high hill is what the Castel del Monte, in the Italian province of Apulia, looks like from a distance. The Staufer emperor Friedrich II (ruled 1212–1225) had it built in the last ten years of his rule, on an octagonal ground outline as a monumental hunting lodge but also as a demonstration of his power highly visible from afar in the open undulating landscape. With its eight likewise octagonal towers and octagonal rooms it is one of the most significant secular buildings in southern Italy. It has been used as a prison from time to time and has been in state ownership since 1876. Since 1996 it has been a UNESCO World Heritage Site.

Perugia, Umbria (facing, centre left)

The Gothic Cathedral of San Lorenzo and the Churches of San Pietro de'Cassinesi, San Bernardino, San Severo (with a fresco by Raphael), the Gothic town hall (in the picture: Piazza Reale), the Renaissance castle as well as numerous other valuable buildings make the Italian town of Perugia in Umbria into the most important art centre of the region. The remains still standing of the ancient ring wall from the Etruscan age have also led to a stream of tourists who boost the already lively goings on in the university city (since 1276) and seat of an archbishop.

Historic Centre, Siena (facing, bottom)

The Piazza del Campo, a narrow crescent-shaped square in the Italian city of Siena in Tuscany, is the venue for one of the most famous horse races in the world, the annual *Palio*, which has been held since medieval times. At the lower end of the Campo stands the Palazzo Pubblico, the town hall erected in 1297–1310 with the Torre del Mangia bell tower (1338–1348). Nothing is any distance here, even the architectural gem of the three-gabled cathedral built from white and black marble. This is one of the most significant examples of Italian Gothic from the 12th to the 14th centuries. Further churches and palaces of the nobility from the 16th century round off the picture, which made the old town into a UNESCO World Heritage Site in 1995.

Hadrian's Villa, Rome (below)

On the slopes of the Tivoli heights in Rome, the Roman Emperor Hadrian (reigned 117–138 AD) built himself a palace-like country home. In the extensive grounds (ten kilometres in circumference) he built imitations of remarkable buildings from all parts of his world empire. Before taking power, he had travelled the empire far and wide and continued to do so afterwards. Furthermore, he established an academy, had a theatre and thermal baths built, all of them decorated with sculptures, busts, reliefs, wall paintings and mosaics. Some of these testimonies to imperial pride can be seen in situ, others in Roman museums. A UNESCO World Heritage Site since 1999.

Historic Centre, Vatican and Rome
(top and centre)

It is impossible to list all the ancient monuments in the Italian capital Rome, once the capital of the world. We will only name the tomb of the Emperor Augustus (died 14 AD) and, as the most visible sight, the Colosseum (picture right) built under the Flavian emperors in the first century. It is the largest amphitheatre in the ancient world with its 50,000 seats, its three-storey façade still standing, together with the ruins of the internal facilities. When the Empire's glory crumbled the church inherited it. However, the external appearance of the city decayed thereafter and it has only been since the Middle Ages that it has recovered. Now religious buildings such as San Paolo fuori le mura (4th century) or St. Peter's Cathedral (built 1505–1624), which is from the new golden age of the Renaissance, set the tone. The ancient and the religious in the heart of Rome have been a UNESCO World Heritage Site since 1980.

Forum Romanum, Rome *(bottom)*

At the foot of the Palatine hill, not far from the banks of the Tiber, the visitor to Rome finds only a field of rubble at the first glance: broken walls, overturned columns or the stumps of broken ones. However, here on the Forum Romanum beat the heart of the Roman World Empire in ancient times, it is where the people's assemblies took place, where the temple to Vesta (goddess of the hearth) stood and where the high priest (*Pontifex maximus*) resided. Laid out in the 6th century BC, the forum was embellished in the time of the emperors. It is from this time that most of the remains originate. These have been uncovered starting from the beginning of the 19th century and can be visited today on an informative guided tour to gain an insight.

Sistine Chapel, Rome *(top)*

A simple hall construction with a rectangular outline, barrel vaulting and arched windows became the summit of Renaissance art: for the Sistine Chapel in the Vatican erected (1473–1481) for, and named after, Pope Sixtus IV who commissioned it, many artists created frescos, amongst them Botticelli (1445–1510) and above all Michelangelo (1475–1564). They were guided in their work by the thought of the Old Testament being the precursor of the New Testament in scenes from the lives of Moses and of Christ. In 1519, the lower part of the walls on the long sides received tapestries as wall coverings (story of the apostles) designed by Raphael (1483–1520). When it was painted for a second time 1536–1541, Michelangelo depicted the 'Judgement Day' on the western altar wall.

Pantheon, Rome *(bottom left)*

At the beginning of the 2nd century AD a temple to all gods, the Pantheon, was erected and furnished in a particularly magnificent way. It is a 43.2-metre-high and equally wide cupola which receives light through a nine-metre-wide opening in the vertex and which is divided up by columns and niches where once the statues of the gods stood. It was reconsecrated as a Christian church, Santa Maria ad Martyres, in 609 and has remained so since then. This is where the painter Raphael (1483–1520) and some early members of the Italian royal family are buried.

Vatican Collections, Rome *(bottom right)*

Since the Renaissance, the popes have seen to it that important cultural treasures have been collected under church supervision: Julius II (1503–1513) installed ancient statues, amongst them the Laokoon group; Benedict XIV (1740–1758) founded the Museo Sacro for archaeological and art treasures of Christian origin. There followed museums for Etruscan antiquities, ancient Egyptian finds, for missionary history and ethnography. In 1932, Pius XI (1922–1939) had a picture galley erected for the papal art collection. In 1973, a collection of contemporary religious art was established under Paul VI (1963–1978). The Vatican library and the Vatican archives, which go back to the 6th century, are also to be counted with these.

Castel Gandolfo (top)

The small Italian town of Castel Gandolfo in the Alban hills near Rome owes its fame to Pope Urban VIII, who had the holy fathers' summer residence there magnificently done up in the early 17th century. On the west bank of the Lago di Albano, situated at over 400 metres, the villa in the fresh mountain air serves as a refreshing place to stay to recover from the stifling and sweltering eternal city. The landscape around the lake, which measures 600 hectares, has a more than 500-metre-high extinct volcano towering over it and in ancient times was already attracting rich Romans to build country homes here. The Pope's country seat is, as part of the Vatican, extra-territorial.

Palazzo Reale, Caserta Vecchia, Aquaduct, San Leucio, Caserta
(bottom)

The honorary title of 'Italian Versailles' is no exaggeration for the palace and its estate in Caserta to the north of Naples: with 1,200 rooms, the Palazzo Reale, built for King Charles IV 1752–1774, with a surface area of 44,000 square metres and the 1.2-square-kilometre-large park is well qualified to be placed on an equal footing with its French counterpart. Furthermore, it stands in a landscape which is steeped in history: five kilometres to the north is Caserta Vecchia and an old Roman aqueduct as well as the hermitage of King Ferdinand IV – San Leuchio with the Baroque Church of Santa Maria delle Grazie. A UNESCO World Heritage Site since 1997.

Blue Grotto, Capri *(top)*

The Roman emperor Tiberius (42 BC to 37 AD), who ruled the empire from 14 AD, ruled from the island of Capri for the last few years. There he had the *Villa Iovis* built on the western summit known today as the Monte Tiberio, which drops abruptly 334 metres into the sea. An opening, which is only one metre high above the surface of the sea, enables small boats to enter a 54-metre-long, 30-metre-wide and 15-metre-high cave – the world-famous Blue Grotto. Its magical, changing blue colour is a result of the sunlight entering through the seawater.

Montecassino, Latium *(bottom left)*

Devout Catholics will think of this place when their time comes: the Montecassino Abbey in the Italian district of Latium (Frosinone province) was founded by St Benedict of Nursia, the patron saint of dying people. In the year 529 AD, he founded the order named after him and gathered his followers at the first monastery in Europe on the 519-metre-high mountain above the town of Cassino. Destroyed several times, the abbey has been rebuilt again and again, the last time in 1945–1959, after it had been reduced to its foundations in spring 1944 as a result of heavy battles and air raids.

Historic Centre, Naples *(bottom right)*

Three medieval castles: Castel dell'Uovo, Castel Nuovo (see picture), Castel Capuano; the religious buildings: Januarius Cathedral (13th century), St. Restituta Cathedral (7th century), the Church of St. Maria del Carmine with the grave of the last Staufer ruler Conradin, beheaded in 1268, the Church of Gesù Nuovo (16th century); the royal palace from the 17th century and the Renaissance gate Porta Capuana; ancient relics and the finds from the cities destroyed by the eruption of Vesuvius, Pompeii and Herculaneum, displayed in the Museo Nazionale – all this and much more can be seen in the southern Italian city of Naples (Napoli), whose Old Town has been a UNESCO World Heritage Site since 1995.

Vesuvius (facing, top)

The evenly rising cone of the only still active composite volcano on the European mainland offers a majestic view over the Bay of Naples. From the currently 1,270-metre-high and 300-metre-wide crater, clouds are emitted continuously, which usually remain harmless; the last eruptions worth mentioning happened a long time ago (1906 and 1944). As a result, tourists stream up to the edge of the crater using the mountain railway and chairlift, the baths at the bottom of the giant are very busy, and only the excavations in the Roman cities of Pompeii and Herculaneum, which fell victim to the volcano in 79 AD, are arresting question marks as to whether one can trust the calm.

Coastal and Cultural Landscape, Amalfi (facing, bottom)

Culture and nature in harmony: between the large southern Italian cities of Naples and Salerno, fishing villages and picturesque seaside resorts like Amalfi hug the rocky coast. Despite, or precisely because of, the relatively dense settlement, the coastal strip is a highly attractive landscape, as the most unspoilt little places with many an architectural gem fit into the overall picture perfectly, as is shown by the Cathedral of Amalfi, which dates from the 11ᵗʰ century. Even the agricultural usage through vineyards or orchards increases the prettiness of the area. A UNESCO World Heritage Site since 1997.

Pompeii and Herculaneum (top right)

The ancient Roman city of Pompeii, near Naples, was buried, together with the neighbouring Herculaneum, when Vesuvius erupted on 24ᵗʰ August 79 AD. Today it has been almost completely excavated and the visitor can walk through the ancient city and get a feel of its lifestyle which was so suddenly extinguished, such as in the 'House of the Faun' or the 'House of the Vettii'. The same is true of Herculaneum, which also sports luxurious houses and old Roman thermal baths. Both places have been UNESCO World Heritage Sites since 1997.

Trulli, Alberobello (centre right)

They exist in other places as well, but nowhere as dense on the ground as in the southern Italian town of Alberobello in the Bari province, where 1,500 so-called *trulli* form entire streets. These are one-room houses built in a mortarless construction technique out of roughly worked limestone boulders, with pyramidal, domed or conical roofs. The method of construction, which seems prehistoric, is surprising as the snow-white houses actually originate from the 14ᵗʰ century and give the town's quarters of Monti and Aja piccolo, where the trulli occur in some numbers, a fairy-tale appearance. A UNESCO World Heritage Site since 1996.

Paestum, Velia, Padula, Cilento e Vallo di Diano National Park (bottom)

Ruins on the coast of the Tyrrhenian Sea, the magnificent mountainous Alburni landscape in the interior, in the Cilento e Vallo di Diano National Park. South of Salerno lies the one-time Greek settlement of Poseidonia, which was called Paestum in Roman times. Doric temples from the time of the Greeks have been preserved. Roman walls still stand, rubble from medieval houses, which fell into ruin after the flight of the inhabitants following raids by Saracens and Normans. A further ruined city not far away is Velia, ancient Elea, famous due to the Eleates School of Philosophy. Finally, of Christian origin is Padula Monastery (founded in 1306), south-east of Teggiano. The natural and cultural monuments have been a UNESCO World Heritage Site since 1998.

Etna, Sicily (top)

Mount Etna, is at 3,323 metres the largest active volcano in Europe. Due to the exceptional fertility of the volcanic soil, the slopes of the fire-spitting mountain have been very densely settled and intensively cultivated. Close together, in terraces one above the other grow wheat, barley and early vegetables, in the next storey vines, figs, olives and almonds, then oranges and lemons. Then follow chestnut and beech woods before the tree-line is reached at 2,000 metres and the paradise turns into a wasteland of lava debris, finally ending in the maw of the crater. Eruptions, above all from the 250 minor craters, are a frequent occurrence.

Sassi di Matera (centre)

The oldest houses in the southern Italian town of Matera (Basilicata) are made of tuff. Some of the very old ones have even been hewn out of tuff rock and, like honeycombs, are stacked over and inside each other. The caves used for living in are known as *sassi* and originated in an age when the area belonged to the Byzantine Empire and, as former cave churches, they show, despite their age and the damp niches, early Christian murals. The largest house of worship in the city is the Church of St. Lucia with its high tower. It looks out over the Old Town, which has been a UNESCO World Heritage Site since 1993.

Segesta, Sicily (bottom, left)

In the north-west of the Italian island of Sicily lies the ancient ruined city of Segesta, founded by the Elymer. This tribe was an enemy of the Greek colonists but allowed itself to be inspired by their superior culture: on a hill the Elymer built a Doric temple of which, though it remained unfinished, the ruins still dominate the countryside today. It stands on 36 strapping, smooth round columns, slightly tapering upwards. The building was erected in the 5th century BC, shortly before enmity broke out with neighbouring Selinunt, which perhaps caused the building work to stall.

Nuraghi, Sardinia (bottom right)

The great Mediterranean powers: the Greeks, Etruscans and Phonecians were always looking for expansion possibilities in ancient times. On the island of Sardinia, buildings bear witness to this, which have never been found anywhere else in the world: the *nuraghi*. Today there are still the remains of about 3,000 of these, most of which are from the first half of the 8th century BC. These amazing structures can be seen mostly on hills; they are the shape of a flattened cone and served as defence and watchtowers. The people living in the vicinity of these chunky fortresses fled to them when sentries reported that strangers were approaching. They were often built next to springs so that the inhabitants were able to withstand a siege for some while. The *nuraghi* of Barumini have been a UNESCO World Heritage Site since 1996.

Greek Theatre, Syracuse *(top)*

The Greeks had been eager to escape the narrow world of the Aegean since the 8th century BC. At the same time as some of them reached out for Asia Minor in the east, other bold colonists ventured a move to the west, to Italy and Sicily. Here, on the island at the toe of the Italian 'boot', arose the western centre of Greek classical culture. And theatre is, of course, a part of the classical tradition. Hence, in addition to temples, there are also numerous amphitheatres amongst the traces of Greek civilisation remaining today. These were built into hillsides or nestling in hollows and could contain large numbers of spectators.

Archaeological Sites, Agrigent *(centre)*

In the 6th century BC, Greek colonists settled on the south coast of Sicily and founded the town of Akragas, present-day Agrigent. Over the course of the following 100 years the colony rose to become one of the leading powers on the island. This is visible in the architectural remains, which include impressive Doric temples, the outlines of houses, equipment and furnishings. The excavations have been a UNESCO World Heritage Site since 1997.

Roman Villa Casale *(bottom)*

In 1950, excavations began to the south-west of Piazza Armerina on Sicily, exposing a Roman country estate from the early 4th century. In the place where Emperor Maximian is thought to have resided for a time, amazing and colourful mosaics were found. On over 3,000 square metres of floor area archaeologists discovered depictions of hunting scenes, chariot races, markets and the famous 'bikini girls' — young Roman girls in two-piece bathing costumes. A UNESCO World Heritage Site since 1997.

Malta

The City of Valletta *(top)*
Following the expulsion of the Order of St. John from Rhodes by the Turks, Emperor Charles V gave them a new home on the Mediterranean island of Malta, where the Grand Master, Jean de La Valette, founded the present capital of the republic. The site benefits from natural harbours which, given its location at the intersection of many Mediterranean trade routes, helped the town to flourish. The Cathedral of San Giovanni (1573–1577) and the many inns, knights' lodges and other religious as well as secular buildings testify to the Order's time on the island, although much had to be rebuilt after the destruction caused by German air-raids during the Second World War. Valletta has been a UNESCO World Heritage Site since 1980.

The Hal Saflieni Hypogeum *(bottom left)*
Five kilometres south-east of the Maltese capital Valetta there is an underground labyrinth, known as the Hypogeum, in the Hal Saflieni district of the town of Paola. 4,000 years ago the original inhabitants of the Mediterranean island buried their dead in the 35 x 25 metre site on several layers of limestone rock. They left jewellery beside the dead and made their last resting place homelier with paintings, which are still partly visible. They were first discovered in 1902 during work on the construction of a house and archaeologically investigated. A UNESCO World Heritage Site since 1980.

The Megalithic Temples of Gozo and Malta *(bottom right)*
Cult-related megalithic constructions have been found in several places on Malta and on the island of Gozo which belongs to it: in Tarxien, south of Valletta, in Hagar Qim and Mnajdra on the south coast of Malta, in Mgarr in the northwest of the island, as well as in Ggantija near Victoria on Gozo. They are the walled temple buildings, up to 6,000 years old, and made of gigantic stone blocks which were used to make circles, houses, gates and which in part show fine ornamentation. These monuments of Stone Age religion eroded and sank over the centuries but were rediscovered in the 19th century and declared a World Heritage Site by UNESCO in 1980.

France

Amiens Cathedral (top)

One of the most significant masterpieces of Gothic architecture stands in the north-western French town of Amiens on the River Somme: the Cathedral of Notre Dame, which was built between 1220 and 1288 and only completed in the second half of the 14th century. The triple-naved basilica with its two squat towers, nave and transept is regarded as an incomparable example of medieval architectural design and it may have served as the model for Cologne Cathedral. The portals of the west front are perfect examples of Gothic cathedral statuary, richly decorated with statues, in particular the Christ figure of the central portal known as 'Beau Dieu' (Beautiful God). A UNESCO World Heritage Site since 1981.

Falaises, Normandy (bottom left)

The Normandy coast at Fécamp and Etretat looks as if it has been chopped off by a giant axe: its cliffs are called falaises and are interrupted at several points by valleys of pebbles. As you approach the beach, a curious noise swells up like a goods trains rattling past. It can be heard long before you can see who or what produces this strange music. Only once you are directly next to the sea, stumbling along the sliding pebble slopes does it become clear: the monotonous noise is caused by the stones jostling together when the water, carried forward into the shingle by the swell, comes rushing back through it. If you are only acquainted with sandy beaches, you cannot imagine such a level of noise; at first it shocks you but then you find yourself missing it almost as much, once you leave the beach. Did the Normans' love of their homeland come from these sounds?

The Bayeux Tapestry, Normandy

(bottom right)

It was from here, nearly 1,000 years ago, that the last successful attempt was made to conquer England militarily on her own soil: in 1066 the Norman Duke William, who then became 'William the Conqueror', set off for Britain and had himself crowned King of England after his victory at Hastings. His achievement is honoured in a 70-metre-long and 0.5-metre-high work of art, portrayed in 58 scenes: the embroidered tapestry of Bayeux, or the Queen Mathilda Tapestry to be precise. The northern French town in the Calvados region exhibits the priceless work in its arts centre, which used to house a seminary.

Mont Saint Michel, Normandy (top)

Founded at angelic instigation: in the 8th century the Archangel Michael appeared several times to the Bishop of Avranches and urged him to build a church on a rocky outcrop just off-shore in the bay. The bishop himself did not succeed, but 200 years later a Benedictine abbey stood here, in the middle of the sea. In the 13th century a Gothic building was erected over the Romanesque one. It towers up high and has become one of the most loved of France's pilgrimage churches, admired as the 'Wonder of the West'. The church sits above a monastery of several storeys and is impressive not only for its location but also for its architecture. A UNESCO World Heritage Site since 1979.

Rock Arch, Etretat (bottom)

It is as if erosion has a plan in mind as it goes about its weathering, producing shapes over millions of years that range from the charming to the bizarre, then destroying them again and creating new ones. As a sculptor it particularly likes to work with sedimentary rock from marine deposits; at the same time it readily accepts tectonic help. As coasts or entire continents rise, it works away gradually, using the crashing and swirling of the waves, splitting by frost and blasting with sand. Conical shapes evolve from rectangular ones, doorways appear in rock walls and steps in steep walls make an ascent possible. Here at Etretat on the Normandy coast in France is a particularly good example of this artist's work.

Dinan, Brittany *(top)*

The River Rance in northern France is famous not only for the tidal power plant located at the mouth of its long funnel-shaped estuary but also for the small town of Dinan which lies upstream where the estuary begins. The town stands guard very picturesquely over the harbour that the bay provides and that at one time was of great importance. It also stands guard over itself, with a 2.5-kilometre-long town wall around it, although today it is breached in two places by a through-road. The protective fortified towers however are still on guard, even if it is hardly likely that an enemy will be trying to approach these days. Instead it is much more likely to be welcome guests in the form of tourists coming to enjoy the sight of the late medieval houses on the Place des Merciers.

The Tidal Power Plant, Saint Malo
(bottom left)

The 110-kilometre-long River Rance flows through Brittany and into the English Channel at Saint Malo. The tidal difference is 8.5 metres at this point, rising to over 13 metres during spring tides. The size of this fall between the two water levels inspired engineers to build a 750-metre-long dam with 24 pipe turbines across the funnel-shaped mouth of the estuary. After a 7-year construction period, the tidal power plant became operational in 1967. It holds back the inflowing water in a storage basin and then lets it flow out through the turbines. The power plant, the first of three that now exist worldwide, thus generates 10 megawatts.

Fougères, Brittany *(bottom right)*

Enemies seldom strayed here, even the Romans at best just passed through. This was because of the Bretons' fighting spirit, which is often reflected in the urban architecture of their towns, many of which are well-preserved. A typical example is the small town of Fougères, north-east of Rennes and south-east of Mont Saint Michel. Here the towers rise up, the bastions threaten and thick walls enclose the old centre. What once chased enemies away now attracts visitors: the Middle Ages have been popular for some time, perhaps because our Modern Age seems to have lost the sense of adventure. The fortified setting inspires you to imagine yourself living in a more dangerous age.

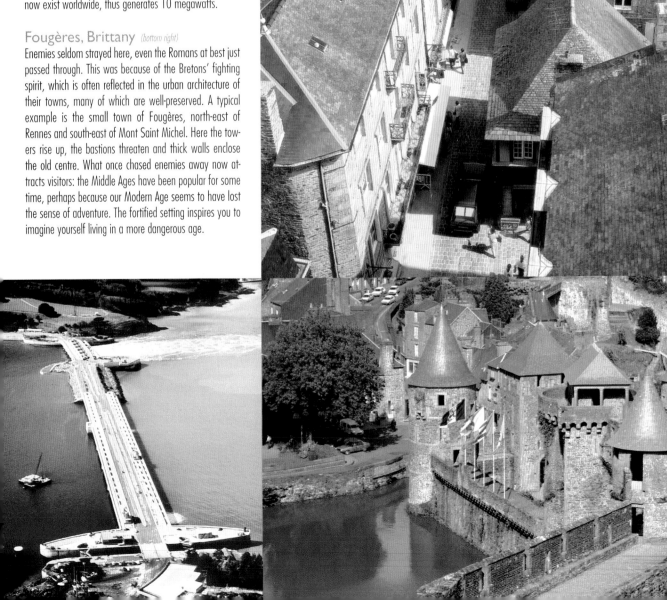

The Cathedral and Palais du Thau, Reims *(top left)*

Here in the capital of Champagne, in 498 AD, Saint Remigius is supposed to have baptised the Frankish King Clovis I a Catholic. In remembrance of this, the coronation and anointing of all French kings took place in Reims from 1179 to 1825. After its founding in the 13th century, these coronations were celebrated in the Gothic cathedral. 2,300 carved figures decorate its west front and its glass windows, badly damaged in both World Wars, were restored and partially modernised by, amongst others, Marc Chagall (1887–1985). In the nearby bishop's residence, the Palais du Thau, valuable church treasures are on display. Together with the cathedral and the abbey church of the Saint Rémi Monastery, this building has been a UNESCO World Heritage Site since 1991.

Monet's Garden, Giverny *(top right)*

'Impressionists' is what the critics scathingly called the school of aritsts around Claude Monet (1840–1926) after his painting of a sunrise 'Impression, soleil levant' in 1872. Today devotees pay millions for the pictures, many of which were created in the garden of Monet's house in Giverny (Eure Départment). An enchanted garden bathed in varying shades of light – as in the art of the impressionists, for whom it was not contours that mattered but expressing what made an impression on him: colours and shadows, the movements of nature and human beings in nature – all joined together in harmony in the garden.

Chantilly Palace *(bottom)*

Between 1527 and 1532 a French field marshal had a palace erected in Chantilly, north of Paris, on the site of an old stronghold that appealed to him for military reasons. There are actually two palaces, a small one (*le petit château*) and a large one (*le grand château*), which were rebuilt and remodelled in the 19th century after they were destroyed by revolutionaries in 1789. Today it houses the *Musée Condé*, where magnificent paintings by Titian, Raphael, Veronese and others are on display. The pièce de résistance, however, is the illuminated manuscript of the 15th century book of hours belonging to the Duke of Berry.

La Défense, Paris *(top)*

"What is there more worthwhile defending than the economy of a country?" the French President François Miterrand asked himself and presented the answer through the medium of architecture. Thus his architects had to orientate themselves on an imperial monument in the heart of the capital Paris, Napoleon's *Arc de Triomphe* from which a particularly good view can be had of the result: the office towers of *La Défense* and the *Grand Arche*, the gigantic gateway to France's modern economy, have been visible from here since 1990. It is triumphant with its 110-metre-high arch, almost twice as grand as that of the emperor's. Then again it does not celebrate any military victories, but that of democracy, which is the most worthwhile thing of all to defend.

The Bibliothèque Nationale, Paris *(bottom)*

With a little imagination, the 80-metre-high towers do actually look like giant open book. The Paris *Biblothèque Nationale*, which has been taking a copy of every new French book published since the 16th century, was overflowing. President Mitterrand, who was a keen supporter of construction projects in any case, therefore commissioned a new library building, thus ensuring his fame for posterity – although he did not live long enough to see its opening in 1998. Despite some initial teething problems, the users as well as the librarians have since grown accustomed to the gigantic temple of books and wouldn't want to be without it – nor is it possible now to imagine the urban landscape of eastern Paris without it.

The Louvre, Paris *(top)*

Elements of Renaissance and Baroque architectural styles as well as Classical and Modern characteristics combine in one of the largest museum complexes in the world: the Louvre in the French capital Paris has grown over centuries and in so doing has changed its appearance. Started in 1546 as the re-modelling of a medieval palace, the Louvre, initially a royal residence, was extended under the 'Sun King', Louis XIV, but was then somewhat sidelined by the removal of the court to Versailles. Emperors Napoleon I and III carried out more building work on the Louvre in the 19th century and, in 1989, the museum and the adjoining Tuileries, with an exhibition space now totalling 60,000 square metres, was given a modern accent with the glass pyramid of the American architect of Chinese origin, Ieoh Ming Pei (born 1917). One example of valuable exhibits is the stele with the Hammurapi Code, the most important collection of laws from the Ancient Orient (approximately 1700 BC).

The Pompidou Centre, Paris *(centre)*

Like his later work on the Lloyd's building in London, the British architect Richard Rogers (b. 1933) together with his Italian colleague Renzo Piano (b. 1937) turned the Parisian Pompidou Centre inside out: supply pipes, lifts and stairs give structure to the façade, which as a result looks futuristic, whilst in the interior they were then able to place a spacious atrium. Critics spoke of the beginnings of a second era of machine aesthetics (the first one having been heralded by the Eiffel Tower). The architects themselves saw their design rather as a synthesis of joy and functionality, a view that has prevailed in the long run.

The Paris Opera House *(bottom)*

A masterpiece of French neo-Baroque style is the Paris Opera House, built between 1861 and 1874 by the architect Charles Garnier (1825–1898). It is one of the key buildings which were part of the improvements to the capital instigated by Napoleon III. The elaborately decorated — critics say: overdone — concert house is strictly symmetrical and the stage is devoid of any non-functional elements. Even the auditorium fulfils its main function perfectly: what matters at the opera is not being able to see but to be seen: the large cloakrooms accentuate a wide marble staircase and a richly decorated foyer provides the elegant gentlemen and, above all, the ladies the ideal setting for making their own entrance.

The Eiffel Tower, Paris *(facing)*

A 'black chimney' of 'dizziness-inducing ugliness' was the fear of many when the plan for a 300-metre-high iron construction for the 1889 Paris World Exhibition was unveiled. Today, the tower constructed by the engineer Gustave Eiffel (1832–1923) is the French capital's most famous landmark, a symbol even of modern France itself. Visitors flock in their millions to the Eiffel Tower, crowding into one of its lifts, to get up higher and higher to where the city on the Seine lies at their feet. Only a year after its completion, the operators had taken in more money than the construction had cost. Today it has grown to a height of 320.75 metres through the addition of a television antenna.

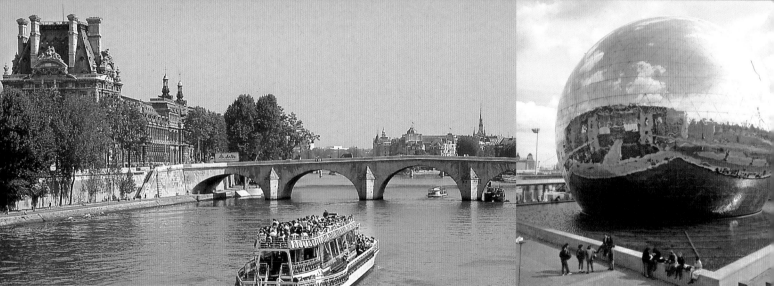

New Opera House, Paris (far top)
François Mitterrand took it as a sign of fate that the 200th anniversary of the storming of the Bastille, which marked the start of the French Revolution in 1789, was to be during his presidency. 10 years before the anniversary he already developed plans to impress the world in 1989. Of course, the most important focus had to be on the site where the 'children of the fatherland' (les enfants de la patrie) first breached the defences of the rotten system of the ancien régime. In the square where the Bastille prison fortress once stood, the president had a new fortress built: the New Opera House. A massive, modern hall for sound, as bright as silver and as clear as glass.

Banks of the Seine, Paris (above left)
Notre Dame, the Louvre and Tuileries, the Place de la Concorde, the Grand and Petit Palais, the Eiffel Tower, the Hôtel des Invalides and the Champs Elysées — between Pont de Sully and Pont d'Iéna, the French capital has more historical and architectural sights to offer than nearly any other city on Earth. Its heritage has therefore been specially protected as a UNESCO World Heritage Site since 1991.

Parc de Villette, Paris (above right)
It was not only the prestige of the centre of his capital that was close to the heart of French president, François Mitterrand (in office 1981–1995). He was also concerned with features in the suburbs. One of the most colourful and most pleasant is the Parc de Villette: the high-tech 35-hectare park, designed by Swiss architect Bernard Tschumi (b. 1944) not only radiates with the colours of the flowers in its various show gardens and the colourful children's play areas, but above all because of its scarlet red follies. With them, Tschumi gave a meaningful structure to the extensive area and combined functionality with fun.

Versailles Palace and Park (opposite, top)
19 kilometres to the west of Paris, set in a splendid park, lies the Palace of Versailles. Designed in 1624 as a hunting palace for Louis XIII (reigned 1610–1643), his successor the 'Sun King' Louis XIV (1643–1705) made Versailles into his residence in 1682. His successors and Napoleon I also used the palace, continually extending and improving it. The Hall of Mirrors with its 17 large windows and the same number of mirrors became famous because it was here that the German empire was proclaimed on 18th January 1871, after the war with France. Revenge was exacted in 1919 when German emissaries had to sign acceptance of harsh conditions for peace in a treaty at Versailles following the First World War. A UNESCO World Heritage Site since 1979.

Notre Dame, Paris (opposite, bottom)
A prototype of French Gothic architecture stands on the south-east bank of Paris' Île de la Cité in the Seine: the Cathedral of Notre Dame, consecrated to the Mother of God. Construction of the basilica with its five nave, transept, choir ambulatory and side chapels began in 1163 and was more or less complete by the middle of the 13th century. Above all, the well-proportioned structure of the west front with the two squat towers, the royal gallery, the glorious rose window, the polygonal apse, the rich statuary on the portals and the tracery became the model for many European Gothic cathedrals.

Fontainebleau Palace *(top)*

Emperor Napoleon made Fontainebleau Palace, which lies 62 kilometres to the south-east of Paris, into the monumental building it is today. The palace was in existence as early as the 12th century when Louis VII (reigned 1137–1180) had a hunting lodge built here when he came to the throne. Later the building fell into ruin, but Francis I (1515–1547) remembered the beautiful location and had it restored as a residence again and extended. The Renaissance parts of the building go back to this time. Empire style elements were added to these during the reign of the Emperors. The park and the palace have been a UNESCO World Heritage Site since 1979.

Chartres Cathedral *(bottom)*

It took two attempts to build this cathedral: the Early Gothic cathedral in the town of Chartres to the south-west of Paris was consecrated in 1120 but burned down shortly afterwards. A completely new cathedral was built between 1194 and 1260. In the years that followed it was magnificently adorned with statues, chapels and altars. Pilgrims stream to this place to admire the works of art in the huge church with its five naves and to worship in the vast, tall space which is warmly illuminated by magnificent glass windows. To do so, they step through three enormous portals, which are decorated with many life-sized figures of rulers and saints. A UNESCO World Heritage Site since 1979.

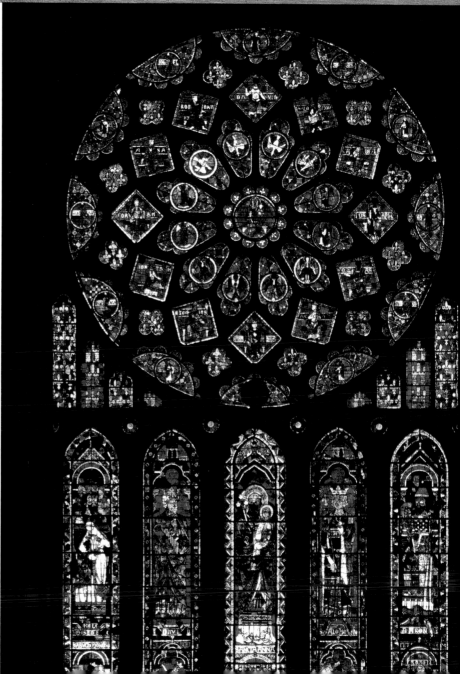

Chambord Palace (top left)

In an area of extensive forests and luxuriant parkland to the south-west of the central French town of Orléans not far from the Loire lies the hunting palace of Chambord, built in 1519 for King Francis I. With towers, oriel windows and chimneys the monumental building is reflected in a branch of the river especially re-routed for this purpose. The confusing multiplicity of parts of the building disentangle themselves after one climbs the double spiral staircase in the internal courtyard, reputedly designed by Leonardo da Vinci (1452–1519), from which one looks down onto a harmonious whole. The building was never completed because the monarchs hardly ever used the remote country estate. Today it belongs to the state and, as a UNESCO World Heritage Site since 1981, has become a magnet for tourists.

Palaces of the Loire (top right)

Sully, Loches, Chinon, Langeais, Chambord, Blois, Amboise, Villandry, Azay-le-Rideau — the palaces of the French nobility and royalty are strung like pearls on the shiny thread of the Loire river. They started out as hill-top castles, and from the 12th to the 17th centuries served as Renaissance palaces in parks, for hunting, feudal conviviality, as love nests and for entertainment purposes. Today tourists ensure they include them on their itineraries and enjoy the charming harmony between culture and nature.

Palace at Angers and Abbey Church of Saint Serge (centre)

Actually, it is more a castle than a palace — in the middle of the industrial French town of Angers on the River Maine it bears witness to bygone times: surrounded by a 950-metre-long circular wall, interspersed with 17 massive fortified towers, lies the palace, built in 1228–1238, highly conspicuous with the amount of its fortified structures. Inside, visitors are enchanted by a cycle of 80 scenes from the Book of Revelations on the *Apocalypse d'Angers* as the tapestry is called, the oldest in France (1375). It was created in the nearby cathedral (see picture), a Gothic construction from the 12th/13th centuries with magnificent stained glass windows. The older parts of the Abbey Church of Saint Serge originate from the same period, and it was only completed in the 15th century.

Menhirs and Dolmens, Carnac (bottom)

Like gigantic punctuation marks whose words have gone missing, the large stones stand up to five metres high in rows (alignments), in circles (cromlechs), individually (menhirs) or on graves (dolmens) near the French seaside resort of Carnac on the south coast of Brittany. On closer acquaintance, the words surface and speak of a Celtic culture which flourished here over 4,000 years ago and which then died out. The names of the fields of stones underline the strangeness of this megalithic culture: Kerzerho, Locmariaquer and Gavrinis. There are similar monuments in other parts of the world as well, but nowhere in such quantity and so well-preserved.

Old Town, Strasburg (far top and above right)

"How the giant building with firm foundations rises so lightly into the air, how broken through everything is, but is nevertheless for eternity." This is how in 1770 Germany's master of words, Goethe enthused about the Minster of the town of Strasburg in Alsace. The Gothic construction, which was begun in the 12th century, only has one 142-metre-high spire, which was completed in 1439. It towers over the Old Town, *le Petite France*, which lies between the two branches of the river Ill, with its half-timbered houses and Renaissance buildings, the Palais Rohan, the prefecture and the town hall (formerly the Hanau Court) dating from the 18th century, as well as more Gothic churches. UNESCO World Heritage Site since 1988.

Nancy (left)

Nancy lies in Lorraine and is the administrative headquarter of the French département Meurthe sur Moselle. It has a deposed king to thank for the splendid Rococo design: Stanislaw Leszczynski (1677–1766) could not assert himself as Polish king and was compensated by his son-in-law, King Louis XV, with the Dukedom of Lorraine in 1738. Here, in his residence at Nancy, he showed the qualities of an enlightened monarch in renovating the infrastructure of the town and created a public space with the Place Stanislaw (see picture), which harmoniously connects administrative buildings and residences. Together with Place de la Carrière and Place d'Alliance, Place Stanislaw has been a UNESCO World Heritage Site since 1983.

The Way of St James (top)

The longer section of it belongs to Spain but it was often also called the 'French Way': the pilgrims' route to the grave of the Apostle St. James the Elder in Santiago de Compostela begins in Central France, passes by the vast cathedrals of Vézelay (see picture), Tours, Limoges and Toulouse, then over the Pyrenees via Roncevalles through Burgos and León to the furthermost north-west corner of the Iberian peninsula. In the Middle Ages, millions of pilgrims followed the route, which is still full of great charm today thanks to the places of worship and inns built along the way, and it has thus been a UNESCO World Heritage Site since 1988.

Church of Mary Magdalene, Vézelay (bottom left)

The small Burgundy town of Vézelay, on the northern edge of the French Massif Central, became famous from a world history point of view in 1146 when Bernard von Clairvaux (1091–1153) called for a second crusade in an inflammatory sermon. The high Romanesque Church of Saint Madeleine (Church of Mary Magdalene) had at that time been under construction for half a century and already had the fascinating portico with statuary columns and the richly decorated portal with steps. When the troops of French King Philipp II August (1180–1223) and the English troops belonging to Richard Lionheart (1189–1198) gathered here for the third crusade, the priceless construction with a Gothic choir was nearly completed. Together with the picturesque hill town, the Church of Mary Magdalene has been a UNESCO World Heritage Site since 1979.

Cistercian Abbey, Fontenay (bottom right)

Saint Bernard of Clairvaux (1091–1153) was responsible for founding a total of 70 monasteries. One of the first was in 1119, a Cistercian Abbey, consecrated in 1147, in Fontenay to the north-west of Dijon in the French département of Côte d'Or (Burgundy). The monastery church and the buildings for the monks comprising a refectory, dormitory, kitchen, workshops and other buildings needed for running the household are a perfect example of the self-sufficiency, organisational talent and efficiency of the medieval Cistercians. A UNESCO World Heritage Site since 1981.

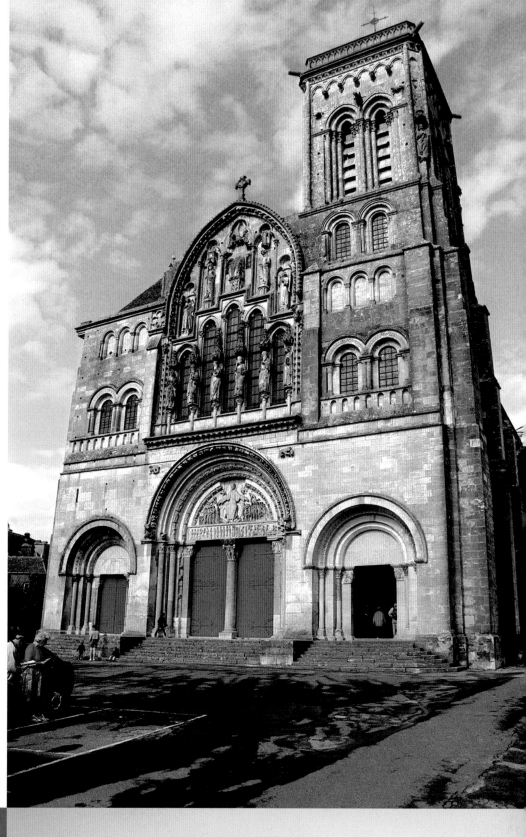

Hôtel-Dieu Hospice, Beaune *(top left)*

When it came to thinking about death, feudal lords who were otherwise renowned for their resoluteness became troubled by their conscience. The Burgundy Chancellor Nicolas Rolin was no exception and in 1443 he decided to found a hospital in Beaune in order to at least have something to show for himself when he finally came before his Maker. The roof of this impressive creation is covered with tiles that are so colourful that your eyes automatically look up to heaven. The interior too holds several select treasures and in the 'Ward for the Poor' you can see reproductions of original medieval beds on which the patients had to lie just two to a mattress – an unheard-of luxury in those days.

Notre Dame du Haut, Ronchamp *(top right)*

Built like a castle but without fortifications, small windows, a sacred place but at the same time very much of the world: such is the effect created by the pilgrimage Church of Notre Dame du Haut. It was designed by Le Corbusier (1887–1965) and built in 1950–1954 in the town of Ronchamp, north-west of Belfort (département Haute-Saône). The curved roof and the white, softly-contoured tower allow the building to nestle gently into the landscape. An outside pulpit and an altar on the external wall emphasise the pilgrimage character of the church and enhance its sculptural appearance. A late work of the Modernist master, this building is a final architectural testament of an unconventional designer.

Cathedral, Bourges *(bottom)*

It was as the capital of the dukedom of Berry in the High Middle Ages that the town of Bourges, situated in Central France, reached the zenith of its prosperity and importance. The Cathedral of Saint Etienne (1195–1280) is testimony to this period. It has five naves but no transept. Whilst you may be overwhelmed by the sense of space of this vast sacred building, you should not forget to also admire its detail: the sculpture of the richly decorated west portal, the stained glass window in the choir, the Late Gothic side chapel extensions. A UNESCO World Heritage Site since 1992.

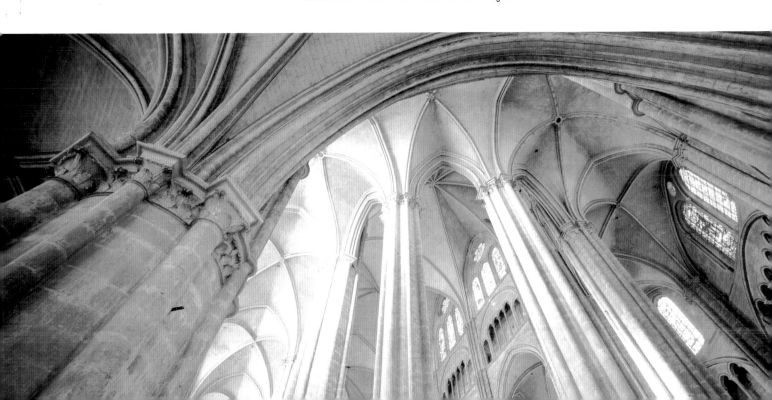

Cluny Monastery (top left)

First came the abbey and then the town: it was thanks to the Benedictines who founded a monastery here in 909 that the small town of Cluny (4,400 inhabitants) became established in the French département Saône-et-Loire. The monastery secured its place in world history with the Cluniac Reforms, reforms named after it, which brought the church back to the spiritual roots of Christianity, and which spread throughout the whole of the Western World during the early Middle Ages. They even found expression in what might almost be described as an ascetic style of building to be seen in the abbey church of the 10th century. By contrast, the vast new building, which was built 100 years later, again displays great splendour.

Beynac, Dordogne (top right)

The concept 'national' was of little importance in the Middle Ages, what really mattered was 'dynastic'. For example, an area of land in the middle of Germany could be 'Russian' just as a large part of France had long been 'English'. Where two powers collided, such as in Périgord in the present day département of Dordogne, old fortifications will occur in abundance. Especially river valleys, which were important transport routes, needed to be secured by means of castles on the hilltops above. The castle of Beynac dates from this period in the 13th and 14th centuries. Anyone wishing to pass here, along the Dordogne river, was well-advised to find favour with the lord of the castle first, or be prepared to face a barrage of rocks from above.

The Lascaux Caves, Vézère Valley (bottom)

In south-west France, on the lower reaches of the River Vézère, a tributary of the Dordogne, lies the birthplace of European man. This may be an exaggeration, but there is some truth in it: at Cromagnon in 1868 the first traces were found of Homo sapiens, our direct ancestors, dating back around 35,000 years. Here in the caves of Lascaux, Stone Age drawings of animals and hunters can be admired. Since 1963, however, only copies and not the originals have been displayed, as the breath of the crowds of visitors was threatening to destroy the original paintings. A UNESCO World Heritage Site since 1979.

Dune du Pilat, Arcachon *(top left)*

The Atlantic coast near the French town of Arcachon, southwest of Bordeaux, runs in an absolutely straight line. Behind the coastal dunes lie lakes which are linked to the ocean by water courses, so-called 'courants' – a real holidaymakers' paradise. At Cap Ferrat there is a special attraction: the *Dune du Pilat*, Europe's largest shifting sand dune. The enormous hill of sand stands 118 metres high, is 500 metres wide and three kilometres long. Every year it shifts a little to the east and from it you can see clearly for miles across the flat coastal countryside.

Saint Emilion *(upper centre)*

Nature and culture alike can be enjoyed in the southwestern French wine-growing area of Saint Emilion on the right bank of the Dordogne and in the town of the same name. In places the hills are as round and gentle as the red wine of this region to the east of Bordeaux. The vines grow right up to the boundary wall of the small town. Here visitors can marvel at the Monolithic Church, which is cut into the rock. What began as a mere chapel in a cave has grown since the 8th century and is now a triple-naved basilica with a splendid Gothic front and a huge bell tower. The Saint Emilion district has been a UNESCO World Heritage Site since 1999.

Lyon *(lower centre)*

Known in Roman times as Lugdunum, the capital of the Province of Gallia Lugdunensis, Lyon is now the second largest city in France. The ruins of an aqueduct and two theatres on what was the former Forum Vetus, the present day historic quarter of Fourvière, testify to the city's ancient past, more of which is packed into the Lyon archaeological museum. Also to be found in the city is a collection of medieval buildings with the cathedral and the Church of Saint Paul, both begun in the 12th century. However, a newer construction towers over all of these: the pilgrimage Church of Notre Dame de la Fourvière (see picture) which dates from the end of the 19th century. On the narrow peninsula between the Rivers Rhône and Saône stand a range of striking buildings including the town hall (1646–1655), the Benedictine Monastery of Saint Peter and a late medieval church. A UNESCO World Heritage Site since 1998.

Amphitheatre and Triumphal Arch, Orange *(bottom)*

The strong influence of the long years of Roman rule on the south of France can still be seen today in many towns. In Orange, a medium-sized town not far from the Rhône in the département of Vaucluse, the remains of the ancient amphitheatre (picture) are impressive: its semi-circular rows of seats had room for 10,000 spectators. A triumphal arch is evidence today of the power, now long gone, of Rome, while the cathedral, consecrated in 1208, shows that the Church became the heir to that empire. The Roman remains have been a UNESCO World Heritage Site since 1981.

Pont du Gard (top)

What master engineers they were! At the time of Emperor Augustus (30 BC to 14 AD) Roman engineers built a bridge across the valley of the River Gard, a tributary of the Rhône, between Nîmes and Avignon. It was not designed to carry people however – although doubtless engineers crossed it as they carried out maintenance work – it was, instead, an aqueduct that brought pure spring water to the town. In total the water channel was 50 kilometres long, and the three-storey arched bridge spans 245 metres at a height of 49 metres. A UNESCO World Heritage Site since 1985.

Chauvet Cave, Vallon-Pont d'Arc (centre)

They are nearly as old as the first traces of the Cromagnon man: the oldest evidence of Ice Age art from the Neo-Palaeolithic Age, which were found in 1994, also in France, in a limestone cave near Vallon-Pont d'Arc (Départment Ardèche). The rock paintings from the nearby Cosquet grotto and those from the Lascaux cave (Vézère valley), estimated to be between 20,000 and 25,000 years old, had until then been regarded as the oldest, only to be beaten by nearly 10,000 years by the Chauvet findings.

The Papal Palace and Old Town, Avignon (bottom)

In the southern French city of Avignon in Provence, the Papal Palace towers over everything. The Holy Fathers ruled the Church from here for 70 years in the 14th century, and erected this fortress-like residence. Many tourists who stream into the town on the Rhône come to see just this – and to admire the Gothic architecture, the frescos in the chapel and the private chambers of the popes. In summer, events are staged in the first courtyard as part of the Avignon Festival. An excursion to the Pont d'Avignon, the ruins of the bridge across the Rhône, celebrated in the well-known song, is as much a Must as a stroll through the narrow streets of the city's Old Town.

Roman Monuments, Nîmes *(top left)*

The Pont du Gard, 19 kilometres away, is a remainder of a Roman aqueduct, built to supply Nemausus (Nîmes). The podium temple (see picture), now known as *Maison Carrée*, was built for the grandsons of Emperor Augustus (reigned from 30 BC to 14 AD). Over the course of the centuries it has lost its surrounding pillared hall. The gladiators' combat arena is now used for bullfights. Also remarkable is the temple to Diana from the 1st century AD.

Carcassonne *(top right)*

The double-walled, upper town of the city of Carcassonne looks like the Middle Ages frozen in time. The fortifications have been fully preserved and restored, as have the Romanesque-Gothic cathedral from the 13th century, the older castle, and the 38 towers: together their silhouettes rise up above the town as a landmark. The town has King Louis IX to thank for its defiant fortified appearance. He ruled for almost half a century (1226–1270). Due to its uniquely homogenous appearance the Old Town of Carcassonne has been a UNESCO World Heritage Site since 1997.

Roman and Romanesque Monuments, Arles *(bottom)*

Today it is back in use: the amphitheatre of the southwestern French town of Arles (département Bouches du Rhône), which dates from the time of the Roman ruler Julius Caesar but was built over in the Middle Ages. It is just one of the Roman remains in Arles which also include the Circus Maximus and the subterranean galleries of the Cryptoportica. By contrast, the testimonies to the Middle Ages tower on high, like the Romanesque Church of Saint Trophine, named after its triumphal arch-like portal through which the Emperor Frederick Barbarossa stepped on his way to be crowned. The Old Town has been a UNESCO World Heritage Site since 1981.

Scandola Nature Reserve, Corsica *(top)*

A peninsula on an island: the western part of the French Mediterranean island of Corsica is rugged and in many barely accessible places provides a habitat for endangered plants and animals. Added to this is the charming scenery of this still largely unspoilt coast. It was made a nature reserve in 1975, to ensure that any man-made changes to it can only take place with the express permission of the environment minister. This applies to the shore as well as to the sea off-shore. Of particular importance in this area is the 1,000-hectare Scandola peninsula, a porphyritic rock mass in the north-west; together with the Girolata and Porto Bay, it has been a UNESCO World Heritage Site under special protection since 1983.

Gallery in the Grimaldi Castle, Antibes *(centre)*

On the French Côte d'Azur the traveller seeks rest, adventure or nerve-tingling excitement in the casino. Lovers of antiquities also get their money's worth. However, that modern art can also be enjoyed here, is something only few are aware of: Pablo Picasso spent some time in 1946 in the coastal town of Antibes with its Grimaldi Castle, situated next to the sea. When he left he gave all the works he had created here to the town, which put them on display in the castle. They document a decisive phase in Picasso's creative development.

Canal du Midi *(bottom left)*

An astonishing technical feat for the period in which it was built: in 1666 France's 'Sun King', Louis XIV, launched a project to link the Mediterranean with the Atlantic. The Canal du Midi was built from Toulouse on the River Garonne over 241 kilometres through the most difficult terrain of the Languedoc to Sète on the Mediterranean. 101 lock gates, the bridge at Béziers on which the canal crosses the river Orb, and the *Ecluse de Fontséranes*, a series of eight locks further to the south-west, all bear witness to the problems which the French hydraulic engineers managed to overcome in less than 20 years (completed in 1684). A UNESCO World Heritage Site since 1996.

Coastal Fortification, Marseilles *(bottom right)*

A painting by J. Vernet hangs in the Louvre, which shows what is now France's second largest city and its harbour as it was in the 18th century: left – the mole with the gun tower, right – the fortress' casemates rising in terraces on the steep coast. It was the only route into the interior of the harbour basin. Anyone who came with hostile intent would have been sure of a fiery reception. Today modern Marseilles, close to the Rhône estuary, has allowed the vast forts to fade into the background somewhat, but they still symbolise the confidence of this Mediterranean metropolis which was founded as a Greek colony as long ago as the 6th century BC.

Spain

Old Town, Santiago de Compostela (top)

The end point of the most important pilgrimage route in Christendom was and is the town of Santiago de Compostela in Galicia in the extreme north-west corner of the Iberian peninsula. After the grave of the Apostle James was discovered here in 813, thousands and thousands of people made their way via the path of St. James from France over the Pyrenees to Santiago, which because of this is also richly decorated with holy buildings from many centuries. In first place stands the Romanesque cathedral (see picture), which was given a front in the churriguerist style, a playful Spanish take on the Baroque, in the 18th century. As well as a further 40 churches, other buildings, which should be mentioned, are: the archbishop's palace, the Hostel de los Reyes Católicas (1511) inn and the monastery of San Martín Pinario. They give the Old Town its stamp and it has been a UNESCO World Heritage Site since 1985.

Guggenheim Museum, Bilbao (top)
It only took California-based architect Frank Owen Gehry (born 1929) a few days to sketch this building — or so architectural legend will have it. Construction of the ship-like structure on the River Nervión took a little longer, seven years, from 1991 to 1997, to be precise. But it was worth it: the Guggenheim Museum, named after the famous American patron of the arts (1861–1949), now draws crowds of admirers from all over the World to the city of Bilbao in the Basque country. The gleaming titanium dream offers a fitting architectural setting for the priceless art collection inside.

The Way of St James (bottom left)
According to legend, St James the Apostle (Santiago in Spanish), arrived in north-west Spain in 44 AD where he wanted to do missionary work. Other reports claim that only the remains of the martyr ended up here and were laid to rest in Santiago de Compostela, which was then named after him. It was only in the early Middle Ages, in the 9th century, when the grave was rediscovered, that pilgrims from over the whole of Europe set out on the difficult St. James' Way. The Spanish section alone covers more than 800 kilometres. The tradition has endured and today only those who have covered at least 100 kilometres on foot or 200 kilometres by bicycle through the grandiose Spanish landscape, past and through places such as Burgos, Frómista, León and Villafranca del Bierzo, are recognised as true pilgrims. The way itself is a destination and has been a UNESCO World Heritage Site since 1993.

Altamira Cave, Cantabria (bottom right)
The cave system of Altamira stretches over several large grottos with a total length of 280 metres, close to the Spanish town of Santillana in Cantabria. An underground world like this is a fascinating place in itself. But what a Spanish explorer discovered there in 1879 took his breath away: the walls are painted with numerous pictures of hunting game. In the Sala de las Pinturas in particular, they gleam magnificently in red, brown and yellow. Some of the animals, such as bison, wild boar or deer, are depicted life-size and are painted accurately in great detail. The discoverer was at first accused of forgery and was only redeemed after similar discoveries in France. Today we know that the works we have before us here were created up to 15,000 years ago by Ice Age artists from the Late Stone Age (Neo-Palaeolithic). A UNESCO World Heritage Site since 1985.

Cathedral and Monastery, Burgos
(far top)

The Spanish national hero Rodrigo (Ruy) Díaz de Vivar, better known by his Moorish epithet El Cid, was born in Burgos, a provincial capital in the north-east of the plateau of Old Castile. Here a finely proportioned Gothic cathedral rises up in a breathtaking manner. Its foundation stone was laid in 1221. Building work continued right into the 16th century before it began to look the way it does today. The best-known detail of the building is a clock figure that opens its mouth wide when the bell rings and which for this reason was christened by the locals as the 'flycatcher' (*Papamoscas*). Just as worthwhile seeing, however, is the interior with its statues and tombs, including those of El Cid and his spouse Doña Jimena. As well as this UNESCO World Heritage Site (since 1984), it is worth paying a visit to the *Las Huelgas Reales* Monastery which dates from the 12th century and has finely proportioned Romanesque cloisters. The building once served as the burial place for Castilian kings.

Historic Centre, Salamanca *(above left)*

The Punic General Hannibal passed through here on his march on Italy. Soon afterwards his Roman opponents took up position here and left behind them a bridge over the Rio Tormes (see picture), which is preserved to this day. As well as these ancient remains, the Spanish town of Salamanca is noted for its monasteries, churches, and the Jesuit College, which today houses the papal university and boasts a vast Baroque church. Other religious buildings date back to the 12th century: the old cathedral, the round Church of San Marcos and the Church of San Martín. The pulsating focus of the town became the Plaza Mayor, which was built in the 18th century in the Churriguerist style. This historic centre, in which so many styles coexist, was elevated by UNESCO to a World Heritage Site in 1988.

Old Town and Aquaduct, Segovia *(above right)*

At an altitude of 1,000 metres on the southern edge of the plateau of Old Castile lies the Spanish provincial capital Segovia. A Roman aqueduct, known as *el Puente* which spans a 700-metre-wide valley on 29-metre-high supporting arches, bears witness to the venerable age of the town on the mountain crest. Its silhouette is dominated by the towering medieval Alcazár castle as well as many religious buildings, including the Late Gothic cathedral, which was completed in the 16th century. The Romanesque churches appear simple in comparison, but the Monastery of San Antonio el Real, founded in 1445, is very impressive, as are several palace façades built in the Gothic-Moorish Mudéjar style. The ancient and medieval remains have been a UNESCO World Heritage Site since 1985.

Old Town, Churches and Town Wall, Ávila *(far top)*

On the northern edge of the Castilian mountain divide, at an altitude of over 1,100 metres, lies the capital which bears the same name as the province, Avila, the 'town of the Saint and the stones'. The first epithet relates in particular to the fact that Saint Theresa was born here in 1515, the latter signifies a rocky landscape but also refers to the buildings, of which the three-metre-thick, 12-metre-high town wall with its 82 towers and nine gates is the one you notice first. It was built in the 12th century and encloses a historic quarter which, with its Gothic cathedral, has been largely preserved as a medieval town. Several Romanesque churches remained outside the encircling wall but belong to the overall historic picture, which predestined Avila to become a UNESCO World Heritage Site in 1985.

La Granja Palace, Castile *(above left)*

In the historic Castilian heart of Spain, north-west of the capital Madrid, lies the former royal summer residence of La Granja, where in 1784 a queen gave birth to the future ruler Ferdinand VII. However, either the stars were not favourable or the newborn royal was unimpressed by the magnificence of his birthplace. At any rate, neither brought any real luck. In 1808 Napoleon chased the young king off the throne and following his return in 1814, Ferdinand turned the so-called Carlists against him when he introduced the female succession, which it was thought would lead to unending disputes. And yet it seems as if the palace, with its elegant Baroque façade and gardens had been made as the cradle for real rulers. Obviously, though, the cradle alone is not enough.

Black Madonna, Montserrat *(above right)*

50 kilometres to the north-west of the Spanish city of Barcelona the jagged mountain mass of the Catalan mountains rises 1,241 metres into the sky. At an altitude of 720 metres, in front of the bizarre limestone backdrop of Montserrat (Catalan for 'sawn mountain') lies the Benedictine monastery of the same name. Although it can only be reached on foot via a steep eight-kilometre-long path, believers and tourists flock there in masses, for here a unique painting can be admired: the Black Madonna of Montserrat (*La Moreneta*), a representation of Mary from the 12th century, which, according to legend, was found by hermits in a grotto (the *Santa Cava*) during the Reconquista campaign against the Muslim Moors. By touching this picture, many people hope for spiritual and possibly also physical fortification.

Poblet Monastery *(opposite, top left)*

40 kilometres north-west of Tarragona in Spain, in the province of the same name, stands the Poblet Monastery which was founded in the 12th century by the Cistercians and which today partially serves them as an abbey. This royal monastery ranks as one of the most significant monastic centres of Catalonia. With its three encircling walls it looks extremely well fortified. Between the first and the second walls artisans and peasants settled, behind the second there was a pilgrims' inn and a hospital. The monks themselves lived, prayed and worked in their buildings around the *Plaza Mayor* which lay entirely within all the walls. The complex was begun in Romanesque style and continued in Gothic, only for it to suffer plundering and destruction in 1835. It was restored to its original form in 1940 and declared a UNESCO World Heritage Site in 1991.

Palau de la Música Catalana, Hospital of Sant Pau, Barcelona *(facing, top right)*

During the Art Nouveau era, two modernistic features were added to the varied architecture of Barcelona by the architect Lluís Domènech i Montaner. With the Palace of Catalan Music, the imaginative artist created a magnificently ornamented building, which was further decorated by famous designers. His hospital of Sant Pau (see picture) was likewise a bold construction, richly ornamented and dynamically structured. This was honoured by UNESCO in 1997 by being elevated to World Heritage Site status.

Parc Güell, Palais Güell and Casa Milà, Barcelona *(facing, bottom)*

The Spanish architect Antoni Gaudí (1852–1926) created fairytale-like works for Barcelona: a five-storey house that looks like a rugged rock wall with cast iron balcony railings in the form of leafy creepers and a park bench on the roof – this is the *Casa Mila* (1905–1910, see picture). A house like a sculpture with a corrugated arch in parabola form, a roof garden on top with pointed chimneys – this is the Palais Güell (1900–1914). It is named after one of the architect's sponsors who also challenged him to transform the district of the city called Eixample with gardens, which he did painstakingly with Parc Güell: park benches with magnificent mosaics and tile fragments, a hall with 100 columns, serpentines winding through wild landscapes, a magical garden. A UNESCO World Heritage Site since 1984.

Sagrada Família Cathedral, Barcelona *(right)*

It was to be a 'sermon made out of stone', the *Sagrada Família* Cathedral designed by the Spanish architect Antoni Gaudí (1852–1926) in Barcelona, the capital of Catalonia. It was not completed during his lifetime, only the north front was standing, together with only one of the 18 planned towers (for the 16 apostles and evangelists as well as for the mother of God and her son). It is still unfinished today, although several artists have taken on the task. However, the towers are now standing, the body of the structure has been closed over and Gaudí's vision has turned to stone, to the extent that some people are afraid that the cathedral, which is modelled on natural forms, might actually one day reach completion.

Old Town, Toledo (top)

The governors of cities have always had a predilection for utilising hills to build fortresses on. The Romans were no exception and did so in Toletum, now Toledo, in the Spanish province of La Mancha: on the site where today the Alcazár national monument stands, they built a castle, the remains of which can still be found in the new castle erected by Charles V in the 16th century and renovated after the Civil War of 1936–1939. Elsewhere in the town, buildings from the time of the Moors (712–1085) characterise the 'town of three religions' (Muslims, Christians and Jews). Many Christian churches were originally Islamic places of worship and have been kept in the Gothic-Moorish Mudejár style. The most important religious building is the five-naved Gothic Cathedral of San Juan de los Reyes (1226–1493). A UNESCO World Heritage Site since 1986.

El Escorial (bottom)

Despite some Baroque elements, this is the largest Renaissance building in the world, a closed rectangle of 207 x 162 metres; the *Escorial* was built as a residence and a monastery in 1563–1584. King Phillip II of Spain had it built in order to reign from here – with Madrid some 50 kilometres away, just in sight – and to create a burial place for his dynasty. The rigidly symmetrical buildings in cold, grey granite testify to austerity, stern power and dogmatic faith. 2,000 windows look onto 16 inner courtyards, 15 cloisters and 88 fountains. The basilica is, after the model of St. Peter's in Rome, a central building with a cupola roof. The buildings include a library containing 130,000 volumes as well as collections of paintings, Gobelin tapestries and manuscripts. A UNESCO World Heritage Site since 1984.

Santa María de Guadalupe Monastery *(top)*

Shepherds in the 13th century in the Spanish town of Guadalupe, which stands on the river of the same name in Estremadura, stumbled across a buried picture of the Virgin Mary. Soon a rumour was going round that Saint Luke had carved it and a busy stream of pilgrims began to descend on the small town, where, in 1340, the monastery of Nuestra Señora de Guadalupe was founded. The vast building with its two cloisters, partly maintained in Moorish-Gothic Mudéjar style, grew into the best-loved Marian pilgrimage site in the country and became one of the richest monasteries in Spain. As a result of its school of medicine, inspired by Arab science, and its theological importance it became known as the 'Spanish Vatican' and in 1993 was awarded the title and protection of a UNESCO World Heritage Site.

Roman and Early Medieval Buildings, Mérida *(bottom)*

Most of it may still be slumbering undisturbed underground, but much has either been excavated by archaeologists or has survived, only slightly weathered, in the places that remained above ground: the eastern edge of the Old Town of Mérida, on the Guadiana in Estremadura, features an entire *zona arqueológica,* with a Roman theatre, amphitheatre, a Roman villa with well-preserved mosaics, a 792-metre-long bridge, the remains of an aqueduct, as well as a museum of Roman art displaying ancient sculptures and utensils. In addition to these relics, which date from a time when the town was still called Emerita Augusta, there are impressive churches and other religious buildings from the early Middle Ages. A UNESCO World Heritage Site since 1993.

Historic Fortifications, Cuenca *(top)*

On the western edge of the Serrania lies the Spanish city of Cuenca, the capital of the province of the same name. It is situated at a height of 900 metres on a steep, bare rock at the confluence of the Júcar and the Huécar rivers, across which the 42-metre-high San Paolo Bridge was erected in 1523. The walled town has a beautiful Gothic cathedral — the first in Spain — many distinguished palaces of the nobility, and the famous 'hanging houses' (*casas colgadas*), which are suspended from sheer cliffs above the valley. Many a visitor has wondered how they manage not to crash down into the abyss. These unique medieval buildings and the protective fortifications made Cuenca's Old Town a UNESCO World Heritage Site in 1996.

Doñana National Park *(centre)*

Even the status of a UNESCO World Heritage Site (since 1994) does not always protect cultural and natural treasures from damage: in 1998 the collapse of the dam to a sewage treatment pond belonging to a nearby ore mine destroyed large parts of the irreplaceable Spanish Coto de Doñana National Park in the estuary of the River Guadalquivir. At 75,000 hectares it is the largest nature reserve in the country and is important for its unique flora and fauna. Many species of birds live in the bushy terrain and marshes as well as in the cork oak and pine forests of the Doñana area, such as flamingos, storks, spoonbills, falcons and geese. The damage it suffered is healing slowly but steadily, thanks to international support. The picture shows the El Rocío, a place of pilgrimage on the northern edge of the marshes.

Cathedral, Alcázar and Arhivo De Indias, Seville *(bottom)*

Founded by the Phoenicians, subjugated by the Romans, conquered in the 5th century, first by Vandals and then by Visigoths, the Andalusian city of Seville, the Hispalis of ancient times, was ruled by the Moors for around 100 years from 1147. It was only won back by the Spanish in the course of the Reconquista. Its turbulent history is reflected in the buildings of the Old Town, which is characterised in particular by Islamic elements such as the mosque courtyard, the Patio de los Naranjos, or the Alcázar, but also by Christian buildings, the most important of which is the Gothic Cathedral of Santa María de la Sede (see picture) where Columbus found his last resting place. Valuable testimonies of the Spanish colonial period in America are kept in the *Archivo General de Indias*. A UNESCO World Heritage Site in 1987.

Mosque-Cathedral and Jewish Quarter, Córdoba *(opposite)*

The centre of what was probably the most powerful caliphate during the Moorish rule of Spain was the Andalusian town of Córdoba. The mosque *La Mezquita*, erected here in 785–990 by the Umayyids, still draws admiration and wonder at the skill of the Arab architects: 856 columns and double-tiered horseshoe-shaped arches in red and white marble support the vast hall. It is adorned with an extravagance of rich architectural detail in jasper and granite as well as mosaics and finely engraved reliefs. In 1523 the building was reconsecrated as a cathedral. Together with the Old Town and its former Jewish quarter, the *Judería*, it has been a UNESCO World Heritage Site in 1984.

Alhambra and Generalife Palace, Granada (top)

The last Moorish stronghold on the Iberian peninsula, which only fell in 1492, was Granada, high in the Andalusian mountains. One of the most famous buildings of the Islamic era stands here: the Sultan's 'red fortress', the *Alhambra* on La Sabika hill. On the occasion of his marriage to Isabella of Portugal in 1526, Emperor Charles V had a palace extension built onto it, 207 x 162 metres in size, including a hall of pillars in Renaissance style. The pièce de resistance of the Moorish part is the *Patio de los Leones* (Lion courtyard), in which twelve lion sculptures support a fountain. To the side of this, behind 124 columns, are the private apartments (harem). The Alhambra and the 13th century Generalife Palace have been a UNESCO World Heritage Site since 1984.

Ibiza, Biodiversity and Culture, Balearic Islands (bottom)

A good example of the interaction of marine and coastal eco-systems is provided by the Spanish Balearic island of Ibiza. The fields of seaweed offshore safeguard a large variety of underwater species and flora and fauna on land. At the same time the island has been densely populated since prehistoric times and bears the marks of the cultural influences that crossed here. Experience and good care of the natural resources has led to this harmonious accord of culture and nature, which can be traced back to the time of the Phoenicians and Romans and also did not suffer during the time that the island was being developed militarily, as represented in the Renaissance fortress in the Alta Vila of Ibiza town. A UNESCO World Heritage Site since 1999.

Portugal

Historic Centre, Porto *(top)*

Powerful Christian features were put in place by the new rulers after they had put an end in 997 to the Moorish rule of Porto, today capital of the Portuguese district of the same name. The most important was the cathedral which was only finished in the 12th century and decorated with a splendid silver altar. From later times stem the São Pedro dos Clérigos Church (1732–1750) with the 75 metres high free-standing bell tower and the Baroque archbishop's palace presiding above the town, which rises in terraces, on the right bank of the Douro. Its historic centre has been a UNESCO World Heritage Site in 1996.

Cistercian Monastery, Alcobaça *(bottom)*

Reunited for ever, here rest Dom Pedro of Portugal and his lover Inês de Castro, who was murdered in 1355 with the approval of the king, Pedro's father. After he had taken power, Pedro had her named as his rightful spouse and interred in the royal crypt of the monastery church built 1153–1252, where he himself, twelve years later, found his last resting place next to her. A more worthy place can scarcely be imagined, for in Santa María de Alcobaça (Estremadura) the Cistercians have brought their early Gothic architectural style to its fulfilment. A UNESCO World Heritage Site since 1989.

131

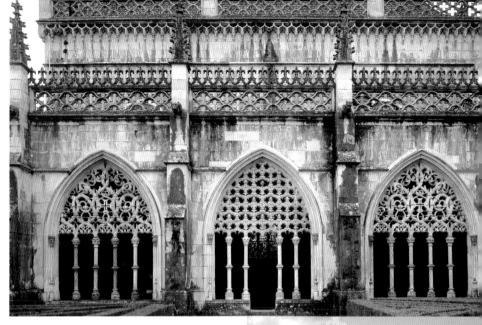

Monastery of Batalha (top)

An architectural style is named after the Portuguese King Emanuel I (reigned 1495–1521), which combines late Gothic elements with the nautical and exotic. An often-cited example of this is the former Monastery of Santa María da Vitória to the north of Lisbon, erected in proud memory of the victory of Portugal over Castile in 1385. The 32-metre-high monastery church is impressive, as is the Royal Cloister (*Claustro Real*) with the finest tracery. As an expression of a highly original Portuguese architectural style, the complex has been a UNESCO World Heritage Site since 1993.

Convent of Christ, Tomar (centre)

Inside the sixteen-sided church building lies the octagonal sanctuary of the Templars, the core of the monastery complex which is usually simply called *O Convento*, and which belongs to the Knights Templar of Tomar (transferred in 1344 to the Knights of the Order of Christ) in Portugal. Built in the 12th century in the style of a fortress, the ablutions cloister (*claustro da lavagem*) was added in the 14th century and thereafter the cemetery cloister. Renaissance elements (the large cloister) were added 200 years later. The cloister represents not only the successful Reconquista but also Portuguese missionary work in the Age of Discoveries. It has been a UNESCO World Heritage Site since 1983.

Cabo da Roca, Sintra (bottom)

The western Irish Dingle peninsula with its point at Slea Head and the central Portuguese Cabo da Roca are in competition for the title of the most westerly point of Europe. Depending on how you look at it, they both deserve it: Ireland is definitely part of Europe and, on the point of contention, it clearly extends further west than its southern rival. However, the latter can cite being part of the continental mainland and therefore claim the record for being the most westerly point on the continent. They both have their charms: the Irish promontory is raw, the Portuguese headland sunny – it was the last thing to sink below the horizon when the bold explorers from Lisbon set sails in the direction of the New World.

Sintra and Sintra Mountains (opposite)

The fact that the landscape has inspired architects and that they in turn have left their mark on the landscape, makes the town, castle and heights of Sintra to the north-west of Lisbon, on the slope of the Sierra de Sintra, a striking sight: the town climbs the hill and reaches its peak in two curious white cone shapes that are the kitchen chimneys of the royal palace, which for a long time was the monarch's summer residence. Outside the town is a dream palace à la Disney, which the Prince Regent Ferdinand had built in the middle of the 19th century on the site of the ruins of a Hieronymite monastery. On the summit opposite are two squat fortified towers from the Islamic period, the Castelo dos Mouros. The neo-Gothic Montserrat Palace completes this UNESCO World Heritage Site (1995).

Old Town (Alfama), Lisbon *(opposite, top)*

When a horrific earthquake struck Lisbon in 1755, it divided the core of the Portuguese capital in two. The lower town, Cidad Baixa, had to be fully rebuilt, whereas the old town, Alfama, was only partially damaged. Here, below the São Jorge Castle from Moorish times, some precious medieval buildings still stand such as the Cathedral of Sé Patriarcal from the 12th century, which only had to be repaired, the Church of São Vicente de Fora from the late Renaissance and the somewhat more recent Pantheon — a beautiful counterpoint to the new Old Town.

Tejo Bridge, Lisbon *(facing, bottom)*

The Tejo is the longest river on the Iberian peninsula, the last 179 kilometres of which traverse central Portugal before broadening out in Lisbon into a wide funnel — good for the harbour, but a problem for the bridge. For the 1998 World Exhibition the Portuguese government delved deep into its pockets and had a 17.2-kilometre-long bridge built across the river, at a cost of 900 million euros. It has thus become the longest bridge in the whole of Europe and, with its white pylons and cables, it is also one of the most magnificent. It was named after the great explorer Vasco da Gama (approx. 1469–1524), who sailed from here in 1497, and was the first European to round the Cape of Good Hope on his way to India.

Belém Tower, Lisbon *(top right)*

On the mouth of the Tejo, opposite the Portuguese capital of Lisbon, stands one of the most famous towers of Europe, the Torre de Belém. It stands in water, but is nowadays connected to the mainland. It commemorates the bold seamen who, in the 14th and 15th centuries, sailed from here to India and the New World. They always did so with the blessing of the Church, who was equally interested in extending its power. In the district of Belém, the Church is represented with an even more magnificent building: the Hieronymite monastery consecrated in 1572. Both buildings have been a UNESCO World Heritage Site since 1983.

Historic Centre of Evora *(bottom right)*

In Evora, in the Portuguese province of Alentejoo, there is no need to go underground to get back to Roman times: the ruins of Roman buildings, in particular those of a temple to Diana with 14 Corinthian columns from the 2nd century, have all been excavated. The medieval church buildings are also well-preserved and are still in use: the Gothic 12th century cathedral, the massive Church of São Brás, built 300 years later, the building of the former Lóios Monastery in the Emanuel style with its hint of the exotic. The Old University is 450 years old and likewise stands as an example of this architectural style. A UNESCO World Heritage Site since 1986.

Russia

Churches, Kizhi Pogost *(top left)*

A religious museum without parallel: on the Russian island of Kizhi in Lake Onega (South Karelia), north-east of Petrozavodsk, you might think you are dreaming when looking at the *Preobrajensky*, or Church of the Transfiguration in Kizhi Pogost. The wooden construction has 22 slate domes, each crowned with a cross that glints like silver in the sun. Inside, a magnificent wall with over 100 icons summons one to prayer. In addition, the island also offers the Church of Mary's Protection and Intercession, built 50 years earlier, which does not have quite so many domes, but instead has a large, 27-metre-high central dome. As a masterpiece of Russian log building and as a monument to the piety of the ordinary people, Kizhi Pogost has been a UNESCO World Heritage Site since 1990.

Lake Ladoga, Northern Russia *(top right)*

The whole of Wales would easily fit into it: the 18,135-square-kilometre Lake Ladoga in Northern Russia is the largest inland lake in Europe. It has 600 islands, is fed by four rivers (Volkhov, Svir, Vuoksi and Sjas) and water flows out of it courtesy of the River Neva in the direction of Saint Petersburg. As a part of the Volga-Baltic Waterway it is of great economic significance and also offers fishermen a livelihood. The fact that Leningrad, as it used to be called, did not completely starve to death during the German siege of 1941–1944, was in part due to the occasional supplies reaching it via the lake by boat or, in winter, by horse-drawn sledge.

Historic Centre, Saint Petersburg *(bottom)*

Compared to some other time-honoured Russian cities, St Petersburg is relatively young. Czar Peter (I) the Great (reigned 1682–1725) created the 'Venice of the North', as the city is called, partly on account of its many canals and its picturesque location on the River Neva, but also because it was designed by Italian architects. Wherever you look in the city centre there are architectural masterpieces: the vibrant Hermitage (1764–1767) with its breathtaking stairway, the Winter Palace (1754–1762), the foundations of the Peter and Paul Fortress (1703) with the cathedral of the same name (1712–1732), St. Isaac Cathedral (1818) with its magnificent cupola – a symphony in Baroque and Classicism, which fully deserves its designation as a UNESCO World Heritage Site since 1990.

Catherine's Palace, Pushkin (top left)

At the beginning of October 1941, in the Russian town of Pushkin, south of what was then called Leningrad, the 3rd company of the German 553 supply battalion dismantled the Amber Room, installed in Catherine's Palace in 1755 as a present from the King of Prussia, and sent it to Kaliningrad where it disappeared without trace in 1945. In a painstaking effort it has been rebuilt over the last few years. Yet Catherine's Palace is worth a visit not just to see the reconstructed Amber Room but also for its Baroque (by Rastrelli amongst others) and Classicist buildings (including, among others, the Alexander Palace designed by Quarenghi) in the 'Old Garden', together with the palace kitchen and the orangery.

Church of the Resurrection, Saint Petersburg (top right)

In the very place where Czar Alexander II was assassinated in 1881, the Russian Church erected the Church of the Resurrection — "On Spilt Blood" — with almost excessive opulence, particularly when it is reflected in the waters of the Griboyedov Canal. No expense was spared on the colours, gold, turrets, ornaments and pictures. If heaven could be summoned by decoration alone then here would be the place for it.

Petrodvorets Palaces (bottom)

Many Russian Czars did not reign long enough to try out all their summer residences in the then capital city, St Petersburg. As well as the Pavlovsk and Pushkin Palaces they also had the palace collection of Petrodvorets, construction of which began in 1714 under Peter (I) the Great (reigned 1682–1725). The work was completed under his heirs by the architect Bartholomeo Francesco Count Rostrelli (1700–1771). In the end there was a choice of the Great Palace (see picture), the water palaces of the Hermitage and Marly, the little palace of Monplaisir and, of course, the park with its charming fountains.

Historic Monuments of Novgorod and Surroundings (top left)

Special mention is due, even among this abundance of remarkable buildings, to the five-naved Sophia Cathedral (1045–1050, picture) in the Kremlin, the oldest building of Russia's first capital, with its Romanesque bronze door. Other than this, a list of examples will have to suffice: the Kremlin with its 1,385-metre-long wall, the Court Church in Yaroslav Palace (1113–1136), the Church of the Transfiguration of Christ on Ilya Street (1374), wall paintings by Theophanes the Greek, the Church of Fiodor Stratilat (14th century). Outside town: Yuryev Monastery, St. Anthony's Monastery, the Church of the Redeemer (12th/13th centuries), the Church of the Transfiguration of Christ at Kovalevo (1345), the Church of Mary's Assumption into Heaven (1363). A UNESCO World Heritage Site since 1992.

Monasteries and Churches, Suzdal and Kideksha (top right)

In the town of Suzdal, the site of the former royal residence and home of the princes of Vladimir-Suzdal, numerous religious buildings bear testimony to Russia's Golden Age at the height of the Middle Ages, such as the Rozhdestvenski Cathedral, which was erected in the 13th century on top of earlier churches, the Spasso-Yefimi Monastery, consecrated in 1352, the Pokrovski Monastery, consecrated 12 years later, and the, admittedly considerably younger, Rispoloschenski Monastery, which was built in the 16th century. The princes also maintained a residence in nearby Kideksha where you can still visit the Boris and Gleb Cathedral from the 12th century, which underwent Baroque renovation in the 18th century. Both sites have been a joint UNESCO World Heritage Site since 1992.

Yaroslavl (above)

Named after its founder Yaroslavl the Wise, the Grand Prince of Kiev from 1019 to 1054, the town on the Volga began to develop from as early as 1024 but only became significant centuries later. Testimony to this can be seen in the numerous monastic buildings and churches from the 16th to 18th centuries. Amongst these, two in particular deserve mention: the Church of Elijah the Prophet, which was erected in only three years between 1647 and 1650, with its gleaming, precious interior, and the only slightly more recent Church of John the Baptist (1671–1687) whose 15 domes tower over the suburb of Korovniki. Also important is the Baroque theatre, built in 1750, which is the oldest in the whole country.

Trinity Sergius Lavra Monastery, Sergiev Posad (top)

The Trinity Church of St Sergius Lavra in the Russian town of Sergiev Posad, also named after the Saint, became Russia's national holy site soon after it was founded in 1340. Czar Boris Godunov (1598–1605) took a particular interest in it after the Russian Church had severed from Constantinople and appointed a Moscow patriarch, who was, and is once again, the nominal abbot of this monastery and its many subsidiaries. Fortified in the 16th century, the complex comprises several churches, including the Uspenski Cathedral (picture) dating from the 16th/17th centuries and containing the Czar's tomb. Together they form a fine example of a working Orthodox monastery and have been a UNESCO World Heritage Site since 1993.

Cathedral and Historic Centre, Vladimir (bottom)

One of the oldest towns in Russia, Vladimir, which lies on the Klyaz'ma, was founded and fortified in 1108 to secure the border. Shortly afterwards the Russian grand princes of the most powerful Russian territory moved their capital here and developed the town accordingly. What has survived, amongst other things, are the Golden Gate, the remains of the city wall, the Uspenski Cathedral in which the princes were crowned and which contains frescos by the famous Andrei Rublyov, and the Demetrius Cathedral which is remarkable for its stone masonry – a family of buildings which has been a UNESCO World Heritage Site since 1992.

Kremlin and Red Square, Moscow *(far top)*

Many will know the heart of Moscow from books, films or television footage of the massive communist May Day parades on Red Square which demonstrated on the one hand the size of this showplace of Russian power and on the other the magnificent collection of buildings grouped around the square, including the 16th century Cathedral of St. Basil. Inside the fortress of the Russian capital, the Kremlin, which sits on the west side of Red Square, are numerous religious buildings with golden onion-shaped turrets, and many secular buildings. The Kremlin is seen as the embodiment of Russian politics and its claim to sovereignty over the largest country on earth. The square and its buildings have been a UNESCO World Heritage Site since 1990.

White House, Moscow *(above left)*

The White House is actually the Duma building, the seat of the Russian parliament in Moscow: However, the bright building which gleams from afar, inspired journalists as well as locals to draw a parallel with the most famous political building in Washington, hence the name 'White House' came about. The Russians use it not without pride. Their White House is much bigger than the American one, in which only the US President rules, whereas here the people have their say. And at least on one occasion the gigantic building has withstood a baptism of fire: it was here in 1991, for example, that Boris Yeltsin defended the reform policies of Mikhail Gorbachev against those who were bent on a coup in Gorbachev's absence.

Lomonosov University, Moscow *(above right)*

'Morning reflections on the Majesty of God' is the title of an essay by the Russian academic Lomonosov (1711–1765). The chemist, mathematician and philologist was one of the last polymaths and so highly regarded that even the communists did not rename Moscow's university, which was named after him, when it re-opened after the Second World War, in 1953, in a gigantic new building on the Lenin Hills. Presumably, Lomonosov had a different definition of 'majesty', but the vastness of the new building and the so-called 'gingerbread style' of Soviet architecture, which recalls elements of old Russian decorative traditions, might still have impressed him.

Western Caucasus (far top)

The foothill area on the outermost edge of the western Caucasus in southern Russia, about 50 kilometres to the north-east of the Black Sea, is one of the few large mountain regions that remain largely unspoilt by man. The foothills of the mountain range have been protected as a UNESCO World Heritage Site since 1999 and encompass 2,750 square kilometres. From its grasslands in the lower reaches to virgin mountain forests in the sub-alpine zones, it offers unique landscapes. In this diverse ecosystem, many plant and animal species exist which are only found here, such as the mountain bison sub-species to name but one example.

GUM Department Store, Moscow (above left)

Wherever you look on Moscow's Red Square there are towers, turrets and cathedrals. Even the vast three-storey building on the east side of the square turns out to be a temple, albeit a highly profane one: it is GUM, the temple of consumerism, the acronym standing for *Gosudarstvenniy Universalniy Magazin* (State Universal Department Store). For a long time, GUM was unable to compete with department stores such as London's Harrods or Berlin's KaDeWe in terms of the goods on offer, but at least it could match them easily in terms of decor. The 90-metre-wide and 250-metre-long 'basilica of the world of merchandise', built at the end of the 19th century, offers a unique shopping experience.

Church of the Ascension, Kolomenskoye (above right)

An unusual church was built to celebrate the birth of a ruler who was to become an exceptionally harsh one. In 1532, the Russian Czar Vassily III ordered the construction of the Church of the Ascension in Kolomenskoye, now a district of Moscow, when his son Ivan came into the world – a world which would later learn to fear him as 'Ivan the Terrible'. The church, by contrast, is highly attractive and unique among Russian religious buildings, with a wooden tent roof construction on a stone and brick substructure on cruciform outline. A UNESCO World Heritage Site since 1994.

Estonia

Old Town, Tallinn *(top)*

First of all came the Danes, then the Germans, the Swedes, the Russians, then the Germans again and finally the Russians once again. It is only since 1991 that the Estonians have at last been able to determine their own fate from the capital city and port of Tallinn, formerly Reval, on the Gulf of Finland. The city's varied history has marked it with the Alexander Nevski Cathedral as a symbol of the Russian rule, with the Gothic cathedral and the fortifications of 13th century origin from the German era, and numerous medieval buildings, rising up the cathedral hill and adding a sense of elevation to the town's appearance. A UNESCO World Heritage Site since 1997.

Latvia

Historic Town Centre, Riga *(bottom)*

Like other Baltic cities, the Latvian capital Riga, located where the Duna flows into the Baltic, suffered heavily in the Second World War. It has since been possible to restore the historic centre on the right bank of the river to a large extent and it sights now include the Cathedral of Mary, begun in 1215, in late Romanesque style, the medieval 'Black Heads House', which was later remodelled in Renaissance style, the likewise several times remodelled Palace of the Teutonic Order, a row of charming Baroque buildings and the Swedish Gate, the last remaining town gate. This restored splendour has been a UNESCO World Heritage Site since 1997.

Lithuania

The Curonian Spit *(top)*

In the north of the now Russian East Prussia and in Lithuania, a narrow strip of dunes separates the open Baltic from a large but shallow coastal lake of 1,613 square kilometres, the Curonian Lagoon. The sand spit, which is between 400 metres and four kilometres wide, is called the Curonian Spit and stretches from the former seaside resort of Cranz to Memel (Klaipeda), where the spit ends in front of the narrow opening of the Memel Channel. Shifting dunes, up to 70 metres high on the lagoon side, together with a small woodland on the spit create a natural paradise, where the Rossitten research station is situated.

Old Town, Vilnius *(centre)*

A bouquet of glorious buildings bears witness to the heyday of the Lithuanian capital Vilnius in the Middle Ages and in the Early Modern Age: the Church of Saint Anna (completed in 1580, see picture), built in Gothic brick style, and Saint Bernard's (completed in 1513), the Church of St. Michael (built 1594–1625) and the Church of St. Peter and St. Paul (1668–1676) decorated with 2,000 statues. They characterise the Baltic Baroque and the so-called Vilnius Baroque. Even the remains of late medieval fortifications such as the Gedimin Tower have been preserved as well as the Classical town hall and the Russian Orthodox Church of the Assumption which also deserve a long look. A UNESCO World Heritage Site since 1994.

Belarus

Pripyet Marshes *(bottom)*

Bogs and wetlands are incredibly rich habitats for moisture-loving plants, birds of all kinds and amphibians. The largest marshland in the world is the catchment area of the Pripyet, a 775-kilometre-long tributary of the Dnieper. The largest part of the marshes lies in the Polesian landscape in the south of Belarus and encompasses almost 100,000 square kilometres. Although it has been possible in the meantime to drain some areas at enormous expense, the lion's share is still inaccessible moor. Nature has placed itself under protection through lack of firm ground and man benefits from the giant 'lungs' of the vast open land interspersed with the occasional woodland.

Ukraine

Church of St. Andrew, Kiev (top left)
On the highest point of the Old Town of the Ukrainian city of Kiev, a church was consecrated to the apostle Saint Andrew, in the presence of Czarina Elizabeth in 1744. According to legend, he was a missionary in Constantinople and Russia. The church is unmistakably Russian Orthodox in style. However, the influence of Western European Baroque is also clearly visible in the building's central construction, rich decor and pastel colours. Its central dome is crowned by a small onion cupola, signalling the confidence of the Russian Church, based as it was on a deeply rooted piety of the people. This, together with the support it enjoyed – at the time – from the state, gave the Russian Church a secure sense of power it would never experience again.

Historic Centre, Lviv (far top right)
Lviv, then known as Lemberg, belonged to the Austro-Hungarian double monarchy for a long time before becoming Polish (under the name of Lvov) and now Ukrainian. Despite its turbulent history, the city managed to save all kinds of architectural treasures and has been a UNESCO World Heritage Site since 1998 for the remains of its medieval fortress, the gunpowder tower (around 1550), the late Gothic cathedral – later remodelled in Baroque style, the Armenian cathedral from the 14th century, the front of which was renovated in 1908, the Uspenski Cathedral from the early 17th century, the Baroque Church of Saint George and the Dominican Church, of about the same age, as well as the provincial parliament building, which now houses the university, and the town hall, both built in the 19th century under Austrian rule (in the picture: the Cathedral of the Assumption).

Petcherskaia Caves Monastery, Kiev (centre)
The buildings in the oldest Russian monastery in the Ukrainian capital Kiev are magnificent, and yet the main visitor magnet is another sight: the Kiev Petcherskaia Monastery, which originated in caves above the steep bank of the Dnieper, when monks settled here in the 11th century. Later numerous churches and living quarters were built above ground and the labyrinthine cave system below became the burial place for deceased monks. Their mummified corpses can still be seen in the flickering candlelight of the caves. Together with the Cathedral of St. Sophia in the city, the caves have been a UNESCO World Heritage Site since 1990.

Cathedral of St. Sophia, Kiev (bottom)
In the year 988 AD, the Grand Prince Vladimir of Kiev sent out envoys to all different countries, for he had decided an official religion was necessary for his country but was unsure which one to choose. His counsellors returned with reports of the Bulgarians having a 'bad smell' and the Germans being 'joyless'. However, "when we were with the Greeks" they continued, "we knew not whether we were in heaven or on earth. For on earth there is no such splendour or such beauty, and we are at a loss how to describe it. We know only that God dwells there among them." Thus, as the oldest Russian chronicle has it, the Grand Princedom became Greek Orthodox and the Cathedral of St. Sophia, erected from 1037, proves that Vladimir's architects had learnt their lesson about beauty. They were rewarded in 1990 with the title of World Heritage Site by UNESCO.

Poland

Malbork *(top)*

Built by Knights of the Teutonic Order in the 13th century, the *Marienburg* castle, situated on the estuary of the Vistula River, became the capital of the Order shortly after and a town of the same name developed around it. The locality now belongs to northern Poland and is called Malbork. The mighty brick fortress, which doubles in size as a result of its reflection in the waters of the river, had only been preserved in parts — the rest was rebuilt after the war: the convent house, the tower, the Chapel of Mary and Ann, the middle palace and outer ward. A UNESCO World Heritage Site since 1997.

Masurian Lake District *(bottom)*

Masuria, or *Mazury* in Polish, with its great lakes belongs to the Baltic Ridge and its largest area of water is Lake Spirding at 122 square kilometres and Lake Mauer at 104. The area's crystal lakes and beautiful scenery make it a popular tourist destination. However, in the past, peasants who had to live off the land in this area had only a meagre income, as the soils are poor and the extensive forests often belonged to rich landowners.

Old Town, Warsaw *(top left)*

In the Second World War, the Polish capital was the first European capital to suffer concentrated air raids. Further destruction was later caused during the Warsaw Uprising in 1944. Visitors are therefore thoroughly amazed to find the Old Town on the west bank of the river Vistula fully restored to its old glory. The restorers have accomplished a miracle: palace and town walls, parts of which actually managed to survive the war, are standing once again just like the colourful Baroque and Renaissance houses on the Old Market Square (see picture) and the numerous churches and monasteries from the Middle Ages. Even the incomparable palaces of the nobility, which today of course serve other purposes, have risen again from the ashes. A UNESCO World Heritage Site since 1980.

Torun *(top right)*

Although not as magnificent as the one in Pisa, it is definitely leaning: the lopsided tower of Torun (Thorn until 1945). The city on the Vistula, in the Polish province of Kajawsko Pomorskie, is so full of architectural gems that UNESCO declared its entire centre a World Heritage Site in 1997. Particularly worth mentioning are the Gothic town hall (today a museum), the medieval town fortifications, the Gothic Churches of St. James, St. John and St. Mary (see picture), with wall paintings from the 14th century, the Baroque Church of the Holy Ghost (1735–1756), the former Bishop's Palace (1693), the armoury (1824), built in Classicist style, and the theatre in Art Nouveau style. The astronomer Copernicus was born here in 1473, and is commemorated by a monument (1853) and a museum.

National Park Bialowieza and Belovezhskaya Pushcha *(bottom)*

A nature reserve since 1947, the Bialowieza Forest in Poland together with the *Belovezhskaya Pushcha* in Belarus straddles the border between the two countries over an area of 1,250 square kilometres. Vast stretches of this area consist of unspoilt marshland and dense, evergreen and deciduous forests. Bison, wolves and wild horses roam here as do other protected species such as eagle owls, sea eagles and white storks. This undisturbed paradise and haven for rare fauna and flora received the status of World Heritage Site from UNESCO in 1992.

Barbican, Warsaw *(top)*

In the Middle Ages, bridgeheads and outworks of fortifications were referred to by the Italian word *barbacane*, which has become 'barbican' in English. And for a bastion as imposing and powerful as the one at the entrance to Warsaw's Old Town, the term becomes the name itself. The Warsaw Barbican, north-east of the town centre is enthroned above a brick gate with two massive towers, fortified with battlements, as a reminder of the time of the crusades, when this type of opening in town walls and the security it implied was adopted from Arab fortifications. Comparable constructions can still be found in Cracow and in some French towns.

St. John's Cathedral, Warsaw *(centre)*

Only one street along from the Old Town's market square, in the heart of the Polish capital rises the Cathedral of St. John. It surpasses the many other churches of Warsaw in dignity, size and furnishings. The Gothic building with its star-shaped vaulting is the burial place of significant dignitaries, including Henry Sienkiewicz, the author of the novel *Quo Vadis?* – in which Jesus Christ appears to the fugitive St Peter and to his question "Where are you going?" replies with: "Since you are abandoning my flock, I am going to Rome to let myself be crucified for a second time." A perfect analogy to the martyrdom of the Polish Church, which has stood by its flock even through the most difficult times, most recently under the Communist rule.

Royal Palace and Palace Square, Warsaw *(bottom)*

The decision to rebuild the old city of Warsaw was taken soon after the Second World War. Only the Royal Palace on the southern edge of the Old Town posed a slight conundrum to the Communists in power. However, in 1971, they decided, after all, to close this gap and spared no expense in having a reconstruction carried out which was faithful in every minute detail. In this they were helped by a treasure belonging to the building, which had survived the war in storage elsewhere: landscape paintings by the Italian painter Canaletto (1720–1780), who had spent twelve years in Poland and to whom a whole room in the magnificently reconstructed 16th century building has been dedicated. Palaces can only look this prestigious and impressive when they have the corresponding space in front of them. This is the case in Warsaw. The enormous space also provides tourists with a suitable subject for their photographs: in the middle of the square a Baroque column rises up, from the top of which the figure of a saint or a bishop appears to be raising his hand in a blessing. At least this is what many people think, because the figure is holding an oversized cross in his left hand. The truth is that it represents the Polish King Sigismund III Vasa (reigned 1587–1632), a fervent Catholic, who successfully prevented the Reformation spreading to Poland – whilst being much less successful on the political front: he lost Livand to Sweden and the Polish coastal cities to Prussia.

147

Sacramentalists' Church and Church of St. Mary *(top)*

To the north of Warsaw's historic Old Town lies the historic New Town which contains two small but beautiful churches. The Sacramentalists' Church (see picture) designed by Tylman van Gameren, the Dutch master of the Polish Baroque, is a central construction with a monastery. A short distance away, in the direction of the River Vistula, stands the bell tower of the Gothic Church of St. Mary. From its terrace one can enjoy an uninterrupted view across green parkland and the broad river to the suburb of Praga on its eastern bank.

Royal Way, Warsaw *(centre)*

From the palace a straight boulevard runs out of the Old Town through the Marian city southwards. This is called the Royal Way not only because it starts at the palace but also because of some architectural gems: St. Ann's Church (see picture) directly behind the town wall, a Gothic construction with a remodelled front in Classicist style, then the monument to the Polish National Poet Mickiewicz (1798–1855) and the Radzwill Palace in which the state president resides today. Going past the opulent Baroque Visitants Church one reaches the extensive grounds of the university on the left and finally the Copernicus monument (1473–1543) whose origins, whether German or Polish, has been the subject of some debate.

Wilanov Palace, Warsaw *(bottom)*

In an imaginary extension of the Royal Way from Warsaw to the south stands another royal item: the Wilanov Palace, built from 1677–1696, one of the most beautiful Baroque establishments in Poland. This applies to the tastefully ornamented building of the actual palace as well as to the ancillary buildings and above all to the park. One might think the former master of this summer residence, King Jan III Sobieski, who in 1683 relieved the Viennese from a Turkish siege during the battle of Kahlenberg, was still strolling around his estate.

Gothic Town Hall, Wrocław (top)

Although Silesia was outside the range of the allied bombers, only a heap of rubble was left of its capital Breslau, *Wrocław* in Polish, after the bitterly fought battle in spring 1945. The German population was expelled and in their place came mainly Poles, themselves expelled from eastern Poland by the Russians. They restored the old town centre to a great extent, in particular its centrepiece: the magnificent Gothic-style town hall which was started in the 13th century and took over 200 years to complete. It stands on the old market square which, with its Baroque houses and Renaissance palaces provides a worthy framework.

Old Town, Cracow (bottom)

For over 400 years the Polish kings were crowned here: the Polish town of Cracow, situated in the south-west on the River Vistula, has some correspondingly splendid architecture. In the south, the Wawel towers over it, the castle hill with a palace where the kings resided until 1596 and the cathedral with their burial place. Further religious buildings dominate the skyline with their towers and attract visitors with their treasures. The cloth halls and the magnificence of the business houses bear testimony to the economic significance of this town, which lies at the intersection of important trade routes. A UNESCO World Heritage Site since 1998.

Cloth Halls, Cracow *(top)*

The Market Square in the Old Town in the south-western Polish town of Cracow is gigantic and in its centre stands an imposing monument to the city's former commercial power: the cloth halls, a purpose-built construction which strikes us as an architectural gem today. The complex with the long arcade on the front side came into being in the 14th century and was, a little later, expensively re-modelled in Renaissance style. It is difficult not to buy something at the stalls, which still offer their wares in the halls, for rarely is one in such an atmospheric place and faced with such attractive goods on sale.

Town Hall Tower, Cracow *(centre left)*

The town would be governed from elsewhere today any-way, but that the old town hall of Cracow has simply disappeared is nevertheless regretted by the visitor to the town's big Market Square. For there stands, alone and abandoned, the tower which belonged to the building and shows with its Gothic design what has probably been lost of architectural value in the town hall. After a fire in the 19th century, the Cracow town councillors shied away from the expense involved in repairing their place of work, or rather perhaps just wanted a new one. At any rate, the ruins were pulled down and the tower was left all alone.

Church of St. Mary, Cracow *(centre right)*

In the Middle Ages, church towers also had to serve as watchtowers when danger of war threatened or for spott-ing fires. For this the left tower on the front of the Church of St. Mary in Cracow is better suited as it is clearly higher than its partner and prettier into the bargain. Here a signal from a trumpet once even warned of the approaching Mongols. The watchers in the tower must have been asleep as a few of the fast archers had already reached it and one of their arrows pierced the trumpeter so that the signal was broken off abruptly. In memory of this, a flour-ishing fanfare still rings out today from the tower on the hour, breaking off abruptly. In contrast, the main altar by the wood carver Veit Stoss of Nuremberg in the triple-naved church tells stories of a religious nature. At 13 me-tres high it is the largest medieval altar anywhere.

St. Adalbert's Church, Cracow *(bottom)*

Cracow lies on the upper reaches of the Vistula and is said to have the largest town square in Europe. Modestly situ-ated in one corner of this large market square, which is dominated by the cloth halls, huddles a little church that actually deserves more than such an existence on the edge of things: St. Adalbert's Church is much older than every-thing around it, originating in parts from as early as the 10th century, when there was already a market here, albeit not such a magnificent one. The reason that the old age of the little church is not apparent at first glance, is that it was partially remodelled in Baroque style in the 17th cen-tury. Inside is an exhibition with information about the his-tory of the market and the church.

Wawel, Cracow (top)

Here on top of the Wawel castle hill, the Polish kings resided for a long time looking down on their capital Cracow with the River Vistula winding its way through it. So that they did not lose touch with reality, the cathedral next to their castle was a reminder that everything temporal is vain. Upon their coronation in this Gothic house of God they knew that the crypt was not far away in which their ancestors rested and in which they in good time would also sleep the eternal sleep. They financed many a chapel for the cathedral (see picture), including what is perhaps the most magnificent of all, the Sigismund Chapel with its golden cupola. Once back in their residence they took pleasure in works of art, of which many can still be seen or can be seen again, despite the German Governor General in the Second World War having taken everything that seemed to be of any value.

Barbican and Florian Gate, Cracow (centre left)

Unfortunately the town councillors had the town walls torn down in the 19th century. They were in the way of the expansion planned for the centre of Cracow and therefore gave way to a greenbelt which is, of course, much prettier and does not look so warlike. How defensive the old fortifications must have looked can still be seen in the Barbican, a mighty outer fort with a tower bulwark and passage originating from the 15th century. Behind this is the Florian gate (see picture), from which a few remnants of the wall continue. These have however lost some respect, as there is a throng of artists here offering their pictures for sale.

Wieliczka Salt Mine (centre right)

A document from the year 1119 mentions the name Wielika Sol for the first time as a place where salt was being mined in the southern Polish Carpathian foothills. Today the place is called Wieliczka and is able to look back on 750 years of salt mining. Visitors can do this too as they are able to venture into some of the 2,100 chambers and shafts, spread over nine levels and up to 342 metres deep, from this long operational period. A salt works museum is situated at a depth of 130 metres and a spa for people suffering from respiratory problems at a depth of 211 metres. A UNESCO World Heritage Site since 1999.

Kalwaria Zebrzydowska (bottom)

Approximately 20 kilometres south of Cracow and about 15 kilometres to the east of Vadovice, the birthplace of the late Pope John Paul II, a pilgrimage park set in the southwestern Polish countryside summons the Catholic faithful to meditate on the Passion of Jesus Christ. In *Kalwaria Zebrzydowska* a series of symbolic stations relating to the Passion of Christ and the life of the Virgin Mary were laid out at the beginning of 17th century and have remained virtually unchanged since then. The park with chapels and avenues representing the stations of the cross, from the house of Pilate, who condemned the Saviour to death, to the hill of Calvary (*calvaria* = skull in Latin), Golgotha, with the cross of Jesus and the two thieves, is still a place of pilgrimage to this day, and a UNESCO World Heritage Site since 1999.

The Czech Republic

Cheb (below left)

In February 1634, at a time when the north-western Czech spa town was known under the German name Eger, a bloody deed of historic significance took place here: General Wallenstein fell victim to a murder plot. How it was done is graphically illustrated at the scene of the crime, the former town hall and present day museum. However, the town also has more pleasant things to offer, such as the partially reconstructed imperial castle, the Gothic Church of St. Nicholas and Elizabeth, the quarter known as *Stöckl* with eleven medieval houses in the former Franciscan monastery.

Ceský Ráj, Turnov (centre)

What the Elbe Sandstone Mountains are to the Saxons, the *Ceský ráj* is to the Czechs. This is the 'Bohemian Paradise', south of the town of Turnov. Thousands of years have shaped the sandstone plateau here into bizarre shapes: pillars and crevasses, steep walls and deep fissures form a stone landscape of great charm. In the early 19th century the Romantic poets discovered this rock garden and celebrated it in verse. Today it is one of the favourite day-trip destinations for the inhabitants of Prague who only live an hour away by car. Whilst there, they also visit the picturesque castles in the area, including Waldstein Palace of Generalissimus Wallenstein, the Emperor's commander-in-chief in the Thirty Years' War.

Czech Spa Towns (below right, far bottom left and right)

Formerly known as Karlsbad, Marienbad and Franzensbad, today the three north-western Czech spa towns are called Karlovy Vary, Mariánské Lázne and Frantiskovy Lázne, respectively. Having lost their polularity under Communist rule, the spa towns are now once again 'in'. 'Goethe tourism' alone accounts for a considerable proportion of visitor numbers: Karlsbad, the largest of the three spa towns (picture below right) is the place whence the poet fled to Italy in 1786 under cover of the night. In Marienbad (picture bottom right), the 74-year-old man fell in love with a 19-year-old girl called Ulrike, resulting in one of the most beautiful poems about renunciation. And Franzensbad (picture bottom left) sports the beautifully painted half-timbered façade of the 'Three Lilies' inn where Goethe stayed. Yet many others simply come here for the pulsating spa life and the healing properties of the northern Bohemian water.

Historic Town Centre, Prague *(bottom)*

"On the bed of the Moldau the stones are shifting./Three emperors lie buried in Prague./The great won't stay great and the small won't stay small./The night has twelve hours and then comes the day." What Bertolt Brecht tried to express with these verses from his famous 'Song of the Moldau' is both confirmed and contradicted by the city he refers to in these lines – Prague. The monuments have remained grande, but gone is the power and often the fame of those who created them. What is left is one of Europe's most history-laden city centres. It's main highlights being the historic town hall from the 14ᵗʰ century on the Old Town Ring, facing it the Teyn Church with its many turreted towers, the Carolinum as the seat of the first central European university (1348), the Gothic Bethlehem Chapel, now rebuilt, where the Reformist Jan Hus preached, the Clementinum Jesuit College and the Baroque Clam Gallas Palace. A UNESCO World Heritage Site since 1992.

Charles Bridge, Prague *(top)*

In the Czech capital, Prague, many bridges span the Vltava River, but none reaches the aesthetic rank of the 515-metres-long Charles Bridge named after Emperor Charles IV (1355–1378). Built from 1357 onwards by Peter Parler at the behest of the Emperor, the stone bridge was given magnificent Gothic bridge turrets. Sculptures of the emperor and his son and successor, Wenceslas, decorate the façade of the western one. Wenceslas in particular had a special connection with the bridge, as he had the priest John of Nepomuk thrown off it into the Vltava in 1393 for refusing to break confessional confidence. A statue of the priest, canonised in 1729, now decorates the bridge's parapet, together with other Baroque statues, and he is celebrated on 16th May in the whole of Europe as the patron saint of bridges.

Hradshin, Prague (top left)

In 1618, high above the Czech capital, the Bohemians threw two imperial councillors out of the window – an act, known historically as the 'Defenestration of Prague', which sparked off the Thirty Years' War. Prague Castle, or the Hradshin, the foundation walls of which originate from the first millennium, has often played a key role in history. Crowned by the Gothic St. Vitus Cathedral (see picture), which was only fully completed in the 20th century, it received its outward appearance from Peter Parler in the 14th century. The complex also contains the old palace with beautiful Renaissance rooms and the Monastery of St. George with its Romanesque basilica. Outside the castle complex stand several palaces, including the Baroque Sternberg Palace, which now houses the National Gallery.

Malá Strana, Prague (far top right)

At the foot of the Hradshin stretching to the Vltava is the quarter known as *Malá Strana* ('small side'). It contains the palaces of the nobility from Prague's feudal days. The most important one is that of the Emperor's Commander, General Wallenstein, who had 20 houses pulled down in order to build his Waldstein Palace in the shadow of the mighty Prague Castle. The centre and focal point of this lower part of town is the Baroque St. Nicholas Church with its mighty green dome, built from 1703 by Christoph Dientzenhofer (1655–1722) and his son Kilian Ignaz (1689–1751). From Malá Strana one reaches the Old Town on the other bank of the river via the Charles Bridge.

Golden Alley, Prague (above right)

The name 'Golden Alley' is not – as one might think – derived from some splendid decoration made from valuable ore. Instead, it refers to the profession of those once resident in these colourful 16th century buildings: this is where alchemists were based, employed by a slightly excentric Emperor Rudolph II (1576–1612), with the task of manufacturing gold for him. The idea was that he would thus increase his power, which was crumbling away in the rivalry with his brother, who eventually succeeded him and ruled from 1612 to 1619.

Strahov Monastery, Prague *(top left)*

This is a library with so much to look at, you're in danger of forgetting about the books altogether: the Strahov Monastery of the Premonstratensians was consecrated in 1148 and expanded and remodelled in the 16th/17th centuries. 100 years later it received its Baroque appearance together with the Philosophy Library in a dedicated two-storey building. Above the glass display cases and book shelves arches a ceiling painting – created by Franz Anton Maulpertsch, the most famous Austrian Baroque painter – of such magnificence that visitors stare up at the ceiling for a long time rather than down at their reading desks. The other rooms were also decorated by famous artists.

Wenceslas Square, Prague *(top right)*

By a town square most people imagine something square to rectangular or even something round to oval in shape. However in the Czech capital they have to revise their opinions when faced with its main square. The square, named after the holy Duke Wenceslas I (921–929 AD), christianiser and patron saint of Bohemia, is a 750-metres-long and 60-metres-wide double boulevard. Everyone comes together here to see and be seen, and not least the elegant window-shoppers, who find shops of all kinds on Wenceslas Square. The square is also well-known for political reasons: this is where in 1968 students stood opposite Soviet tanks, sent in to crush the 'Prague Spring', and this is where Jan Palach burned himself alive in 1969 in protest at this brutal suppression.

Astronomical Clock, Prague *(centre)*

That such a thing could be built as early as 1490 astonishes new visitors to Prague daily: on the town hall in the historic quarter, the astronomical clock shows the year, month, day, hour, minute, phase of the moon, position of the planets and sign of the zodiac, with extreme accuracy and also very picturesquely, using a combination of hands and images. The crowd gathers on the hour when the two windows above the clock face open and each allows six of the twelve apostles to pass by. Then they close again, a cockerel lets out a raucous crow and the grim reaper turns the hour glass over as a reminder that every minute brings us nearer to the end.

Historic Centre, Kutná Hora *(bottom)*

Mining was carried out here as early as the Bronze Age, making the former town of Kuttenberg, now Kutná Hora, in central Bohemia a flourishing town. The preserved, precious buildings in the historic centre speak eloquently of this: right above all of them the focal point is the five-naved Late Gothic Church of St. Barbara with its three pavilion roofs over fine tracery (see picture). It was begun in 1388 by Peter Parler (1330–1399) but only completed in 1565. Both the secular buildings are also significant: the old mint known as the 'Italian Court' from the 14th century and the 'Stone House' from the 15th century, built for the town council. A UNESCO World Heritage Site since 1995.

Litomysl Palace *(top)*

There is music in this town – in two ways: firstly the magnificent buildings in the Czech town of Litomysl (East Bohemia) produce an architectural harmony, secondly an annual festival takes place here, in honour of the town's greatest son, the composer Friedrich Smetana (1824–1884). The tone for the buildings is definitely set by the Renaissance palace, where the sgraffito façades in the large palace courtyard provide a feeling of elation in themselves. This feeling is backed up by the palace brewery from the same era, and by the somewhat later Baroque palace theatre. The 'Knight's House' should also be mentioned as a particularly beautiful building.

Historic Centre, Telc *(centre)*

The fountain in the town centre of Telc, south-west of Moravia, is a popular meeting point for the city's teenagers as well as a magnet for the tourists; in the centre of the fountain rises a fabulous sculptured column in Baroque style, tapered towards the top, providing an exhilarating centrepiece against the backdrop of the more sensible town houses surrounding the market square. It is because of this column that the town is also referred to as the 'White Pearl' on the 'Czech Renaissance Route'. Palace, town hall and Church of the Holy Ghost likewise derive from this architectural period and, in 1992, brought Telc the rank of a UNESCO World Heritage Site.

Old Town, Brno *(bottom)*

'What we are, you will become,' stands as a *memento mori* on a tablet in the Capuchin crypt in the Monastery on the square of the same name in the Czech town of Brno. This reminder from the monks buried here, that our days on Earth are numbered, hurts particularly, as in the capital of the southern Moravian district one feels like feasting one's eyes forever, looking at this beautiful place surrounded by hills and all its architectural monuments. Above the town, the 15th century citadel stands guard on Spil Hill; the cathedral (in the centre of the picture), remodelled in the Baroque style, dominates the Old Town, where Gothic and Baroque churches, the monastery mentioned above and its crypt, the old and new town halls, palaces and the remains of the town fortifications make a visit worthwhile.

Austerlitz *(top left)*

Exactly a year to the day after he crowned himself Emperor of the French, on 2 December 1805, Napoleon I 'met' two 'colleagues' near the present day Czech town of Slavkov u Brno, then called Austerlitz, in western Moravia. As a result of this encounter the town entered world history, as it was an extremely lead-filled meeting, from which the short Corsican took away a great victory over the Austrian and Russian emperors. For this reason the battle is also known as the 'Battle of the Three Emperors'. That 7,000 Frenchmen as well as 27,000 Russians and Austrians lost their lives in the process, is commemorated in a memorial on the Peace Hill, ten kilometres west of Austerlitz.

Kromeríz Palace and Park *(upper centre)*

In Germany, the Church of St. Paul in Frankfurt represents a symbol of thwarted hopes of democracy during the 1848/49 Revolution. The present day Czech town of Kromeríz, then Kremsier, holds the same meaning for Austria. For this is where the Austrian parliament withdrew for consultation over a federal constitution for the Danube monarchy's multi-ethnic state. However, the members of parliament failed to achieve their aim in the gold-leaf decorated ballroom of the splendid Kromeríz Palace (a UNESCO World Heritage Site since 1998). Walks in the equally beautiful park and gardens with its 233-metre-long colonnades would have offered little comfort to them in the face of their powerlessness vis-à-vis the armed counter-revolution. The picture shows one of the treasures on display in the palace: 'The Flaying of Marsyas' by Titian (circa 1490–1576).

Cultural Landscape of Lednice and Valtice *(lower centre)*

One of the appealing features of English landscape gardens is that the human influence in their creation only becomes apparent at second glance. So when a landscape is as vast as the area around the Czech towns of Valtice and Lednice, which are linked via a magnificent tree-lined avenue, namely a whopping 160 square kilometres, then the boundaries between nature and culture merge in a pleasant communion to form one single whole. The Princes of Liechtenstein had this sheer endless park laid out at the beginning of the 17th century. One by one, Baroque, Classicist and Neo-Gothic buildings were placed in the open landscape, carefully sited by their architects, thus creating a Romantic treasure at a time when the term had not even been invented. A UNESCO World Heritage Site since 1996.

Holasovicé *(bottom)*

Built on medieval outlines, some houses from the 18th and 19th centuries stand in the Czech village of Holasovicé to the west of Budweis as if time had stood still. Their façades are resplendent with geometric decorations and floral imagery as fresh as they were at the time of building – the most glorious southern Bohemian Peasant Baroque. Lovingly restored, they can be visited today, as they are an open air museum. The solid farmsteads are grouped with stables and living quarters around quiet inner courtyards and present the picture of an agrarian era when agricultural machinery was still for the most part unknown. A UNESCO World Heritage Site since 1998.

Historic Centre, Ceský Krumlov *(top right)*

The Czech town of Cesky Krumlov lies within two curves of the Vltava, south-west of Budweis, and is home to a traditional annual beer festival. The best view is experienced from the wonderfully shaped and painted Maselnice tower of the palace, where you can look down onto the chess-board-like layout of the town with the Renaissance town hall and the Gothic St. Vitus Church. Also to be enjoyed are works by the painter Egon Schiele (1890–1918), found in the cultural centre named after him. A UNESCO World Heritage Site since 1992, as an outstanding example of a small central European medieval town whose architectural heritage has remained intact thanks to its peaceful evolution over more than five centuries.

Slovakia

High Tatra *(top)*

Yes, they do seem bottomless when seen from the summits, the lakes — called 'sea eyes' by the locals — in the high mountain range of the High Tatra. And they are by no means the only attractions in this fascinating landscape, which rises steeply and abruptly from the Spis Basin in the south and the Neumarkt Basin in the north. It reaches its highest point with the summit of the Gerlsdorfer Peak at 2,655 metres and in the north of Slovakia it marks the border with Poland. The granite massif shows traces of past glaciation and now also of increasing tourism, as conditions for skiing and sledging are so ideal in some locations that chairlifts and hotels are multiplying rapidly. In an attempt to counteract this, other areas have now been declared nature reserves.

Cultural Monuments, Spisský Hrad
(bottom)

The religious people in the northern Slovakian landscape of Spis always looked up towards the peaks of the High Tatra to the north-west. Suspicious glances on the other hand were cast in the opposite direction, where potential danger was lurking. The religious needs were served by the triple-naved Romanesque Cathedral Church of St. Martin in Spisský, while Spisský Hrad Castle (see picture) was there to protect the population from danger. Still standing is a round tower from the 13th century, even older remains of walls, massive fortifications from the time of the Hussite wars and the Chapel of St. Elizabeth — for even war could not be waged without support from above. A UNESCO World Heritage Site since 1993.

Hungary

Bank of the Danube and Castle Hill, Budapest *(top left)*

On the chain bridge in the Hungarian capital you can pass from one side of the city, Buda, over the Danube, approximately 600 metres wide at this point, to the other side, Pest. There the Dunakorzó road along the riverbank runs past town palaces of the nobility of former times and other magnificent buildings now recycled for other uses, amongst which is the parliament building erected in 1885–1902 modelled on the London Houses of Parliament, which sets the overall architectural tone. Before the war this boulevard was a promenade and after the collapse of Communist rule in 1989/90 it developed once again into a place where the rich and the beautiful go to see and be seen. The riverbank and the castle hill in Buda have been a UNESCO World Heritage Site since 1987.

Castle Quarter, Buda, Budapest *(top right)*

On the right bank of the beautiful Danube, the ground rises steeply 150 metres to the castle hill of the Hungarian capital. This is where the old castle (circa 1250) of the *Ofen*, as this part of the city was once called, can be found. Even more impressive than the mighty building, which houses the National Gallery, the History Museum and the National Library, is the view from here over the whole city and also of the Romanesque Gothic Church of St. Matthew (1255–1269), where the Hungarian kings were crowned. Next door is the neo-Romanesque Fisher Bastion (1901–1905, see picture) and not far away the old town hall. Together with the Danube riverbank, this historic centre of Budapest has been a UNESCO World Heritage Site since 1987.

Caves of Aggtelek and Slovak Karst *(upper centre)*

The Slovakian Ore Mountains are called thus despite the fact that they extend into northern Hungary and, here as there, caves have formed in the karst. The most beautiful and biggest lies on Hungarian territory at Aggtelek: the Baradla Cave is 22 kilometres long, with bizarre rock formations, subterranean rivers and lakes. At eight kilometres evidently smaller but, if possible, even more fascinating, is the ice cave of Dobschau, in which a 13-metre-high frozen waterfall gleams in all the colours of the rainbow. Caves, flora and fauna of the Aggtelek National Park have been a UNESCO World Heritage Site since 1995.

Old Village of Hollókö *(lower centre)*

In the northern part of the Hungarian mountains lies the village of Hollókö, where the hunched medieval houses with hipped roofs and carved wooden summer houses are picturesquely built on a slope. The remote village in which 500 people still live today has kept its individual charm. Now a hot tip among tourists, Hollókö bears the stream of visitors with composure. An old fortification built on a precipitous rock watches over the comings and goings. A UNESCO World Heritage Site since 1987.

Hortobágy National Park *(bottom)*

An endless, almost completely treeless steppe in the broad Hungarian lowlands: the puszta and its wide open sky, across which King Árpád's horses bound at night. Not too much of this image remains, as economic pressure has turned it into vast agricultural monocultures. Only Hortobágy in the west of Debrecen, a National Park of 30,000 hectares, still offers puszta in its original state and therefore has been a UNESCO World Heritage Site since 1999.

Slovenia

Old Town and Palace, Ljubljana (top)

As early as the time of the Romans, a significant settlement, called Emona, stood on the site of the Slovenian capital. A water channel, which even provided part of the town's supply right up into the 19th century, is still evidence of this. It was as early as the 12th century that Ljubljana in the Springs is mentioned for the first time. The city's agreeable present-day appearance stems from the pleasant grouping of the town quarters around the 77-metre-high Castle Hill, so called for the 12th century castle on top of it. Of the public buildings, which mostly came into being in the 17th and 18th centuries, the Cathedral Church of St. Nicholas with its beautiful frescos and stucco ornaments deserves special mention, as does the Franciscan church near the Three Bridges (see picture), the Renaissance town hall and the Bishop's house.

Skocjan Caves (bottom left)

'Grand Hall', 'Paradise', 'Hall of the Sinter Baths', 'Silent Cave' are just a few of the evocative names given to caves within the five-kilometre-long cave system near Skocjan, east of Triest. However, 'cosy' is probably not quite the word that comes to mind when experiencing this rugged underworld: as you cross bridges 45 metres high above the River Reka, which roars through the caves or cascades downwards in some places, or step from narrow passages into mighty cauldrons such as the Martelova Dvorana Cave, measuring 308 by 123 by 146 metres. In the outer reaches of the cave system traces of prehistoric settlements have been found in sheltered caves, today only inhabited by bats. A UNESCO World Heritage Site since 1986.

Postojna Caves (bottom right)

The town of Postojna in Slovenia has an odd creature on its coat of arms: it represents itself with a Proteus anguineus, the olm or cave salamander. The pale creature has received this heraldic honour as it occurs in the area's main tourist attraction: in the stalactite and stalagmite paradise of *Postojna Jama*. The caves were scoured out by the subterranean river Pivna and proffer a magical maze of standing (stalagmites) and hanging (stalactites) limestone deposits. Today the cave system can be reached by means of a mine train and is even used for cultural purposes: in one of the natural cathedrals in the rock, a concert hall has been installed, the appearance and acoustics of which guarantee an unforgettable listening experience.

Croatia

Amphitheatre, Pula *(top)*

Up to 5,000 people still crowd in today to the open-air performances in the amphitheatre in the Croatian town of Pula, close to the southernmost point of Istria. It originated in the time of the Emperor Augustus (30 BC to 14 AD) and has survived the past 2,000 years well. Ruins, albeit enchanting ones, are the temple built at the start of the Christian era and the *Porta Aurea* (Golden Gate). The remains of the Roman military camp of *Pietas Iulia*, as it was called, provide evidence of the great strategic significance that the world empire gave this outpost in the Adriatic.

Old Town, Porec *(centre left)*

Traces of Roman times can be found everywhere in Dalmatia; at that time the present-day Croatia belonged to the province of Illyria. The Roman emperor Diocletian (circa 245–313 AD, ruled 284–305 AD) came from here and many Roman remains originate from this epoch. Very beautiful temples and the forum in Porec, a town on a peninsula on the west coast of Istria (harbour, see picture) are examples; later Christian buildings joined them, above all the Euphrasius Basilica from the 6th century in which the relics of Saint Mauros, the patron saint of the town, are stored. Together with other religious and secular buildings, the Old Town has been a UNESCO World Heritage Site since 1997.

Historic Town, Trogir *(centre right)*

Dalmatia, the classic transit country, shows, above all on the coast, the traces of many cultures. Here the Croatian town of Trogir is no exception: founded by the Greeks as Traugurion, it became Roman in 56 BC and in Catholic Croatia was a Bishop's seat from 1062 to 1822. Of course most cultural monuments that have been preserved are from the most recent period in the form of religious and secular buildings, thus we have: the cathedral (started in the 13th century, only finished in the 16th), Church of St. Barbara, the smaller, but originating from as early as the 9th century, and nobles' palaces from the 14th to 17th centuries as well as two castles from the late Middle Ages. A UNESCO World Heritage Site since 1997.

National Park, Plitvicer Lakes *(bottom)*

South of Karlovac in the border area with Bosnia-Herzegovina lie the Croatian hills of Plitvice, cut through by the river Korana. Chalk and dolomite formations make the terrain difficult to traverse in places and only permit a scant mixed woodland, mainly of birches and pines. Although the war was not influenced by UNESCO making the 192 square kilometre area, which is dotted picturesquely with 16 lakes, into a World Heritage Site in 1979, it was spared the fighting to the extent that the numbers of the rare brown bears and wolves did not become endangered. Even the eagle owl nests here and with it 126 other types of bird.

Church of Saint Donat, Zadar *(top left)*

The Croatian town of Zadar, a port on the Adriatic coast, developed from a Roman settlement in the first century BC. According to legend its oldest church building is said to have been developed from a Roman temple. In the 9th century the monks symbolically built over what was a temple to Juno as a stand against paganism. This interpretation is supported by various things, amongst them the fact that the central building looks more Roman and warlike than Christian and religious. Put together from high, rounded constructions, which look like bastions, and given only a few small windows, the light-coloured house of worship looks more like the 'strong fortress' Luther sang about centuries later.

Old Town and Imperial Palace, Split *(top right)*

After ten years as emperor, in the year 395 AD, Diocletian began to look around for a place to retire to and found a suitable spot in Aspalatos, or *Spalatum* in Latin, today's Split, on a peninsula on the Croatian coast. On a 215 by 180 metres large piece of land he had a palace built over a period of ten years. The two-metre-thick walls surrounding it gave the appearance of a fortress, and it still evokes respect today. Awe of another kind is inspired by a religious building from the time after the victory of Christianity, which the emperor had so mercilessly persecuted: the cathedral developed out of the imperial mausoleum, which unfortunately suffered severe damage in the war against Serbia in 1990/91. A UNESCO World Heritage Site since 1979.

Old Town, Dubrovnik *(bottom)*

Extolled as 'Queen of the Adriatic', the now Croatian Dubrovnik (Ragusa in Italian) competed for a long time with Venice, the major power. The town has a splendid location at the foot of the Sergius Hill on a spit of land extending into the Adriatic. Unfortunately, this also made it only too exposed for artillery bombardment from above during the war against Serbia 1990/91, leading to much destruction in what up until then had been an almost unaltered medieval townscape. Much has been restored, the six-metre-thick and up to 25-metre-high town walls, the towers and bastions still stand or stand again, the monasteries, the cathedral and other churches ranging from Gothic to Baroque styles have been repaired and restored. UNESCO had recognised Dubrovnik as a World Heritage Site in 1979 and strengthened this protection in 1994.

Serbia and Montenegro

Stari Ras and Sopocani Monastery, Serbia *(top)*

In the Church of the Trinity in Stari Ras, an old and run-down town on the Raška, west of Novi Pazar in Serbia, one can see the oldest Byzantine frescos (12th/13th centuries). Particularly striking is the 'Birth of the Mother of God' (see picture). Not far away stands the even older Church of St. Peter, with the remains of the medieval castle towering above. Somewhat further to the west visitors reach the Sopocani Monastery which was founded as the final resting place for King Uroš I (reigned 1243–1276), at the 'point where the Eastern and Western Churches meet'. It is likewise decorated with artistic frescos by old Serbian painters. A UNESCO World Heritage Site since 1979.

Studenica Monastery, Kralyevo *(centre)*

With an eye on the eternal salvation of his soul, the Serbian king Stefan Nemanya founded Studenica Monastery in 1190 at Kralyevo. There he retired in 1196 and where in the end he was buried. His grave is in the Mother of God Church (see picture), which was finished during his lifetime. This was followed in the 13th century by the construction of the Church of St. Nicholas and 100 years later by the construction of the Royal Church, which is actually called the Church of St. Joachim and St. Anna. The walled complex with house-hold and accommodation buildings forms the biggest and most richly furnished monastery in Serbia (with 'Crucifixion' from 1209 amongst other Byzantine wall paintings) and has been a UNESCO World Heritage Site since 1986.

Durmitor National Park, Montenegro *(bottom left)*

In the high country of Montenegro a 320-square-kilometre large area was made a nature reserve in 1952. Durmitor National Park was declared a UNESCO World Heritage Site in 1980. It climbs from 450 to 2,522 metres in Bobotov kuk and is wooded right up to the tree line; in the Tara gorge the terrain drops abruptly 1,300 metres, 16 lakes and the Tara with its tributaries provide a habitat for brown trout and huchen, also known as Danube salmon. Rare alpine plants such as a type of gentian thrive here and endangered animals such as the brown bear and wolf roam the area.

Kotor Bay and Region *(bottom right)*

In 1979 an earthquake destroyed a cultural paradise that lay in the middle of a natural one. The town of Kotor on a bay that penetrates 28 kilometres into the land on the Montenegrin coast is of Greek origin, became Roman in 168 BC and then, in the Middle Ages under changing rulers, was an independent city state and a favoured anchorage due to its sheltered position. The wealth achieved is mirrored in the buildings reconstructed, such as the cathedral or the church dedicated to 'Our Lady on the Rock' from the beginning of the 17th century. Surrounded by mountain ranges, Kotor has been a UNESCO World Heritage Site since the commencement of reconstruction in 1979.

Romania

Moldau Monasteries *(top)*

Humor, Moldovita, Arbore, Probota, Sucevita, Voronet — resonant names, but little known. And yet they represent architectural rarities of the first order: monastery buildings, whose churches deserve attention due to the integration of Byzantine and Gothic elements and which captivate with their richly painted façades. They are complexes erected in the 15th and 16th centuries in the Romanian part of Bukovina, which bear witness to the rural piety in this remote area. UNESCO raised the buildings with their overhanging saddle roofs to World Heritage Site in 1999.

Wooden Churches, Maramures

(bottom right)

Eight churches, eight different architectural answers to the problems of using wood as a construction material: in the low-lying Romanian landscape of Maramures, between the wooded Carpathians and the Rodnau Mountains, masterpieces of wood construction from several epochs have remained preserved. They provide a living picture of the design possibilities of the material and the skills of the craftsmen, who were just as capable of building slim high towers as stable shingle roofs. As typical examples of native cultural monuments they have been a UNESCO World Heritage Site since 1999.

Historic Centre, Sighisoara *(bottom left)*

Since the opening up of the East European states, many inhabitants of impoverished Romania have been attracted to the West. In particular the German settlers, who had built a flourishing culture here since the height of the Middle Ages and who were known as Transylvanian Saxons, are turning their backs on the country. There is a danger that their cultural legacy will decay. For this reason, UNESCO put the town of Sighisoara under protection as a UNESCO World Heritage Site in 1999. Situated on the Great Kokel in Transylvania, the town formerly known as Schäßburg in German boasts a particularly successful ensemble of monuments to the German period, such as the clock tower (see picture), the Church of Mary and the mountain church, all built in the late Middle Ages.

Fortified Church, Transylvania *(top)*

The community of Biertan, in the district of Sibiu (formerly Hermannstadt) in rural Transylvania, is now only small. The German inhabitants have left it and the country in droves. At the beginning of the 16th century, when the place was still called Birthälm and inhabited almost exclusively by Transylvanian Saxons, a fortified church was built here, above the village on the church hill. Under its protection, Birthälm established itself as a Protestant diocesan town (1572–1867). The Kleinschenk church fort is regarded as a typical example of a fortified Transylvanian church.

Royal Palace, Sinaia *(centre left)*

Kings and vampires have apparently an odd weakness for each other. Why else did the Prince of Walachia in present-day Romania move his summer residence to the valley through which the Prahova river roars in the southern Carpathians, and why, in erecting the new building of Peles Palace in 1875–1883, did he entice the bloodsuckers even more through the splendid half-timber work in the inner courtyard? Don't they like blue blood? Perhaps though, through the charming decoration of the walls, he wanted only to divert their thirst for strangers' blood and make them lust after his in lasting fashion. In the long term, it seems not to have worked as the monarchy came to a violent end. Only such beautiful pearls set in the landscape as the palace of Sinaia are what are left of their crown.

Hill Fort of the Dakar, Orastie *(centre right)*

Similarly tough resistance as that put up by the Germanic tribes was put up by the Dakar in what is present-day Romania to the Roman expansion around the start of the first century. They did not appreciate the achievements of Roman civilisation, in some things they were after all further advanced than the world empire (in the picture: a decorated cauldron cart in bronze, 8th century BC). To a certain extent, this also applied to technical matters as the ruins of the Dakar fortresses in the Orestie hills (western Romania) prove. These were built to defend against Roman attacks. It was not until Emperor Trajan (98–117 AD) that the Romans managed to subjugate the Dakar and make part of their country into a Roman province. As a memorial to their tough resistance and to a martial culture, the Dakars' fortifications have been a UNESCO World Heritage Site since 1999.

Biosphere Reserve, Danube Delta *(bottom)*

In spring 2000, environmentalists suffered a blow when the storage pond of a Romanian gold mine collapsed and poured its poison into the Theiss and then on into the Danube. Yet there was luck in the midst of misfortune: the toxic water was so diluted by the time it got to the Danube delta in Romania, where the Danube eventually flows into the sea, that it caused barely any harm to the Biosphere Reserve created there. For here lies the largest reed bed area in the world at 1,700 square kilometres. It is incomparably rich in plant and animal species, from pink pelicans to catfish, from black poplars to wild hops. A UNESCO World Heritage Site since 1991.

Bulgaria

Srebarna Biosphere Reserve *(top)*

Srebarna Lake, near the Bulgarian town of the same name, is only six square kilometres large and, at two metres deep, it is not exactly bottomless. However, this ensures its significance: the big pond on the Danube, to which it is connected by a channel, provides the best prerequisites for marsh and water birds, due to its silting up along the edges. Dalmatian pelicans gather here for their migration to the south, great egrets nest in the extensive reedbeds, the glossy ibis sails over the reeds, spoonbills and diverse species of ducks breed in sheltered corners and in winter blue-throats and red-breasted geese drop by. This small paradise has been a UNESCO World Heritage Site since 1983.

Church of Bojana, Sofia *(bottom left)*

In a suburb nestling on the slopes of the Vitosha foothills of the Bulgarian capital, Sofia, chapels built on the church there display medieval wall paintings with vivid drawings and vital colours. The works of art, created in the 13th century, show a total of 89 scenes from the life of Jesus, in which the figures were depicted in the likeness of important people of the time of their creation. Thus one can make out portraits of the then Czar Constantine Assen and his spouse Irina. A UNESCO World Heritage Site since 1979.

Old Town, Nessebar *(bottom right)*

South of Bulgarian Varna, on a tiny peninsula, lies what was a medieval church town and is now a residential town of the modern era: in the most cramped space Nessebar offers educational viewing of Byzantine religious architecture and secular architecture of the 19th century. Church buildings with a surfeit of religious frescos such as that of St. Stephen or massive ones erected out of differently coloured stone layers such as the Pantocrator Church from the 13th to the 16th centuries together with houses rich in oriel windows and with broad roof parapets result in a completely unique architectural accord: a UNESCO World Heritage Site since 1983.

Rila Monastery, *(far top)*

The monk Ivan Rilski, also known as John of Rila, founded a monastery in a valley in the Rila mountains to the south of Sofia. Nothing remains standing of the original buildings and the complex received its present appearance for the most part only in the 19th century. However, some wall paintings in the Church of Mary's Birth and manuscripts preserved in the monastery's library date further back. What was more important was the spiritual influence emanating from here, which contributed to the development of a Bulgarian sense of tradition and nationhood. The complex crowned by cupolas has been a UNESCO World Heritage Site since 1983.

Alexander Nevski Cathedral, Sofia
(above left)

Until 1878, the country belonged to the Ottoman Empire and could only develop its orthodox religion to a limited extent. Then however, thanks to Russian help, they freed themselves from foreign rule and a new religious awakening set in. In 1904, after a long planning period, the construction of a diocesan church began, which upon its consecration in 1912 received the name of the 13th century Russian patron saint, Alexander Nevski. One is tempted to designate the style of the full, rounded and massive central construction with its golden main dome and the gleaming gold cupola on the tower as Bulgarian Baroque.

Pirin National Park *(above right)*

A 400-square-kilometre sizable chunk of the northern Pirin Mountains in south-western Bulgaria has been a nature reserve from as far back as 1963. In Wichren it reaches a height of 2,915 metres and the Mesta and Stuma rivers run through it. Rich alpine flora is found there. Densely forested, the National Park provides a habitat for wild cats, brown bears, otters, martens and polecats and a table richly laid with their animals of prey. Endangered bird species too, such as eagle owls and golden eagles find protection here, especially since UNESCO declared the mountain landscape to be a World Heritage Site in 1983.

Albania

Straits of Otranto *(top)*

Can a narrow channel in the sea be a cultural monument? Not in itself, but perhaps as an enticement to building bridges. It would almost be an architectural impossibility to build a bridge across the Straits of Otranto, between the Albanian town of Durrës and the Italian town of Otranto, Apulia (see picture), as one would have to span 70 kilometres. The east-west connection in the Mediterranean is therefore easiest done by sea. The currents of reciprocal influence ran through the straits during the time of the ancient Greek colonisation of Italy, Otranto itself was a Greek colony, just as the currents ran in the opposite direction when Rome reached out to the east. The same applied to Norman expansion to the east in the Middle Ages and also for later Turkish pushes towards the west.

Butrint *(bottom)*

On a peninsula in the south of Albania on the Straits of Corfu lies Butrint, which was established in pre-historic times. It later became Greek and then part of the Roman province of Epirus. This was followed by Byzantine and then Venetian rule, before the place was abandoned in the late Middle Ages. The ruins of the town, which today have been investigated by archaeologists, clearly demonstrate the different layers and thus show the development over the millennia. Not only the unwalled ancient town of Buthroton, which only covers an area of 16 hectares, has therefore been a UNESCO World Heritage Site since 1999, but also its surroundings with traces from the different epochs.

Macedonia

Ohrid, Lake Ohrid *(top & bottom)*

It has been established that there was a settlement as far back as the 6th century BC in the place where the town of Ohrid is located, on the lake of the same name in Macedonia. In the 4th century BC, the Macedonian King Phillip II appropriated the area. There then followed Roman, Byzantine and Ottoman rule. There are remains from all these epochs, though the Byzantine ones have a particular charm due to the simplicity of the piety that speaks through them. Valuable icons and frescos (picture left: 'Christ in the Garden of Gethsemene', 14th century) can be seen in the Church of the Archangel, which belongs to a former monastery. It stands on the southern shore of the lake, which, for its part, is a natural wonder. You can see down to a depth of 22 metres through the crystal clear waters with their 17 species of native fish. A UNESCO World Heritage Site since 1979.

Greece

Early Christian and Byzantine Monuments, Thessaloniki *(top)*

Between the Aegean Sea and the River Evros lies Thessaloniki, the second largest city in Greece. It was founded in the 4th century BC and ancient monuments feature in its historic centre. Particularly precious are those that bear witness to the early centuries of Christianity and those from Byzantine times. Amongst the richly furnished religious buildings, the Church of Ossios David is worth particular mention due to its magnificent mosaics. Also notable is the Rotunda, a Roman mausoleum, which was converted into a church in the 4th century (in the picture: the Church of St. Demetrios).

Athos Monastery and Mount Athos
(bottom)

This state within the state of Greece, on the 50-kilometre-long and 10-kilometre-wide most easterly peninsula of Halkidiki, is unique in the world: 20 large monasteries with small settlements form the 336-square-kilometre large monks' republic of Athos, inhabited by 1,500 men. Visitors, exclusively male, are only allowed in after a strict check. However, they do get to see venerable and highly picturesque monasteries with rich art treasures and valuable collections of manuscripts and icons. The monasteries lie in partly wild terrain on the southern tip of the peninsula, which rises to 2,033 metres with Mount Athos. As a cultural as well as a natural monument it has been a UNESCO World Heritage Site since 1988.

Acropolis, Athens (top)

Even today's high buildings are towered over by the Acropolis, the fortress hill of the Greek capital Athens, and by the temples built on it in classical ancient times. These are: the Parthenon (447–432 BC), the temple to the goddess Athena Parthenos; the Propylaea (438–432 BC) through which one walks to the shrines, the Erechtheion, the small temple to Nike on a bastion next to the Propylaea. The buildings, which were nearly all built under the supervision of Phidias, probably the most famous sculptor of antiquity, are individually, and also as an ensemble, masterpieces of ancient Greek art and have been a UNESCO World Heritage Site since 1987.

Metéora Monasteries and Rocks, Pindiós Valley (bottom)

Hermits discovered them very early on as the optimum places for a retreat from the contemptible world: the rocks that tower up to 300 metres like giant fingers in the central Greek Pindiós Valley. Settlement on the summit began in the 14th century. At a dizzying height monks constructed monastery buildings for which every stone and every beam had to be brought up via neck-breaking paths or swaying rope ladders. They made 'pillars of Heaven' out of the chilly giant towers, admonitions visible from afar to live a pious life. Only six out of the original two dozen abbeys are still being run and they are real tourist magnets, not however for people who suffer from vertigo. A UNESCO World Heritage Site since 1988.

Tholos Athena, Delphi (top left)

There is proof that the temple to Apollo in the ancient Greek town of Delphi in rural Phokis dates back to as early as the 9th/8th century BC. During excavations since 1832, the remains of the sanctuary came to light. We can now just imagine how the priestess Pythia sat with a bowl in her hand here at the 'navel of the world' and every month proclaimed, in artful riddles, what the gods had revealed to her about the future, after her bath in the Castalian spring. One can also visit the Tholos in the sanctuary of Athena Pronaia on the southern slope of Mt. Parnassus (picture above), a UNESCO World Heritage Site since 1987.

Mycenae, Tiryns (top right)

On the Peleponnese to the north-east of Athens, long before Sparta, lay the power centre of the peninsula: in Mycenae the Achaeans erected a fort in the 19th century BC. It became the focus point of a cultural circle (home of the Atrides saga) and went under around 1100 BC. Ancient Mycenae was partially excavated from 1874–1876 by Heinrich Schliemann; during these excavations cyclopean fortifications, the mighty Lion Gate (see picture) and richly furnished graves were revealed. A second centre of the culture lay in Tiryns, where the fort fell victim to an earthquake in 1200 BC and likewise was partially excavated by Schliemann. UNESCO World Heritage Sites since 1999.

Erechtheion, Athens (bottom)

On the fortress hill of the Greek capital Athens stands the Attic-Ionic building of the Erechtheion, which was erected to the patron goddess of the city, Athena, and the god Poseidon Erechthus in 421–406 BC. The three rows of columns are striking, as are the casements on both sides of the eastern portal and the Caryatids, female figures, which bear the roof of the Caryatid Porch, whose burden takes nothing away from their loveliness. Together with the other buildings on the Acropolis, the Erechtheion has been a UNESCO World Heritage Site since 1987.

Ancient Ruins, Olympia *(top)*

Renowned right up to the present day, the ancient Greek city of Olympia, 18 kilometres from the Ilia coast, owes its fame to the Olympic Games held from 776 to 393 BC, and only recommenced in 1896. It was a centre of the Cult of Zeus and correspondingly rich in remarkable buildings, amongst which the Nymphaeum (water fountain) is worth a particular mention. With its facing of gleaming white pentelican marble it made an imposing sight against the green background of Kronos Hill. The Zeus Temple, the stadium (120 by 220 metres) and baths are no lesser sights. The excavation site has been a UNESCO World Heritage Site since 1989.

Apollo Temple, Bassae *(bottom left)*

He is in Arcadia as well: on the western Peloponnese in the antiquity there was a mountain village called Bassai, which in the 5th century BC was endowed with a temple to the god Apollo, responsible for the sun and the art of healing, by the inhabitants of the neighbouring town of Phigaleia. The classical Doric design makes the ruins in the remote mountain area very attractive. The temple's orientation towards the north is really unusual as temples from this time almost always look east. The cella frieze from the inner chamber of the temple was removed to the British Museum in 1811. A UNESCO World Heritage Site since 1986.

Epidauros, Peloponnese *(bottom right)*

On the Peloponnese in the countryside of Argolis on the Gulf of Saroni there was a religious centre in ancient times: Epidauros with the sanctuary of Asclepios, the god of healing, the Asclepeion. It was a spa and a centre for medical treatment at one and the same time, as the priests of the sanctuary were also doctors, who tried to restore the patients to health with the sayings of an oracle as well as orthodox medicine. The gigantic amphitheatre assisted in this: it had seating for 14,000 spectators and is being used again today. Together with the buildings belonging to the Asclepeion (bath, stadium, temple, holy grove), it has been a UNESCO World Heritage Site since 1988.

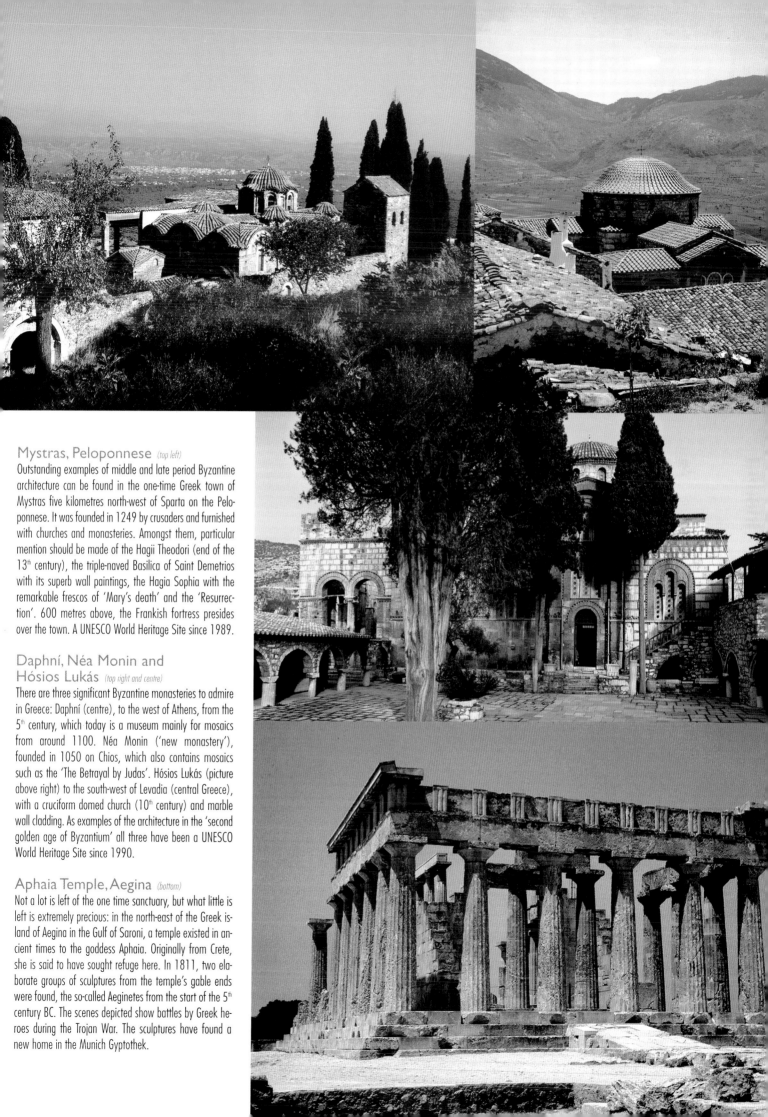

Mystras, Peloponnese (top left)

Outstanding examples of middle and late period Byzantine architecture can be found in the one-time Greek town of Mystras five kilometres north-west of Sparta on the Peloponnese. It was founded in 1249 by crusaders and furnished with churches and monasteries. Amongst them, particular mention should be made of the Hagii Theodori (end of the 13th century), the triple-naved Basilica of Saint Demetrios with its superb wall paintings, the Hagia Sophia with the remarkable frescos of 'Mary's death' and the 'Resurrection'. 600 metres above, the Frankish fortress presides over the town. A UNESCO World Heritage Site since 1989.

Daphní, Néa Monin and Hósios Lukás (top right and centre)

There are three significant Byzantine monasteries to admire in Greece: Daphní (centre), to the west of Athens, from the 5th century, which today is a museum mainly for mosaics from around 1100. Néa Monin ('new monastery'), founded in 1050 on Chios, which also contains mosaics such as the 'The Betrayal by Judas'. Hósios Lukás (picture above right) to the south-west of Levadia (central Greece), with a cruciform domed church (10th century) and marble wall cladding. As examples of the architecture in the 'second golden age of Byzantium' all three have been a UNESCO World Heritage Site since 1990.

Aphaia Temple, Aegina (bottom)

Not a lot is left of the one time sanctuary, but what little is left is extremely precious: in the north-east of the Greek island of Aegina in the Gulf of Saroni, a temple existed in ancient times to the goddess Aphaia. Originally from Crete, she is said to have sought refuge here. In 1811, two elaborate groups of sculptures from the temple's gable ends were found, the so-called Aeginetes from the start of the 5th century BC. The scenes depicted show battles by Greek heroes during the Trojan War. The sculptures have found a new home in the Munich Gyptothek.

Pythagoreion and Heraion, Samos
(top left and right)

Many civilizations have inhabited this small Aegean island, near Asia Minor, since the 3rd millennium BC. The most significant ruler of the island was Polycrates, who ruled in the 6th century BC. This was also the time the Heraion, temple of the Samian Hera, wife of Zeus, and the largest temple of the classical period, was built. This, together with the remains of Pythagoreion, an ancient fortified port with Greek and Roman monuments and a spectacular tunnel aqueduct, can still be seen and forms a UNESCO World Heritage Site since 1992.

Chorá, Monastery and Cave of the Apocalypse, Patmos *(bottom left)*

According to Christian legend, the apostle John, who was also the author of the Apocalypse, was banished to the 34-square-kilometre Greek island of Patmos (Dodecanese). This is where he is said to have composed his New Testament writings and to have experienced the 'revelation' about the apocalyptic end of the world on Judgement Day. A monastery (see picture) dedicated to Jesus' 'favourite disciple' was built in the 10th century linked to the old Roman settlement of Chorá near the very cave where the angel is supposed to have appeared to John with God's message. A UNESCO World Heritage Site since 1999.

Delos *(bottom right)*

The ancient Greek God of Light, Apollo, could not have found a much smaller place of birth: he is said to have come into the world on the barren Cycladean island of Delos, which subsequently was a centre of Apollo worship for centuries. Today, excavations on the small, no longer inhabited, 3.4-square-kilometre island are proof of this. Many large places for worshipping the god have been uncovered, including the Temple of Seven Statues and a processional avenue. Also discovered were a theatre and an ancient residential town. The excavations are a magnet for tourists and have been a UNESCO World Heritage Site since 1990.

Medieval Town, Rhodes (top)

Not only significant ancient ruins make Greek towns and islands worth seeing. Rhodes town, on the island of Rhodes, which is also the largest in the Dodecanese, bears the marks of the Knights of the Order of St. John who resided here from crusader times right up until 1522: the Palace of the Grand Master, the Crusaders' Inn, the triple naved Basilica of St. Mary and the town wall on which the 150 coats of arms of the Order's Grand Masters are resplendent. The charm of the medieval townscape lies in the connection with the later Ottoman buildings. A UNESCO World Heritage Site since 1988.

Santorini (centre)

Seen from the air, the southernmost Greek island in the Cyclades, Santorini, looks like a burst ring. This was not always the case: until the year 1628 BC it was round and beautiful. Beautiful it still is, but the middle is missing. It went up in the air together with the central cone of the volcano that once made up the middle bit of the island. The explosion was so gigantic that a tidal wave spread throughout the Mediterranean, bringing destruction to the shores of the islands around. Santorini itself remained as a 'broken ring' consisting of a larger part, Thera, and a smaller part, Therasia, while the sea flooded into what was once the volcano's crater and surrounding the two small islets Nea and Palaea Kaimeni. An architectural characteristic of the island are the white buildings with blue cupolas.

Knossos, Crete (bottom left)

About two kilometres inland lies the ancient Palace of Knossos on the north coast of the Greek island of Crete. Its origins date back to the 6th millennium BC. The main building however is 4,000 years younger. It covers an area of 150 by 200 metres, the inner courtyard alone encloses 1,500 square metres. Prayer and ceremonial rooms, living quarters, workshops, baths and storerooms can be made out from the ruins. The thick outer walls are like fortifications, although the then ruling Minoan culture was peaceable in its relatively secure island location. Around 1450 BC, Knossos became the victim of a natural catastrophe.

Odeion, Gortyn on Crete (bottom right)

Many amphitheatres from Greek and Roman times have been preserved. In ancient times there also existed theatres, as we understand them, as a building, in which musical or dramatic performances took place. Of these only a few examples have remained. One stands in the ruins of Gortyn on the south coast of Crete. The excavation site is better known through the inscription of the 'Law of Gortyn' which was found here in 1884 and which furnished valuable information on Greek slave, family and criminal law of the 5th century BC.

Turkey

Selim Mosque, Edirne (top)

On the spot where Turkey projects the furthest towards Europe, lies the town of Edirne, the Adrianople of ancient times. It carries its oriental features with confidence, setting the tone with its most important one — a mosque by the Ottoman empire's court architect Sinan (around 1490–1588), which he completed in 1575 and which was named after Sultan Selim II. Its four 80-metre-high minarets tower above everything else in town and the 42-metre-high central cupola appears to have been built in premonition of the safety containment dome of a nuclear reactor. Mighty decorated pillars and arches support it in the interior and shape the space, which is bathed in a reverential twilight.

Safranbolu, Anatolia (bottom left)

For millennia Anatolia has been a cultural country and even Safranbolu, which lies to the north and north-east of Karabük and which has only been called Safranbolu since 1940, was already settled at the time of the Hittites. Little remains of that settlement, there is more from Roman times when there were thermal baths here. The charm of the town today however mainly derives from its Islamic heritage such as the many religious buildings, including the Suleiman Pasha Madrese and the Old Mosque from the 14th century. In the market quarter, the character of a trading town from the days of the caravans has been preserved. A UNESCO World Heritage Site since 1994.

Blue Mosque, Istanbul (bottom right)

The Sultan Ahmet Mosque belongs to the ensemble making up the UNESCO World Heritage Site of the Old City quarter in Istanbul. It is in competition for the status of symbol of the city with the nearby Hagia Sophia. In this, its mighty dome, 24 metres in diameter, helps as well as the tiles from Iznik, which have brought it the name by which it is known: 'the Blue Mosque'. It also has six, instead of the usual four, slim minarets, which draw attention to it. Built 1609 to 1616 by the Sultan who gave it its name, it is the last of the great houses of worship with which the rulers distinguished their city of residence.

Hagia Sophia, Istanbul (top)

Church of the 'Divine Wisdom' is the English name of the mighty house of worship in Istanbul, which was rebuilt in its present form by Emperor Justinian I (527–565 AD) in the space of only five years, after a fire in the year 404 AD. A huge dome, 32 metres in diameter, rises above a monumental base, a marvel of engineering at the time. Inside, it offered an unparalleled richness of colours and shapes, further enhancing the overwhelming sense of space: marble-clad pillars and walls, mosaic floors, carpets, silk curtains and precious liturgical implements. A day after the Turks conquered Constantinople, Hagia Sophia was turned into a mosque; it has been a museum since 1934.

Suspension Bridges and Üsküdar, Istanbul (bottom)

Today the quickest way to reach the Asian part of the Turkish metropolis Istanbul is via two suspension bridges, each of which is over one kilometre long. It is also nice to take the ferry across because of the silhouette of Üsküdar (formerly Skutari), which appears even higher when seen from the water. Offshore from it stands the Leander Tower, the first thing you see in the Bosporus, which is more gallantly called 'Maiden Tower' by the Turks. This is where Aphrodite's priestess Hero is said to have waited every night for her lover, Leander, who used to swim over the Hellespont, as this stretch of sea was then called, to meet her. When he drowned in a storm, Hero threw herself into the waves too.

Süleymaniye Mosque, Istanbul *(top left)*

The Turkish sultan Süleyman, who was Emperor Charles V's opponent in the 16th century, bore the epithet 'the Magnificent'. This also suits the mosque built for him in the Old City of Istanbul between 1550 and 1557, which was named after him. It can be regarded as the most artistically successful creation in the city on the Bosporus. Its 53-metre-high and, at 26.5 metres, half as wide dome is nearly the size of that of Hagia Sophia. Its 136 windows make it a 'mosque of light', which the marble of the interior reflects. With its adjoining buildings for baths, educational facilities, kitchens and libraries, it has developed into a religious complex — or indeed an entire quarter of the city.

Topkapi Seraglio, Istanbul *(top right)*

Directly behind the Hagia Sophia in the Old City of Istanbul, only separated from the Bosporus by a railway line, the mighty complex of the Topkapi Seraglio is situated, the one-time palace of the sultan. It was started in 1465, that is immediately after the Turks took Constantinople, and has gone through all kinds of extension and remodelling work so that today it appears to be a regular city of palaces. Its extent becomes clear in the Seraglio courtyard, which is bounded by the kitchen buildings to the right (today housing a china collection) with their ten chimneys and to its left by the stables, with the harem's quarters opposite. The living quarters and state buildings, gardens with ponds, religious buildings and many other establishments give an impression of the power and glory of the sultan's court.

Church of the Holy Cross, Ahtamar Island in Lake Van *(bottom)*

As early as 1000 BC, the Urartu empire blossomed here, which, thanks to the remote location, lasted a long time: the land on and around the eastern Turkish Lake Van, situated at 1,650 metres above sea level, was only occasionally disturbed by wars. For this reason, 2,000 years later, the Armenian kingdom of Vaspurakan lasted from 908 to 1026. It was at this time that the Church of the Holy Cross was built on Ahtamar island, once the residing place of the kings, in the southern part of the lake. It is a jewel of Armenian architecture of the time: almost over-abundant external reliefs show not only religious themes but also something of the people's everyday life.

Göreme National Park (top left)

It is as if the memory of the time in which we lived in caves never entirely leaves us: about 150 kilometres to the south-east of the Turkish capital, Ankara, erosion has scoured the tuff plateau into bizarre shapes. Large cones, which have arisen this way, particularly enticed Byzantine builders and artists to carve apartments, houses, even multi-naved churches out of the stone and to decorate their walls and ceilings with frescos. Although of course structurally not required, mock supporting columns and pillars have been added. Items of furniture and altars are carved from the stone and some of the hills look as if attacked by so many moles. These fantastic monuments from the Middle Ages have been a UNESCO World Heritage Site since 1985.

Hattusa (top right)

In 1834, a French traveller discovered ruins close to the Turkish village of Bogazkale, 200 kilometres to the east of Ankara. He thought they were Roman remains but excavations carried out since 1907 found that they were the remains of Hattusa, the capital of the Hittite empire which fell around 1200 BC. Smaller finds have been displayed in a museum since 1966, the larger ones have been opened up and can be walked around in. The town encompassed a high plateau and several rocky hills. The 250-metre-long King's castle presided over it all, the mighty walls of which bear witness to highly developed architectural skills, with their towers, casemates, gates decorated with reliefs and broad steep staircases. Considered to be of even greater significance are the cuneiform archives also found here. A UNESCO World Heritage Site since 1986.

Rock Monuments, Ürgüp (centre)

It is nice and cool inside whilst the sun burns down mercilessly on the stony Anatolian landscape: in the Göreme Valley near Ürgüp, 40 kilometres as the crow flies and 60 kilometres by road to the west of Kayseri, the oldest cave dwellings and churches of Cappodocia can be found. They developed from the 4th century onwards from hermitages in the natural caves of the karst landscape. The hermits who had retreated here from the world wanted to create houses of prayer for their god and used the soft tuff stone to hollow out entire hills. Today these hills are partially broken open, showing the lovingly chiselled-out living quarters within.

Nemrut Dagi Ruins (bottom)

Hellenism, that is the culture which developed in the Oriental empires conquered by Alexander the Great, with influences from Persian and Greek, also flourished in Anatolia. One particular piece of evidence for this is in south-eastern Turkey, in Malatya, a very remote location at 2,150 metres above sea level on the Nemrut Dagi mountain massif. This is where King Antiochos I of Kommegene (69–34 BC) had a mausoleum erected, to which two sanctuary terraces lead. The processional route is lined with colossal statues such as the one of a bearded Zeus wearing a Persian helmet, presumably a deification of the king, and many other sculptures. UNESCO declared the ruins a World Heritage Site in 1987.

Ancient Port, Ephesus *(top left)*

Ionian Greeks settled on the coast of Asia Minor as early as the 10th century BC in, amongst other places, Ephesus, a rapidly growing port at the mouth of the Caistros River. The Persians, who ruled here right up into the 4th century, did not impinge on the profitable Greek independence and even when Alexander the Great came to power and after him the Seleucides, Ephesos remained a booming trading metropolis and centre of the Artemis (Diana) cult. Many thousands of tourists annually wonder at everything from the splendid remnants of the triumphal avenue to the goddess's sanctuary.

Archaeological Site, Troy *(centre)*

The junior commercial clerk Heinrich Schliemann had heard of the Greek legends in school and would spend much time day-dreaming about the heroic world of Homer and about being able to wander in its tracks. With enormous energy, he taught himself Greek and worked hard until he became a multi-millionaire. With the determination of the self-made man, he took Homer at his word and had excavations carried out in the place Homer had described: on the ruins of Hissarlik on the Turkish north-western point of Asia Minor. Despite all prophecies of doom he found his promised town, although in many layers, which took decades of research to identify. The town from the time of the Trojan Wars probably covered an area of 2,000 hectares. The historic National Park of Troy has been a UNESCO World Heritage Site since 1998.

Ancient Hierapolis, Pamukkale *(bottom)*

The ruins of the town of Hierapolis in western Anatolia, to the south of the Turkish town of Denizli, are forced to compete with the Pamukkale limestone terrace. The name is Turkish for the more picturesque 'cotton castle'. The water from warm springs flows here for a length of 2,700 metres and a width of 300 metres down steps to the valley as if in a gigantic Roman fountain and, due to limestone deposits, has formed basins with white stalactite borders that look like cotton plaits. The ruins of the ancient town are really Roman: thermal baths, a theatre for 12,000 spectators, a cemetery and a temple. The testimonies of eternal nature and of an extinct culture have been a UNESCO World Heritage Site since 1988.

Ruins and Sanctuary of Latona, Xanthos *(top right)*

How do you imagine a daughter of Titan who gave herself to the father of the gods, Zeus, and through him became the mother of Apollo and Artemis? The residents of Xanthos, once the largest town in Lycia on the river of the same name (now Koçaçay), 120 km south of Antalya, dedicated a magnificent shrine to the mighty Leto (*Latona* in Latin), only ruins remain of this after its destruction during the Roman Civil War in 42 BC. Reliefs from other monuments have been taken to the British Museum. The copies, which can be seen in situ, are just as good. A UNESCO World Heritage Site since 1988.

Cyprus *(Turkish)*

Salamis *(centre)*
The name is well-known from the Persian Wars of Athens and Sparta and this is where it is said to come from: a Greek from the island of Salamis in the Gulf of Saroni between Attica and the Pelopennese, where the Persian fleet got themselves bloody noses in 480 BC, is named as the founder of the Cypriot place of the same name, which today lies in the Turkish part of the island, 10 kilometres to the north of Famagusta. In Greek as well as in Roman times it was a wealthy town, which profited from the copper trade (*kyprios* in Greek = copper, hence the name of the island). However, Salamis had to be abandoned after a powerful earthquake and following Arab attacks in Byzantine times. Today only an excavation site, the largest on the island, provides evidence of the ancient past.

Cyprus *(Greek)*

Stavrovouni Monastery *(top)*
On the journey from Nicosia to Limassol, the traveller can see the oldest of the many monasteries of Cyprus from afar; Stavrovouni, the founding of which goes back to the year 327 AD. This can be dated so precisely because Saint Helen, the mother of Emperor Constantine the Great, was the founder and is known to have spent time on Cyprus that year. She arrived from a journey on which she is said to have discovered Christ's cross in Jerusalem and made a fragment of it available as a relic to the monastery, whose name in English means 'mountain of the cross'. This name also refers to the cross in which the relic was housed.

Archaeological Site, Khirokitia *(bottom)*
The finds made by archaeologists on the south coast of the Mediterranean island of Cyprus at Khirokitia indicate prehistoric times. The area between Larnaca and Limassol was settled as early as 7000 BC and so-called *tholoi*, the remains of roundhouses, are proof of this. Close by, the researchers also discovered a cemetery and were able to get a picture of the customs and everyday life of the prehistoric inhabitants on the basis of the burial gifts: obsidian blades, necklaces and storage containers. The excavation site has been a UNESCO World Heritage Site since 1998.

Makheras Monastery (far top left)

In summer 1152, two hermits were travelling through the eastern Troodos Mountains on Cyprus. One of them injured himself in a fall and drank from a nearby spring, decorated with an icon, and was healed immediately. This is the story explaining the founding and location of the Makheras Monastery. Whether such miracles can still be reported today is by the by. What is certain, however, is that the monastery, which was restored in 1892, is a miracle in itself: in its sense of security and in its successful architectural solution. The living and household quarters form a defensive wall around the church, which almost completely fills the courtyard with its multi-roofed construction and the octagonal central tower.

Chrysorroyiatissa Monastery (far top right)

There is no need to have learnt how to meditate, the place alone will teach you how to do it. At Paphos in the south of Cyprus lies the town of Pano Panayia, which is worth a short stop beforehand, as the Archbishop Makarios was born here who led Cyprus to independence in 1960. A further three kilometres to the south and you reach the Chrysorroyiatissa Monastery. It is said to have been founded in the 15th century at the place where, according to legend, the evangelist Luke once painted a crown of Mary on the rock wall. The church of the abbey stands in an obliquely angled inner courtyard whose positively visible silence causes those in a hurry to pause.

Byzantine Churches, Troodos Mountains (above)

Nine churches in the Byzantine style hide away in the Troodos mountains in the south-west of Cyprus. Especially the churches of Lagoudera, Platanistasa, Kalopanagiotis and Asinin, the Kykko Monastery and Saint Nicholas of the Roof near Kakopetria stand out for their interiors of gleaming colour. The frescos, which stem mainly from the 11th and 12th centuries, show many scenes from the New Testament such as 'Three Angels at Supper' or 'The Raising of Lazarus'. As testimonies to Byzantine wall painting the churches have been a UNESCO World Heritage Site since 1985.

Kourion (far top)

Barely 20 kilometres to the west of Limassol, the traveller in Cyprus stumbles across an area of ruins that lies on high cliffs over Episkopi Bay. They are principally Roman ruins, although Kourion was settled from as far back as the Neolithic age. The wealth of what is presented here cannot be listed in full, so examples will need to suffice: the house with the Achilles mosaic is recommended to fans of art and mythology; the aqueduct, the baths and the spring house will attract those with a technical bent; the stadium for 6,000 spectators on the road to Paphos is rewarding for those with an interest in architecture; and the Apollo temple a bit further on is the oldest on the whole island.

Pissouri Bay (above left)

Tourists have a tendency to stay with the herd. Thus it happens that even on completely overrun islands and near overcrowded beaches, just a few kilometres further on, silence returns and nature comes into its own. This can also be said for Limassol on Cyprus. A short distance to the east of the heaving holiday resort, the Greek goddess of beauty would be able to live out her famous epithet: in the quiet bay of Pissouri the *Anadyomene* ('the one who rose from the surf') would hardly have to hide behind the rocks in the middle of the water, even today. However someone must have seen her at some time, as the beautiful wave-breakers in the azure sea are called 'the Rocks of Aphrodite'.

Ruins, Paphos (above right)

The poet plucks the lyre to accompany his love song, the beauty inclines her ear towards him, the faun blows on his flute loud and clear, the beaker passes round: scenes from Roman mosaics that have not been found in such a colourful and complete form anywhere, perhaps with the exception of Pompeii. In the ruins of Paphos on south-western Cyprus, archaeologists distinguish between the Greek features acquired through the cult of Aphrodite that flourished here in *Palaepaphos* (old Paphos) and the ruins of buildings by the Romans who succeeded the Greek in the year 58 BC and made *Nea Paphos* (new Paphos) the capital of the province. For the combination of these two ancient cultures, it has been a UNESCO World Heritage Site in 1980.

Asia

A step away from heaven

The largest of the continents, Asia stretches almost halfway round the world from eastern Siberia to the Bosporus and from the huge mouth of the Ob estuary in the Arctic Ocean to the Equator, with the Sunda Islands actually in the southern hemisphere. It contains every conceivable landscape feature and all climate zones. These attractions became known around the globe, casting their spell over us then as now. The yearning for oriental wisdom proclaimed by the temples and the beauty of Asia's shoreline illuminated by the rising sun will remain forever.

Russia *(Asia)*

Golden Mountains, Altai *(top)*

In south Siberia the Russian Altai Massif rises up, extending southeast into the Mongolian and then the Gobi Altai, climbing to 4,506 metres at Belukha. The area has been able to support a rich mountain flora, including 212 plant species only found here, because 16,000 square kilometres of the Russian section is protected by law. The animal world has also remained mostly intact: the snow leopard, which has become very rare, and 71 other mammal species can be seen here. The most important bird species here are the imperial eagle and the Altai falcon (gyrfalcon). In 1998 the nature paradise was declared a UNESCO World Heritage Site.

River Estuary of the Ob *(bottom left)*

Whether the Ob, which together with its tributary, the Irtysh, forms the gigantic river system with a 3 million square kilometre catchment area in West Siberia, ends in a bay of the Kara Sea downstream of Salekhard, or whether the Ob is still a river beyond that point is really just splitting hairs. What is clear is that the bay, which pushes 885 kilometres inland, initially takes so much water from the river that the salinity level is still considerably lower than that of the ocean. However, by the time the river reaches the opening east of the White Island, salinity is at ocean level. There can certainly be no argument over the amazing endless tundra landscape, through which the Ob's lower stretch flows to its destination.

Boreal Virgin Forest, Komi *(bottom right)*

At the crossroads between Europe and Asia at the foot of the western slopes of the Ural Mountains, there is a typical natural landscape: 32,000 square kilometres of tundra and mountain tundra. They are protected by law and extend right into the glacier regions of the mountain range. The lower altitudes are dominated by moorland with fauna and flora: the wolf, brown bear, otter, elk and sable live here. In areas where it floods, willows and also mountain ash thrive. The virgin boreal forest consists of pine, spruce and Siberian larch. UNESCO World Heritage Site since 1995.

Lake Baikal *(top left)*

Located between high, forested mountains, the deepest lake on earth, extending up to 1,637 metres in depth, is in south Siberia, Russia. It contains 20 percent of all unfrozen freshwater and, at 48 kilometres wide and 636 kilometres long, it covers an area of 31,500 square kilometres (about the same size as Belgium). With more than 50,000 square kilometres of surrounding land, the clear waters (visibility to 40 metres depth) of the inland sea have been protected by law as a UNESCO World Heritage Site since 1996, as industrialisation in the region had started to endanger its unique diversity of life. Many species, such as the Baikal nerpa or gammarids, are only found here. That also applies to land animals, such as the steppe pika or the Siberian red deer and to bird species, such as the northern hawk owl.

Trans-Siberian Railway *(centre)*

The 7,512 kilometre long railway track of the Trans-Siberian Railway runs from Vladivostok on the southeast edge of Russian Siberia via Khabarovsk, Chita and then with electrification via Ulan Ude, Irkutsk on Lake Baikal, Krasnoyarsk, Novosibirsk and Omsk to Chelyabinsk on the eastern slopes of the Urals; continuing on to Moscow, the railway line is actually 9,289 kilometres long. Built between 1891 and 1916 and extended to a double track in 1938, it is an essential transport link for the economic, human and political cohesion of the vast Russian federation and now also the ideal way for tourists to get to know the vastness of southern Siberia.

Tatar Strait *(bottom left)*

The Pacific island of Sakhalin extends almost 1,000 kilometres practically parallel to the east coast of Russian Siberia. And the sound between the Sea of Okhotsk in the north and the Sea of Japan in the south is correspondingly long, in fact, the longest in the world at 633 kilometres. At the southern point this Tartary or Tatar Strait measures 324 kilometres in width, but islands and the Asian mainland in the Nevelskoy Strait section narrow it down to 7.3 kilometres, after which it widens again quite rapidly to the north.

Volcanoes, Kamchatka *(bottom right)*

At 370,000 square kilometres, the Kamchatka Peninsula in the northeast corner of Russia, where it separates the Sea of Okhotsk from the Bering Sea, is more than one and a half times bigger than the UK. There are about 160 volcanoes, of which 28 are still active; the highest cone, Kluchevskaya Sopka, is 4,835 metres high (compared to Mont Blanc's 4,807 metres). Due to its isolation, human interference in the ecosystem and landscape of the peninsula has remained low, and in order for it to stay that way, huge areas have been protected by law, in particular south Kamchatka containing the ten most active volcanoes. In front of this backdrop, a rich diversity in animal and plant life has developed that led to the peninsula being inscribed in the list of UNESCO World Heritage Sites in 1996.

Georgia

Bagrati Cathedral and Gelati Monastery, Kutaisi *(top)*

Founded in the 10th century and one-time residence of the princes, the town of Kutaisi lies on the Rioni, northwest of Tbilisi in Georgia. The ruins of the Bagrati Church, named after Bagrat III (973–1014 AD), date from its beginnings. In 1003 AD it was dedicated to the Virgin Mother and is also called Death of the Virgin Cathedral. About 100 years more recent is the nearby monastery complex of Gelati, which was destroyed, as was the church, by the Turks in the 16th/17th centuries. Yet still today, the ruins are such an impressive example of the flourishing of Georgian architecture that they were declared a UNESCO World Heritage Site in 1994 (photo shows fresco).

Historical Churches, Mtskheta *(bottom)*

North of the Georgian capital of Tbilisi, the kings of the Caucasian land resided for some time in Mtskheta and decked it out with religious structures. Of particular note are the Cross or Zhvari Church dating from the 6th/7th centuries, the Samtavro Church built 400 years later and the cathedral dating roughly from the same time also, which is as important to Georgian Christians as St. Peter's Basilica is to Catholics. During excavations there, archaeologists came across an earlier church, a pillared basilica, which stood here in Byzantine times in the 5th century. The religious centre of Mtskheta was declared a UNESCO World Heritage Site in 1994.

Syria

Ruins, Palmyra *(top)*

It is as if the gods had been ten-pin bowling, but not had a very good aim, for there are many glorious pins, i.e. columns, still standing from the old Roman city of Palmyra in the north Syrian Desert. They belong to temples, baths or other public buildings and extend over an area of ten square kilometres. The main attraction is the mighty 200 by 200 metres Baal Temple (see photo), which Emperor Hadrian was even able to admire on his visit in the year 129 AD. Just fifteen years later the then prince of the province, Odaenathus, and his wife, Zenobia, rose up against Rome, so that Emperor Aurelius destroyed the city in 273 AD and thus was the author of the ruins that were declared a UNESCO World Heritage Site in 1980.

Old City, Aleppo *(right above)*

The cities in the Near East are saturated in history, and Aleppo in north Syria especially so. The city already existed during the reign of the Hittites at the beginning of the 2nd millennium BC. For a time it declined in importance, but grew again during the Hellenist era. Aleppo really flourished under Islam, when the Abraham Mosque, the Grand Mosque and most importantly the palace and citadel on the hill fort were built in the 13th/14th centuries. Up there, a throne room, 700 square metres in size, and a sumptuous bath are glittering examples of all that Arab craftsmen were capable of. The old city and the bazaar (see photo) were declared a UNESCO World Heritage Site in 1988.

Old City, Damascus *(right centre)*

With its two million inhabitants, the Syrian capital of Damascus is steadily eating into the countryside of the eastern slopes of the Anti-Lebanon. But the historic heart of the ancient metropolis has hardly altered over centuries. The ring wall, which displays Roman parts as well as parts from the Arabic and Turkish eras, is preserved, and evidence that there was a religious centre here even in the early Islam period is provided by 75 mosques, among them the famous Umayyad mosque (8th century) and the Sultan Selim Mosque; the Madrasa Zahiriye is today still a famous theological college. UNESCO World Heritage Site since 1979.

Old City, Bosra *(right below)*

The townscape of the south Syrian town of Bosra to the west of Jebel Druze is characterised by ancient Roman, early Christian-Byzantine and Arab-Islamic elements. Where once 80,000 people populated the market and streets of the capital of the Roman province of Arabia, there are now only 1,000 inhabitants. The reason why it is still lively is due to its many tourists, who are interested in the ancient amphitheatre with its 15,000 seats, the ruins of the Roman public baths, the Byzantine cathedral and the al-Khider Mosque, and fascinated by the atmosphere of its varied history, which helped old Bosra to become a UNESCO World Heritage Site in 1980.

Lebanon

Ruins, Byblos *(far top left)*

In the history of mankind, the alphabet is quite a recent achievement and our alphabet even more recent. While the Egyptians were already painting their hieroglyphics 3,000 years BC and the Sumerians were covering their clay tablets with cuneiform script at the same time, it was a thousand years later that the Phoenicians developed an alphabet. This linear alphabet, however, influenced Greek and Latin, and therefore ours, considerably. Some information about this has also been found in Byblos, the oldest city in Lebanon, north of Beirut. An inscription from the 13th century BC using these letters was found here in the Phoenician ruins. This and the ancient structures made Byblos a UNESCO World Heritage Site in 1984.

Cedar Forest, Qadisha Valley *(above left)*

Early monk settlements, some of which became complete monasteries, gave the Qadisha Valley in the Mount Lebanon range the epithet of 'Holy Valley'. But the brothers and settlers made another contribution in their construction of churches and chapels, by decimating the forest of Cedars of Lebanon that once covered all the mountain range, for its timber was considered by craftsmen to be the best for huge religious structures. The remnants of that wonderful natural environment can be seen here in the valley, where there are some trees over 1,000 years old, forming the grove called 'The Cedars of God' (Arz el-Rab), in which there is also a chapel. As a monument to piety and to the forest mentioned in the bible, the valley was declared a UNESCO World Heritage Site in 1998.

Ruins of Umayyad City, Aanjar *(top right)*

In 705 the Arab founders laid out the city of Aanjar in Lebanon, south of Baalbek, in the style of the Greek city architect, Hippodamus of Milet (5th century BC) in a grid pattern with streets at right angles to each other. It served as a summer residence for the caliphs of the Umayyad dynasty for only a few decades, because Aanjar then fell into decay after a defeat at the hands of the Abbasids around 750. The ruins covering the site of 12 hectares still give an impression of the courtly life in the lavishly built city dominated by the palace, and justify its designation (1984) as a UNESCO World Heritage Site.

Ruins, Baalbek (top)

In the year 47 BC, the former City of the Sun, Baalbek, northeast of Beirut, became a Roman garrison town. Now there are only ruins left, but quite spectacular for all that. They are mainly remains of structures dating from the 1st to 3rd centuries, whose sun-drenched columns tell of past greatness. A particular example is the Jupiter Temple, nearly 20 metres tall, (see photo), which swarmed with crowds of pilgrims in its time. Today, the crowds are back again, for, due to its sights of antiquity, Baalbek is a must-see for Middle East travellers and a UNESCO World Heritage Site since 1984.

Ruins, Tyre (bottom)

In the first half of the 1st century BC, the Phoenician people were under the rule of the big powers in the Mediterranean world. In 950 BC their capital Tyre (modern Sour in central Lebanon) was in its heyday: it owed its wealth from the trade in purple dye and cedarwood across the whole of the Mediterranean to its shipbuilders and its security to its position on a rocky island off the Lebanese coast. There are still remains of the Phoenician city wall, the Hadrian arch, which records the Roman victory over its rivals, bathhouse and temple ruins. Tyre, which fell into decline towards the end of the Crusaders era, was declared a UNESCO World Heritage Site in 1984.

Israel

Bahai Temple, Haifa *(top)*

The north Israeli port of Haifa terraces its way up Mount Carmel, from whence the Christian Carmelites got their name. But the mountain and city also play an important part in the other main Mediterranean religions, Islam and Judaism. The Druze and an Islamic sect also profit from this juxtaposition: the Bahais, who preach tolerance and combine different elements of the other faiths' teaching, were able to build their central shrine on Mount Carmel in 1953 in the architectural style of a mosque, a clear sign that in the Holy Land there are different paths to God.

Jericho *(above centre)*

In the baking Jordan rift valley, 300 metres below sea level, the ancient city of Jericho lies northwest of the Dead Sea. Founded way back in the dim and distant past, it was destroyed several times, once, according to the Bible, by the noise of trumpets, but always rebuilt afresh. Excavations on the Tell es-Sultan have revealed the 'oldest city in the world' here (about 6,500 BC), other archaeological examinations have produced finds from the pre-ceramic early Stone Age and some from the Bronze Age, which was beginning in the Middle East in 3,000 BC. Only at the time of the birth of Jesus, when King Herod had his winter palace built here (70 AD destroyed by Emperor Titus), did Jericho become important again. Today it leads the way in the Israeli-Palestinian peace process (Treaty of 13ᵗʰ September 1993).

Golan Heights *(below centre)*

A bone of contention in world history: whoever possesses the high plateau south of Mount Hermon across Jordan also controls the valley. In the 1967 Six Day War, Israel was able to snatch these strategically important Golan Heights away from Syria, after the Jewish settlements had had to put up with continuous shelling from Syrian artillery from the Heights. In the 1973 war, in heavy fighting, Israel retained the area, where Jewish settlers meanwhile had put down roots. But there will be no lasting peace if Syrians and Israelis do not find agreement. The peace process in the Near East will be decided here.

Al-Aksa Mosque, Jerusalem *(bottom)*

'The most distant mosque' is the translation of the second most important Muslim cult site after the Dome of the Rock in the city of Jerusalem, which is sacred to all three main Mediterranean religions: the huge Al-Aksa Mosque with seven bays, first founded by Emperor Justinian in the 6ᵗʰ century as St. Mary's Church, marks the spot where the prophet Mohammed was furthest away from Mecca. The church and latterly the mosque were built on top of the rubble of the Jewish temple mount and thus constructively unite all three religions.

Dome of the Rock, Jerusalem *(top)*

Its golden dome is the symbol of the holy city of Jerusalem, whether Christian, Jewish or Muslim. In the Israeli capital, the temple complex, where the temple of Solomon once stood, forms the intersection of these world religions. From these rocks the prophet Mohammed was supposed to have made his Night Journey, his fiery horse leaving hoof prints on the stone, and on which Caliph Abd al-Malik built the Dome of the Rock on an octagonal base between 669 and 692 AD. Later its interior was decorated with costly marble cladding, mosaics and rich ornaments in vibrant colours, while in the 16th century the exterior was tiled. The Dome of the Rock and the other structures in the old city were declared a UNESCO World Heritage Site in 1981.

Western Wall, Jerusalem *(bottom)*

The remains of the temple, which stood during the reign of King Herod at the time of Christ's birth, constitute the holiest site of Judaism in Jerusalem's temple district. The typical praying gestures of the Jews performing their worship have given that part of the preserved western retaining wall its more common name of 'The Wailing Wall'. Together with the Muslim mosques and the Christian Church of the Holy Sepulchre, they form a kind of holy ensemble that, as part of the Old City of Jerusalem, was declared a UNESCO World Heritage Site in 1981.

Church of the Holy Sepulchre, Jerusalem *(top left)*

At the place where Jesus is supposed to have crucified, Emperor Constantine the Great founded a church (built 326–335 AD) that was later destroyed, rebuilt, altered and embellished several times. In it is reflected the chequered fate of the modern Israeli capital, Jerusalem, where the Church of the Holy Sepulchre, as the most important Christian shrine, together with the Islamic cult sites and the Jewish Western Wall, form the centre of the Holy Land. Since 1852, it is in the custody of six Christian creeds that continue inside the church the external tolerance of the three world religions. Together with other structures in the Old City of Jerusalem, it was declared a UNESCO World Heritage Site in 1981.

Masada *(top right)*

It was on a rock with a sheer drop on all sides, situated on the left bank of the Dead Sea, that in 30 BC the Jewish King Herod the Great built his fortress castle, Masada, guarded by a white wall over 5 metres in height. The walled area measured 630 by 130 to 230 metres, with dugouts and 37 high towers for added security. The royal 'hanging' palace was built on the north tip of the ship-like platform and therefore accessible neither from below nor the side, but only from above. It was only after a siege lasting months that the Romans were able to seize Masada in 73 AD. Today the Jews make a pilgrimage to the top of the mountain where the ruins tell a story and swear an oath there: "Masada shall not fall again."

Bethlehem *(centre)*

Jesus of Nazareth, founder of Christianity, was born in Bethlehem (Beit Lahm) in West Jordan, now Israel, according to the New Testament records, because Emperor Augustus had ordered all the people in his kingdom to return to their place of birth for a census. In the place where the manger stood, in which Mary had to lay her child, Emperor Constantine the Great built a basilica with five bays in 326 AD. It forms the core of today's Church of the Nativity, which, situated between a Roman Catholic, an Armenian and a Greek Orthodox monastery, includes all three creeds. They each have their own entrance to the Grotto of the Nativity underneath the main altar; a silver star marks the birthplace. In the east of the city lies the field where the birth of the saviour is supposed to have been proclaimed to the shepherds.

Dead Sea *(bottom)*

It is hardly possible to do the breaststroke here, because one's legs keep sticking up out of the water. The buoyancy in the Dead Sea tides in the Jordan rift valley between Israel and Jordan is so great due to the salinity (26 percent), that, even in the deepest part where it is 500 metres deep, non-swimmers would not get into difficulties. And they are swimming almost 400 metres below sea level, which is how deep the river and lake have carved the landscape. The lake, actually called a sea, is 80 kilometres long and 18 kilometres wide. It drains nowhere and is so salty and so 'dead' on account of the high level of evaporation in the hot desert region. However, its water has healing properties: people suffering from psoriasis find relief here.

Jordan

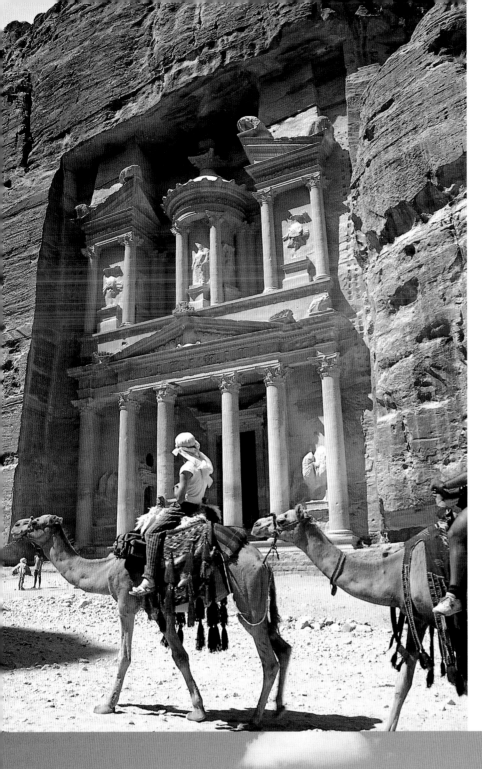

Ruins, Petra (top)

The Nabataean King Aretas IV ruled a mighty kingdom from 9 BC to 40 AD. Today the ruins of his capital, Petra, in south Jordan are a tourist trap. This is due to the amazing sights, such as the ten pear-shaped water chambers, which were hewn by the inhabitants out of the mountain now called Umm el-Biyara ('Mother of Cisterns'), or the shrines, for instance the ad Deir mausoleum with its 42 metre high facade in the Graeco-Roman style and particularly the horse stables. The stables with their thick, cooling walls and service and storeroom in the centre are arranged in an exemplary fashion. The ruins were declared a UNESCO World Heritage Site in 1985.

Desert Palace, Qusr Amra (bottom)

It is not certain whether it was built by a caliph or just a very wealthy nobleman in the Omayyad kingdom. However, there can be no question that it is the most magnificent country seat in Jordan dating from the 8th century: Qusr Amra is a palace complex with a three-bay audience hall and adjoining baths, situated east of Amman in the middle of the desert. In the hall there are frescoes, one of which, 'The Large Bather', is especially captivating: a beautiful, young woman, bejewelled with diadem, necklace and armlets, decoratively positioned in front of arcades. The pleasure palace was declared a UNESCO World Heritage Site in 1985.

Iraq

Royal Tombs, Ur *(top left)*

Under the hill ruins of Tell Mukajir in south Mesopotamia (modern Iraq) lies Ur, one of Babylon's metropolises and home of the biblical progenitor, Abraham. Over 4,000 years ago the city was the influential centre of an already advanced civilisation. We know this from the extensive excavations in the 19th/20th centuries, when elaborate temple complexes and the royal cemetery were revealed.

Ruins of the Parthian City, Hatra *(bottom)*

The Parthian city of Hatra, about 100 kilometres southwest of modern Mosul in Iraq, withstood a siege in 116 AD by the army of Emperor Trajan (ruled 98–117 AD), who was otherwise the most successful emperor, as well as three attempts at conquest by Emperor Septimius Severus (193–211 AD). In the year 240 AD, however, Hatra succumbed to the Sassanians. The circular city walls crumbled, the Parthian palace became a ruin, the temples collapsed. It was only in the 20th century that archaeologists excavated much of it, including several hundred statues of marble and limestone, important evidence of Hellenic-Middle Eastern art. UNESCO World Heritage Site since 1985.

Mosaic Standards, Ur *(top right)*

Only the hill ruins of Tell Mukajir remain in south Iraq, where once in the 3rd century BC a mighty city of Mesopotamia stood: Ur in Chaldea was such a pulsating metropolis in the Sumerian kingdom that the Gilgamesh Epic said of it: "Enlil heard the roaring and advised the gods: 'This tumult of people is unbearable and it is no longer possible to sleep.' And that was how the gods were moved to send the flood." That was the first fall of the city, which rose again several times and made quite a name for itself again — partly through works of art, of which some like the mosaic standards have been handed down: wonderful inlaid work with lapis lazuli, mussels and limestone on wood (about 2,500 BC).

Iran

Caspian Sea (top left)
It is the largest inland water in the world, covering about 400,000 square kilometres, bordered by Azerbaijan, Russia, Kazakhstan, Turkmenistan and Iran, which has 15 percent of the coast in the south. The scenery is particularly charming there, where the Caucausus slopes down to the sea at Baku and on the Iranian coast, encircled by the Alborz Mountains. At 5,671 metres, Mount Demâvend, the highest peak, looks down on the sea and seaside towns such as Resht, Bender Ansali and Babol. For a long time, the Caspi Sea, as many call this giant stretch of water, was in danger of silting up, but recently the water table has risen again due to geological movements.

Ruins, Choqâ Zanbil (top right)
In the 13th century BC in eastern Mesopotamia, the ancient eastern kingdom of Elam (modern southwest Iran) flourished. The city of Dur Untash grew up at this time near to modern Choqâ Zanbil and north of Abadan. The walled city, one square kilometre in size, belonged to a shrine and Iranian-French excavations have now uncovered its tower, now just 25 metres tall. Unlike the Babylonian ziggurats, this was reached by a covered staircase inside. Together with three palace ruins it was declared a UNESCO World Heritage Site in 1979.

Royal Square Meidan-e Shâh, Esfahan (centre)
For 150 years, this was the heart of Persia, and nowhere is this better observed than in the Royal Square Meidan-e Shâh in the southwest of Esfahan, which was the capital city from 1598 to the middle of the 18th century. Surrounded by extravagantly decorated mosques, in an array of colours, the square is a favourite meeting place for the faithful and tourists alike. The Shâh Mosque (now Masjed-e Imam), built by Abbâs the Great at the beginning of the 17th century, is the showpiece of Islamic houses of God with it countless faïence tiles. UNESCO World Heritage Site since 1979.

Ancient Ruins, Persepolis (bottom)
About 80 kilometres northeast of Shiraz in southwest Iran, travellers come across a ruined site, which even in decay reveals the power long ago of the ancient Persian ruler of the Achaemenian dynasty who resided here in the summer. Darius I the Great (550–486 BC) began the layout of the city with a throne room. The stone head of a horse (see photo) was part of that. Of particular note is the staircase leading to this room showing reliefs of homages from vassal nations in his large kingdom. His successor, Xerxes I (486–465 BC), added the 'Hall of a Hundred Columns'. Excavated in the 1930s, the city was declared a UNESCO World Heritage Site in 1979.

Turkmenistan

Ruins of the Old City of Merw, Mary *(top)*

The benefits must have been great, because the efforts were indeed enormous. Ancient and mediaeval merchants, who wanted to bring goods from the Far East to wealthy customers in the Mediterranean region, had to contend with mountain ranges and inhospitable steppes. The old oasis city of Merw, modern Mary, in the Turkmenistan desert of Kara Kum, was one of a handful of resting places on the central Asian Silk Road, leading from China to central Europe. Ruins of structures from the time when Merw belonged to the kingdom of Parthia (2nd century BC to 3rd century AD) have been preserved alongside later remains from Sassanian, Arabic and Mongolian times. UNESCO World Heritage Site since 1999.

Uzbekistan

Historic Centre, Bukhara (top)

Due to its masterpieces of Islamic architecture, the Uzbek city of Bukhara on the Zeravshan in an oasis in the Kyzyl Kum Desert was declared a UNESCO World Heritage Site in 1993. The citadel with its round towers on the gate commanding respect, the small, compact Ishmael Samani Mausoleum 1,000 years old, the Mir-i Arab Koran School dating from the 16th century, the Grand Mosque, finished in 1514, with its 46 metre high minaret that looks like a fortified tower. After the collapse of the Soviet Union in 1991, religious life was able to develop again.

Samarkand (bottom)

The old city of Samarkand on the Zeravshan river in Uzbekistan goes back in time as it unfolds its important structures: relatively 'young' are the Tillya Kari Koran School (1646–1660) and the Medrese Shir Dor (1619–1636), considerably older are the Ulug Beg Medrese (1417–1420), the Bibi Chanym Mosque (1399–1404) and the Gur Emir Mausoleum, which was completed in 1404/05 after a long period of construction to serve as the grave of the rulers of the Timuridian dynasty. The madrasas (theological colleges) with their splendid gates decorated with mosaic and faïence are located in Registan, the central square in Samarkand, where the grand bazaar was held and where even today every discovery trail through the 'Paradise of the East' begins.

203

Saudi Arabia

Mecca (top)

Every Muslim, who is medically and financially able, has a duty to make the pilgrimage ('hajj') to Mecca to the holy site of Islam once in their lifetime. The birthplace of the prophet Mohammed in the west of Saudi Arabia on the edge of the Central Arabian plateau is home to the Ka'aba ('Cube'), a building in which the Hajar al-Aswad ('Black Stone') meteorite is lodged and which is also called 'House of God'. This building is in the courtyard of the main mosque with its seven minarets. This main shrine and many Koran schools (madrasas) and mosques have turned Mecca into the 'Holy City', which the faithful face every time they pray.

Grand Mosque, Medina (bottom left)

The centre of Islam is Mecca with the Ka'aba, but at least as many pilgrims are attracted to Medina in Hejaz (west Saudi Arabia), where the prophet Mohammed is buried in the incomparable El Haram Grande Mosque ('The Shrine'). His youngest daughter, Fatima, is also buried here, and in the Islamic tradition she has high standing, so that to the Shiites she is actually a member of the 'Holy Family'. Mohammed himself came here at the end of September 622 AD, when he had to flee from his birthplace, Mecca, and on this Hejira ('migration') found both recognition and a new home in Medina. The Islamic calendar starts from the Hejira.

Royal Palace, Riyadh (bottom right)

In the middle of nowhere so to speak, in other words, deep in the desert of the Arabian Peninsula, lies Riyadh, the capital of Saudi Arabia. Already built in the middle of the 18th century, it then became the seat of the Ibn Saud family in 1824 and 100 years after the founding of the Kingdom of Saudi Arabia, which today has 2 million inhabitants. The traditional form of the palace, a massive fortress-style complex with battlemented walls, mosque and residential sections for the large royal family and servants, was not quite sufficient for the demands and self-image of a traditional, yet modern monarchy. Large parts of it were demolished at the end of the 1970s and the remainder subjected to a thorough makeover.

Yemen

Old City, Sana'a *(top)*

Such splendour in a desert land! The first glimpse of Yemen's capital city, Sana'a, situated in a fertile valley 2,350 metres above sea level, with its almost completely preserved city wall and colourful facades, is straight out of a fairy tale. Minarets of over 100 mosques point up out of a sea of tall, five to nine-storey tower houses, built from stone blocks or mud bricks and imaginatively decorated with painted friezes. The Old City with its buildings mainly dating from the 18th/19th centuries was declared a UNESCO World Heritage Site in 1988.

Medina, Zabid *(bottom left)*

In contrast to the European districts, the old centres of Arab cities are called medina, which more or less means town. Part of the medina of Zabid on the eastern edge of Tihama on the coast of Yemen was established as long ago as the 9th century, and the original buildings have been preserved to an amazing extent. As a religious centre, the Grand Mosque and the Ashair Mosque set on an oval base, are impressive. You venture deep into Arabia when you enter the narrow, winding alleyways to admire the friezes, which are even to be found on old, plain houses. It was not until the 15th century that the present capital, Sana'a, situated in the northeast, outshone its rival, Zabid, whose beauty earned it the status of a UNESCO World Heritage Site in 1993.

Marib Dam *(bottom right)*

As rich 'as the Queen of Sheba', a familiar quotation. But where was Sheba? It flourished where in today's desert state of Yemen the population scratch a meagre living, and included the metropolis of Marib. Its wealth was due to a dam, marvelled at as the 'eighth wonder of the world' and whose remains can still be seen: it appears to have been completed in its final fortified form at the end of the 5th century BC: 600 metres long with a 15 metre high dam wall, it blocked the present-day Wadi Dana. There were weirs on the mountainsides. Their regular opening enabled the fertile, but arid, land around Marib to be thoroughly watered all year round. Frankincense trees grew there at that time as well as 'spices', which the queen was supposed to have given to Solomon when she visited him.

Old City, Shibam (top left)

About 500 houses are squeezed into the confined space inside the 6 to 9 metre high, fortified wall, which is preserved in an almost undamaged state, encircling the Yemeni city of Shibam in Wadi Hadhramaut. The area is only 400 by 500 metres in size, so that some of the high-rise structures have to be up to 30 metres tall to house the population of about 8,000 inhabitants. The almost uniformly yellow-brown facades with tiny windows and the flat roofs of these slim buildings make the skyline of Shibam look like a mini-Manhattan.

Cemetery of the Seven Graves, Inat/Hadhramaut (top right)

Life in the environs of Hadhramaut in the east of Yemen is modest, even meagre. Only sheikhs and princes live better, but they still die. Nothing is too good for the afterlife and even in the desert at Inat the worthy white mausoleums of noble families stand out in the Cemetery of the Seven Graves. They look like little mosques with their dome shape and beautiful doorways, while the simple folk get only plain graves. Even death does not eliminate class differences.

Al Midhar Mosque, Tarim/Hadhramaut (bottom)

Not much grows in the highlands of Hadhramaut north of Al Mukalla in east Yemen. To compensate for this, however, the mosque minarets reach even farther towards the sky, for they are symbols of hope, and the people have to make do with this tenet instead of earthly goods, usually until the end of their lives, which is the real beginning for faithful Muslims and Christians alike. The lofty towers also point towards that, like this one on the Al Midhar Mosque in Tarim, a few kilometres northeast of Seiyun. The light, two-storey sandstone structure with its seven-storey tower is an inspiring example of the sun-drenched architecture of the desert.

Oman

Fort Nakhl (top left)

It was after the Crusades, when the knights returned from those lands in which, according to the ballad, "there were many rocks but little bread", that forts were built in Europe that deserved the name. The fortress builders in the Middle East had learned from the Arabs, and how skilled they were in their fortifications is shown by later structures such as Fort Nakhl before the Al Hajar Mountains in Oman, on the eastern corner of the Arabian Peninsula. The wonderfully preserved complex, still in use, seems to have influenced the style of civil architecture as well, as it serves not just to fend off human enemies, but also protects against the sun beating down.

Wildlife Reserve in Oman Desert (top right)

The desert is alive – if we did not know before, we certainly did after the famous Disney film of the 1950s. And those responsible in the desert state of Oman in the south of the Arabian Peninsula have recognised that life in this barely accessible landscape also requires protection and have declared a 27,000 square kilometre area of the desert region, Jiddat al Harasis, a national park. The protection is especially intended for the only herd of Arabian oryx still living wild, a subspecies of the antelope, but other rare animals such as the Arabian wolf, honey badger, gerbil and 168 bird species also live there. UNESCO declared the area a World Heritage Site in 1994.

Ruins of Jissa Muscat (bottom)

Up until the 20th century, the region covered by modern-day Oman on the east tip was of no interest to the world, but then all that was changed by oil. Not only nomads populated the area, but also settled peoples, such as the inhabitants of Jissa near the capital, Muscat, who tried to protect themselves from belligerent desert tribes. The defensive structures are now just ruins, but they reveal something of the difficulties of past times, when the black gold lay yet untouched underground.

Pakistan

Karakoram Massif (top)

The Pakistani Karakoram can only boast the second highest mountain in the world, the K2 (Mount Goodwin Austen). However, this summit resisted human mountaineering skills for one year longer than the highest, Mount Everest. It was only on 31st July 1954 that an Italian team managed to reach the top. There are three other 8,000 metre peaks soaring into the sky, making the Karakoram a record-breaking mountain range. It also includes a glacier: the Siachen is the longest single ice river in the world and from a high altitude rolls more than 76 kilometres down to the valley, which is still at a higher altitude than the summits of the Swiss Alps.

Buddhist Rock Inscriptions, Skardu (centre)

'Little Tibet' is the name given to the mountainous landscape of Baltistan in north Pakistan due to its position between the Himalayas and the Karakoram mountains and the many holy Buddhist sites found there. One lies on the way from the main town of Skardu to the Satpara Lake at Manthal: a rock face rises up vertically to the sky and obviously inspired artist monks to carve a Buddha homage in the rock. 'The Enlightened One' is enthroned amid smaller figures, sunk in meditation high above the world. The artistic line drawings alone are amazing enough, never mind the climbing ability necessary to produce this relief.

Nanga Parbat (bottom)

Although it is more than 700 m lower than Mount Everest, the first ascent was not made until 6 weeks later: the summit of Nanga Parbat, at 8,125 metres the highest mountain in the Western Himalayas, saw its first human on 3rd July 1953 in the shape of the Austrian mountaineer, Hermann Buhl (1924–1957). In seven previous, unsuccessful efforts, 31 people had been killed. The Nanga Parbat region, situated in the Pakistani part of Kashmir, belongs to the best-explored regions of the Himalayas. The mountain massif, formed of gneiss, is heavily jointed on the north side, while on the south side there is a sheer drop down to the Rupal Valley.

Fort and Shalimar Gardens, Lahore
(top)

The two showpieces of Old Lahore, now capital of the Pakistani province of Punjab near the Indian border, could not be swallowed up by the giant city of three million inhabitants: in the northwest of the Old City, Akbar the Great (1556–1605) built a fortress town, whose military function was practically lost amongst the splendour of mosque and palace structures. The ruler and his descendants were evidently more interested in prestige and political influence through extravagance. In 1641–42 his son, Jehangir, then added the Shalimar Gardens to the complex, a masterpiece of landscaping covering 16 hectares and three terraces with baths, ponds and pavilions of refined taste. UNESCO World Heritage Site since 1981.

Moenjodaro *(above centre)*
In the Pakistani Indus Valley archaeologists have been excavating ancient towns belonging to the so-called Harappa civilisation since the 1920s, of which the most important of these unique settlements from this early epoch is Moenjodaro. At the beginning of the 3rd century BC, the town planners built an incomparable sewage system there that used natural flowing water sources. Wells and baths, including a large public open-air bath, are evidence of highly developed hygiene awareness. Built for roughly 30,000 inhabitants, the two to three-storey houses, constructed from clean moulded and carefully fired bricks, were arranged in a square, so that their rooms were accessible from an inner courtyard. This example of a lost civilisation was declared a UNESCO World Heritage Site in 1980.

Buddhist Ruins, Takht-e Bahi *(below centre)*
The ruins of the Buddhist monastery complex, Takht-e Bahi, and those of the old fortress town of Sahr-e Bahlol, also with monastery structures, lie 30 kilometres east of Peshawar on a rocky hill (photo: sitting Buddha, 2nd/3rd century AD). It dates back to the 1st century BC and was extended subsequently by the main stupa and other stupas in several courtyards. They fell into disrepair and were forgotten, until, in 1836 during the British Raj, they were discovered again by travellers and later examined more closely by archaeologists. Restored in the 1920s, the remains were declared a UNESCO World Heritage Site in 1980.

Ruined City, Taxila *(bottom)*
The British colonial officers of the 19th century were the first to penetrate so far into Asia, following Alexander the Great. He conquered Bactria (north Afghanistan) in 329 BC and two years later was also here in Taxila, north Pakistan, 30 kilometres away from Rawalpindi. The Greeks, who stayed behind in the region, founded the town of Sirkap. Along with the ruins of Bhir Mound, 200 years older, and of Sirsukh, founded by the Parthians in the 2nd century AD, these ruins have since been examined and in the Greek settlement the royal palace, a shrine, a temple and other structures have been excavated. The ruins site was declared a UNESCO World Heritage Site in 1980.

India

Golden Temple, Amritsar *(top)*

About 30 kilometres from the border with Pakistan lies Amritsar in the Indian state of Punjab. The showpiece of the buildings in the Old Town is the Golden Temple with the holy lake (16th century), the Sikhs' main shrine. They are members of a religious community influenced by Islam and Hinduism, yet, or perhaps on account of it, are not in harmony with either. Following the partition of Pakistan and India, the Sikhs demanded their own state, Khalistan, but were met with refusal in New Delhi. The conflict escalated and in 1984 Indian troops stormed the Golden Temple, resulting in the burning of the Granth, the original of the Holy Book of the Sikhs. Fanatical Sikhs then murdered the Prime Minister, Indira Ghandhi.

Nanda Devi National Park *(bottom left)*

In 1939 the Indian authorities set up a wildlife nature reserve and in 1980 a national park of 630 square kilometres around the 7,816 metre high Nanda Devi, the second highest mountain in India, in the Himalaya region of Uttar Pradesh. A chain of snow-capped peaks towers over the impassable primeval landscape, through which snow leopards move in large numbers. Brown and black bears, langur and blue sheep, musk deer, mountain goats and gorals are safe in this nature reserve as are 27 butterfly and 620 plant species. UNESCO World Heritage Site since 1988.

Chandigarh, Punjab *(bottom right)*

A city created by a master hand: the architect, Le Corbusier (1887–1965) drew up the plans for the northwest Indian city of Chandigarh, capital of the Punjab, in 1950/51 and it was finished in 1965. The administration, high court, university and parliament buildings are imposing and functional. The power and simultaneous lightness are typical of designs made of bare concrete. Overhanging roofs and sources of shade serve to protect against the monsoon winds and the boiling summer heat. Many Indian architects have deliberately followed Le Corbusier's example. The photo shows the 26 metre high 'open hand', symbol of the city.

Emperor Humayun's Tomb, Delhi *(top)*

In the 16th century, Haji Begum, the widow of Emperor Humayun, had an octagonal mausoleum built for her husband on the southeast edge of Delhi in northern India. It marks one of the first high points in early Moghul architecture (1526–1828) and was an influence on the Taj Mahal of Agra, built just 100 years later. Constructed of red marble and also black and white marble in parts, the huge domed temple with its long colonnade has an artificial lake in front of it.

Red Fort, Delhi *(bottom left)*

'City of Seven Cities': the capital of India has sometimes been called this, for the seat of government is only in the southern part of New Delhi, while the other districts in this metropolis of seven million inhabitants are situated on older settlements. It is said that a total of seven cities have been built on this site. Which of these is the Old Delhi with the important buildings from the time of the Moghul kingdom (1526–1828), depends on how one counts them. It is the most impressive, due not least to the Red Fort, which was built under Shah Jahan between 1636 and 1648: a massive complex with turreted outer walls of red sandstone and numerous palaces, marble structures and mosques inside.

Qutb Minar, Delhi *(bottom right)*

With the advent of Islamic rule over North India in the 12th century, a victory tower, 73 metres tall, was built 15 kilometres from Delhi. The five-storey Qutb Minar tower tapers from 15 metres at its base to 2.5 metres at the top. Using red sandstone and marble from remains of old Hindu shrines, the Quwwat-ul-Islam ('Power of Islam') was also built with a courtyard complex and mausoleums for the rulers. As a valuable example of early Indo-Muslim architecture, the complex was declared a UNESCO World Heritage Site in 1993.

Havelis, Jaisalmer *(top left)*

An oasis offering water in the Thar Desert in the western-most corner of Indian Rajasthan once made Jaisalmer one of the richest cities in the region. Reminders of this are the massive yellow sandstone fort on top of the castle mound and the many havelis, by which Jaisalmer became known as the 'Golden City'. These havelis were the palaces of the rich merchant families, constructed from honey yellow stone with extravagant ornamentation, balconies and bay windows, turrets, embellished arches and porticos, parapets and latticework.

Umaid Bhawan Palace, Jodhpur *(top right)*

The Thar Desert in northwest India is an impossible place to survive in and that may be the reason why the cities on its edge exude vitality with their glittering style. Jodhpur in the southeast is one of these cities. A fortress towers so high above it that the noise of the city hardly reaches it: the inhabitants call it 'whispering of the gods'. And, in truth, they are godly, these palace buildings, particularly Umaid Bhawan (18th century), which is built of pink sand-stone. It is both a citadel and a castle, with a soaring central dome and angular towers. It becomes quite magical when lit up at night.

Fatehpur Sikri *(bottom)*

Even the most powerful of the great Moghuls could achieve nothing without water: in 1569 Akbar the Great (1542– 1605) built the city of Fatehpur Sikri, west of northwest Agra, designed to be his residence. Three years later the Friday Mosque was built, a long magnificent building with a colonnade at the front and domed canopies arranged like battlements on the ridge. Fifteen years later, it had to be abandoned, as the water supply could not be guaranteed. Palace buildings, more mosques, the treasury and many other notable buildings remain. They survived undisturbed for centuries and now, as a UNESCO World Heritage Site (since 1986), are a tourist attraction.

Keoladeo National Park (top)

When the Maharaja of Bharatpur went hunting, it was to the Keoladeo area in Rajasthan, south of today's capital, Delhi. No shots are fired here now, for the area, 29 square kilometres in size, of which a third is swamp, has been a national park and bird sanctuary since 1982, home to 364 bird species: Siberian crane, Indian gannets, purple herons, spoonbills, Dalmatian pelicans, pintail ducks, ring-necked parakeets — they and many more can be seen here and many migratory species also stop in this lush green park. UNESCO World Heritage Site since 1985.

Palace of Winds, Jaipur (bottom)

A planned city: Jaipur in the Aravelli Mountains, built in the 18th century in the middle of the desert in Indian Rajasthan, is noted for its grid street network and some notable buildings dating back to its early period. Besides the observatory, the most important of these is the Palace of Winds (1799, see photo). Without being observed, the ladies of the maharaja's court could watch the daily bustle in front of the five-storey, red sandstone palace from a total of 953 bay windows. Like a honeycomb, the intricately decorated 'eyes' are piled up on top of each other in this huge building, like something out of a fairy tale.

Taj Mahal, Agra (top)

Apart from the Red Fort in Agra, the most famous building in the sub-continent is the snow-white Taj Mahal, the marble mausoleum for the favourite wife of the Moghul ruler Shah Jahan, who died in 1631 after the birth of her 14th child. The 73 metre high building, topped with its enormous onion dome and flanked by four pointed minarets soaring up 41 metres, is a perfect example of Islamic architecture and the 300 metre wide garden in front of it with its large central tank simply emphasises this. UNESCO World Heritage Site since 1983.

Red Fort, Agra (centre)

Akbar the Great (1542–1605) rebuilt the destroyed city of Agra in today's Indian state of Uttar Pradesh and made it the residence of his Moghul kingdom. It was splendidly arranged and very secure: in 1566 the Red Fort was finished, a fortress of red sandstone with a 2.5 kilometre enclosure wall and a 10 metre wide moat. His grandson, Shah Jahan (1628–1658), added further buildings such as the Pearl Mosque (completed in 1653) and the Hall of Private Audience, Diwan-i-Khas (1636/37). The complex was declared a UNESCO World Heritage Site in 1983.

Akbar's Mausoleum, Sikandra (bottom)

Fame in this life means nothing in the afterlife. For this reason, kings and potentates have always provided for suitable memorial sites. One of the first was Mausolos of Caries in the 4th century BC, who had a magnificent tomb. This is why these temples of posthumous reputation are now all called mausoleums. The Indian Great Moghul Akbar the Great (1542–1605, ruled from 1556) had one built in Sikandra, not far from his Agra residence. It displays elements of several religions to underline the tolerance that Akbar instilled into his subjects. However, his son and heir put three-storey, red sandstone minarets on the four corners and thus gave the mausoleum a more Islamic character.

Manas Wildlife Sanctuary *(top)*
The tiger sanctuary on the Manas, a tributary of the Brahmaputra in Assam, northern India, south of the small state of Bhutan, covers over 2,800 square kilometres (an area not much smaller than Cornwall). The actual national park occupies an area of about 300 square kilometres. Endangered animals such as the Bengal tiger, one-horned rhino, golden langur (a species of leaf monkey), clouded leopard, meerkats and many more are given a safe refuge here. Despite elevating the Manas National Park to a UNESCO World Heritage Site (1985), civil war unrest has resulted in serious poaching since 1990. Yet there is a wonderful variety of species here in this transition zone between tropical rainforest and steppe foothills.

Himalaya Railway, Darjeeling *(centre)*
Just as Switzerland has its Glacier express, India has its Himalayan railway, which in 1881 reached its terminus in northeast Darjeeling (West Bengal, see photo) at 2,185 metres above sea level. Like its Swiss counterpart, it takes its passengers through breathtaking, magnificent mountain scenery, yet it is more than just a tourist trail. Roads are rare and caravans are not just slow but have very limited transport capability. The remote region benefited considerably in terms of development because of the railway. It was declared a UNESCO World Heritage Site in 1999.

Kaziranga National Park *(bottom)*
The one-horned rhino and the hog deer live companionably together here: in the northeast Indian state of Assam, an area of 430 square kilometres covers one of the last almost undisturbed nature paradises in the sub-continent: the Kaziranga National Park. With large parts being regularly submerged by the Brahmaputra, the marshland offers excellent living conditions for endangered flora and fauna species, as do the drier parts, where elephants move through the tall grasses of the same name. Leopards and tigers are at home here, sloth bears drink at the river, where the Ganges dolphins, which have become rarer, splash about and leap over the great storks. UNESCO World Heritage Site since 1985.

Observatory, Varanasi (top)

According to Indian legend, the gods once put heaven and all the stars on one side of the scales and the holy city of Varanasi (Benares) in the other. And the city of light was heavier and fell to the ground. That's why the faithful come here to seek access to heaven. Not only them, but, as often happens in sacred places, the astronomers too. As in other highly developed societies, the priests took charge of astronomy and astrology here, which is why Varanasi observatory was built like a temple and with such solid walls.

Mausoleum, Aurangabad (bottom)

India was not only a land where widows threw themselves on their husband's funeral pyre, but also a land where widowers fell into the depths of despair, shown in the wonderful mausoleums they built for their favourite wives. The Taj Mahal just happens to be the most famous. In addition to it, there are many more similar monuments to love beyond the grave. In Aurangabad in the state of Maharashtra stands the mausoleum for the great love of the Great Moghul Auranseb (1618–1707, ruled from 1658): a wide walkway with water channels leads up to the central domed structure, which is flanked by four minarets also topped with domes.

Chitaurgarh *(bottom)*

About 100 kilometres northeast of Udaipur in the Indian state of Rajasthan lies the martial citadel of Chitaurgarh, a memorial to the resistance of the Rajputis against their Islamic conquerors. Three times in their history the city had to admit defeat and three times the defenders committed johar, a type of Indian hara-kiri. The men would ride to their death wearing red robes and the women and their children would burn themselves alive. Today the old, strong walls enclose a ghost town.

Maharaja Residence, Udaipur
(far bottom left)

Due to its charming location between wooded slopes, Udaipur in the Aravelli Mountains in the southwest of Rajasthan is one of the romantic pearls of India. On natural and artificial lakes palaces are to be found, the most magnificent of which belonged to the maharaja Udai Singh, who founded Udaipur in 1567. The enormous building with many turrets and storeys matches the self-confidence of the immeasurably wealthy ruling family of the Maharana, who epitomised the picture of the maharaja's luxury life. On the other hand, the population of Rajasthan belong to the poorest of the poor in India.

Temple Complex, Khajuraho
(far bottom right)

It is just as well that the sculptures are so old and therefore venerable, otherwise they might bring moralisers on the scene: in the 10th/11th centuries, Indian artists near the modern village of Khajuraho (Madhya Pradesh state) southeast of Agra created 80 temples, of which 23 with 872 sculptures still remain. Some of them show figures in uncompromisingly erotic positions, which have given the temple complex the name 'Kama Sutra in stone'. The affirmation of the physical side of the human body in Hinduism has seldom been expressed so openly. UNESCO World Heritage Site since 1986.

Buddhist Shrine, Sanchi (top)

On a hill northeast of Bhopal in the Indian state of Madhya Pradesh stands the early Buddhist cult site of Sanchi. It dates back to the 3rd century BC when it was established by King Ashoka. The oldest stupa, which was originally 17 metres high and 37 metres wide at its base, dates from this time. More stupas and reliefs with scenes from the life and previous incarnations of Buddha, later monasteries and temples form a religious complex of particular impressiveness. UNESCO World Heritage Site since 1989.

Cave Temples, Ajanta (bottom left)

Five temples and 24 monasteries hewn out of the rock for eternity: the word 'bomb-proof' instinctively springs to mind when you look at the cult sites in Ajanta in northern India (state of Maharashtra). And the wish for seclusion will have been the reason for such a time-consuming construction design. The outstanding feature in the Buddhist complex, where there is even one cave with more than one storey, is the colonnaded caves and also the murals. The oldest parts date back to the 2nd century BC and the most recent to the 7th century AD. Thereafter, Ajanta lay forgotten and was only re-discovered in 1819 by a British hunting expedition. UNESCO World Heritage Site since 1983.

Sunderbans National Park (bottom right)

Mangrove forest is the only vegetation covering an enclosed area of 2,300 square kilometres in the amphibious delta region of the Ganges, Brahmaputra and Meghna in Bengal, which is approximately 80,000 square kilometres in size. In 1973, together with adjoining areas, it became a tiger reserve and in 1984 a national park, in which about 250 Royal Bengal tigers still live. There is a very wide variety of other fauna, with Ganges dolphins, fish otters, crocodiles, pythons and macaques, in addition to over 260 bird species and flora that is probably even more diverse. In particular, rare halophytes flourish due to continual submersion by the sea, which also provides ideal spawning grounds for many fish species. UNESCO World Heritage Site since 1987.

Lingaraj Mandir, Bhubaneswar (top)

In Bhubaneswar in northeast India (state of Orissa), Hindu temples pop up one after the other like gigantic beehives. They date from the late Gupta era (8th century) and are surrounded by later cult structures (up to the 15th century). The Lingaraj temple city includes hundreds of Hindu shrines and attracts pilgrims and tourists. The holy Shikkara tower, shaped like a corn on the cob and soaring up 55 metres, has a flat, ribbed sphere and its crowning motif supported by lion sculptures.

Cave Temples, Ellora (bottom left)

Northwest of Aurangabad in the Indian state of Maharashtra in the village of Ellora, shrines of three religious communities grew up together in devout harmony. There are 17 Hindu, 12 Buddhist and 5 Jain temples and monasteries hewn out of the basalt cliffs along a stretch of two kilometres. The oldest are Buddhist and date from the 7th/8th centuries, the Hindu, including the famous Shiva temple, Kailasanatha, and the Jain ones date from around 1000 AD. This 'ensemble of tolerance' has been protected by international law as a UNESCO World Heritage Site since 1983.

Sun Temple, Konarak (bottom right)

'Place of the sun' is the literal translation of the northeast village of Konarak in the state of Orissa, 30 kilometres away from Puri. Hindu pilgrims and tourists from all over the world visit the 'black pagoda', so called because of the dark colour of the Sun god's stone chariot flanked by elephants. The shrine has 24 stone wheels, each up to 3 metres high with 8 spokes, and forms the decorative base for the 13th century Surya temple. Recognised as the pinnacle of temple art in Orissa, it was declared a UNESCO World Heritage Site in 1984.

Main Railway Station, Mumbai (top)
Mumbai (Bombay) with its ten million inhabitants is the second largest city and the largest port in India. The main railway station welcomes the traveller with a splendour that puts all similar European railway stations in the shade. And yet it owes this to European influence mixed with Indian ornamentation, which has produced a type of Asian baroque: domes and towers, decorative detail and colonnades literally dress up this functional building.

Churches and Monasteries, Goa (centre)
For almost 500 years (from (1510) the Portuguese colonial masters occupied the region of Goa in today's Indian state of the same name on the west coast. Once the capital and situated east of today's Panjim, Old Goa (Velha Goa) has historic reminders of this in its religious buildings from early times. The churches and monasteries have only been partially preserved intact, but are evidence of the European conquerors' intense efforts to spread Christianity and are also outposts of their Baroque architectural style. UNESCO World Heritage Site since 1983.

Temple Complex, Hampi (bottom left)
Vijayanagar, the southern Indian 'city of victory' came to an end after the devastating defeat of the Vijayanagar empire in 1565 against the central Indian sultanates. On the right bank of the Tungabhadra in today's village of Hampi (Karnataka state) the ruins, which have been systematically investigated and excavated since 1981, tell of its dazzling period. There are temples with artistic sculptures, an impressive palace complex, gateways, the 'Bath House of the Queens' and the ruler's elephant stables, whose arches already display Islamic influences. UNESCO World Heritage Site since 1986.

Temple District, Mamallapuram (bottom right)
The Pallava king, Narasimharvarman I Mahamalla (about 630–668) founded the city of Mamallapuram (Maha-balipuram) on the Coromandel coast in today's Indian state of Tamil Nadu, 60 kilometres south of Chennai (Madras). Later generations extended their city with various temples (some hewn out of rock). In particular, the bas-relief, 'Arjuna's Penance', draws pilgrims and travellers on account of its size alone: 32 by 14 metres, it depicts pictorially the mythology of the Ganges river. UNESCO World Heritage Site since 1984.

Sri Lanka

Ruined City, Polonnaruwa *(top)*

Some researchers date the rise of the city of Polonnaruwa, northeast of Colombo, to a royal residence of the Sinhalese in the 8th century, whereas others accept a much later date. What is certain is that the city played a role in the monarchy until the 13th century and was vested with appropriate powers and then abandoned. Numerous ruins, reclaimed since 1900 from the jungle, tell of its old glory: the Buddha image house, 'Monastery of the Cremation Grounds', the house of 60 reliquaries and the once seven-storey royal palace with the audience hall of the ruler, all decorated with works of art of Sinhalese sculpture. UNESCO World Heritage Site since 1982.

The Sacred City, Anuradhapura
(centre and bottom left)

From here, Ceylon, now Sri Lanka, was ruled by a total of 119 Sinhalese kings over a period of 1,000 years, from the 3rd century BC to the 8th century AD. The old city of Anuradhapura is now just extensive ruins, with some Buddhist shrines, palaces and the almshouse preserved. The latter is remarkable due to an 8 metre long stone trough, called the rice trough, which contained rice for 6,000 hungry people. What led to the city being abandoned in the 12th century can only be left to conjecture. It declined anyway and was swallowed up by the jungle, until a British expedition re-discovered it in 1820 and archaeological studies were later begun. The Sacred City of the Sinhalese was declared a UNESCO World Heritage Site in 1982.

Ruined City, Sigiriya *(bottom right)*

Damsels in diaphanous garments, rising out of the clouds, offering flowers: this charming picture was painted by Sinhalese artists in the 5th century on a rendered, over-hanging rock wall in the granite hillock of Sigiriya, which rises 200 metres above the surrounding countryside 90 kilometres north of Kandy. In those days the king's citadel stood here and its ruins, spread over the 12 hectares of land, still lord it over the land below. The delightful juxta-position of delicate art and imposing walls led to the site being declared a UNESCO World Heritage Site in 1982.

Golden Cave Temple, Dambulla *(top)*

The monastery caves in Dambulla in the centre of Sri Lanka were started BC. They developed in the following centuries into proper cave monasteries, five in all. In every room there are Buddha statues; mostly sitting in utter relaxation, in one cave reclining. The room is 15 metres long and is completely filled by the gold-painted figure, just as following the Noble Eightfold Way should completely fulfil the followers of Buddha. The white facade of the complex and the precious murals also contributed to its status as a UNESCO World Heritage Site (since 1991).

Sinharaja Forest Nature Reserve *(centre)*

In the southwest of Sri Lanka, the authorities have turned an area of 89 square kilometres into a nature reserve. It covers the hill country of Sabaragamuva, which is between 500 and 1,170 metres above sea level. The Sinharaja Forest has been established as a biosphere reserve, in order to save the very rare tree and orchid species, many of which are only endemic here. The area is part of the remaining regions of virgin tropical mountain rainforest, in which leopards and Indian elephants can still be found. The diverse stock of endemic bird species is also a contributing factor to the forest reserve being declared a UNESCO World Heritage Site in 1988.

Old Town and Fortifications, Galle
(bottom left)

Ceylon enjoys such an attractive position on all trade routes to the Far East that the greed of the colonial powers could not be ruled out. As early as 1505 the Portuguese landed, established themselves in the harbour now called Galle, south of Colombo, built a city, but had to give way in 1640 to the Dutch, who in turn were driven out in 1796 by British colonial troops. All three occupying powers left their architectural mark on the harbour city. It is therefore a typical monument of a fortified European settlement on Sri Lanka, which is reflected in its status as a UNESCO World Heritage Site since 1988.

Holy City, Kandy *(bottom right)*

It is thanks to the Buddha's tooth that Kandy, situated in the hill country in the centre of Sri Lanka, got the honorary title 'holy'. The tooth is kept in the temple of Dalada Maligawa, nearly 300 years old, and many Buddhists make a pilgrimage there. They also visit the nearby cave temple of Degaldoruwa, which was hewn out of the rock also in the 18th century. At that time, Kandy was the residence of Sinhalese kings and was able to remain independent until 1815, when British troops advanced. UNESCO World Heritage Site since 1988.

Maldives

Maldives

An area of 760 by 130 kilometres would definitely put the Republic of the Maldives into the medium size states of the world. However, solid ground only accounts for 300 square kilometres, and thus this country, consisting of 19 atolls and 2,000 coral islands, is only a miniature state. But the motto here is: small is beautiful. The view of islands fringed with white beaches and palm trees explains why 300,000 tourists come every year to join the 250,000 inhabitants. And if the flight was not so expensive, there would certainly be more. But the only other way to get to the tiny paradises is to take a slow sea voyage.

Nepal

Mount Everest, Sagarmatha National Park *(top left)*

Nowhere else on earth is the law of gravitation so strikingly demonstrated: a pendulum deviates noticeably from the perpendicular because of the effect of the mighty Mount Everest massif. The Nepalese region, Sagarmatha, certainly did not need to become a nature reserve for that reason, but because it attracted tourists. Trekking tours and deforestation of the mountain forests have severely disturbed the ecological balance in this region covering 1,150 square kilometres and between 2,845 and 8,848 metres in height. The situation is gradually improving since Sagarmatha was designated a national park and became a UNESCO World Heritage Site in 1979.

Valley Region, Kathmandu *(top right)*

The Nepalese capital, Kathmandu, lies in a valley approximately 30 kilometres long and 20 kilometres wide. Its townscape, mainly dating from the 16th to 18th centuries, characterised with red brick buildings, is sprinkled with religious architecture that indicates a peaceful harmony of Hindu and Buddhist elements. The oldest structures are the royal palace and the main temples, Taleju and Degutale. Not far from the town there are Buddhist monasteries, amongst which is Bodnath, with the gleaming white dome-shaped stupa and golden spire (see photo). The Krishna and Shiwa shrines complete the spiritual cultural impression in this valley situated more than 1,300 metres above sea level in the heart of the country. UNESCO World Heritage Site since 1979.

Temple of Bhadgaon, Kathmandu *(centre)*

No country is so poor that its religious structures at least could not show off their sumptuous decoration. This is the case in the Himalayan kingdom of Nepal and its capital, Kathmandu: anything spare was invested by the people in their salvation, which the monks and priests look after in the wonderful temples. Bhadgaon, built in the typical red brick style of the town, is especially fascinating, but distinguished by its overhanging canopies, because they are supported by beams painted with colourful fantastic figures: blue or yellow figures with crossed legs and strange crowns. The rest of the facade is decorated with black relief carving, also framing the doors and windows.

Chitwan National Park *(below)*

For over 100 years, the kings of the Himalaya state hunted in this Nepalese-Indian border area, before it was declared a nature reserve in 1962 and a national park in 1973. It covers 932 square kilometres and its subtropical climate supports mixed woodland of sal, palisander and chir pine as well as lush grassland, in which the endangered one-horned rhino and other rare animals such as the sloth bear, Himalayan marten, leaf monkey, Indian python and marsh crocodile have a home. Of the 489 bird species, there are some that are scarcely found anywhere else. UNESCO supported the Nepalese efforts, by declaring the park a World Heritage Site in 1984.

Bangladesh

Ruins of the Buddhist Vihara, Paharpur (far top left)

In west Bangladesh, northeast from Rajshahi, there is a Buddhist monastery complex, which rises 80 metres up on terraces. It covers an area of 90 hectares and has cells for 177 monks. The 'Great Moon City Monastery', as it is called, was built around the year 800 of brick with terracotta decoration. Its length was 273 metres, making it the largest monastery structure south of the Himalayas, but in the 12th century it was abandoned, possibly due to a devastating flood. With UNESCO assistance, restoration work began in 1979 and it was declared a UNESCO World Heritage Site (1985) as a monument to the heyday of Mahayana Buddhism.

Mangrove Forest, Sundarbans (far top right)

It begins south of Calcutta in India, crosses the border to Bangladesh and extends up to the estuaries of the Ganges/Brahmaputra. The Sundarbans is a unique damp, even wet, landscape and is protected by law in Bangladesh. This area of about 6,000 square kilometres is mostly mangrove forest, which, with its impenetrable aerial root undergrowth, acts as a silt trap, thus offering optimum living conditions to amphibian creatures. To the north, the land becomes gradually drier, so that 350 Bengal tigers, hog deer and wild cats have found protection here. Ganges dolphins splash about in the countless stretches of water, while ospreys circle above. UNESCO World Heritage Site since 1997.

Mouth of the Brahmaputra Delta (top)

Rising in the north Himalayas, the Brahmaputra river ('Son of Brahma') reaches the lowlands of Bangladesh after 2,900 kilometres and branches into an enormous delta. The main arm is the Yamuna, which joins the Ganges at Goalundo becoming the Padma, then, forming a wide estuary with many distributaries, flows into the Gulf of Bengal. It is about one kilometre in width when it enters the plain, whereupon it soon widens to eight kilometres and transports up to 15,000 cubic metres of water per second to the south. Continually threatened by flooding, the fertile Ganges-Brahmaputra delta is the biggest in the world and covers an area of 80,000 square kilometres.

Myanmar *(Burma)*

Kutho Daw Pagoda, Royal Mausoleum, Mandalay *(top left)*

The Kutho Daw Pagoda is a symbol of the central Burmese city of Mandalay, built in 1857 and situated on the Irrawaddy River. Shining from afar, it announces to the world that Buddha wished a shrine to be built here; nearer at hand, surrounding the soaring centrepiece there are another 729 small white gleaming pagodas. The sacred scriptures of Buddha are continuously engraved on these devotional cells and altogether thus form, in a way, the biggest book in the world. No less splendid, with its extravagent ornamentation, pediments, roofs and a four-storey tower, is the mausoleum of King Mindon, the founder of the city.

Sandamani Pagoda, Mandalay *(top right)*

The British colonial powers exiled the last Burmese king in 1885. When the Japanese pushed up the Irrawaddy from China during the Second World War and fought the British in bloody battles, irreplaceable cultural artefacts were lost through artillery and air attacks. Mandalay was lucky, as the fighting was limited both during the invasion and the retreat. Among the surviving treasures was the Sandamani Pagoda, built in the 19th century of white sandstone. Its countless, little devotional structures with their pointed towers change colour from white to red, depending on the time of day.

Arakan Pagoda, Mandalay *(bottom)*

The central tower of this 19th century structure points so decisively upwards with its roof cap as if to proclaim to the world that salvation can never be found in this world but only in the heavens above. It is flanked by a host of much smaller offspring that give the building, ornamented on all sides by beautiful, white pediments, the appearance of a pincushion.

U Bein Bridge made of Teakwood at Amarapura *(top)*

The name has no intrinsic meaning, but refers to a mayor by the name of U Bein, who ruled here at the end of the 18th century. Not far from Mandalay in central Burma, Amarapura was an old royal residence like Ava, which the last monarch had, however, just given up. Not being a lazy person, U Bein requisitioned the teakwood from the royal palace and used it to construct the strange pedestrian bridge on stilts with its cosy bridge house. Almost 1.5 kilometres long, it still stands today.

Maha Muni Temple, Mandalay *(centre)*

The glorification of Buddha in statues and temples like the Maha Muni in Mandalay, central Burma, is supposed to urge the faithful to follow in his footsteps. No expense is spared in this effort, so that even in poor Buddhist countries the temples are always looked after and magnificently decorated. This has also led to an ornamental architecture, which is used especially in extravagant roof designs: the tapering storeys rise up in steps to the gleaming, golden spire. In contrast, therefore, the inner rooms of the temple are arranged solely to serve meditative contemplation, which does not mean talking to God, but rather practising the rejection of all things earthly.

Bell, Mandalay *(bottom left)*

In the Mingun Pagoda in Mandalay in central Burma, there hangs a bell of massive dimensions, which is very difficult to move, certainly not as in Schiller's poem, "Walled up in the earth so steady" (The Song of the Bell), but simply by virtue of its own weight. It is guarded by two sculptures of predators. Bell-founding in fact originated in Asia, from where it spread to Europe in the early Middle Ages. But, whereas here bell-ringing calls us to worship or sounds the death knell, it is different in Asia, where bell-ringing and especially that of such enormous bells are primarily to banish evil and bad spirits.

Maha Lawka Pagoda, Mandalay *(bottom right)*

If Myanmar was not ruled by such an unyielding military dictatorship, UNESCO would certainly have already selected a number of world heritage sites. One of those would certainly be the Maha Lawka Pagoda in Mandalay on the River Irrawaddy in the centre of the country. As in many such complexes, hundreds of small, white pagodas are grouped around a central shrine with a tall spire and coloured decoration. They give the area the appearance of a tented city from the time of Genghis Khan, whose hordes also passed through here, 700 years earlier, although the pagoda city was built in the second half of the 19th century.

Ananda Temple, Pagan *(top left)*

In 850 a town was built, which just 200 years later was to be the capital of the Burmese kingdom: Pagan, 150 kilometres southwest of Mandalay. The capital was to flourish for another 200 years before it fell victim to a Mongol assault. Of the original 5,000 or thereabouts temples and pagodas, about 1,000 are still standing, of which the best preserved must be the Ananda Temple, with its central tower, 55 metres tall, sitting on top of the building like a tiara. A white gate, beautifully decorated by stonemasons, gives entry to it across a broad flight of steps. Little towers also decorate the corners of the terraced structure.

Shwe Dagon Pagoda, Yangon *(far top right)*

Gold in plenty and plenty of poverty, they go hand in hand in Burma. The symbol of the country, the Shwe Dagon Pagoda in the capital, Yangon (formerly Rangoon), in the south of the country, only wallows in gold, however. The whole of its enormous dome and the 110 metre tall tower are gold-plated, the towers both big and small around it have a golden gleam and, entering through golden doors, one is faced by the gleaming golden smiles of Buddha statues. Moreover, the sculpted decoration is sumptuous and reflects the advanced skills of the Burmese sculptors in the 18th century, when the building was built.

Temple Precinct, Pagan *(top right)*

On the left bank of the Irrawaddy river in the Burmese province of Mandalay, there is an expanse of rubble: Pagan, capital of the country in the Middle Ages, fell victim to the advancing Mongols in 1287. However, they were not alone to blame for the total destruction of 5,000 temples and pagodas in the city; many of the religious structures, which had suffered weathering over the centuries anyway, collapsed after severe earthquakes in 1975 and 1980. Nevertheless, many hundreds still stand, even if damaged, and a small number of the cultural monuments, mainly built of brick, have since been restored thanks to a UNESCO assistance programme.

Karaweik Barque, Lake Inle *(bottom)*

Although Myanmar is mainly secularised, Buddhist cult elements still play an important role in public life. Processions are part of that and those performed on water represent a special high point. Many monasteries use boats, even ships, of such splendour, that Western kings and emperors would have become green with envy upon seeing them. The king of them all is the Karaweik Barque with the monk shaded by canopies, travelling across Lake Inle, 1,000 metres above sea level and southeast of Mandalay, to visit shrines along the shore.

Thailand

Wat Phra Singh Temple and Doi Suthep Temple, Chiang Mai
(top left and centre)

The largest temple in Chiang Mai in northwest Thailand stands in the west of the historic centre and is called Wat Phra Singh (photo above). It houses a precious Buddha relic in a special shrine and is thus the religious centre of the city and a place of pilgrimage. Behind the main building a temple is almost tucked away, which is richly decorated with murals and has fantastically carved pediments. Sixteen kilometres northwest of the city, Doi Suthep rises up 1,600 metres. The best view of the city can be had from just beneath its summit, at probably the most important Thai temple, Wat Phra That Doi Suthep (photo, centre), where one can admire the golden chedi (a relic chamber) in the complex.

Chedi Group in Temple Complex of Wat Suan Dok, Chiang Mai (bottom)

The cultural heart of north Thailand beats in Chiang Mai, in a fertile valley at the foot of Doi Suthep. The tourists are especially attracted by the religious structures, in particular the temple complex of Wat Suan Dok dating back to the

13th century. Typical of this Buddhist shrine is the so-called Chedi group, a complex with a tall, white pagoda, which displays a square intermediate section on top of which the round tower tapers upwards to a point, like a tiered wedding cake. It is brightly painted with a golden crown; the ashes of the Thai kings were kept here. All around this central tower are smaller, simpler, yet still beautifully constructed temples, which also line the entrance to the complex.

Wat Phra That Hariphunchai, Lamphun (top right)

When King Athittayarat had the temple (wat) built in 1157, the capital city of Chiang Mai, 25 kilometres to the north, did not exist. It was not until 1296 that it took control of north Thailand. Up until then, Lamphun, built in 660 AD, led a relatively independent existence with such magnificent buildings such as the Phra That Hariphunchai Temple, which has a pagoda that soars up 45 metres with a golden umbrella on top. Special mention should be made of the reliquary (chedi) with its golden roof bulging in imitation of the Buddha figures. It gives the building a feeling of inner peace.

Ruins of Sukhothai *(top left)*

Monumental Buddha statues in all the temples tell of religious life in the mediaeval Siam Kingdom of Sukhothai in north Thailand, where the remains of this capital have been excavated. It flourished only from 1238 to 1378 and then lost its independence to the Ayutthaya Kingdom. The archaeologists have counted 37 temple complexes in the centre of the city, which was the cradle of the powerful Thai architecture. Especially worth mentioning is the royal temple, Wat Mahathat, with standing Buddhas and the 185 chedis, as the relic shrines are called. UNESCO World Heritage Site since 1991.

Wat Phra Si Ratana Mahathat, Phitsanulok *(bottom left)*

Situated north of Bangkok, almost in the centre of Thailand, the city of Phitsanulok has an extremely beautifully decorated royal temple. The ordination hall of this Wat Phra Si Ratana Mahathat is lined with pillars, whose golden background is decorated with geometric patterns and which shimmer in the reflection of the all-over golden Buddha statue. The Buddha, which is several metres tall, sits at the head under a canopy with latticework, disciples stand on either side of him. He is actually only radiating the light from the candles lined up in front of him, but it seems as if he is illuminated from within and thus is literally 'the Enlightened One', the equivalent in English of the word 'Buddha'

Thung Yai Wildlife Nature Reserve *(right)*

In Thung Yai ('large field') on the border with Myanmar in west Thailand, 3,200 square kilometres are now protected by law, which, together with the adjacent Huai Kha Khaeng Park, 2,575 square kilometres in size, was declared a UNESCO World Heritage Site in 1991. Around a central, grassy plain there are bamboo, dry and gallery forests, karst landscapes and old villages. The vegetation includes subtropical and tropical and offers a corresponding diversity in species. In addition to 400 bird species, numerous amphibians and reptiles, mammals also live here, such as the tiger, cloud leopard, elephant, tapir and the Sumatran rhino. UNESCO World Heritage Site since 1991.

Ruins of Ayutthaya *(top left)*

Siam, modern-day Thailand, was ruled by 33 kings from 1350 to 1767 from Ayutthaya, situated north of Bangkok. The first city became a pearl of Buddhist architecture on account of its extensive palace, monastery and temple complex and it developed a unique Ayutthaya style that was distinguished by its exact symmetry, before the Burmese attacked and put an end to its glory. In 1956 work started on carefully restoring the most important buildings, which, together with the ruins, were declared a UNESCO World Heritage Site in 1991.

Phra Pathom Chedi, Nakhon Pathom *(top right)*

The temple attains the majesty of a cathedral: not content that the relic chamber (chedi) in the Phra Pathom complex in Nakhon Pathom, central Thailand, is 116 metres in height, the architects then placed it on top of a hill. A bell with a handle for a tower: the tallest religious structure in the country owes its awesome appearance to a later design, for the original building dating from the 5th century was smaller. In addition, there are prayer halls at the four corners of the complex, in which Buddha statues in various poses draw in the faithful. The favourite one is the standing Buddha in the north hall.

Summer Palace, Bang Pa In *(centre)*

The kings of the Chakri dynasty have been on the Thai throne since 1782, and they have understood how to spare their country, the only one in Mainland South East Asia, from becoming a colony. Similar skills are evident in their choice of architects, for they created truly majestic structures. The summer palace in Bang Pa In, north of Bangkok, is proof of that: the pavilion is so wonderfully situated that its roofs, pillars and turrets create their double in the reflection of the lake. Standing half in the water, it has rolled out a white staircase for good spirits from the deep or for young ladies silently arriving for a lovers' tryst.

Wat Phra Keo (shrine), Bangkok *(bottom)*

The most important religious buildings in Thailand are naturally to be found in the capital, Bangkok, upstream from the mouth of the Mae Nam Ping. The Wat (temple) Phra Keo was built in 1782 at the same time as the city and contains the royal pantheon with its stylish faïence decoration and sculptures on the outer walls. In the square 'bot' (ordination hall), with its staggered roof decorated with snakes and bells, the Emerald Buddha (so-called simply because of its colour) sits enthroned as the central shrine. In reality, it is formed from a piece of green jade. It has a special link to the royal family.

Wat Phra Keo (Grand Palace), Bangkok *(far top left)*

The Thai royal family resides in the Grand Palace of Bangkok, which is entered from the rear of the Wat (temple) Phra Keo through a gateway. Measuring 500 by 400 metres, the palace complex far exceeds the temple precinct in size and is guarded by a wall topped with battlements. Entry is through the 'Gate of Supreme Victory' in the north of the area. Visitors may only see the audience hall with its gold-plated throne set on top of nine steps and another public hall with a mother-of-pearl altar, in which deceased members of the dynasty lie in state. The 'Door to the Seat of Victory' bars entry to the Inner Palace.

Temple, Bangkok *(far top right and all above)*

Although the Thai capital, Bangkok, was only built in the 18th century, it displays a wealth of Buddhist shrines. Po is the largest and oldest temple (wat), situated south of the Grand Palace (photo above right). It has four assembly halls, 95 relic chambers and 400 Buddha statues. On the opposite riverbank stands the 'Temple of Dawn' (Wat Arun) with its 79 metre high tower (prang) and four more towers on the corners of the complex (photo far top right: temple guards). The Wat Saket lies in the far east of the Old City on the Golden Mount and offers a splendid view from 60 metres up. In the north of the city centre is the Wat Benchamabophit, a complex built of white marble with red roofs (photo above left). And finally the Wat Traimit at Lamphong Station (photo above centre) with its solid gold Buddha weighing almost 5 tons.

Kampuchea

Angkor

In the 19th century, French explorers discovered the ruins of Angkor in the jungle of Kampuchea (Cambodia). Massive sculptures, incorporating amazing detail, on the remains of temple complexes and palaces showed them to be the residence of the Kmer kings, whose dominion once reached as far as Thailand. Destroyed three times since it was built, it has lain in ruins since 1431. There are many ponds in the town centre, whose 45 square kilometres are well fortified, and in the surrounding temple precinct. Angkor Wat mausoleum built by Suryavarman II (1113–1152) is the biggest structure in the whole of South East Asia, covering an area of 1,500 by 1,300 metres, and the tomb itself is 200 metres wide. The actual temple is almost 200 square metres in size.

Laos

Mekong (top)

4,500 kilometres in length and covering an area of more than 8,000 square kilometres, the Mekong is the largest river in Southeast Asia. It rises on the eastern border with Tibet, for a short while forms the Burmese-Lao border and then for the longest stretch the western border of Laos. In the Cambodian basin the lower reaches attain their widest span. Below the capital Phnom Penh it breaks up into a delta of five large arms that takes in the southern part of Vietnam. Larger tributaries join the Mekong, particularly in central Laos near the capital, Vientiane. Here, in places, rapids and waterfalls hinder shipping, which is mainly made up of junks.

Wat That Luang Nuea Monastery, Vientiane (centre left)

The capital of Laos was formerly called Vieng Chang ('City of Sandalwood'), which turned into Vientiane. That it deserves its name is nowhere better seen or smelt than in the temple (wat) of the That Luang Nuea Monastery. It is resplendent with sandalwood carvings and smells of incense sticks. Its facade, decorated richly with the most delicate of reliefs, its stupa, 35 metres high and built on a square plinth, and the gold-plated door in the huge stone gateway date in their present form from the 19th century, for the previous structures were destroyed by Siamese (Thai) soldiers in 1827/28.

Khone Falls (centre right)

The Khone waterfalls in Laos are not particularly high, but instead so wide that they have no rival in the world: over a 10.8 kilometre front, 42,500 cubic metres of water per second fall over a precipice 15 to 21 metres deep. The Mekong is not just any river, but the artery of Mainland South East Asia, and it would be an even better shipping waterway, if it did not have treacherous rapids and precipices like the Khone Falls. If they were better situated on the main tourist trails and not in the almost inaccessible interior, then income from foreign currencies could make up for the economic disadvantages. The Far East operators are working on attractive package deals to this water wonder.

Royal Palace and Buddhist Monastery, Luang Prabang (bottom)

North of the Lao capital, Vientiane, where the Mekong, after bending sharply westwards, forms the broadest valley width in its upper reaches, lies the former Luang Prabang residence. Only the religious structures and the royal palace remind one of the splendour of the pilgrimage centre, originally founded by Buddhist missionaries, with a pagoda that conceals a miraculous Buddha statue. Otherwise it is a mixture of traditional South-East Asian architecture and French colonial elements from the 19th and 20th century. This mixture, however, is exactly what gave the city the status of a UNESCO World Heritage Site in 1995.

Wat Xieng Khuan, Vientiane *(top)*

Buddhism is literally a 'godless' religion. That does not mean that Buddha denied the existence of gods, but he considered them beings in need of salvation, just like people. In other words, to obtain salvation from one's own evil: from the 'thirst' for existence. And, according to Buddhist teaching, one only loses oneself by extinction of self through transcending to Nirvana, where the eternal circle of reincarnation is broken. Buddhist believers, therefore, do not pray, as in other religions, to Buddha as a God, but search for the example of his life that reached this breakthrough. The reclining Buddha figure, as can be seen in the Buddha Park in Vientiane, symbolises for them the decisive moment at the end of that journey.

Victory Gate, Vientiane *(bottom)*

Quite obviously, the Paris Arc de Triomphe was the influence behind the construction of the Anousavari Monument in the Lao capital of Vientiane. However, contrary to the French counterpart, the Far East arch is not dedicated to military victory — at least not directly — but to Lao victims of war. It is thus more of a posthumous victory, for Laos has been independent since 1949 and with full sovereignty, following the French defeat in the Indochina war, since 1954. The arch with its almost overloaded roof is thus rightly regarded as a symbol of its capital.

Vietnam

Ha-Long Bay *(top)*

South of the Vietnamese capital, Hanoi, there is a wide bay in Tonkin Gulf with 1,600 islands, some of which tower up to 200 metres out of the sea. Formed from limestone, they give rise to peculiar shapes, caves and grottoes, in which archaeologists have made important prehistoric finds. Some of the Stone Age finds are up to 8,000 years old. These cultural gems, together with the natural charms of the sea and rock landscape, have made the archipelago a UNESCO World Heritage Site (1994). Its protection also benefits about 1,000 fish species, which are to be found in the bay.

Ho Chi Minh Mausoleum, Hanoi
(bottom left)

When the Vietnamese revolutionary leader, Ho Chi Minh, died in 1969, 540,000 US soldiers were stationed in the south of the country and it was hard to see whether the war that Ho implacably waged against them would ever be successful. However, by 1975 it was, Vietnam was re-unified, and the Father of the Victory enjoyed almost as much veneration from the rebellious youth of Europe as he did back home, where a socialist-realist mausoleum was built in his capital, Hanoi, for the man originally called Nguyen That Thanh, inscribed with his honorary name, which means in English: 'bringer of light'.

Hué *(bottom right)*

Anyone who remembers the reports of the Vietnam War at the beginning of the 1970s knows that Hué, situated halfway down the coast, was never mentioned without the epithet 'the old imperial city'. It would have been important to the presenters to make it clear to listeners the contrast between the lost cultural values and the indiscriminate killing and destruction of the war. And in fact, the grief and sorrow over loss is quite understandable in view of what has been preserved. The 'Palace of Supreme Harmony', in which the emperor resided, and the city wall with the fantastically painted and decorated gates are the only outstanding examples of feudal architecture.

Marble Mountains, Danang (top left)
Here is the explanation as to why Vietnam's temples and palaces are splendidly clad in marble. Not far from Danang, south of Hué, which the US troops developed into a military marine and air base during the 1960s and 1970s in the war against the Communist Vietcong, the coveted stone gleams through the green vegetation. It is quarried here and sold both to domestic and foreign customers. The giant Marble Mountains show that the builders will not be running out of this majestic stone for a long time to come.

Great Buddha, Danang (top right)
It is almost absurd that a war could be fought right under his nose, but Danang was actually one of the most important air and marine bases for the US army during the Vietnam War in the 1960s and 1970s. But, sitting on his lotus leaf, he calmly observed even this murderous activity in the same way as all other human activity, in the same way as he would rather observe his inner self and with his overgrown ears, as the philosopher Kant would say, appears to be listening to music of the heavenly stars above him and moral law within him.

Eight-storey Pagoda, Quang Am
(bottom)
The reason why builders love marble so much can be discovered at the quarry itself: in the mid-Vietnamese mountains near Danang the precious stone is not only cut and polished but also used prolifically: the eight-storey pagoda in Quang Am village is resplendent with abundant marble decoration, and other buildings are also preserved in this light stone. Tapering only slightly upwards, the religious structure stands on a square base and each storey is distinguished from the other by a white cornice. The tiled roof is crowned with fantastic sculpted scenes.

Old Town, Hoi An (top left)

A quarter of a century of war did not make Vietnam better off. When the Americans left in 1975, so did the dollars, which had lent an air of temporary wealth at least to the US army bases and surrounding area. The town of Hoi An is immediately south of Danang, which was the main base for the air force and navy in the Vietnam war. Fortunately, the shooting has long stopped, but the struggle for daily existence goes on. Nevertheless, the Vietnamese do not let that stop them from grabbing every opportunity to beautify their everyday life. If they cannot afford decoration, then they use colour, as this modest house facade shows. The Old Town of Hoi An was declared a UNESCO World Heritage Site in 1999.

Town Hall, Ho Chi Minh City (Saigon) (top right)

To represent the population of Indochina, the French colonial masters naturally required 'dignified' administrative buildings. However, they had to ensure that the people also shared their idea of dignity. In the South Vietnamese city of Saigon, changed to Ho Chi Minh City in 1975 after the Communist victory, they achieved a town hall of European style mixed with Oriental grace and ornamentation. The symmetrical, gleaming yellow and white building has an arcade facade, two flanking fortress-style towers and a taller, tapered clock tower in the middle. For a long time now, of course, the red flag has taken the place of the tricolour at the front of the building.

Caodai Temple, Tay Ninh (below)

Cochinchina province lies in one of the most fertile rice growing areas in the Mekong lowlands in South Vietnam. Judging by its capital, Tay Ninh, prosperity seems the norm here: it would be really hard to find such a magnificent double-towered temple anywhere else. The exterior of the Caodai ('high palace') is bright yellow; it is decorated with blue pictures, golden ornaments, coloured arcades along the long front wall and multi-tiered red roofs. On entering beneath a wonderful balcony through the main door into the prayer hall, one is met by a breathtaking sight. The extreme opulence of the room is reflected in its cool tiles and sky blue vaulted ceiling, supported by brightly coloured columns. Caodaism is an Oriental religion founded in 1926.

China

The Great Wall (top)

Although it is no longer intact, it is still the biggest structure in the world and the only one that astronauts in outer space can apparently see with the naked eye: the Great Wall that stretches over 6,250 kilometres through north China from the Pacific to Turkestan. It is an astonishing feat of engineering that allowed no physical obstacle to get in its way. Started in the 3rd century, the gigantic barricade was built 6–9 metres high and 5 metres wide and was completed during the Ming Dynasty (1368–1644). This stone ribbon crossing mountains and valleys is crowned with numerous massive watchtowers.

Silk Road (below)

For the inhabitants of the desert in Xinjiang, the camel caravans still represent an important means of transport, even if they are no longer necessary for maintaining the link between Europe and the Far East. The costly silk, which, because of its great trading importance, gave its name to the oriental route, can now be shipped by air, if the requirement is for silkworm-produced Chinese silk. Locally, however, the camel is still by far the cheapest method of transport.

239

Summer Residence and Temple, Chengde *(top left and right)*

Did the rulers here really want to 'earn virtue', as the name of the Chinese town in Hebei Province suggests? That may have been the case for some, for the Emperor's summer residence, built in the 18th century, did actually offer just that. For example, one could bury oneself among the 36,000 volumes in the library or worship at one of the numerous temples in the monastery complex, with names as evocative as that of the town: 'Monastery of Universal Love', 'of Universal Goodness', etc. There is also the Puning Temple ('Temple of the Great Buddha') or the Xumi Fushou Miao ('Temple of Bliss and Longevity', photo top right). In 1820, the heavens displayed their displeasure at the feudal pomp when Emperor Jiaqing was killed by lightning, and in 1911 the people rose up and swept away for ever all the imperial glory. What remained in Chengde was declared a UNESCO World Heritage Site in 1994.

Grand Canal from Peking to Hangzhou *(bottom)*

What the forefathers began thousands of years ago is still without a doubt producing prosperity today. In the 6th century BC, Chinese traders recognised that transporting goods by water was preferable to all other forms of transport, and in many cases this is still true today. The Middle Kingdom had sufficient natural arteries: Yangtze, Huai He and Yellow. If there were links between them, then the whole country could be reached by junk or ship. The work was begun, but the first two waterways were not linked until 1,000 years later, and in the 13th century the Grand Canal was extended up to Beijing. In 1958, the Communists had it enlarged to take large ships.

Imperial Palace of Ming and Qing Dynasties, Beijing *(top)*

The Mongolian rulers of China had their residence in Beijing, but the third emperor of the Ming Dynasty (1368–1644) had the invaders' palace torn down and in 1407 started building a new one on the site, which over a 500 year period of additions and changes now looks as it does today. The emperors of the succeeding Qing Dynasty (1644–1911) also ruled from the heart of the 'Forbidden City'. Today the apartments and other palace buildings are just a museum, crowded with Chinese and foreigners, who marvel at the splendour or imagine how it was made possible by the exploitation of the people. As an example of classical Chinese and feudal architecture, the building complex was declared a UNESCO World Heritage Site in 1987.

Square of Heavenly Peace, Beijing *(bottom left)*

Bigger than St. Peter's Square in Rome, the 'Square of Heavenly Peace' (Tian'anmen) extends in front of the former Imperial Palace in Beijing. It is designed to symbolise the immense vastness of the Middle Kingdom, as China is called, and was laid out as far back as 1651. Under the rule of Mao Tse Tung, who proclaimed the People's Republic of China from here in 1949, it was extended in 1958 to its present size. The 'Great Chairman' is still present here today, in the form of his embalmed body in his mausoleum on the south side of the square.

Temple of Heaven with Imperial Altar of Sacrifice, Beijing *(bottom right)*

The Chinese heaven controlled the fate of the people, but it was empty, no god and no special place embodied it. Believers could only make contact with it in temples specially created for that purpose. That also applied to the emperor, who every year had to have his power blessed in the Temple of Heaven in the south of his capital, Beijing, and pray for success. He would walk from the 'Palace of Abstinence' in the west of the complex to the special circular temple with the three-storey roof made of blue glazed tiles and would perform the harvest sacrifice in the specially designed hall to bring prosperity to his land. The temple was built at the same time as the Imperial Palace, in 1421 to be exact.

Seventeen Arched Bridge, Beijing (top)

The former lords and masters may have been sacked, but China's Communists have not refused their inheritance, neither as regards pride in their history, nor concerning the material estate. For, indeed, the cultural monuments were not created by feudal 'parasites' but by artists and workers. Anyway, the people certainly paid for them. And why shouldn't mandarins and burghers also have had good taste. An example of how good it sometimes was is shown in the Seventeen Arched Bridge, which spans a lake inlet in the Summer Palace Park with a grace that has never been achieved since under the 'dictatorship of the proletariat'.

'Imperial Gardens' of Summer Palace, Beijing (centre)

No matter how huge the dimensions of the city palace complex in the heart of the capital, Beijing, might be, it was not enough to satisfy the emperors: as long ago as the 12th century they had a summer residence built 20 kilometres to the northwest, which by the 18th century had reached its present-day size of 290 hectares. The majority of it consists of charming gardens with the artificial Kunming Lake, islets, pavilions, teahouses, temples and sculpture parks. Alongside the lakeside there is a long, covered promenade with vivid paintings that leads to the 'Tower of Buddhist Incense'. Passing through the 'Garden of Harmonious Joy' brings one to the 'Palace of Jade Waves', a residential building in the complex. UNESCO World Heritage Site since 1998.

Cemetery, Turpan (bottom left)

The Tombs of Astana lie to the east of the city of Turpan. This 1,800 year-old graveyard is comprised of more than 1,000 tombs, including those of the former rulers of Gaochang and covers an area of approx. 10 km². It was not only reserved to the upper echelons of society, but also provided final resting places for farmers, traders, soldiers and civil servants. The graveyard became famous for its many relics such as terracotta figurines and its murals.

'Peking Man' Site, Zhoukoudian (bottom right)

Today it is widely agreed that the cradle of mankind is in Africa. As to when hominids turned up on other continents is more difficult to answer. In 1921 and 1929 important pieces of the jigsaw puzzle were found southwest of the Chinese capital, Beijing: remains of Homo erectus type humans, who are known to have lived in Africa 1.5 million years ago and whose Chinese 'mates' date back 400,000 to 250,000 years. It was 1966 before the next find: jaw and cheekbones of a Peking Man were discovered and can now be seen, as part of a complete skull, in the National Museum in the capital. The excavation site at Zhoukoudian was declared a UNESCO World Heritage Site in 1987.

Town Mosque, Turpan (below)

'Flaming Mountains'? What that means in Turpan, a small desert town in Sinkiang Province, becomes clear in the early morning when the mountain range in the west is alight with a red glow. Then the town start to come alive too. It represents a strange cultural mixture: situated on the ancient Silk Road, the ruins and semi-intact buildings of old Turpan display both Chinese and Iranian, Buddhist and Muslim elements. The most important Muslim monument is the green, town mosque with its six minarets, a massive structure with a central facade decorated with tiles and faïence and capped with a dome, decorated with sophisticated simplicity.

Ruins of Gaochang (far bottom left)

There have been trading links, called Silk Roads on account of the most expensive export, between the Far East and Europe since the Chinese Han dynasty from 206 BC to 220 AD. The Northern Silk Route led from the edge of northwest China through the modern province of the Uigurs, where there is a large number of ruined Silk Road towns. One of those, about 45 kilometres southeast of the Turpan oasis, was Gaochang. It flourished as long ago as the 1st century BC and, as the seat of a small kingdom, it enjoyed its heyday in the 4th and 5th centuries. Later its importance declined and today the ruins are used as a temporary shelter by the local shepherds and their sheep.

Caves and Cave Sanctuaries, Mogao (far bottom right)

As long ago as the 3rd century BC, there was a Silk Road running between the Gobi Desert and the inhospitable Tibetan highlands for the Chinese 'East-West' trade. One of its staging posts was the modern oasis town of Dunhuang, in the vicinity of which the Buddhist cave temples of Mogao were formed over the course of the following centuries: almost 500 of them, over 1,200 years old, in sanctuaries and cells with several thousand painted sculptures, some over 30 metres in size, hewn out of a 1.5 kilometre long rock face. 45 hectares of wall paintings and countless manuscripts provide information about the religious life in this desert seclusion. UNESCO World Heritage Site since 1987.

Bezeklik Caves, Turpan *(far top)*

Takla Makan, 'Desert of No Return', is the name of the giant dried-up basin in northwest China, on the northern edge of which, even in ancient times, a Silk Road led to Europe. This is the only explanation for there being a chain of villages in the infrequent oases, where the merchants would stop and in so doing bring a degree of prosperity to them. This found expression in amazing structures, mostly religious, and created a whole sacred town near Turpan: the Bezeklik Caves, also known as 'Caves of 1,000 Buddhas'. And that is no exaggeration. In the easily carved tufa rock, artists have filled natural and created grottoes, niches and caves with countless Buddha statues.

Fortress, Jiayuguan *(above left)*

The camel era is not yet completely over in the deserts of northwest China. On seeing the picturesque riders, one is taken back in time to when the merchants took on the risky operation of transporting the much sought-after silk through these barren wastes. But the rulers did not leave them completely without protection. That was offered by the walls and battlements of the fortifications built roughly along the trade routes, such as at the western end of the Great Wall at Jiayuguan in Gansu Province. Its mighty wall was respected from afar and was a contrast to the friendly buildings behind, which kept a lookout over and beyond it.

Mount Taishan *(above right)*

A climb of over nine kilometres and 6,293 steps in the east of the Shandong mountains and the followers of Taoism reach the 'Peak to Watch the Sunrise', as the holy Taishan mountain is called. Laotse, the philosopher from the 3rd century BC, declared it a shrine, so that thereafter it was endowed with temples, with the 'Hall of Heavenly Gifts', with the 'Shrine of the Mountain God', with the 'Tomb of the White Mule' (an imperial beast of burden), the 'Monastery of Universal Enlightenment' and stelae and inscriptions. From 1759 onwards the Chinese rulers made an annual sacrificial visit to Taishan, which is now a UNESCO World Heritage Site (since 1987).

Huanglong Scenic and Historic Interest Area *(top left)*

Huanglong means 'Yellow Dragon', and the scenery in the north of Sichuan Province got its name from a very steep limestone tufa slope and perhaps also because of the yellow limestone terraces, nearly five kilometres long, with water pools that look like blue or green eyes. The area, 700 square kilometres in size and rising to 5,588 metres at Xuebaoding, is one of the few refuges where the giant panda can live and has a chance of survival. Two-thirds forested, Huanglong offers protection to other endangered animal and plant species. UNESCO World Heritage Site since 1995.

Longmen Grottoes, Luoyuang
(top right)

In all religions there existed and exists the desire to find and worship the deity in nature. Whether a procession in Christianity, a rain dance in Animism or the building of cave monasteries in Buddhism – in creating, the believer is nearest to the Creator. This can be seen in the Longmen Grottoes, situated on either side of the River Jishui in the Chinese town of Luoyang in Henan Province, which have been formed into shrines. The town existed before them, as it was already the capital of the Zhou dynasty, when Buddha was born. It was the capital again several times, as, for example, when most of the important stone Buddha statues were sculpted in the grottoes (5th/6th centuries).

Temple of Confucius, Tomb of Confucius, Qufu *(bottom left and right)*

In Qufu, situated south of Beijing, where Confucius (551–479 BC) lived and taught, there is now a building complex, which exerts an influence just like the petrified wisdom of the teacher (photo bottom right). For him, the most important value was the integration of self in the family, state and traditional morality. This principle was the state doctrine in China up until the end of the imperial epoch (1911). Only the Imperial Palace in the capital is bigger than this building complex, which comprises of the Confucius Temple and the Apricot Altar as well as the residence of the Kong family, the descendants of Confucius, for the last 1,000 years. Beside all this splendour, however, the grave of Confucius is marked only with a simple headstone (photo bottom right). UNESCO World Heritage Site since 1991.

Tomb of the First Emperor of China, Xi-an *(top)*

Whether or not Qin Shi Huangdi (emperor from 259–210 BC) really was the 'first emperor of China' can be left to the experts to decide. His burial chamber at Lintong near Xi-an in Shaanxi Province is certainly super-imperial. The ruler had an army of more than 7,000 life-size terracotta soldiers marching around the actual tumulus. All ranks, from general to archer, are represented, and there are chariots and armoured horses too, in order that the respect due their ruler would continue in the afterlife. They were known about from old reports, but nobody really believed it until the warriors began to be excavated in the 1970s and were declared a UNESCO World Heritage Site in 1987.

Jiuzhaigou Valley Scenic and Historic Interest Area *(bottom right)*

Children and other animal lovers are completely bowled over by the 'cute' panda bears in the zoo. But how long they will be able to enjoy them depends not least on Jiuzhaigou Valley. It lies in the northwest of Sichuan Province and until a few decades ago was barely accessible due to its terrain and therefore remained undisturbed. However, when the habitat for the endemic wild panda began to dwindle alarmingly, it had to be protected. The area covering 720 square kilometres offers such beautiful scenery with its surrounding peaks and large tracts of virgin forest that it was declared a UNESCO World Heritage Site in 1992.

Classical Gardens, Suzhou *(bottom left)*

Since the country's economy has been opened up, stress is part and parcel of everyday life in the biggest Chinese port, Shanghai. So there is no better way of relaxing than to visit Suzhou, situated to the west. Over the centuries, 200 gardens have been created here, with 6,000 bridges both big and small, whose beautiful landscapes radiate calm: 1044 'Pavilion of Azure Blue Waves', 1342 'Lion Grove', 1620 'Garden To Linger In', 1860 'The Humble Administrator's Garden' – just a few examples of the many landscapes filled with temples and pagodas, sculptures and foliage, which helped the city on the Grand Canal to achieve UNESCO World Heritage Site status in 1997.

Potala Palace, Lhasa *(top)*
If one is thinking of a valley 3,700 metres above sea level, then it must be in the Himalayas, the highest of all mountain ranges. In one such valley at such a height lie the cities Lhasa and Potala. The Red Palace is situated inside the White Palace and was built 50 years later, although also in the 17th century. UNESCO World Heritage Site since 1994.

Gyantse *(bottom)*
On the road from Lhasa to Kashmir, in the present-day Chinese province, lies the old town of Gyantse at a height of 4,000 metres above sea level, unimaginable in Europe. The 15th century monastery area is well preserved. The stupa tower, topped with gleaming gold latticework, and the multi-storey meeting hall are looked after by the monks. The fortress-style building constructed into the slope may keep their hopes up.

Mount Huangshan Scenic Beauty and Historic Interest Site *(top)*

1,450 endemic plant species, many of which are endangered, 48 mammal species, 170 bird, 38 reptile, 20 amphibian and 24 fish species. This diversity alone would have merited its successful achievement as a UNESCO World Heritage Site in 1990; in addition, its status is enhanced by the charm and in places splendour of the accompanying scenery. The mountainous Huangshan area, 154 square kilometres in size, in which the many peaks, some strangely shaped, rise up to 1,899 metres high, is situated southwest of Shanghai in Anhui Province and has been celebrated by poets and artists, the wooded valleys with their swathes of mist exactly captures the Chinese ideal of landscape.

Mount Emei Scenic Area, 'Giant Buddha of Leshan' *(bottom left and centre)*

You might feel uncomfortable if you met a giant Chinese salamander in Mount Emei on the southwest edge of the Sichuan Basin. Yet, we should be glad that these threatened (but hardly threatening) reptiles, up to 1.5 metres long, and other rare animal and plant species are still to be found here. There is also tranquillity here for the many monks in the monasteries built on the slopes and on top of the Jinding, the 3,099 metre high holy mountain. The Buddha statue at the foot of the mountain in Leshan on the steep bank of the Min Miang is a special attraction of the pilgrimage centre. It is 71 metres tall and was finished in the year 803. UNESCO World Heritage Site since 1996.

Wulingyuan Scenic and Historic Interest Area *(bottom right)*

The Wulingyuan National Park, 264 square kilometres in size, displays eroded rock formations, waterfalls, limestone caves, more than 3,000 quartzite sandstone pillars up to 200 metres tall and, as the main attraction, two natural bridges of incredible dimensions: one crosses a ravine at a height of 100 metres, it is 26 metres long, 2 metres thick and 1.5 metres wide The other spans a crevasse with a record-breaking 40 metre arch, it is 357 metres high, 15 metres thick and 10 metres wide. In addition, the park is a refuge for many animal species threatened with extinction, for example the panda bear. UNESCO World Heritage Site since 1992.

Hongkong and Shanghai Bank (top)

After 150 years of British rule, the south Chinese port and trading centre of Hongkong was returned to its motherland in 1997. Everywhere in the Central District of the city has a British feel to it, and its Hongkong and Shanghai Bank was actually built by a Briton 1979–1986: the famous architect, Norman Foster (b. 1935). The elegant hi-tech tower consists of three parts of differing heights 'fused' together and has a glass-steel facade linked by girders. A system of mirrors catches the sunlight and thus illuminates a boldly constructed atrium using bridge building engineering.

Po Lin Monastery, Hongkong (bottom left)

It seems impossible that there could be anywhere isolated in this pulsating trading centre of Hongkong, which has more than 6,000 people per square kilometre. Yet on Landao Island this is possible at least some of the time, when the visitors depart leaving only those who have retreated to the mountains here to meditate: the monks of Po Lin Monastery. The mountain location of this complex, however, attracts so many tourists that tranquillity has become a very rare commodity. Nevertheless, a 23 metre high Buddha reminds everyone to behave respectfully, so that amid the bustle there is still a little calm.

Old Town, Lijiang (bottom right)

China is populated by Chinese people — in such a huge country as that of the Middle Kingdom this can only be a gross propagandist simplification that completely ignores the complex structure of the nation. Around the northwest of the south Chinese Yunnan Province the Naxi live, a Tibeto-Burmese people with a very individual culture, which has its centre in Lijiang. The Old Town has been preserved in this 'Oriental Venice', 2,000 metres above sea level with its ancient water supply system, and it possesses a unique character with its gardens surrounded by brightly painted houses made of 'five-coloured stone'. Built in the 12th/13th centuries, it was declared a UNESCO World Heritage Site in 1997.

Korea *(South)*

Changdok Palace, Seoul *(top)*

The Korean traveller in the capital city of Seoul enters the old royal residence of Changdok, in English 'Palace of Wonderful Blessings', through a magnificent entrance gateway. For a long time only the inhabitants, namely members of the royal family, could enjoy this and only the ruler himself was allowed to enter the 'Secret Garden'. Nowadays, the public can enjoy the 'Hall of Radiating Government' as well as the extensive and fantasy-filled garden areas. In 1872, the palace stopped being the royal residence; in 1907, renovation work began. UNESCO World Heritage Site since 1997.

Kyongbok Palace, Seoul *(centre left)*

As the central tourist attraction in the South Korean capital, Seoul, the palace seems to bear its name in defiance: it is called Kyongbok, meaning 'Palace of Shining Happiness'. Yet the building dating from the 14th century has been burnt down several times by the Japanese and other enemies, the last time during the Second World War. Undeterred, however, Korean artists have repaired and renovated it, so that once again it offers a place to visit, full of landscaping and architectural charm: from graceful bridges spanning ponds, pavilions on islets full of blossom, pagodas and residential quarters of refined taste.

Jongmyo Shrine, Seoul *(centre right)*

Confucianism's commandment of reverence towards an individual after their death applies to the descendants. In China and Korea, which is much influenced by China, this developed into ancestor worship, most prominently found in the upper classes and still to some extent today. The ancestors of the kings received special veneration, of course, as can be witnessed in the Jongmyo Shrine, in the South Korean capital, Seoul. With music and sacrifices, the deceased rulers and their most senior advisers were venerated in the 'Hall of Eternal Comfort' or in that of the 'Most Commendable Followers'. Built in 1394, the building is still used today for ritual ceremonies. UNESCO World Heritage Site since 1995.

Seokguram Grottoes and Bulguksa Temple *(bottom)*

At the foot of Mount T'oham, three kilometres away from the old residence town of Kyongju, lies the Buddhist temple complex of Bulguksa. It dates from the period of the Three Kingdoms (8th century) and displays two of the most beautiful Korean pagodas. In addition, there is the bridge 'of the White' and that 'of the Blue Cloud', the bell pavilion and the paradise hall. The complex is 'blessed' from on high by the Seokguram Cave Temple on the mountain top. It is placed in an artificial grotto, whose showpiece is a 3.5 metre high Buddha and a whole array of 'Enlightened Beings'. UNESCO World Heritage Site since 1995.

Haein-sa Temple, Kaya Mountain
(top)

The woodblocks in the mediaeval monasteries in the Far East were not yet 'set' with movable characters, but could certainly be used in printing. One of these monasteries, still inhabited today by 250 monks and nuns, houses the most comprehensive collection of sacred scriptures of Mahajana Buddhism: 81,000 of the woodblocks are kept in the Haein-sa Monastery on Mount Kaya in central South Korea. This is the 'Tripitaka', which draws a steady flow of pilgrims to the sanctuary. The monastery consists of 50 buildings, which date back to a hermitage in 802 AD. Lovingly built on a wooded slope, the complex was declared a UNESCO World Heritage Site in 1995.

Korea *(North)*

Triumphal Arch, P'yongyang *(right)*

In the North Korean capital of P'yongyang there won't be many happy folk in front of the triumphal gesture of the arch, which the new Communist leaders of the country erected to celebrate the 1945 victory over the Japanese. It was not even their victory nor that of their protector, the USSR, which only attached itself to the American victory at the last minute. And the losers have long since become an economic power in the world again, whereas the triumphant Socialist-realist victor urgently needs their assistance. Still, the Koreans certainly had reason to celebrate the end of Japanese occupation.

Japan

Shirakami Mountains *(far top)*

Japan is about one and a half times bigger than the UK, but it has twice the number of inhabitants and in some parts is even uninhabitable. The remnants of natural landscape, such as the Shirakami Mountains in the north of the main island of Honshu, are thus immensely valuable. In this nature park, 170 square kilometres in size, there are still virgin beech forests that once covered the whole of the north. The mountains and forest areas are a refuge for black bears, monkeys (the most northerly in the world), reptiles, golden eagles and black woodpeckers, as well as several thousand insect and 500 plant species. UNESCO World Heritage Site since 1993.

Shirakawa and Gokayama *(top left)*

Half-timbered houses in Japan? The old Gassho architecture is similar, although the timbers are very small thus giving rise to the term 'folded hands style'. These houses can be found in villages in the previously fairly inaccessible mountains of Shirakawa and Gokayama in the centre of Honshu, north of Tokyo. The surprisingly large farmhouses have very steep, three-sided gable roofs and this roof space is used for silkworm breeding. UNESCO World Heritage Site since 1995.

Shinto Shrine, Nikko *(top right)*

In Nikko, in east Japan, a Shinto shrine was dedicated as a mausoleum for Tokugawa (1543–1616), founder of the last Shogun Dynasty in 1603, a year after his death. It is in exemplary style with its extensive layout and numerous buildings. What is noticeable is how much attention has been given by the architects and in subsequent extensions to integrate the architecture into the landscape and nature with its ancient trees. In so doing, they were fulfilling a Shintoist principle, according to which human action goes hand in hand with veneration of nature. UNESCO declared the complex a World Heritage Site in 1999.

Ginkaku-ji Temple, Kyoto *(top left)*

In the city centre of the Japanese city of Kyoto on Honshu, everywhere one looks one is sure to find at least one temple, Buddhist or Shintoist. There are some richly ornamented, while others are more simple, like the two-storey Ginkaku-ji pagoda set on an artificial pond amid the lush green of one of the many gardens. The sweeping reed roofs on both storeys give the building an air of gravity and at the same time refuge, which is what the faithful pray for in their worship.

Historic Monuments and Gardens, Kyoto *(top right)*

Myoshin-ji, Ninna-ji, Nishi Hongan-ji, Ryoan-ji, Seiryo-ji, Tenryu-ji, To-ji, and in nearby Otsu Enryaku-ji and in Uji Byodo-in — these are just a few of the 1,500 Buddhist temple complexes that grace Kyoto and its surrounding area, capital of the prefecture of the same name on Japan's main island of Honshu. Also of cultural value are the 200 Shinto shrines, some standing in enchanting gardens (photo shows the Heian shrine), and palaces such as the emperor's residence, rebuilt to the original design in 1856, and the Nijo palace dating from the beginning of the 17th century. UNESCO World Heritage Site since 1994.

Matsumoto Castle *(bottom)*

One castle but two pagodas: built next to each other in Matsumoto, a city in Nagano prefecture on Honshu, it comprises a three-storey and a five-storey structure dating from the 16th century and was a Shogun residence (military commanders of the emperor and the real holders of power in the land). Both buildings sit on a strong stone base and are enclosed by a moat. Their object was to exude power and the windows give an unwelcoming appearance because of their wooden grilles constructed for defensive purposes. However, from the top storey there is an excellent view over the grounds.

Golden Pavilion, Kyoto *(top left)*

However small and winding the gardens might be in the old town of Kyoto, the Japanese industrial metropolis on Honshu, there is always room for temples of all shapes and sizes. The famous Golden Pavilion of 1395 (rebuilt after the Second World War) stands in the middle of a park on an artificial lake. Does it have three or only two storeys? There is no pagoda roof over the ground floor, instead it is crowned with a golden balustrade that encompasses the second storey. It has the typical sweeping roof and also a gold crown, the balustrade for the top storey.

Yakushima Forest *(top right)*

Over ten metres of rain fall annually in the 108 square kilometre Yakushima Nature Reserve in the south of the Japanese island of Kyushu and on Yaku Island just offshore, where Myanoura rises to almost 2,000 metres. There are 1,000 year old Japanese cedars growing here and macaques and Sika deer enjoy protection. The 150 species of birds include rare Japanese wood pigeon species and there are 1,500 insect species represented. The flora ranges from subtropical plants in the lower regions to winter-hardy Alpine plants in the mountains. UNESCO World Heritage Site since 1993.

Buddhist Monuments at Horyu-ji, Nara *(bottom)*

Nara, on the main island of Honshu, was the capital of Japan in the 8th century, and nearby a Buddhist temple complex 'of the sublime law', consisting of 45 buildings spread out over a large area was built in the year 607 AD. Horyu-ji is made up of two complexes, the Western Precinct (Sai-in) with the double-storey Golden Hall, the Central Gate (Chumon) and the five-storey pagoda and the Eastern Precinct (To-in), where the fabulous Hall of Dreams can be gazed at. They are all masterpieces of early Japanese wood sculpture and together were declared a UNESCO World Heritage Site in 1993.

Kofuku-ji Hall, Nara *(top left)*

Together with other temples in the Japanese town of Nara on Honshu, the Kofuku-ji complex was declared a UNESCO World Heritage Site in 1998. The temple complex dates from the 12th century and deserves special attention due to its multi-storey pagoda and its large Assembly Hall with the elegant sweeping roof. Jutting far out, this shades the beautifully arranged facade and displays exquisite carving. The location of the sacred precinct in a carefully maintained park satisfies the Japanese wish to set religion within a framework of nature.

Historic Monuments and Gardens, Nara *(top right)*

Although Nara, on the island of Honshu, lost its capital city status in 784 AD, the Japanese rulers still beautified their one-time emperor's city by adding temples and gardens. The preserved shrines include the 'Sanctuary of the Great Buddha', the Kofuku-ji with multi-storey pagodas dating from the 12th century, the Todai-ji dedicated in 752 AD and the Kasuga Taisha Shrine in Kasugajama Forest dating from the Heian period (794–1185 AD). The palaces in the beautifully landscaped gardens have also made Nara a favourite destination and in 1988 it was declared a UNESCO World Heritage Site.

Fuji-san *(bottom)*

It has few equals in its supremacy and it is no accident that it is a Japanese shrine, 'Seat of the Gods': Fuji-san or Fuji for short on the main island of Honshu is the highest mountain in the country at 3,776 metres, a regular volcanic cone approximately 100 kilometres southwest of the capital, Tokyo. Visible from far away, it has become Japan's symbol, which people from all over come to, especially in the snow-free period during July and August. The last eruption was recorded in 1707, and the inactivity since then has led to research installations, hotels and temples being built on the edge of the 600 metre wide crater.

Himeji Castle (top)

The oriental archipelago of Japan is not really well known for castles and yet there are forts that are worth seeing, such as the one on the Himeyama in Himeji on the main island of Honshu, northwest of Kobe. Built in the 14th century and later extended, the complex is also called the 'White Egret Castle' because of its light-coloured, six-storey facade. It was surrounded by three moats and there were three donjons of up to 92 metres in height (accommodation and defensive towers). All that remains is the central part, so we can only guess how extensive the original fortifications must have been. UNESCO World Heritage Site since 1993.

Peace Memorial, Hiroshima (bottom left)

The start of the atomic era claimed 200,000 victims: on 6th August 1945 the US bomber 'Enola Gay' dropped the first nuclear bomb in history, nicknamed 'little boy' by the American military, on the Japanese city of Hiroshima in the southwest of the main island of Honshu. People and buildings were vaporised in the atomic blast, even far away from the hypocentre of the explosion there was only rubble, among which was the annealed, three-storey domed structure of the Industry Promotion Hall. Today these ruins are called the 'A-Bomb Dome' (Genbaku Dome) and were declared a UNESCO World Heritage Site in 1996 to serve as a warning for peace.

Shinto Shrine, Itsukushima (bottom)

Over 100 metres from the shore there is a kind of gateway, which in Japanese is called torii and when translated means 'bird perch'. It forms the entrance to the Shinto shrine on the formerly forbidden sacred island of Itsukushima on the Japanese Inland Sea, southwest from Hiroshima. It was first mentioned in 811 AD, repaired in the 12th century after fires and completely renovated and rebuilt in 1556. The extensive complex is dedicated to goddesses and includes amongst others the 'Hall of Cleansing', other halls and the torii mentioned above. As an example of the Shintoist philosophy of nature and culture, it was declared a UNESCO World Heritage Site in 1996.

Hiroshima Castle (top)

It had resisted many attacks and sieges in the past, but on 6th August 1945 even the fortified castle of Hiroshima was wiped out in the nuclear blast. It stood for almost 400 years on a really solid hillock, whose careful reconstruction using old drawings was completed in 1958. Charmingly situated on the Ota river delta, the fortress now bears no reminder of the atomic disaster, for in 1989 the interior was also renovated in the style once appreciated by the various aristocratic families. A museum has been added, featuring the "Samurai culture" and the town's history. There are old weapons to look at as well as documents describing the main stages in Hiroshima's development.

Fortified castle, Hirosaki (bottom)

At first sight, it does not seem possible that this idyll could have been built to ward off attackers. The castle at Hirosaki, situated in the far north on Honshu (Hondo), floats majestically above the red bridge and the water lilies in the moat. The reason for this effect is due to a massive, ochre-brown stone base set in the middle of a relatively flat landscape, barely visible between the bridge piers and upon which the castle stands. It thus seems as if the white castle tower is almost off the ground, especially as the gracefully curved roofs of the stories give the impression of wings. This castle, like most of the fortified castles in the country, was built during the troubled times of the civil war (finished in 1576).

257

Philippines

Rice Terraces, Mountains of Ifugao
(top)

Probably the biggest rice-growing terraces in the world in the Central Cordilleras in the north of the Philippine island of Luzon, they are testimony of the necessity not to spoil or indeed destroy nature through human exploitation: the paddy fields of the rice farmers at Ifugao cover an area of over 250 square kilometres rising up to 1,500 metres above sea level and have been cultivated in this way for over 2,000 years. The 'steps to heaven' are shored up with six to ten metre high stone walls and by means of these breaks in the slope ensure optimum irrigation of the areas under cultivation. UNESCO World Heritage Site since 1995.

Baroque Churches in Manila, Santa María, Paoay and Miag-ao *(top)*

The Philippines do not quite fit into the picture of the Far East, because, unlike the surrounding countries, Christianity has a stronger influence here. The reason for this is that early in the 16th century they were introduced to Spanish Catholicism, in contrast to other countries that were colonised later by Dutch merchants or British seafarers. In 1521 the remnants of Ferdinand Magellan's (Magalhães) world circumnavigation expedition reached Manila and in 1571 it became the centre of the mission colony run by Augustinians, Franciscans and Jesuits. Their baroque churches on the island of Luzon in Manila, Santa María, Poay and Miag-ao are splendid edifices of their faith and were declared a UNESCO World Heritage Site in 1993.

Tubbataha Reef Marine Park *(centre left)*

About 180 kilometres southeast of Puerto Princesa, the capital of the Philippine island of Palawan, lies a marine nature reserve covering 332 square kilometres in the middle of the Sulu Sea. There are two flat atolls here, with coral reefs that barely protrude a metre above the surface of the sea, yet plunge steeply 100 metres downwards. These reefs have formed lagoons that offer ideal breeding and nesting sites for seabirds and marine turtles. The shallow waters also provide a nursery for many fish species and a total habitat for others. UNESCO World Heritage Site since 1993.

Puerto Princesa Subterranean River National Park *(centre right)*

Erosion has formed absurd rock formations and caves in a vast karst landscape in the Saint Paul Mountain Range near Puerto Princesa, the capital of the Philippine island of Pulawan. An underground river was discovered in one of the caves. What is remarkable about it is that it flows underground right into the sea, so that its lower reaches are subject to tidal influences. Amphibian animals and plants find an ideal habitat in its brackish water. Named after the capital city, the national park is part of the Palawan Biosphere Reserve and was declared a UNESCO World Heritage Site in 1999.

Stilt Settlement on Mindanao *(bottom)*

Many tourists will experience a pang of conscience when they find out that much of what they find picturesque is the result of utter poverty. The people on Mindanao, the second largest island in the Philippines in the south of the republic, would probably prefer a pretty detached house in a healthy location to their stilt structures. But the descendants of ancient Malayan immigrants have not known anything different for centuries and are mostly too poor to be able to settle on land. Perhaps, though, their home is more important to them than comfort, and anyway their watery location makes them feel a bit safer from intruders such as wild animals.

Indonesia

Ujung Kulon National Park *(top)*

In the extreme southwest of the Indonesian island of Java, the Ujung Kulon peninsula together with the islands of Peucang, Panaitan and Krakatau on the Sunda shelf form the national park named after the peninsula, altogether 1,240 square kilometres in size. Seismologists and zoologists gather here, the former to carry out research into vulcanology and the frequent earthquakes in this region of tectonic instability, the latter to observe animals that have become rare, such as the Javan rhinoceros, sunda deer, estuarine crocodile, Indian python or osprey, all of which have found a home and protection here. UNESCO World Heritage Site since 1991.

Komodo National Park *(bottom left)*

The Komodo National Park, 2,200 square kilometres in size, is made up of a group of tiny and not so tiny Indonesian Sunda Islands as well as part of Flores and the Komodo Islands and provides protection to the Komodo dragon (a predatory lizard), which can be up to 3 metres long and is found nowhere else in the world. The mangrove jungle provides it and other reptiles with a refuge. Mammals and both land and sea-birds also find protection on land and in the sea between the islands, where giants such as the blue whale and the whale shark can be seen from time to time. UNESCO World Heritage Site since 1991.

Archaeological Site, Sangiran *(bottom right)*

The oldest find is at least 700,000 years old, probably a few more 100,000 years older: since the 1930s, fossil remains of human skeletons, belonging to the Homo erectus genus (formerly pithecanthropus = apelike man) continue to be found in the east Indonesian village of Sangiran, north of Surakarta. This is the first early human to be found outside Africa, that closely resembles modern humans in build. During the last few hundred millennia before Homo sapiens appeared, they had developed manual skills and had learnt how to control fire. UNESCO World Heritage Site since 1996.

Buddhist Temple Complex, Borobudur *(top)*

Around the year 800 AD, 10,000 coolies in Borobudur, central Java, set about the task of building over a hill. For 80 years, generations worked on this by building up layer upon layer of mortarless hewn stone, in total 56,640 cubic metres, until the original hill had completely disappeared under the artificial, and artistic, one. This square Buddhist temple is 123 metres long and rises in five square and three round terraces up to a height of 34 metres. Hundreds of Buddha statues decorate the structure, which was re-discovered in the 19th century and on which, with UNESCO assistance, restoration work was started in 1973 (World Heritage Site since 1991).

Hindu Temple Complex, Prambanan *(bottom)*

Twenty kilometres northeast of Yogyakarta in central Java, Indonesia, on the top storey of a terrace sit eight Hindu temples to the gods Shiva, Vishnu and Brahma dating from the 9th/10th centuries. Arranged concentrically on the terrace level beneath are 224 small so-called virgin temples and on the lowest level there is a square, exterior temple area, 390 metres in length. The largest Shiva temple complex in Indonesia, it was declared a UNESCO World Heritage Site in 1991.

Africa

Cradle of civilisation

It is only the north of the 'Dark Continent' that stepped into historical limelight even earlier than the European Old World. The gigantic statues of gods and pharaohs are the first important highlight in the history of mankind. And that it is found here is not only justified by the inimitable cultural achievements of the ancient Egyptians, but also by an achievement in nature that is crucial to us all: it was in Africa that an offshoot of hominids and from them early man, our ancestor, developed from a branch of the primate family. Over millions of years the family of man multiplied under the African sun. What is amazing is that more than half of what we define as prehistory took place between the Mediterranean Sea and the Cape of Good Hope. Other places only entered the history books thereafter. Strangely, after the hey-day of the Egyptians, most of the continent lay forgotten until the era of discovery, which brought it back to light and showed that cultures had flourished here completely overshadowing those of northern climes. A lack of written evidence, however, means that Black Africa's past can only be pieced together from archaeological finds, rock painting and orally handed-down stories. They tell of a unique spiritual link between humans and nature, in a landscape of vast variety from tropical, fertile regions to the picturesque stillness of the dunes.

263

Africa

Azores (Port.)
Terceira
Angra do Heroisme

Madeira (Port.)
Laurisilva

Canary Islands (Spain)
Gomera
Tenerife
San Christóbal
Garajónay National Park

ATLANTIC

OCEAN

St. Helena (Brit.)

GREECE
CYP

Mediterranean

Tipasa
Algier
Djemila
Annaba
Carthage
Kerkouane
Tunis
Hammamet
Timgad
Thugga
Sousse
Kairouan
El-Jem
TUNISIA
Tripolis
Bengasi
Cyrene
Alexandria
Abu Mena
Memphis
Giza
Abus
Saqqa
Dahsh

Tangiers
Tetouan
Oran
Rabat
Fès
Casablanca
Volubilis
Meknès
MOROCCO
Marrakesh
Atlas Mountains
Béchar
Beni Isguen
M'zab Valley
Agadir
Aït-Ben-Haddou
Sabratha
Leptis Magna
Ghadamis

Sahara

Sahara
Sahara

Marsuk
LIBYA
EGYPT

Tassili n'Ajjer
Tadrart Acacus
Hoggar Massif
Tamanrasset

Abu

El Aaiún

Western Sahara (under Moroccan administration)

ALGERIA

MAURETANIA
Nouakchott

MALI

Aïr and Ténéré National Nature Reservat

NIGER

Djoudj National Park
Dakar
SENEGAL
Senegal
Île de Gorée
GAMBIA
Banjul
GUINEA-BISS.
Bissau
GUINEA

Bandiagara
Djenné
Niamey
BURKINA
Ouagadougou
FASO
Bobo-Dioulasso
Niger
Bamako
BENIN

Kano
Zaria
Maiduguri
Ndjamena

CHAD

SUDAN
El

Conakry
Freetown
SIERRA LEONE
Monrovia
LIBERIA

Comoë National Park
IVORY COAST
Yamoussoukro
Taï National Park
Abidjan
Kumasi
GHANA
TOGO
Lomé
Sekondi-Takoradi

Oshogbo
Ibadan
Porto Novo
Lagos
Benin
NIGERIA
Abuja
Enugu
Port Harcourt

St. Floris National Park

CENTRAL AFRICAN REPUBLIC

CAMEROON
Douala
Malabo
Yaoundé
Bangui

EQUATORIAL GUINEA
S. Tomé
S. TOMÉ & PRINCIPE
Libreville
GABON
Dja Faunal Reserve
Ubangi
Congo
CONGO
Mbandadaka
Brazzaville
Kinshasa
Pointe Noire
Cabinda (part of Angola)
Matadi
Kikwit
Kananga
Mbuji-Mayi

Okapi National Park
Kisangani
Virunga National Park
RWAND
Bukavu
BUR
Buju
DEM. REP.
CONGO

Luanda

ANGOLA
Benguela

Likas
Lubu
Kitwe
Lusaka
ZAMBIA
Lake Tangar

Victoria Falls
Bulawa
ZIMBAB
Gt.-Zir

Okavango Delta
Brandberg
Mana Natic
Zambezi

Swakopmund
Walvis Bay
Windhoek
NAMIBIA
BOTSWANA
Gaborone
Pretoria
Mb
Johannesburg
Lüderitz

Kimberley
Oranje
Bloemfontein
Maseru
LESOTHO
Sterkfontein
SOUTH AFRICA
East Londo

Table Mountain
Robben Is
Cape Town
Cape of Good Hope
Port Elisabeth

0   500   1000   1500
km

Azores *(Portugal)*

Angra do Heroísme, Terceira

An earthquake in 1980 showed what would happen if no effort was made to preserve the historic centre of the city of Angra do Heroísmo on the south coast of Terceira Island in the Portuguese Azores. Partly rebuilt since the destruction are the Saviour Cathedral, heavily decorated in the Emanuel style of the 16th century, the São Francisco Monastery, a baroque Jesuit church, and the Castelo São João Batista, Portugal's largest fortification to safeguard this important base on the way to the colonies in the New World. UNESCO World Heritage Site since 1983.

Madeira *(Portugal)*

Laurisilva Forest, Madeira

One of the loveliest landscapes of Portugal lies far out in the Atlantic: the island of Madeira, an attractive destination both for crowned heads and the common tourist. However, the intensive human exploitation of the paradise also threatens it and that is why a natural monument was protected by law as a UNESCO World Heritage Site in 1999: the Laurisilva of Madeira in the centre of the island, the largest connected laurel forest, home to many plant families occurring only here in such an environment and many animals such as the Madeiran long-toed pigeon. 90 % of the area is primeval forest undisturbed by humans.

Canary Islands (Spain)

La Laguna, Tenerife (top right)

Situated 550 metres above sea level, the narrow streets and shuttered house facades with brightly coloured window shutters, wood-carved balconies and decorated doors lend an air of the old colonialism of the 16th century to San Cristóbal de la Laguna on the Spanish Canary Island of Tenerife. Established in 1496, the nucleus on the hill slope was extended by the Lower Town with a grid network of streets and wide squares. The town owed its planned layout to promotion to capital of the island, a role that only passed to Santa Cruz in 1723. That protected La Laguna from too much unchecked modernisation and made this university town since 1817 a UNESCO World Heritage Site in 1999.

Garajonay National Park, La Gomera (bottom)

Laurisilva forest and the grounds of the Garajonay National Park in the mountainous centre cover ten percent of the surface of the Spanish Canary Island of La Gomera. The park was set up to protect the extraordinary flora, especially the massive laurel trees, which have their best chance of survival here. The mist sprays its branches continuously and the mountain springs and streams provide indispensable moisture. The 3,000 hectares of forest are only broken up by rocks, which give bizarre emphasis to the landscape. Of the 450 different plant species in the national park, 34 are unique to here. There are also two species of laurel pigeons here that are found nowhere else. UNESCO World Heritage Site since 1986.

Morocco

Medina, Tetouan *(far top left)*

Islamic tolerance was foreign to the Christians, who had struggled to regain control of the Iberian Peninsula from the Arabs during centuries of fighting. After the victory in 1492, many of the Moors stayed in Spain, but then were driven out by Spain's drastic measures. The refugees settled in North African cities such as Tetouan (Tetuán in Spanish) in north Morocco, imbuing it with their characteristic lifestyle and architecture. The Old City describes this perfectly: a defensive mentality arising from long battles has produced fortresses and the caliph's palace, the city wall and narrow streets. The decoration on the mosques shows features of traditional Moorish elegance. UNESCO World Heritage Site since 1977.

Hassan Tower, Rabat *(left)*

Unfinished buildings sometimes possess a particular charm, and a visit to the Hassan Tower in the Moroccan capital underlines this idea. It is so named because it stands in the former part of the city called Hassane, which does not exist anymore – neither does the mosque for which the tower was designed as a minaret. Back when the city was founded in the 12th century, it was supposed to be the biggest settlement in the Maghreb, but they never got further than building the tower, and in 1755 an earthquake destroyed the actual ruins and also damaged the tower. Still 44 metres high, it is all that remains of a grand plan.

Grand Hassan II Mosque, Casablanca *(centre far left)*

Six years before his death in 1999, King Hassan II of Morocco was able to officially open the tallest religious building in the world in the port of Casablanca: the Hassan II Mosque, which is named after him. It took 35,000 labourers seven years to build, producing a prayer hall 200 x 100 x 60 metres in size for 25,000 believers, and with a 200 metre high minaret towering over another 75,000 people attending prayers on the beach. A laser beam shines 35 kilometres from the tower towards Mecca. The building, which cost around 350 million pounds, summons the people to worship their God.

The Old City of Fès *(bottom)*

East of the Moroccan capital, Rabat, is the double city of Fès, built in the 8th century. The Old City of Fès el-Bali is one of the best-preserved mediaeval medinas in North Africa (the photo shows the view through one of the city walls to the old city). Just as in Christian cities of that period, religious structures were the main focus, such as the Kairaouine Mosque, which was already there 100 years after the city was built and was extended more than once. Its inner courtyards decorated with tiles in a variety of colour designs, the luxurious fountains and the high gateways compel non-Muslims not only to respect, but even to admire. Just as religion is still very much alive here, so the dyers of Fès are busy producing natural dyes in a separate part of city. UNESCO World Heritage Site since 1981.

The Old City of Meknès (top left)

Islam allows a Muslim man to take four wives, but it does not say anything about other types of relationships, so it is no wonder that the development of harems got out of hand in the courts of the caliphs and sultans. In 1672, when Sultan Moulay Ismail had a palace built in Meknès in Morocco, the apartments for his 600 ladies were by far the biggest and most elegant part of his palace buildings. The stables for his 12,000 horses and the accommodation for his soldiers were kept much more simple. The Sultan also had mosques and fortifications built, such as the 25 kilometre long enclosure wall round the Old City, which was designated a UNESCO World Heritage Site in 1996 (the photo shows the view into a bazaar).

The Atlas Mountain Range (top right)

The Atlas mountain range, which extends through Morocco, Algeria and Tunisia, forms a sort of northern frontier to the massive North African Sahara Desert region. Only broken by the Strait of Gibraltar, it forms a bridge in Morocco both geologically and culturally between Africa and Europe. In geological terms, the Atlas Mountains, which were folded upward about 70 million years ago, display Alpine features with their jagged peaks and sheer drops and reach similar heights to the Alps with Morocco's Jebel Toubkal at 4,165 metres in the High Atlas Mountains. They act as a weather divide, even climate divide, by separating the sub-tropical Mediterranean zone with its winter rain from the arid climate of the Sahara. The Atlas Mountains, which are often snow-capped, look especially magnificent when viewed from the barrenness of the Sahara.

Fortress City of Aït Ben Haddou
(above centre)

Until the Arabs conquered North Africa, it was the Europid Berbers who were in charge here. They defended their traditions with tenacity, but were converted to Islam and driven out. Their defensive attitude is seen in their settlement patterns, the largest of which was usually built around a fortified area, called the kasbah. However, there are also settlements that are completely fortified such as Aït Ben Haddou, northwest from Ouarzazate on the southern edge of the High Atlas Mountains. The visitor is met with tall, reddish-yellow mud brick structures consisting of sloping, layered walls with characteristic patterns. UNESCO World Heritage Site since 1987.

Excavation Site at Volubilis (below centre)

In arid Africa, where not all ruins were immediately built over, especially in areas of low population density, travellers have often discovered these antiquities by accident: a Roman city springs up in the middle of the barren landscape. South of Fès, the 2nd and 3rd century ruins of ancient Volubilis rise up majestically and also bear witness to mighty human endeavours of the past. A particularly clear example of this is the triumphal arch of Emperor Caracalla from the year 217 AD, now left standing on its own. However, the temple remains, the facade of the court basilica and the house of columns are all evidence of a past that will not die if we remember it, for without it we would be impoverished. And in order for this not to happen, the ruins were made a UNESCO World Heritage Site in 1998.

The Old City, Marrakesh (bottom)

The epithet 'Red Pearl' was given to the Old City of Marrakesh in the centre of Morocco, because the 12 kilometre long walls and watchtowers are built of red sandstone. Despite the flowery name, they still look extremely fortified: one of the massive city gates is called 'Gate of the Thickened Grape Juice'. You can certainly buy it in the Jemaa el-Fna Square in the centre, where traders from the surrounding area sell everything that appeals to the locals as well as the tourists. Around it are grouped the mosques and the largest Koran school in the whole of the Maghreb, built in the 14th century. UNESCO World Heritage Site since 1985.

Algeria

Roman Ruins, Djemila *(below right)*

A common sight in North Africa: rows of columns, walls, triumphal arches, facades of baths and temples on the edge of Small Kabylie west of Constantine in Algeria. It gives the impression of being part of the spectacular hilly landscape, yet it is just a memorial to its decline. Now there are only ruins where once Rome's symbols of power seemed built to last forever. Where Djemila stands today, the historical ruins tell of the highly developed Roman city of Cuicul, whose streets and plumbing system are evidence of a sophisticated civilisation. In the 7th century it fell victim to Islamic expansion. UNESCO World Heritage Site since 1982.

The Ruined City of Tipasa *(below left)*

The Romans had cause to be grateful to the Numidians in North Africa in the battle against the Phoenicians (Punics) for supremacy in the Mediterranean. As a result, Numidia retained formal independence right into the first century, evidence of which can be seen today in Tipasa, west of Algiers. Outside the modern city, Roman relics dominate the ruins; but there is also a burial mound, 60 metres long and 34 metres high, for King Juba II, who ruled the de facto Roman province at the time of the birth of Jesus. Other signs of Roman life are: an amphitheatre, baths, temple, a 'Fresco Villa', early Christian religious structures. It all fell into decay after the Vandals captured it and came to an end when the Arabs stormed it in the 7th century. UNESCO inscribed Tipasa in the list of World Heritage Sites in 1982.

Roman Ruins, Timgad *(far bottom left)*

Given the splendour of the site, the old name seems more suitable: Colonia Marciana Traiana Thamugadi. The place fell into decline, as did the name, and became a ruin with the modern-day Timgad taking its place. Following its founding by Emperor Trajan (98–117 AD) – see classical name – around 100, the Roman colony flourished on the northern slopes of Aurès, about 40 kilometres east of Batna in Algeria. According to the archaeological finds excavated since 1880, the city was constructed to a grid plan and had everything that Roman civilisation could offer: theatre, triumphal arch, baths, temple and plumbed drinking water. UNESCO honoured that in 1982 by designating Timgad a World Heritage Site.

Kasbah, Algiers *(far bottom right)*

When the Iberian Peninsula was regained in 1492, the Spaniards could not wholly come to terms with the fact that the Reconquista era was at an end. Time and again they tried to spread their power into North Africa. In turn, the Arabs fortified their cities, and the Old City (Kasbah, see picture) of the Algerian capital, Algiers, with its houses towering up the cliff, is both a well-preserved and living example of this. In 1516, Spain relinquished control and in 1541 the city was even able to resist an invasion by Emperor Charles V. Well known for piracy, Algiers was frequently involved in fighting, but was not conquered until 1830 by the French. It was in the Kasbah in the 1950s that the struggle for independence had its roots. The Algerians are proud of their Kasbah and of its status since 1992 as a UNESCO World Heritage Site.

Beni Isguen (top left)

Built in 1347, the 'holy city' of Beni Isguen is the last of the five settlements in the Algerian valley of M'zab established in the Middle Ages by the Mozabites, a Berber tribe converted to Islam. Its layout reflects the societal structure of this uncompromisingly patriarchal, religious world. The honeycomb arrangement of the dwellings stretching upwards to the central mosque, from where the muezzin calls the people to prayers, is a manifestation of a deep faith and at the same time a rejection of today's secular values. Visitors are not allowed to enter the city without a guide and must leave before dark. Along with the other cities in the oasis valley, Beni Isguen became a UNESCO World Heritage Site in 1982.

Hoggar Mountains (top right)

Rising majestically in the central Sahara in the south of Algeria is the Hoggar Massif, a craggy mountainous desert, the only one of its kind. Although the word 'weather' does not really apply in this never-changing shimmering heat, the highly accomplished stonemasonry skills of wind and water are visible here. The temperature fluctuations between day and night have split rocks and created rubble wasteland, the wind has formed precipices and infrequent, but devastating rainfall has gouged out ravines – a destructive beauty.

The M'zab Valley (above centre)

An oasis region in the mid Sahara, the M'zab Valley illustrates particularly well how the devout Islamic inhabitants of the hinterland are worlds apart from the bourgeois intellectuals in the Algerian coastal cities. There is a collection of five strict Muslim Berber cities here, of which Ghardaïa (built in 1048, see photo) and Beni Isguen (1347) are typical: they are all grouped around a mosque, usually built on top of a hill, with its minaret pointing skywards in an almost threatening way. Since their establishment in the Middle Ages, these settlements have scarcely altered, nor has their spiritual world changed much. A clash with the modern world was unavoidable. However, just as they need modern aids, so the modern world needs their monuments to understand their cultural significance. Consequently, M'zab became a UNESCO World Heritage Site in 1982.

Sahara (below centre)

Only the oceans could be a greater wonder of the world than the Sahara in terms of size. Otherwise, there is nothing to match the Sahara, which, extending 6,000 kilometres east-west and 2,000 kilometres north-south, is the largest arid region in the world. Almost all of North Africa, a third of the whole continent, has been swallowed up since the last Ice Age, when a Mediterranean climate flourished. But if you are expecting endless, monotonous, undulating dunes, then you will be amazed at the variety of landscape between the Atlantic and the Red Sea. High mountains alternate with wadis, salt deserts with forests of rock, limestone formations with charming oases. For the Sahara is certainly not dead, its web of life is simply on an enormous scale.

Rock Painting at Tassili n'Ajjer (bottom)

Right in the south-east corner of Algeria, the mountainous Tassili n'Ajjer National Park is probably the best example of the extreme desert landscape. Aeons ago this must have been a much more hospitable area, because in the 80,000 square kilometres of wild country are to be found works of art showing great activity, created by evidently well-nourished stone-age artists. Today's 'Forest of Sandstone Rock' reveals that at that time (around 10,000 years ago) there must have been forests, because, apart from humans, the pictures are full of hippopotami, cattle, elephants and giraffes. UNESCO World Heritage Site since 1982.

Tunisia

Ruins of Carthage *(top)*

"Ceterum censeo, Carthaginem esse delendam" – "Besides, I declare that Carthage must be destroyed" – this was the sentence that the Cato the Elder (234–149 BC) uttered at the end of every political speech in Rome. His wish was granted just three years after his death, when, after winning the 3rd Punic War, the Romans destroyed their old North African rival. Today, the site of the ruins lies to the north of the Tunisian capital, Tunis, and still gives an idea of what a great power was based here or, more precisely, what great powers, for the archaeological treasures also include the relics of the Roman city built on the rubble of Punic Carthage. They have now been excavated (see photo) and smaller finds are on display in museums. The excavation site became a UNESCO World Heritage Site in 1979.

Medina, Hammamet *(bottom left)*

Situated on the gulf of the same name amongst citrus, olive and almond tree groves, Hammamet with its smart fishing harbour is today a favourite holiday resort on the Tunisian coast. A well-preserved ringwall with projecting square towers still surrounds the Old City (medina). Inside the wall there is busy activity. When the Moors were driven out of Spain, some settled here and established this new town of Hammamet in the 15th century.

The Old City, Tunis *(below right)*

The old city of the Tunisian capital of Tunis is worth a visit, with the mosques numbering among its outstanding sights. It fell into Arab hands in 698 AD and blossomed into one of the wealthiest cities in the Mediterranean. This resulted in extravagant religious architecture: one of the first to be built, and later made more splendid, was the Grand or Olive Tree Mosque, which was begun in 732 AD and extended chiefly between the 13th and 15th centuries. During this time the Kasbah mosque was also built, later the Sidi Jussuf mosque and the Dyers mosque. The image of this self-confident Islamic city has also been enhanced by palaces and public buildings, for which it was declared a UNESCO World Heritage Site in 1979.

Punic City and Necropolis, Kerkouane *(far bottom right)*

In 574 BC, Phoenician refugees from Tyre (Lebanese coast), which was threatened by the Persians, were looking for a spot to establish their community and discovered it on the northern point of Cap Bon Peninsula, modern-day Tunisia. Here they built Kerkouane, later destroyed by the Romans, forgotten and covered up by the desert sands. Excavation work has been carried out on it since the 1950s. The only Punic settlement never to be built over, its relics give us an insight into the way of life of a sophisticated society, which must completely overshadow the Graeco-Roman one. A necropolis of 200 graves dating from its beginnings allows us to draw conclusions about the cult of the classical inhabitants. UNESCO World Heritage Site since 1987.

The Old City, Kairouan *(below right)*

Many poets and artists have described the view of the central Tunisian city of Kairouan, south of Tunis, as "a vision". If it enthuses poets and artists, there must be more to it than just sights; they were also taken with the exotic atmosphere and the busy life. Mention must also be made of the Grand Mosque with its vaulted hall supported by a veritable forest of columns with relief capitals and its mihrab (prayer niche) decorated with wonderful tiles. Since 1052 massive city walls have protected this house of God and the palaces of the mighty. UNESCO World Heritage Site since 1988.

The Old City, Sousse *(far bottom right)*

On 12th April 1943, a German armed forces communiqué reported that rearguard units of the German-Italian army section in Africa had brought enemy frontline tanks to a standstill at Sousse in Northern Tunisia. Unfortunately, the consequences of that battle can be seen today, where parts of the city wall dating back to the 9th century were breached. It is indeed fortunate that there was otherwise not much damage to the 9th century Grand Mosque (see photo) and the 8th century fortified monastery (Ribat) in the Old City. In particular, the Roman catacombs, in which about 15,000 people were interred between the 2nd and 4th centuries, remained undamaged. UNESCO World Heritage Site since 1988.

Amphitheatre, El-Jem *(top)*

Many theatres are called 'castle', a fact known not only by the Viennese. Barricading herself in against the advancing Arabs in the Thysdrus amphitheatre, modern-day El-Jem in Tunisia, south of Sousse, a Berber leader showed how the ancient Roman theatres literally lived up to that name. In the end it did not help, but it drew such respect from the attackers that they did not cause unnecessary damage to the giant circle for 35,000 spectators. So much of it is preserved today that one can admire the architecture and planning of these classical buildings. With dimensions of 148 by 122 metres floor area and 36 metres high, it reflects the imperial self-confidence of the architect. UNESCO World Heritage Site since 1979.

Ruins of the Classical City of Thugga *(bottom left)*

Besides the excavation site in Carthage, the most important archaeological site in Tunisia is the village of Dougga, situated to the west of the Hill of Tunis, its name hardly changed from the classical name of Thugga. The Numidian marble from the local quarries was highly prized in classical times and was also used in local buildings, for example the Roman amphitheatre. In the centre of the ruins is the old forum, the traditional centre of communications in Roman towns. The column-lined square is surrounded by temples in which Fortuna, Concordia and Saturn were worshipped. The Capitol (see photo) is the most impressive, its massive portico decorated with reliefs having remained almost intact.

Libya

The Ruins of Sabratha (top left)

As in so many places in North Africa, the Romans took over the Phoenician heritage of Carthage in Sabratha, situated 80 kilometres west of modern-day Tripoli in Libya. After its destruction in 146 BC, the victors immediately took control of the profitable trading city, which stood at the end of the trading route across the Sahara to the Mediterranean coast. The city flourished due to its situation in the vast domestic Roman market, but the Vandals' destruction in 455 AD left it in ruins: an almost intact theatre, the forum, various temples, the marketplace (basilica), early Christian churches. The excavation site became a UNESCO World Heritage Site in 1982.

The Ruins of Cyrene (far top right)

The Libyan region of Cyrenaica got its name from a Greek colony, which was founded by settlers from the island of Santorini in 631 BC: Cyrene lies on the northernmost Mediterranean tip of this region, or more precisely, used to lie, for there are now only ruins. They are mostly Roman relics, since from 96 BC the Romans held sway for many centuries, before the Arabs came in 642 AD and finally wiped out the city that had been rebuilt by Emperor Justinian (527–565 AD) following the destruction by the Vandals. In the 19th and 20th centuries, archaeologists excavated numerous temples, a 118 metre long stoa (covered colonnade with back wall), many hermae and sculptures at this site. UNESCO World Heritage Site since 1982.

The Old City, Ghadames (above right)

You will hardly have noticed the beauties of Libya's Old City of Ghadames, situated on the border of Tunisia and Algeria: the slaves that the Arab traders shipped along with other goods even in the 19th century. Ghadames was in fact the terminus of important caravan routes and the hub of north-south trade and of the east-west link between Cairo and Timbuktu. After the Arabs took over the erstwhile Roman settlement in 666 AD, a flourishing city developed with its traditional two-storey mud buildings. Today they seem picturesque to us and thus were given the status of a UNESCO World Heritage Site in 1988, following the re-housing of the inhabitants to more modern quarters. The photo shows the interior of a typical mud house.

Rock Paintings at Tadrart Acacus (right centre)

The artists could never have guessed that one day a frontier would separate all their artworks, which would force UNESCO to make two world heritage sites out of them. When the pictures in Tassili N'Ajjer in Algeria were given this status, Libya naturally insisted that there were also skilled stone-age artists working in its region in the Tadrart Acacus Mountains. The world organisation awarded it heritage status in 1985, thus honouring rock paintings, whose earliest examples were created around 12,000 BC. However, there is also rock painting thousands of years more recent in recorded history, providing evidence that the weather conditions now making it difficult to access prehistoric evidence did not exist then.

The Ruins of Leptis Magna (bottom)

There are advantages for future generations, when, after a city's destruction, it is left and not rebuilt or built upon – such is the case of the old Roman metropolis of Leptis Magna, situated east of Tripoli. The Arabs did in fact keep the city going for a while after earlier visitations by the Vandals and temporary repairs by Eastern Rome, but its decline finally drove them out in the 11th century. Since then, the desert sand has covered the remains of a great era: imperial baths, temple, town hall, marketplace, circus and forum. Since the 1920s much has been uncovered by excavation, showing that the emperors of the Severus dynasty, in particular, had generously promoted Leptis Magna. UNESCO World Heritage Site since 1982.

Egypt

Muntazah Palace, Alexandria (top)

Egypt is overflowing with classical monuments. One of the most important cities in the country is the Mediterranean city of Alexandria, yet it does not have much to offer. The reason being that the city established by Alexander the Great not much more than 2,300 years ago is relatively new. The cityscape is thus characterised by more recent buildings, of which one deserves special mention: the Muntazah Palace, which the viceroy had built in 1892 in the then Ottoman city, is decorated in the most tasteful neo-Byzantine style, even with a hint of Venetian thanks to the personal style of the Italian architect, Verrucci.

Suez Canal (bottom left)

Even the ancient Egyptian pharaoh Sesostris III (1878–1840 BC) considered linking the Mediterranean and the Red Sea by a navigable waterway. However, it was only in the 19th century, using plans of Ferdinand Lesseps (1805–1894) that the ancient dream of a canal link to shorten the sea route from Europe to India, Australia and the East Asia was realised. Finished in 1869 and with no locks, the Suez Canal from Port Said in the north to Suez at the southern exit is 195 kilometres long, widened from an original width of 52 metres to 365 metres and dredged from an original depth of 12 metres to 20 metres. Around 20,000 ships pass through the waterway annually.

Abu Mena (bottom right)

A Roman officer from Alexandria by the name of Abu Mena or Menas refused to kill Christians during the persecution of Christianity by Emperor Diocletian, declaring that he himself was a Christian. The emperor felt obliged to take severe action against Abu Mena, and on 11th November 296 AD he was executed and buried in a shallow grave 40 kilometres south of Alexandria. However, Christians built a monastery over his grave and venerated him as a saint. According to legend, a spring bubbled up out of Mena's grave, turning the arid land into a paradise. The desert has the upper hand again, since 1961 excavated parts remind us of the monastery. UNESCO World Heritage Site since 1979.

Islamic Cairo

Due to the enormous size of the modern Egyptian capital, it is easy to overlook the richness of its heart. Already inhabited in pre-Christian times and during Roman occupation, Cairo gained its image from the Islamic conquerors, then from the Abbasids in 750 AD and finally from 969 AD onwards, when the Fatimites took possession of the city. The oldest Islamic building is the Mosque of Ibn Tulun (876–879 AD). The Fatimite buildings followed: the Mosque of Azhar (972 AD), the Mosque of al Hakim (990–1013 AD), the Mosque of al Akmar (1125), the fortification gates (1171–1176), the citadel (1179) and especially the Mosque of Sultan Hassan (1356–1362). The ensemble was declared a UNESCO World Heritage Site in 1979.

Mosque of Azhar, Cairo (bottom left)

Just three years after the Fatimites took control in Egypt (969 AD), the Azhar Mosque was built in Cairo as a house of prayer and school dedicated to Mohammed's daughter, Fatima. Worthy of note are the inner courtyard (sahn) surrounded by arcades of depressed arches (see photo) and the three very differently designed minarets. The one above the battlement tower has a double spire and was built at the beginning of the 16th century. The Azhar Mosque is the oldest Islamic university, starting its teaching as early as 975 AD. Together with the other Islamic buildings, it was declared a UNESCO World Heritage Site in 1979.

Mosque of Sultan Hassan, Cairo (below right)

Although designed almost as a fortress, this mosque in Cairo is splendidly ornamented with columns, mosaics and gold decoration. It dates from the 14th century, originally had three minarets, two of which have collapsed. At 80 metres, the one remaining is one of the tallest in the city. Covered by a dome, the well in the inner courtyard (sahn) is used for ritual washing; the sahn is entered from four archways. The mosque houses four schools for the four different Islamic denominations. The mosque was declared a UNESCO World Heritage Site in 1979.

Museum for Islamic Art, Cairo (right centre)

The building itself is a work of art: in the heart of the Egyptian capital, Cairo, is the Museum for Islamic Art, a magnificent cube-shaped building with columns lining the windows and its entrance door extending over the two floors. Its exhibits, of which there are over 80,000, reflect through craft and art works the development of Islamic culture from its beginnings up to the end of the Ottoman Empire in the 20th century. Two whole rooms are given over to textile treasures, rare gold and silver coins, jewellery (see photo) and royal decorations. The library contains a collection of practically all titles on Islamic history and particularly valuable copies of the Koran. UNESCO World Heritage Site since 1979.

Egyptian Museum, Cairo (far bottom right)

Even today the Egyptians profit from their country's long past: the monuments from the time of the pharaohs that are still standing attract visitors like a magnet, but they also pour into the museums, of which the most comprehensive by far is the Egyptian Museum, situated in the centre of the capital city Cairo, with its characteristic skylight dome. Nowhere else in the world can one find such a variety of exhibits, that bring to life one of the first advanced civilisations in human history. Mention should be made of the treasures of the only undamaged pharaoh tomb, which is representative of them all: the possessions from the tomb of the young pharaoh Tutenkhamun are laid out (see photo), giving an insight into the advanced development of splendour in the ancient Egyptian theocracy.

The Pyramids of Giza (top left)

Neither before nor after were such enormous monuments built for the ancient Egyptian pharaohs as for the pharaohs of the 4th Dynasty in the 26th century BC: the three Pyramids of Giza belonged to the Seven Wonders of the Ancient World and still amaze us today. At 147 metres high and 230 metres long at the base, the Pyramid of Cheops is the largest, the pyramid built for the pharaoh Chephren is slightly smaller and that for King Mycerinus much smaller. To the visitor it looks as if the monumental mausoleums are being watched over by the equally colossal figure of the Sphinx. The Pyramids of Giza, together with the Sphinx, were declared a UNESCO World Heritage Site in 1979.

Sphinx (top right)

In order to express the superhuman power of the ancient Egyptian pharaoh, the Egyptians devised the mythological creature of the sphinx, in which human reason (head) is combined with animal strength (lion body). The largest and most famous sphinx is at the Pyramids of Giza, measuring 20 metres high and 73.5 metres long and sculpted out of the rock (UNESCO World Heritage Site since 1979). It is assumed that it represented the pharaoh Chephren (reigned 2520–2494 BC), but it was also identified with the god Horus. The Greeks adopted the figure, turning it into a female demon, however; that's why we refer to the Sphinx as a she.

Mosque of Ibn-Tulun, Cairo

Built during the time of the Abbasids (9th century), the Mosque of Ibn-Tulun is the oldest of the important Islamic buildings in the Egyptian capital Cairo. Its décor is simple; it has an open courtyard in the middle of which stands a well for the ritual washing. It is surrounded by three prayer halls, each with two bays and the sanctuary with four bays. Plaster screens with very beautiful patterns serve as windows on the walls of the mosque. The prayer niche (mihrab) is decorated with gold mosaic and mother of pearl and surrounded by four marble columns. The chancel is made of wood and dates from a slightly more recent period. Together with the other Islamic cultural monuments of Cairo, the mosque was declared a UNESCO World Heritage Site in 1979.

Mosque of Mohammed Ali, Cairo
(below)

Most recent of the largest houses of prayer in the Egyptian capital, Cairo, the Mosque of Mohammed Ali was built in 1830 in the Byzantine-influenced Ottoman style. Its rooms are decorated with ornaments, wall paintings and colourful windows. Due to the extravagant marble cladding, the building is also called the Alabaster Mosque. A courtyard on the eastern side with adjacent halls covered with a dome is designed for worship and prayers; it displays against one wall the clock tower given as a gift by the French King Louis Philippe. A courtyard on the western side offers the best view of the city, the Nile and the Pyramids of Giza. As part of the Old City, the Mosque was declared a UNESCO World Heritage Site in 1979.

Memphis and its Necropolis (top left)

One of the oldest Middle Eastern cities was the ancient Egyptian city of Memphis on the West Bank of the Nile, just south of Cairo. Apparently established by the first known pharaoh Menes in 2900 BC, Memphis was the capital of the kingdom until about 2200 BC. Thereafter, no longer the seat of government, Memphis still remained a significant trading centre, centre of administration and headquarters of the army. The only signs left of its one-time importance are the ruins of temples and some palaces as well as the pyramids and sphinxes nearby (see photo). This necropolis and the relics of Memphis were declared a UNESCO World Heritage Site in 1979.

Saqqara (top right)

The oldest part of the necropolis of ancient Egyptian Memphis is located in the village of Saqqara on the rocky West Bank of the Nile. In the 3rd millennium BC kings and dignitaries of the old kingdom had burial places built here, often in the form of pyramids. The largest and oldest is the step pyramid of Saqqara, which pharaoh Djoser (around 2609–2590 BC) from the 3rd Dynasty had built. It does not display the later, smoother shape. At its feet there are still remains of a replica of the Djoser Palace. After the kings of the next dynasty had their monumental pyramids built at Giza, later pharaohs returned to Saqqara, where a burial place for the sacred Apis bull has also been found.

Abusir Pyramids (centre)

Ten kilometres south of Giza lies an ancient Egyptian cemetery. The pyramids are only slightly younger than the northern giants, yet much more modest, reflecting the waning regal power at that time. Four pharaohs of the 5th Dynasty (around 2300 BC) had their last resting place built here and sanctified by a sun temple in the northwest of the area. The lesser prominence of this royal graveyard could not keep grave robbers at bay, but some of it remains, which anywhere else would have fallen victim to looters or — more politely — collectors.

The Pyramids of Dahshur (bottom)

To the southwest of the capital Cairo there is a large pyramid field. In addition to the mighty structures at Giza and the step pyramids of Saqqara, there are also monuments like these in Dahshur to the south, unfortunately mostly within the military zone. They are differentiated according to their colour: the white, black and, as the first of all 'correct' pyramids, the red pyramid. The strange bent pyramid in Dahshur (see photo) was built in the same way by King Snofru, founder of the 4th Dynasty in the 27th century BC. It got its name from the bent angle of inclination. UNESCO World Heritage Site since 1979.

The Colossi of Memnon, Luxor *(top left)*

They once guarded the funerary temple of pharaoh Amenophis III: the Colossi of Memnon at Thebes in modern Luxor. They have survived. They are gigantic statues, 18 metres high and with 3 metre wide feet, which are supposed to represent the dead. Their name is derived from a legendary king of Ethiopia in Greek mythology, who was killed by Achilles. According to history, following an earthquake in 27 AD that caused tension in the rock, the northerly statue began to 'sing' when warmed by the morning sun. The noise apparently stopped after repair work was carried out at a later date. The colossi was declared a UNESCO World Heritage Site in 1979.

Valley of the Kings, Luxor *(top right)*

Since the beginning of the 18th dynasty (1550 BC) most of the ancient Egyptian pharaohs had their tombs carved out of the rock walls of a desert gorge on the West Bank of the Nile opposite the capital, Thebes. This gorge is thus generally called the Valley of the Kings and allows access only from the north. Yet despite an assuredly careful guard, all the tombs were looted shortly afterwards. What riches and – more regrettably – cultural evidence were thereby lost is substantiated by the only undamaged tomb, that of the young pharaoh Tutenkhamun, certainly not the most magnificent. Together with Thebes and its necropolis, the valley was declared a UNESCO World Heritage Site in 1979.

The Nile *(bottom)*

From its furthest source to its mouth, the Nile measures 6,670 kilometres and is thus the longest river on the Dark Continent. Its catchment area covers almost 3 million square kilometres. After being joined by a number of tributaries, the Nile then flows on over 2,700 kilometres from Khartoum in Sudan to the Mediterranean Sea, bringing 34 billion cubic metres of water annually. Cutting through the Nubian limestone and sandstone table, it forms six cataracts (rapids), then cuts through the Egyptian desert land and branches into delta distributaries before reaching the mouth. With fertility ensured by its flooding, one of the oldest advanced civilisations was established on its banks more than 5 millennia ago.

Medinet Habu, Luxor *(top left)*

South of the Valley of the Kings, opposite modern-day Luxor and part of the Necropolis of Thebes is the Medinet Habu with the shrine of Pharaoh Thutmose III (1490–1436 BC) and the Funerary Temple of Ramesses III (1186–1155 BC). The entrance to the latter (see photo), known as the Syrian Gate, resembles a fortress and is unique in ancient Egypt. The apartments in the gate complex served as a harem. The temple itself displays the usual sequence of rooms: pylons, courtyards, hypostyle hall, sacrificial chamber and the inner sanctum. Left of the entrance there is a scaled-down replica of the Palace of the Pharaoh, for even in the afterlife the pharaoh did not want to miss his familiar surroundings. Together with the Necropolis of Thebes it was declared a UNESCO World Heritage Site in 1979.

Temple of Karnak, Luxor *(top right)*

It took two thousand years to build: the Temple of Karnak in Luxor, upper Egypt, served to venerate Amun, the main god of the empire. His temple forms the nucleus of the complex, whose main attractions, however, are the 'Forest of Columns' comprising 122 columns with papyrus capitals and the ram-sphinx corridor (see photo) in front of the temple complex. There is a central aisle through it, lined with a further twelve columns. Not far away, by the Sacred Lake, the 23 metre high obelisk of the pharaoh Thutmose III (1490–1436 BC) points up to the sky like an exclamation mark. Together with Thebes, the complex was declared a UNESCO World Heritage Site in 1979.

Temple of Hatshepsut, Luxor *(bottom)*

She called herself 'the pharaoh king', for there was not even a word for a female pharaoh: Hatshepsut was also the only woman on the ancient Egyptian throne, but one that put many of her male colleagues in the shade with her political wisdom and energetic dealings. She self-confidently established a remarkable monument by building her funerary temple in modern-day Deir el-Bahri near Luxor on the West Bank of the Nile. It is skilfully integrated into the landscape and rises up the slope of the rock face in three terraces. Rows of mighty columns form the facade of the individual storeys, the top one supporting the actual funerary temple.

Temple of Hathor, Dendereh (top left)

Even today, beauty and fertility belong together in all cults, without people actually being aware of it. But the Egyptians were very aware of it, when they depicted Hathor, the goddess of love, with a cow's head and horns. Not even the Greeks took exception to it, equating Hathor with their goddess of beauty, Aphrodite. Today we need help in forming a picture of the fervour of classical fertility rites. Visitors gain an impression of it when they visit the Temple of Hathor in Dendereh, Upper Egypt, whose preserved shape dates back to the 1st century BC.

Temple of Luxor (top right)

The ancient Egyptian main god, Amun, and the gods Khonsu and Mut form the religious 'Triad of Thebes'. Pharaoh Amenophis III (1402–1364 BC) dedicated a temple to it that lies today in Luxor on the East Bank. Of the original six colossal statues of pharaoh Ramesses II (1290–1224 BC), two remain, which were later positioned at the entrance. Two obelisks also stood here, of which only one remains, the other was presented to Paris in the 19th century by the Egyptian governor, Mehmet Ali, and now adorns the Place de la Concorde. A corridor of sphinxes leads to the temple, which together with Thebes and its necropolis was declared a UNESCO World Heritage Site in 1979.

Philae (centre)

South of Egypt's Aswan lay the former island of Philae on the Nile, which was flooded in the 1960s by Lake Nasser following the construction of the Aswan High Dam. The sacred burial sites dating from the late Pharaonic Era of the 4th to 2nd centuries BC were also more than half submerged, including an Isis and a smaller Hathor temple. Between 1972–1980, it was possible with international support to drain the former island temporarily, move the structures and rebuild them on the island of Agilkia. The relics of Philae, like Abu Simbel, were declared a UNESCO World Heritage Site in 1979. The photo shows the 'Kiosk of Trajan'.

Abu Simbel (bottom)

In the Nubian region of Egypt between the second and third Nile cataract, pharaoh Ramesses II (1290–1224 BC) had two cave temples carved out of the rock face by the river, dedicated to the gods Amun-Re and Re-Horakhty. In front of the pediment, gigantic statues, including those of the king and his wife, guard the richly decorated hypostyle hall inside. The construction of the Aswan High Dam would have drowned the priceless cultural monument in the floods of Lake Nasser. Thanks to international cooperation, the temple was successfully rescued by sawing it into 1036 blocks and re-building it 60 metres higher up under a concrete vault. UNESCO World Heritage Site since 1979.

Senegal

Île de Gorée *(right)*

The painful pages of history turn it into a moral tale that those living can never be reminded of too often. On a rocky island on Cape Verde opposite the Senegalese capital Dakar lies the village of Gorée, established by the Dutch in the 15ᵗʰ century and subsequently under British, then French rule. Before that, Columbus used it at the time of his voyages of discovery to the New World, where there was a need for a human workforce after the Indians were wiped out. If you have read the book 'Roots' by Alex Haley or seen the film, then you will have some idea of the misery of around 10 million people, who set out from here on their journey into slavery. It is as a reminder of this that Gorée was elevated to a UNESCO World Heritage Site (1978).

National Bird Sanctuary at Djoudj
(left)

Tamarisk and water lily, acacia and water ferns thrive in the delta mouth of the Senegal, in which an area of 160 square kilometres north of Saint Louis and Ross-Béthio has been set aside as a nature reserve. It is mainly concentrated around the silted up Djoudj distributary and offers ideal conditions for resident water birds as well as a stopover for migrating species, including European and North Asian ducks. At times, up to three million splashing sea-birds and waders cram into the nature reserve, which does not bother the pink pelicans breeding here at all, as the marshes and the sea nearby offer a rich supply of food. UNESCO World Heritage Site since 1981.

Mali

The Bandiagara Cliffs (top)

The ancient Egyptian gods are not dead. They continue to live in an altered form among the Dogon in south Mali. There are certainly clear links between the cult of the people in West Africa's sandstone country and the Nile culture. The harder living conditions in the rocky environment and the African influences, however, have produced more frugal design and art styles. Particularly good at carving, the Dogon craftsmen also know how to sculpt in stone and decorate their homes with cultic ceilings and facade painting, particularly zig-zag patterns, which evoke the life-giving rain. The 13 villages (see photo) on the plateau of Bandigara were declared a UNESCO World Heritage Site in 1989.

Islamic City and Pre-Islamic Sites, Djenné (below)

Where the upper reaches of the Niger branch out into a delta shape lies Djenné, a little town in the middle of Mali, with its large mosque built in the Sudanese mudbrick style with massive, stepped minaret towers (see photo). Some of the foundation wall dates back to the 13th century, but the present appearance of the house of prayer dates back about 100 years. As a trans-shipment centre for the trans-Saharan traders on the 'gold route' to Timbuktu, the town grew very quickly in importance, but was abandoned around 1400. Not far from the present-day city can be seen the ruins of this old Djenné. As Europeans arrived here very late in the 19th century, much of the old building in the city has remained and it was declared a UNESCO World Heritage Site in 1988.

Niger

Aïr and Ténéré National Nature Reserve

Antelopes and gazelles live on the edges, baboons in the mountains and fennec, the African fox, sometimes trots through the sand dunes. The Aïr Mountains and Ténéré Desert (see photo) together form a 77,000 square kilometre nature reserve in Niger, of which the desert only takes up a good third. Evidence of a saurian find indicates that it was not always so dry; these giant lizards required rich vegetation to survive. Apart from the animals already mentioned, the chief survivors here are plant species managing on little moisture and the Tuaregs, who are resourceful in tapping water supplies. The largest nature reserve in Africa was declared a UNESCO World Heritage Site in 1991.

Ethiopia

Ruins of Aksum *(far left)*

From a European viewpoint, the world and the Roman Empire mean one and the same thing in the term 'classical antiquity'. It's not only China and India that show us how unjust that is. Even within the orbit of the said empire itself and indeed in Africa, which is often underestimated, there were cultures that were more than a match for those of the Mediterranean. From approximately the 1st to 4th century, the kingdom of Aksum flourished, now a site of ruins north of Addis Ababa in Ethiopia. The carved stelae found in Aksum are striking, the largest of which measures 33 metres and lies on the ground broken. The second largest was taken to Italy in 1937 on the orders of Mussolini, the self-pronounced descendant of the Caesars, and the third largest at 24 metres still stands in situ along with many others. UNESCO World Heritage Site since 1980.

Fasil Ghebbi in the Gondar Region *(top left)*

What the British Air Force left undamaged during their battle against the Italian occupation in 1941 is still worth visiting, so much that UNESCO declared Fasil Ghebbi, the old Ethiopian emperor's residence northwest of Addis Ababa in Gondar, a World Heritage Site in 1979. Founded in the middle of the 17th century and developed intensively over 100 years, the city displays architectural elements of Arabic, African and European provenance. Structures such as the Royal Enclosure (1706) or the 'House of Song' (1721) as well as numerous churches are surrounded by a 900 metre long wall with massive watchtowers.

Carved Stelae, Tiya *(centre left)*

Even though it is not quite clear what exactly we have inherited, UNESCO has declared the finds in Tiya in the Ethiopian Sodo region, south of Addis Ababa, a World Heritage Site. What's clear is that these are remains of a culture that flourished long before the birth of Jesus, possibly simultaneously with the pharaonic heyday in Egypt to the north and perhaps even connected to it. Above all, the 32 stelae with their relief decoration (weapons, human-like figures) are highly revealing about the state of the art of stone-masonry at that time. Admittedly, a conclusive interpretation cannot be made.

Rock Churches of Lalibela *(bottom)*

Christianity has survived until the present day, although in a variety of forms. Threatened by Arabic influences, it quickly developed a deep popular piety that found expression in different cultic sites. One very special site contains the 13 rock-hewn churches of Lalibela, on the Amhara Plateau west of Gondar. The churches are hewn out of the stone, the most important is the Saviour Church (Bet Medhane Alem) built during the reign of King Lalibela (1181–1221) and situated at the highest point. Due to the special veneration accorded the Virgin Mother and probably also due to the magnificent design with bright frescoes, the more recent Virgin Mary church (Bet Maryam) matches it in popularity. UNESCO World Heritage Site since 1978.

285

Ivory Coast

Comoë National Park (top)

Covering 11,500 square kilometres, this is a large area protecting a large number of wild animals: with the River Comoë flowing through for 235 kilometres, the National Park in the Ivory Coast Republic is situated in low hills and consists mainly of wet and dry savannah, with only a small part covered by gallery forest, which, however, allows a wide range of rare and endangered plant species to flourish. The animal world is also well represented by leopards and panthers, African buffalo and hippopotami, Nile and slender-snouted crocodiles as well as numerous bird species, particularly herons, and was declared a UNESCO World Heritage Site in 1983.

Taï National Park (bottom)

A green belt of lowland rainforest once stretched from Ghana to Sierra Leone. If the last remnants are to be saved from unscrupulous human destruction, then the area between the Cavally and Sassandra rivers in the Ivory Coast Republic must be protected by law. Accordingly, in 1972 it was classified a National Park and in 1981 its importance was recognised by being elevated to the status of UNESCO World Heritage Site. It is home to Diana monkeys, giant pangolins, bush pigs, water chevrotain, colobus monkeys and 230 bird species with such delightful names as white-breasted guinea fowl or wattled cuckoo shrike.

Ghana

Traditional Ashanti Buildings, Kumasi (top)

The second largest city in the Republic of Ghana and capital of the Ashanti region is Kumasi. Here and in the surrounding villages one can still see the wattle and daub, mudbrick buildings with roofs of palm leaves of the Ashanti people. They are skilled potters, woodcarvers, goldsmiths and weavers, whose products are highly sought after by collectors. They are attracted by the apparently naïve designs, which on closer inspection turn out to be sophisticated abstraction and emphasis of the essential. The buildings and works of art have enjoyed special protection as a UNESCO World Heritage Site since 1980. The photo shows the shrine of a shaman.

Cameroon

Dja Faunal Reserve (below)

Monkeys are in their element here. This vast area of 5,300 square kilometres situated in a loop of the River Dja in Cameroon, southeast of the capital Yaoundé, was protected by law as long ago as 1950 and its large tracts of still undisturbed tropical rainforest offer ideal conditions for primates, such as the western lowland gorilla (see photo), the moustached, white-nosed and crowned guenon, mandrill and potto. While they swing through the trees, the giant forest hog grunts along the ground and the pangolin wiggles through the undergrowth. The Dja animal paradise was declared a UNESCO World Heritage Site in 1987.

287

Congo
(Democratic Republic)

Okapi Faunal Reserve *(top)*

As the name suggests, the reason for placing the area in Ituri in the northeast of the Democratic Republic of Congo (at that time still Zaïre) under protection was to protect the stock of okapis, which are only to be found in large numbers here (see photo). The sparsely populated region covering about 14,000 square kilometres is mostly forested and displays in addition a wonderful wealth of species: large herds of elephants are just as much at home here as leopards, various guenon species, river pig, porcupine, numerous monkey species, crocodiles and birds of all sizes, from the magnificent Congo peacock to the black guinea fowl. UNESCO World Heritage Site since 1996.

Virunga National Park *(below)*

In the border area between the Democratic Republic of Congo, Uganda (Ruwenzori) and Rwanda (Kiwu) there are three national parks. On the Congolese side there is the Virunga area of almost 8,000 square kilometres with numerous volcanic cones that are still active; its forests are home to the last remnants of the endangered mountain gorilla, threatened by political unrest and poaching. Placing it under protection as a UNESCO World Heritage Site (1979) has not changed much, at best it has caught the attention of worldwide publicity, to which even dictators are not indifferent. In addition to the large apes, the park offers a habitat to many other animals, including hippopotami, lions, okapis, warthogs and innumerable birds.

Kenya

Mount Kenya National Park

At 5,194 metres high, the second highest mountain in Africa gave its name to the country on the east coast of the continent: Kenya is proud of the giant, which towers up in the middle of the country, northeast of the capital Nairobi. An area of 584 square kilometres around the peak of the extinct volcano, at over 3,300 metres above sea level, became a national park in 1949 and a UNESCO World Heritage Site in 1997, for this transitional zone from tropical rainforest to the high glaciers is home to rare plants and animals: mountain bamboo, yew pine and lobelias grow here, mongoose (civets), rock hyrax, leopards and black rhinos as well as many bird species can be seen here.

Tanzania

Serengeti National Park I *(top left)*

"Serengeti must not die" – who doesn't remember one of the most important works of the zoologist, Bernhard Grzimek? That was in 1959 and the warning concerned an area that did survive without too much damage because of the worldwide publicity achieved by it. The thinly wooded savannah around Lake Victoria, northern Tanzania, became a nature reserve that year and today contains the largest concentration of wildlife on the whole continent. Measuring almost 15,000 square kilometres, the 'endless plain', translated from the Masai name, still offers space for enormous herds of zebras, giraffes or antelopes to wander and offers predators of all types an abundant supply of food. UNESCO World Heritage Site since 1981.

The Ruins of Kilwa Kisiwani and Songo Mnara *(far top right)*

Off the coast of Tanzania, south of Dar-es-Salaam, lie the two coral islands, Kilwa Kisiwani and Songo Mnara. On the first was to be found in the Middle Ages the much admired city of Kilwa, apparently the most beautiful in East Africa, whose ruins (mosques, forts and palaces) give a hint of what life was like in the golden era of the Arab-Persian gold trade. On Songo too, Arab sultans set up trading posts, but when European competition appeared, decline set in until the jungle completely swallowed up the old buildings. Uncovered again since the 1960s, the two ruined areas were declared UNESCO World Heritage Sites in 1981 (the photo shows the ruins of the Grand Mosque in Kilwa).

Ngorongoro Conservation Area *(top right)*

The 'highlands of the giant craters' rise up in the northeast of Tanzania, in the Arusha Region south of the Serengeti National Park; they are all extinct, the biggest being the Ngorongoro with a diameter of 22 kilometres. The crater walls drop 600 metres to the crater floor, which measures 250 square kilometres. The conservation area also includes about 8,000 square kilometres around the cone. Remnants of a population of black rhino live here as well as hyenas (see photo), and the animals probably wonder what the people armed with magnifying glasses are doing crawling around on the ground. They are palaeontologists, for the park has proved to be a rich source of early human relics. UNESCO World Heritage Site since 1979.

Kilimanjaro National Park *(bottom)*

Three extinct volcanoes of the same age form the mountain massif of Kilimanjaro in the north of Tanzania, with Kibo at 5,895 metres being the highest African elevation. In 1973 about 1,700 square kilometres of the forested region (yew pine, tree ferns) were declared a national park and in 1987 declared a UNESCO World Heritage Site. With glaciers at the highest points, the saddle of the massif displays upland plateau tundra with heath vegetation. Lower down the slopes, the vegetation becomes richer and the fauna more diverse. Bushbucks, duikers, antelopes, elephants, leopards, tree hyrax and other mammals can be seen here.

Zambia

Victoria Falls *(top)*

At Livingstone in Zambia on the border with Zimbabwe, 'thundering smoke' is what the local inhabitants call the water of the Zambezi, which plunges from a width of 1,700 metres 110 metres down into a gorge only 50 metres wide. Once it has gone over the edge you don't actually see the water, instead spray or something like clouds of smoke, in which rainbows appear depending on the light conditions. Up to 500,000 cubic metres per minute fall with a deafening noise into a bottomless abyss. An area of 70 square kilometres around this natural wonder is under protection, so that flora and fauna can also flourish unimpeded. UNESCO World Heritage Site since 1989.

Malawi

Lake Malawi National Park *(bottom)*

Fishing is pure pleasure here, but not permitted everywhere: the southern part of Lake Malawi, a freshwater lake with the most diverse species of fish in the world, is a nature reserve. The area covered is mainly on and around the Nankumba Peninsula, east of the capital Lilongwe, and was declared a UNESCO World Heritage Site in 1984. The nature reserve consists of about 100 square kilometres of water with some islands and is home to all species of chichlid. Hippopotami, leopards, impalas and zebras live on the protected banks and Nile crocodiles and water monitor lizards and white-breasted cormorants have their breeding grounds on the islands.

Zimbabwe

Mana Pools National Park (top)

The environment is also being threatened by the continuing political unrest in Zimbabwe in southern Africa. Nature reserves are therefore especially welcome here, even if attacks still happen in reality. However, as the Mana Pools National Park and the Sapi and Chewore Safari Areas, altogether measuring about 7,000 square kilometres, are an important source of foreign currency, the attacks are limited. As a result, an amazing abundance of wildlife has been preserved here in the Zambezi Valley on the border with Zambia, typical of African dry forests that have not been spoilt much. It ranges from large mammals to several hundred bird species to rare fish species in the river. UNESCO World Heritage Site since 1984.

The Ruins of Great Zimbabwe (bottom)

Strange ruins tossed onto a hill: southeast of Masvango in Central Zimbabwe travellers in the 19th century came across such mighty stone structures, that one would never have imagined at that time in Africa. As archaeological research has shown, these are the remains of the capital of the Great Zimbabwe kingdom of the Shona people. Particularly striking is the 250 metre long and 10 metre high ringwall, called the 'great enclosure' (see photo), which had protected the king's residence and cult sites, as well as the 'acropolis' on the 90 metre high escarpment. The two large monuments of a kingdom dating from the 13th to 15th centuries together with about 100 other structures were declared a UNESCO World Heritage Site in 1988.

Mozambique

Island of Mozambique

Just four kilometres off the coast of northeast Mozambique, now linked to the mainland by a bridge, lies the coral island of Mozambique. It is just 3 kilometres by 300 metres in size, yet its natural harbour offers such a good port that the Arabs established a trading post here in the 10th century. The Portuguese drove them out, fortified the island with forts and palaces and built churches and monasteries for their spiritual life, and located the administrative headquarters of their East African colony here. It lost importance when the Suez Canal was opened, but with its colonial architectural style was declared a UNESCO World Heritage Site in 1991.

Namibia

Rock Paintings in Brandberg (top)

Immediately on leaving the Namibian coastal plain, the land rises to 2,600 metres in the Brandberg Massif, about 100 kilometres north of Swakopmund; the Königstein peak is the highest elevation in the country. The horst mountain range sticking up like a building block is deeply fissured and conceals in its gorges a unique cultural treasure: using different colours, African artists have recorded scenes of everyday life, hunting and cultic themes on the rock faces, these are works of art in rock painting.

Christus Church, Windhoek (bottom)

The Namibian capital, now with over 200,000 inhabitants, has of course long outgrown its once German nucleus. Modern office buildings and housing characterise the townscape. But, near the cavalry memorial for the German Empire's 'peacekeeping force' (they ruled bloodily here between 1890 and 1919), the Christus Church is the finishing touch to a small German colonial ensemble. The church, built at the turn of the century, displays unmistakable Art Nouveau elements in its coloured Dutch brick and arched windows.

Botswana

Okavango Delta

A river that goes nowhere. Emerging from the highlands of Bihé in Angola, the Okavango River, over 1,800 kilometres long, at times forms the border between Angola and Namibia, then flows through progressively drier areas of the Kalahari, dividing into many distributaries, and finally is swallowed up by the desert in northern Botswana. In years when there is plentiful rainfall, the Selina, a distributary, joins the Kwando, so that a tiny portion of the Okavango water actually reaches the ocean via the Zambezi. In such years, another distributary reaches Lake Ngami, but, like the whole Okavango Delta, it is actually just marshland – and a paradise for animals, for even hardened hunters hardly venture into this region of sometimes bottomless ground.

South Africa

Table Mountain (top)

In the early modern age, voyagers to India were overjoyed when they saw this: the Table Mountain towering above today's Cape Town and the Cape of Good Hope. If these geographical features came into sight, then the sailors knew that they would soon have rounded Africa. It is not in fact the most southerly point of the continent, that being Cape Agulhas, but the distinctive shape of the Table Mountain is simply a better beacon for successfully finding the sea route to India. Moreover, the 1,082 metres high table plateau is an excellent lookout point. From any spot, the view over the cape, bay and city is impressive.

Greater St. Lucia Wetland Park (centre)

Not far from Durban in South Africa there is a national park extending 60 kilometres in length around a lagoon parallel to the coast. A chain of sand dunes separates the Greater St. Lucia Wetland Park from the sea, but, because of its high porosity, it makes the lagoon water brackish and extremely rich in nutrients. It is no wonder that large colonies of pelicans and other waterfowl have grown up here, which live in harmony with hippopotami and a large number of crocodiles. With 1,500 large-jawed lizards, the park contains the largest population of all African nature reserves.

Robben Island (bottom left)

From prison to place of pilgrimage – an amazing history: the small Robben Island lies northwest of South Africa's Cape Town, as if specially made for building a high-security wing. The country's white rulers had been using this escape-proof site as early as 1658, when in 1964 a prisoner was sent there, who was the cause of this afore-mentioned history. Nelson Mandela spent 18 of his 28 years in prison here, before he was moved in 1984, released in 1990, awarded the Nobel Peace Prize in 1993 and became president in 1994. In 1997 his place of suffering was made a national monument, recounting the life of the fighter against apartheid from outlaw to idol.

Fossil Excavation Site, Sterkfontein (bottom right)

At Krugersdorp in the Witwaters Rand mountain range in the northeast of the Republic of South Africa, fossil finds are being found in the caves of Sterkfontein and surroundings. Probably the most important to date was found in December 1998 by South African anthropologists: they christened the skeleton of a 3½ million year old Australopithecus africanus 'Little Foot' on account of its daintiness. The fully-grown, oldest known ancestor of modern man only measured 1.20 metres during his lifetime and, although he walked upright, he lived mainly in trees. What is particularly remarkable is the good condition of the bones, which have helped to fill in many gaps in the understanding of early humans in Africa.

Cape of Good Hope *(top)*

Nowadays there is actually a road along the steep cliffs, so that one can drive round them by car. Five hundred years ago, when explorers were looking for the sea route to India, they were glad if they reached this sharp point, which is why they christened it Cape of Good Hope, in other words, for a successful voyage there and back to India, the promised land of silk and spices. At that time they did not realise that Cape Agulhas lay further south and was thus the real southern tip of the Dark Continent. The Table Mountain behind today's Cape Town was a good enough landmark for them to know that they had reached the zenith of their journey.

Seychelles

Vallée de Mai Nature Park *(bottom)*

Praslin Island, north of the main island of Mahé and one of over 100 Seychelles islands, conceals in its mountainous interior a natural jewel: located in the Praslin National Park which measures three square kilometres, the Vallée de Mai, only 20 hectares in size, contains a largely undisturbed virgin palm forest, in which the unique Seychelles nut palm, the 'Coco de Mer' grows. In addition to other endemic palm species, the many birds were also protected, among which the black parrot deserves special mention. The only mammals are the Seychelles flying fox and a species of bat. UNESCO World Heritage Site since 1983.

North and Central America

Where the future has already begun

"America, you are favoured", exclaimed many an eighteenth- and nineteenth-century writer when contemplating Europe's turmoil. Mind you, the New World was not spared and had to suffer some turbulence of its own, since globalisation had early political roots, and in any case such evaluation depends on one's perspective. The 'Indians' certainly have not experienced the last few centuries as a blessing; and for a great many immigrants, the American Dream has long been over. Nevertheless, if voting with one's feet counts for something, it is definitely in favour of the giant continent on the western side of the northern hemisphere. Millions of people from around the world came here to seek a safe haven, new opportunities and challenges, whilst almost nobody embarked on the opposite journey. Everyone who has breathed the air of unlimited possibilities is magically drawn under the spell of the wide open spaces and the spirit of new beginnings. This air blows through the urban canyons and over the skyline of Manhattan, drives the breakers onto the Pacific and Atlantic shores, envelopes the peaks of the Rockies in fog and sways the grass of the prairies. Between the Polar Sea and the Caribbean beaches there is nothing that you can't find, and most of it on an extra-large scale. The rivers flow mightily as nowhere else, the buildings scrape the sky and a many-toothed underworld seems to yawn from the abyss of the canyons. Historically, this part of the globe is a latecomer, since humans only arrived here from Africa via Eurasia a few thousands of years ago. Indeed, for a long time the New World remained enclosed in itself, a world in which fascinating advanced cultures such as those of the Maya and the Aztecs in Mexico developed. With the Europeans came a dramatically accelerated development that transformed the semi-continent fundamentally and made it into a land where the future has already begun.

299

North and Central America

RUSS. FEDERATION

Greenland
(Denmark)

Thule (Qaanaaq)

Qagassairssu
Godthåb

Alaska-Highway

Tuktojaktuk

Denali
National Park

Wrangell-Saint Elias
National Park
Kluane
National Park

Nahanni
National Park

Mendenhall-Glacier
Juneau

Wood-Buffalo
National Park

Hudson
Bay

L'Anse
Nationa

CANADA

Mount Robson
Prov. Park

Edmonton

Banff
National Park
Calgary

Dinosaur
Provincial Park

Regina

Quebec

Montreal

Olympic
National Park
Cape
Alava

Waterton Lakes
National Park

Winnipeg

St. Mary's Lake

Seattle

Glacier National Park

Pictured Rocks

Manitou Lake

Mackinac Bridge

Boston

Niagara Falls

New York

Detroit

Redwood
National Park

Yellowstone
National Park

Rapid City
Mount
Rushmore

Minneapolis

Chicago

Philadelphia

Salt Lake City

Scotts Bluff

Washington

Yosemite
National Park
Mono Lake

Bryce Canyon

Arches
National Park

UNITED STATES

Charlottesville

San Francisco

King's Canyon
National Park

Sequoia National Park

Mesa Verde
National Park

St. Louis

Mammoth Cave
National Park

Great Smoky Mountains
National Park

San Simeon

Las Vegas

Lake Powell

Santa Barbara

Grand Canyon
Meteor Crater

Taos

Chaco
Culture
National Historical Park

Los Angeles

Montezuma Castle

Oklahoma City

Phoenix

Atlanta

El Paso

Dallas

Cape Canaveral

Sierra de
San Francisco

Casas Grandes

Houston

New Orleans

San Antonio

El Vizcaíno

Everglades
National Park

Miami

Gulf
of
Mexico

Havanna

CUBA

Viñales-Valley

Trinidad

Ca
National Histo

Santiago
de Cuba Port

MEXICO

Zacatecas

JAMAICA

Kingsto

Mérida

Guanajuato
Querétaro
El Tajín
Tula
Mexico
City
Teotihuacán
Morelia
Puebla
Xochicalco
Popocatépetl

Chichén Itzá

Uxmal

Sian Ka'an
Bio Reserve

Campeche

Sayil

Palenque

Coastal Islands

Monte Alban

Oaxaca

Tikal

BELIZE

Barrier Reef

HONDURAS

Quiriguá

Río Plátano

Antigua
Guatemala

Tegucigalpa

Copán

GUATEMALA

Joya de Cerén

NICARAGUA

EL
SALVADOR

Managua

Talamanca
Nature
Reserve

Panama

Guanacaste

PANAMA

San José

COSTA RICA

La Amistad
National Park

Darién
National P

PACIFIC OCEAN

0   500   1000   1500
km

COLOME

Greenland *(Denmark)*

Iceberg World near Thule *(top)*

Like an enormous bowl, which far in the interior sinks to a depth of 250 metres below sea level, Greenland supports a covering of ice up to 3,400 metres thick. Out of the entire two million square kilometres of the world's largest island, only 340,000 square kilometres along the shores are free of ice. Even that is not true everywhere, since in the north it is too cold for that; and on the western side near Thule (the Eskimos call this place Qaanaaq), there are mighty glacier-flows that calve into the sea. This is the name given to the process whereby icebergs break off the glacier. The gigantic lumps float out into the open sea, two-thirds of their volume submerged, and search for victims such as the unfortunate Titanic in her day.

Ruins of Eric the Red's Church, Qassiarsuk *(bottom)*

The Vikings were a right rowdy bunch, but even they considered the chieftain Eric the Red to be particularly unpleasant. His behaviour was so wild that the members of his community in Iceland exiled him. But instead of retiring to Europe in comfort, Eric turned even further westward, where in 982 AD he and his people reached Greenland and settled in its south-western corner. He didn't really get along with Christianity, but finally gave in to the pestering of his son, America's discoverer Leif Eriksson, and tolerated the church he built at Qassiarsuk. To what extent this helped redeem his soul after his death in 1005 AD remains open to speculation. All that remains of his church is a stone circle, more reminiscent of the site of a pagan shrine.

Canada

Kluane, Wrangell-Saint Elias, Glacier Bay, Tatshenshini-Alsek National Parks *(top)*

Along the North American western coast, several Canadian and American national parks are ranged in a row across the border. They cover almost 100 000 square kilometres and reach an altitude of up to 6000 metres (at Mount Logan). Here lives the largest closed population of grizzly bears, comprising around 600 individuals. Many other wild animals also find enough space and food here: caribou, black bears, elks, wolves, otters, beavers, sea lions, walruses and 180 bird species, including black-throated divers, whooper swans and whimbrels. Sometimes whales can be observed quite close up in Glacier Bay. UNESCO World Heritage Site since 1979.

Tundra, Tuktoyaktuk *(bottom left)*

Even the Canadian mainland projects considerably further north than Iceland, and at Tuktoyaktuk, east of the Mackenzie River's delta where it flows into the North Polar Sea, reaches almost 70 degrees of northern latitude. Here even in summer the permafrost soil thaws only superficially, and permits at most a sparse tundra vegetation. The rather unimpressive flora is more than compensated for in the Canadian north-west by a natural phenomenon that cannot be observed anywhere else: the grassy landscape curves gracefully in places to hills up to 50 metres tall and 200 metres wide, the so-called pingos. These are conical mounds sitting on top of ice cores, pushed upwards by high hydrostatic pressure.

Nahanni National Park *(bottom right)*

In the south-western part of Canada's Northwest Territories, a 4800 square kilometre area on the South Nahanni River, together with the 100 metres high Virginia Falls, are under protection. This is a mountainous karst region, full of ravines, rising up to 2650 metres in the Ragged Range: canyons three to 20 kilometres long and 1300 metres deep slice through it, underground streams, cave systems and rift craters crisscross it. The region is not easily accessible, and is a sanctuary for grizzlies, red goats, whitetail deer, Dall sheep and beavers. Its flora is highly varied; 325 moss species thrive in the park, which has been a UNESCO World Heritage Site since 1978.

National Parks in the Rocky Mountains *(top)*

The oldest of these was established as far back as 1885, others followed in 1907 and 1920: in the Canadian Rocky Mountains, the chain of national parks consisting of Banff, Jasper, Kootenay, Yoho, Mount Robson, Hamber, Mount Assiniboine and the very productive fossil site of Burgess forms a conservation area covering 23,000 square kilometres. It follows the border of the provinces of Alberta and British Columbia, and reaches an altitude of 3,954 metres at Mount Robson. The grandiose mountain landscape with its alpine flora and diverse fauna (56 mammals and 260 bird species, plus a few reptiles) has been a UNESCO World Heritage Site since 1990.

Wood-Buffalo National Park *(centre left)*

Karl May's complaints were not entirely in vain: time and again, in moving words, the adventure writer described the downfall of North America's great herds of bison through the white man's guns. They had nourished the Native Americans for thousands of years, and a few decades of over-exploitation by the invaders were sufficient to bring them — and to a large extent the Indians, too — to the edge of extinction. But not entirely: in the border country of Northern Alberta and the Canadian Northwest Territories, the authorities established a national park as far back as 1922. With an area of 45,000 square kilometres it is as large as the German province of Lower Saxony, and today is a home for about 4,500 'buffaloes'. This also provides protection to many other animals, in particular the threatened whooping crane of which 40 pairs still breed here. It has been a UNESCO World Heritage Site since 1983.

Gros Morne National Park *(centre right)*

By the north-western shore of the Canadian island of Newfoundland, to the north-west of Deer Lake, explorers have found fossil sites in the lowlands and in the directly adjoining mountains on the Gulf of St Lawrence. In order to protect the 570 million years old evidence of earlier life forms, but also today's fauna and flora, 1,800 square kilometres have been made into a nature reserve. Here the scientists can carry out undisturbed research, while ermines, voles, beavers, lynx, elks and 230 bird species can live unmolested. The former and today's natural paradise have been a UNESCO World Heritage Site since 1987.

L'Anse aux Meadows Historic National Park *(bottom)*

By now it is general knowledge that Columbus was not the first European in America. Almost five hundred years before him, the Vikings under Leif Eriksson came from Greenland to Newfoundland (Canada) and even settled there for a while in the 11th century. We have the remains in the form of several groups of grass-covered timber structures, residential buildings and the workshops of boat builders and metal workers, the outlines of which were exposed during the 1960s and 1970s. The finds included many tools and bronze decorations. In the meantime, scientists have reconstructed the settlement called L'Anse aux Meadows on Epaves Bay. The Viking village has been a UNESCO World Heritage Site since 1978.

303

Banff National Park *(top left)*

Calgary, the largest city in the Canadian province of Alberta, already lies at an altitude of over 1,000 metres. From here you ascend 660 metres to the town of Banff in the national park, which peaks at Mount Forbes (3,630 metres). The road leads through several vegetation zones up into the glaciated high mountain regions, and the flora and fauna protected here is correspondingly varied. That is why the park, covering 6,640 square kilometres, together with the many other conservation areas adjoining it on the north, has been part of the Rocky Mountains UNESCO World Heritage Site since 1984. It offers a haven to many threatened species: even pumas and wolverines, three-toed woodpeckers and golden eagles can be encountered here.

Waterton Glacier International Peace Park *(far top right)*

In the south-west of the Canadian province of Alberta, Waterton Lakes National Park abuts the American Glacier National Park. As far back as 1932, they were joined together into one Peace Park, thus creating a continuous biosphere reserve covering 4,600 square kilometres. Lakes and glaciers – these two words already suggest that a chain of shimmering lakes was formed here through gouging by ice, including St. Mary's Lake in north-western Montana. The mountain lakes are surrounded by alpine tundra and by a sub-alpine forest belt, home to 61 species of mammal such as grizzly bears, coyotes, pumas, mink and bison. UNESCO World Heritage Site since 1995.

Dinosaur Provincial Park *(top right)*

The so-called Judith River Formation is located in the southeastern part of the Canadian province of Alberta, south of the town of Brooks. This is a central mountain massif, around 700 metres high, ca. 75 million years old, displaying strong weather erosion effects. This has brought many fossils to light, with 23,000 finds made between 1979 and 1991 alone, including the remains of ancient reptilians of all kinds, from the flesh-eating Tyrannosaurus Rex to gigantic but herbivorous dinosaurs. Fossilised mammals and marsupials from the Tertiary were also discovered. At the same time, the ca. 75 square kilometres are also a safe sanctuary for living fauna: red deer and hundreds of bird species are in their element here. UNESCO World Heritage Site since 1979.

Historic Quarter, Quebec *(bottom)*

Quebec, although the provincial capital, has long since surrendered to Montreal its predominance as regards size and economic importance. Nevertheless, the government of the Canadian province of Quebec continues to reside here, and historically its glory still exceeds that of any competitor: established in 1608, the city was fundamentally imbued with everything French as the heart of New France. This changed little after Britain took it over in 1759, having bombarded it with 40,000 cannon balls. The British buildings, such as the Anglican Cathedral of the Holy Trinity (1804) constructed after a London model, get along famously with the older French ones, of which those especially worthy of mention include: Hôtel de Dieu; Hôtel Château Frontenac (see picture); Ursuline Convent (1639); Church of Notre-Dame-des-Victoires (1688). The city centre has been a UNESCO World Heritage Site since 1985.

Niagara Falls (top)

The border between the USA and Canada runs at Goat Island, and the island also divides the Niagara River (Niagara means 'the narrow place' in the Iroquois language) into two arms and thus splits a natural wonder between the two neighbours, although not entirely equitably: at 790 metres wide, the Canadians have more than double the American share of 350 metres. Perhaps the Americans are consoled by the fact that their falls, at 51 metres tall, drop two metres further than the Canadian or Horseshoe Falls. But because the border between the two countries is hardly noticed by the tourists who come here in their millions, quite often on their honeymoon, both sides enjoy an equal share in the boom.

Biosphere, Montreal (bottom left)

It's hard to believe: the American architect Richard Buckminster Fuller (1895–1983) was over 70 years old when he created this futuristic USA pavilion for the 1967 World Fair in Montreal. The 20 storeys and 80 metres tall almost-sphere made of struts linked to each other at crossing points realises on a massive scale Fuller's 'geodesic' construction method, that has ensured for him a permanent place in architectural history – and in chemistry: an artificially created macromolecule made of 60 or more carbon atoms resembles his spheres amazingly closely, and thus is called Fullerene.

Stadium and Olympic Tower, Montreal (bottom right)

When the world's youth assembles in a city for the Olympic contest, it should find the best possible conditions. This is true for the accommodation, but even more for the stadiums. The Canadian metropolis of Montreal went deep into debt in 1976 in order to do justice to these requirements. The covered Olympic stadium was naturally the centrepoint, specially exposed to the world's gaze, which is why nothing was skimped on here. A high, oval hall was built, and it only looks flat because the angled tower with its cathedral-like dimensions, 190 metres tall, leaves it far behind. It gives to the whole thing a catapult-like appearance and permits unusual camera perspectives.

United States of America *(USA)*

Alaska Highway *(top)*

A little-known fact is that part of the USA was occupied by the Japanese in World War Two. In the summer of 1942 they took a few small islands in the Aleutian chain that arches into the Pacific at Alaska's south-western tip. The Americans had not been able to prevent this, but hurried to shorten the supply roads into the region: the 2,450 kilometre long Alaska Highway, from Dawson Creek in north-western Canada to Fairbanks in central Alaska, was built in a record time of eight months. Today the military objective is only seen in the uncompromising way the route was laid out; other than that, the road through these wild regions enjoys great popularity with tourists.

Denali National Park *(bottom left)*

North America rises highest in the far north: at Mount McKinley, the Alaska range reaches an altitude of 6198 metres and exceeds the highest point of Europe (Mont Blanc) by almost 1,500 metres. By 1917 the USA had already established a conservation area around the giant, renamed Denali National Park in 1980 after the mountain's Native American name. It covers an area of about 19,000 square kilometres. Heavily glaciated in the high regions, the park displays species-rich flora and fauna in the lower parts. Black and grey bears (grizzlies), caribou, mountain sheep and innumerable smaller mammals romp on the long, forested flanks of the massif.

Olympic National Park *(bottom right)*

When the clouds from the Pacific penetrate the land, they are forced by the Olympic Mountains – rising to 2,428 metres at Mount Olympus – to rise and thus to release their rain. That's why it is so wet in the extreme north-western corner of Washington State, the most north-westerly in the contiguous USA. 3,700 square kilometres of the mountain massif have been under protection since 1938, because here are remains of untouched temperate rain forest, magical glaciated high mountain regions with varied flora, primarily hemlock and giant pines, Sitka spruce, Douglas fir, maple. Over 50 species of mammal are indigenous: wapitis, pumas, black bears and marmots. UNESCO World Heritage Site since 1981.

Mendenhall Glacier, Juneau *(top)*

The government of the state of Alaska decided to have its seat as far south in the state as possible, since the centre would have been even less hospitable, to say nothing of the North Polar Sea coast. Even in Juneau, behind the skerries along the Pacific coast, it's not all that cosy. In the winter it does get pretty cold here, as shown by the glacier tongues that emerge from the snow-covered coastal mountains and lick right down into the lowlands. They include the Mendenhall Glacier, whose white ribbon flows between and through the rocky slopes.

Cape Alava *(centre)*

Only a few kilometres before Cape Mendocino near Eureka in California, Cape Alava in Washington State, at the foot of the Olympic Mountains, lies as one of the most westerly points in the USA (apart from Alaska and Hawaii, of course). To be on the safe side, the cape has a few rocks strewn in the sea, which at low tide are connected to the mainland and are then definitely the most westerly. And certainly picturesque, too: the largest among them bears a crown of trees that struggle to hold onto the draughty peak — only suitable for picnics at less than force four winds.

Pictured Rocks *(bottom)*

In Michigan, not on lake Michigan but on the southeast shore of Lake Superior, the rocks form a steep shore as though a brilliant artist has painted them there. Tectonic uplift has raised the land out of the water, and now only its shining red flanks are wetted. The rock layers are clearly visible, and a few prominences have been undercut by the water over the millennia to such an extent that they form doorways, through which one can see into the distance. The name Pictured Rocks is very appropriate, given that nature has even added an artistic tiara of green forest on top of the ridge.

Mackinac Bridge (top)

There must be some sort of record involved: the bridge that American engineers built in 1957 over the Mackinac Straits between Lake Michigan and Lake Huron is a suspended construction. Its span of 1,158 metres is not the greatest, nor is its overall length of 7.1 kilometres: it is exceeded by the San-Francisco-Oakland-Bay Bridge built in 1936, which trumps it by 1,200 metres. But there is something else: the Californian colleague spans a marine bay, i.e. salt water. The harp-like Mackinac Bridge is therefore the world's longest suspension bridge over freshwater.

Flora and Fauna in Yellowstone National Park (top centre)

Since 1872, rangers and wardens have been making sure that the visitors flowing from around the world into the American Yellowstone National Park, south of Great Falls in the Rocky Mountains, treat this natural jewel with care. It captivates not only through its fascinating geological formations, but also as a biosphere reserve. The long period of protection has allowed the creation of a peerless plant and animal paradise, which of course is why it has been a UNESCO World Heritage Site since 1978. Forested across 80 percent of its area, this oldest national park in the world offers a sanctuary to over 1,000 plant species, one through which about 200 grizzlies wander at leisure. In addition one can encounter elks, bison, bighorn sheep, mountain lions and mountain goats.

Geysers in Yellowstone National Park (bottom centre)

The earth is restless in the southern part of the Rocky Mountains in the American states of Idaho, Wyoming and Montana. Three times in recent earth history, i.e. two million and one million years ago as well as 630 000 years ago, the region was thoroughly reshaped through eruptions that created an overwhelming landscape. By 1872 the authorities became convinced that it should be protected from human destruction. Almost 9,000 square kilometres by the Yellowstone River were joined into the world's first and probably most famous national park, where countless fumaroles puff away and 250 geysers spray their fountains. UNESCO World Heritage Site since 1978.

Redwood National Park (bottom left)

Coastal sequoias (Sequoiadendron giganteum) were once widely distributed in North America, but now they must be saved and protected. This is what is happening in an 80 kilometres long and around ten kilometres wide redwood forest in north-eastern California, north of San Francisco. Three national parks were integrated into one in 1968. The result is a park in which 865 plant species, 75 species of mammal and 398 bird species flourish. In addition to the up to 110 metre tall giant trees, it is mainly threatened animals that need the park's protection: grey foxes, otters, skunks, pumas, brown pelicans, falcons and elks. Since 1980 UNESCO World Heritage Site.

Mammoth Hot Springs in Yellowstone National Park (bottom right)

About 30 kilometres north of Norris Junction on the Gardiner River, hot spring water falls in steps down to the valley. Through sintering, these Mammoth Hot Springs have created limestone terraces that glow white, but also display all kinds of other colours as a result of algae growth or bacterial chemistry. Visitors can walk through the Main Terrace Area along secure paths and boardwalks, admire the springs and listen to their hissing and gurgling.

Mount Rushmore Monument, South Dakota (top)

Had he lived longer, the American sculptor Gutzon Borglum (1867–1941) might have swapped Theodore ('Teddy') for Franklin Delano Roosevelt. But the artist did not see the latter's triumph in World War Two, and thus the Black Hills in south-western South Dakota are decorated with the monumental stone heads of the four presidents, Washington, Jefferson, Lincoln and T. Roosevelt. The faces, chiselled out of the granite rock face, are very lifelike, about 20 metres tall and a singular patriotic memorial very much in the style of the Land of Unlimited Possibilities. They have served as a backdrop to quite a few Hollywood films.

Scotts Bluff, Nebraska (bottom)

In great treks, the Whites pushed their North American settlement boundaries further and further west during the 18th and 19th centuries. The so-called Oregon Trail that snaked across 3,200 kilometres, all the way to the northwest of today's USA, became famous: countless treks chose it even though it led through deserts and dangerous Indian territories. However, compared with other routes it had terrain advantages, such as the sandstone Sentinel Rock in the Nebraska plain. Rising 244 metres above its surroundings, it showed the way reliably from afar. Therefore Scotts Bluff, as the place was named, played an important part in opening up the West, and today is protected as a National Monument. The Oregon Trail Museum tells the story of the treks, the wagon tracks of which are still visible on the ground.

Sears Tower, Chicago (left)

SOM is the name of the builder of one of the world's tallest buildings, but SOM is not an individual: it is the architectural firm of Skidmore, Owings and Merril, established in the 1930s. Between 1969–1974 they created the 443 metre tall Sears Tower in Chicago for a department store group. 100 lifts take 16 000 people to work every weekday up to the 110 floors, and those at the very top have a view across the entire city and on a good day far over Lake Michigan. The harmonic mixture of old and new in this greatest city in Illinois is expressed here, too: in front of the modern steel and glass titan stands an old water tower, a reminder of days past.

Illinois State Center, Chicago (bottom)

'Form follows function' is one of the demands of modern architecture, where every function naturally leaves some leeway for a variety of forms. In the 1960s, when the largest city in Illinois planned a State Center with administrative and commercial facilities, the task was given to the German Bauhaus architect Mies van der Rohe (1886–1969), already over 80 years old, whose work was continued and brought to bold completion by the young Helmut Jahn (born 1940). He followed the requirement perfectly, whereby a house does not consist of a roof and walls but of a surrounded space, and therefore must be built from the inside outwards.

Renaissance Center, Detroit *(top)*

More cars are built here than anywhere else in the world, since the big three – Ford, General Motors and Chrysler – are all based here: Detroit, nicknamed Motown, sitting on the river of the same name that forms the border with Canada in the American state of Michigan, used to be the world capital of car making. The fact that monopolies have their weaknesses became clear at a stroke in 1973 when the oil price crisis hit automotive manufacturers very badly, and thus also the city. Only rapid recovery from the automotive depression saved the companies and Detroit. In 1977 Henry Ford II put up an emblem to this rebirth, with the Renaissance Center that stands 73 storeys tall, houses 50 stores and 25 restaurants and offers visitors a marvellous view across the water to Canada.

Niagara Falls *(bottom right)*

One theory about the name 'Niagara' is that it means Thundering Water, although for 99 percent of its 55 kilometre length the Niagara River, which connects Lake Erie with Lake Ontario, flows as quietly as most rivers. But that last one percent is different: as you get closer you hear the swelling of a tremendous roar, where the river on the American side, 350 metres wide, falls 51 metres and then drops another 60 metres into the maw it had previously excavated. On the Canadian side, the arm separated by Goat Island is wider but drops 'only' 49 metres. Although an annoying obstacle to shipping that needs to be bypassed via canals, the two Niagara Falls are a unique natural attraction for tourists.

Wrigley Building, Chicago *(bottom left)*

The Americans have always wanted to go onward and upward, and architecturally this became possible with the invention of the steel frame construction method by William Le Baron Jenney (1832–1907) and of the safety lift. The architect Louis Henri Sullivan (1856–1932), who put his own stamp on the type of modern commercial high-rise building represented by the Wrigley Building in Chicago, became a virtuoso of the new technology. Of course, against the backdrop of the newest glass palaces and super-skyscrapers such as the Sears Tower, the earlier concrete solutions seem a little 'ancient', especially as the Art Nouveau decor speaks a different formal language.

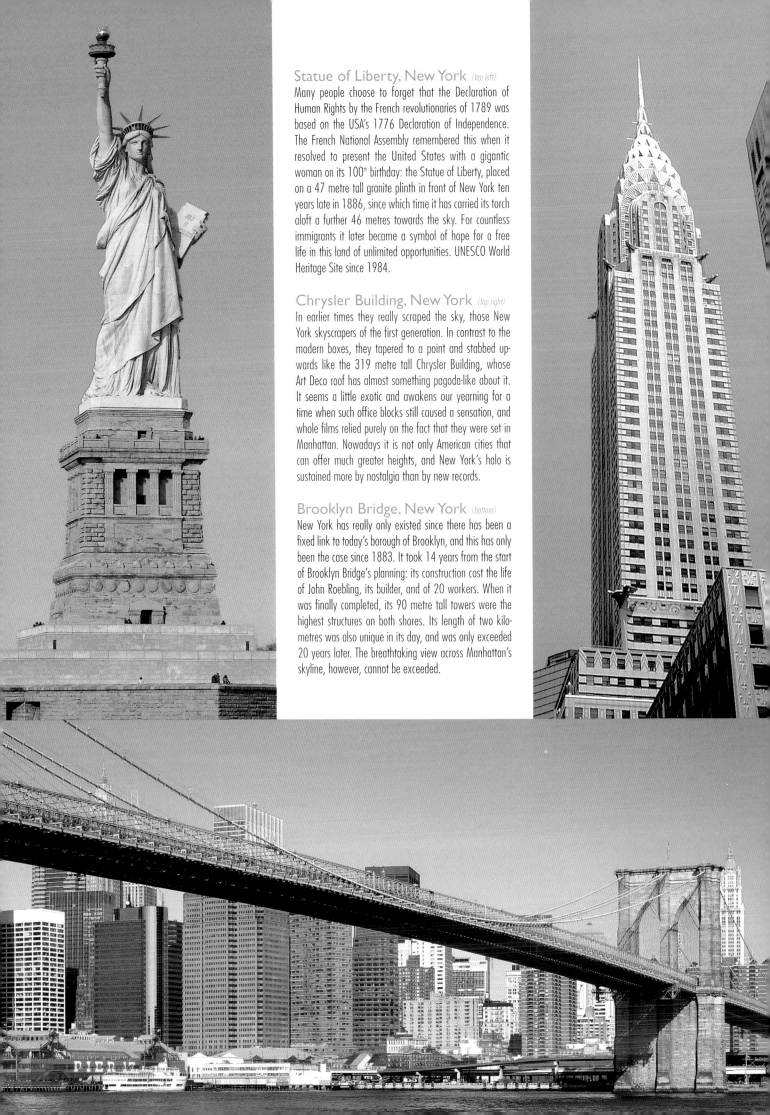

Statue of Liberty, New York (top left)

Many people choose to forget that the Declaration of Human Rights by the French revolutionaries of 1789 was based on the USA's 1776 Declaration of Independence. The French National Assembly remembered this when it resolved to present the United States with a gigantic woman on its 100th birthday: the Statue of Liberty, placed on a 47 metre tall granite plinth in front of New York ten years late in 1886, since which time it has carried its torch aloft a further 46 metres towards the sky. For countless immigrants it later became a symbol of hope for a free life in this land of unlimited opportunities. UNESCO World Heritage Site since 1984.

Chrysler Building, New York (top right)

In earlier times they really scraped the sky, those New York skyscrapers of the first generation. In contrast to the modern boxes, they tapered to a point and stabbed upwards like the 319 metre tall Chrysler Building, whose Art Deco roof has almost something pagoda-like about it. It seems a little exotic and awakens our yearning for a time when such office blocks still caused a sensation, and whole films relied purely on the fact that they were set in Manhattan. Nowadays it is not only American cities that can offer much greater heights, and New York's halo is sustained more by nostalgia than by new records.

Brooklyn Bridge, New York (bottom)

New York has really only existed since there has been a fixed link to today's borough of Brooklyn, and this has only been the case since 1883. It took 14 years from the start of Brooklyn Bridge's planning: its construction cost the life of John Roebling, its builder, and of 20 workers. When it was finally completed, its 90 metre tall towers were the highest structures on both shores. Its length of two kilometres was also unique in its day, and was only exceeded 20 years later. The breathtaking view across Manhattan's skyline, however, cannot be exceeded.

Empire State Building, New York (top)

George Washington, the first president of the USA, liked to refer to New York State as the Empire State, being so-to-speak the heart of the new country, at that time still clinging to the east coast of North America. This was in the minds of the Architect William Frederick Lamb and his clients in 1931 when they named the Empire State Building, at that time the world's tallest and admired all around the globe. This expressed pride and the assertion of having set an unsurpassable benchmark in Manhattan. After 1970, when finally the giant's 381 metres and 102 storeys were surpassed after all, its elegant lines continued to exert a special magic: there may be taller skyscrapers these days, but none more beautiful.

Guggenheim Museum, New York
(bottom right)

The architectural legacy of one of the most important architects of the modern era: Frank Lloyd Wright (1867–1959) was almost 90 when he designed this New York building as the home of the art collections donated by Salomon Guggenheim (1861–1949). Having dispensed with all external decorations, between 1956–1959 he created a complex that in its organic form markedly differs from its utilitarian surroundings, without itself losing sight of its purpose. It rises in a flat spiral that widens upwards, giving the impression of being made up of discs with apertures to let in the light.

Museum of Modern Art, New York
(bottom left)

When three ladies of rank and status established the Museum of Modern Art in 1929, now known worldwide as MoMA, the most prominent among them, Abby Aldrich Rockefeller, the wife of John D. Rockefeller Junior, made her townhouse on W 54th Street available for it. Soon the building no longer sufficed for the rapidly growing collection. It was the first museum to focus its exhibitions and its programme completely on modern art, which at the time was barely appreciated, thus helping the modern movement to break through. The requirements placed on the museum's new home, built in 1939, were in line with this approach. The American architect Edward Durell Stone erected a monument to the modern building style.

Manhattan, New York *(top left)*

Skyline by skyscrapers – this is Manhattan, the best-known borough of New York on the narrow island between the Hudson and the East River. Long dominated by buildings such as the Rockefeller Center or the Empire State Building, until September 2001 the high-rise capital drew attention first and foremost with the two 412 metre towers of the World Trade Center. Until the events of the 11th September, the towers symbolised the city's dual life between the hectic glittering lifestyle in the deep urban canyons with their bars, cinemas, theatres, museums and boutiques, and the frantic pursuits taking place in the office pools, during the week a home to whole hosts of secretaries, managers, typists and service staff.

Flatiron Building, New York *(top right)*

Here, where Broadway meets Fifth Avenue at 23rd Street, Daniel Burnham, the famous architect from Chicago, built in 1902 one of the world's first high-rises using the steel frame method. The steeply tapering plot dictated the overall shape, reminiscent of a hot iron. At 100 metres, this skyscraper is by far not the tallest in New York, but certainly one of the best known.

Capitol, Washington Monument, Lincoln Memorial, Washington *(bottom)*

Borrowings from the ancient world characterise the main axis of the American capital Washington. From the Capitol (built 1793–1824), the temple as it were of the two Houses of Parliament, named after the Roman model, via the Washington Monument with the classical exclamation mark of the 169 metres tall obelisk (1888) to the Lincoln Memorial (1915–1922) in the style of the Athenian Parthenon, everything is designed for eternity. By spreading the historic arc as wide as this, architecturally speaking, something of the patina of the great past is meant to colour the short history of the United States.

White House, Washington *(top left)*

Only the first president of the United States, who gave his name to the capital, did not reside here. However, in 1792 George Washington commissioned the building of his successor's official residence in the Classicist style. At the time, nobody thought to use the later nickname and to-day's official name for the building: this came later in 1814 when the British, during the war against the young renegade state, their former colony, burned down Washington, the heart of the detested new power. Dolly Madison, wife of the president then in office, is supposed to have had the blackened building whitewashed again later. Images of the American president's command centre, the Oval Office, are shown on television around the world almost on a daily basis.

Independence Hall, Philadelphia
(top right)

Originally, the lovely colonial building with the central bell tower on its facade was the home of the people's assembly of the British colony of Pennsylvania. Built in 1732–1740, the Second American Continental Congress chose the building for its conference in 1775 after falling out with the English motherland. The Declaration of Independence was signed here on 4 July 1776. The building is named Independence Hall to commemorate the birth certificate of today's mightiest country. Together with the separate glass pavilion where the Liberty Bell is kept, it has been a UNESCO World Heritage Site since 1979.

Extension of the National Gallery, Washington *(centre)*

When the city fathers of Washington decided in the 1970s to extend the National Gallery, which was coming apart at the seams, they wanted a building that would make such measures unnecessary for a long time. Thus, the Chinese-American Architect Ieoh Ming Pei (born 1917) had to overcome quite a large construction problem. It could have become quite a bunker, given the need for large wall and partition surfaces and therefore fewer windows. But the geometric formal language, which Pei also liked using in later assignments, for example in 1989 at the glass pyramid of the Louvre in Paris, created a landscape of pyramidal and angled features, in which the heavy and defiant monumentality appears to be resolved. The light-coloured variation in the brick walls supports this effect.

Monticello, Charlottesville *(bottom)*

The American president Kennedy invited all living American Nobel laureates to dinner at the White House, and began his toast with the words: "There is in this room more intelligence than at any time in the history of the White House, with the possible exception of nights when Thomas Jefferson dined alone". The homage was meant for the man who formulated the 1776 Declaration of Independence, and as president between 1801–1809 consolidated the young USA. His words resonated with admiration for Jefferson the intellectual, who occupied his mind with classical architecture and had his country seat at Monticello in Charlottesville, Virginia, built in this style, with a white portico fronting a red facade. Together with the buildings of the university also founded by him there in 1819, this has been a UNESCO World Heritage Site since 1987.

Golden Gate Bridge, San Francisco
(bottom left)

At the time of the gold rush, California was regarded as Eldorado, and the five kilometre long entrance into the natural harbour of San Francisco Bay was accordingly known as Golden Gate. The narrowest point, only 1.6 kilometres wide, called for a bridge that was started in 1933 and completed in 1937. The Golden Gate Bridge, with its elegant suspension, really made this entrance into a gate and considerably shortened the journey to the neighbouring town Sausalito, and thus to the coastal road towards the north. But what is that compared with the inspiring effect – unfortunately also on those tired of life – to which we can thank many cinematic scenes filmed in front of this 2.8 kilometre long background, floating 72 metres above the water?

University of Virginia, Charlottesville *(top)*

The American president Jefferson (1743–1826, president between 1801–1809) wanted the University of Virginia, which he founded in Charlottesville in 1819, to be like his villa: rustic and classical. The result was an ensemble that probably needed some getting used to, consisting of dignified urban buildings in a rural setting. Grouped in the shape of a U and with their noble pediments supported on columns, the ten pavilions for the ten faculties seem like ancient temples standing in a sacred grove. The founder's statue is lent thereby something of the character of a central deity. Together with his country seat, the campus has been a UNESCO World Heritage Site since 1987.

Alcatraz Prison Island, San Francisco *(centre)*

This jail was regarded as so secure that even the most notorious criminal of the 20th century, Al 'Scarface' Capone, was detained here: the rock of Alcatraz in San Francisco Bay, California, fortified in 1855 and converted into a high-security prison in 1934, was considered impossible to break out of. In the three decades of its existence (closed in 1963), the toughest guys in the USA experienced here the hard regime of a justice system embodying the Old Testament's ideas of penitence. Directors have always been keen to use the island as the background for prison thrillers. Today, with its endless rows of cells, it is an attraction for tourists.

TransAmerica Pyramid, San Francisco *(bottom right)*

It is neither the capital of California, a title that belongs to Sacramento, nor the largest metropolis in the state, which is Los Angeles. Nevertheless San Francisco, or Frisco for short, is regarded as 'the City'. This has to do with its cosmopolitan outlook, with its wonderful location on the bay, but also with its architecture. Largely destroyed by a severe earthquake in 1906, old buildings are hard to come by. Instead it impresses with plenty of modern ones, which is almost literally true for the rocket-like design of the 260 metre high Trans-Am building. With the two tiny, stubby wings below the pointy roof, it declares: 'Ready for take-off'. This can only mean one thing: up into the 21st century.

Mono Lake, Sierra Nevada (top)

Mono Lake in the Sierra Nevada, east of San Francisco, is almost circular and probably of volcanic origin. It really is a rather 'mono', i.e. lone lake, currently covering about 175 square kilometres and therefore around three times the size of Loch Lomond. It is extremely salty, being without an outlet and lying on the dry eastern slopes of the mountains. It is almost 2,000 metres in altitude, one and a half times that of Ben Nevis, hence the sparse vegetation around the lake in front of the backdrop of mountain ranges, high-alpine in character.

General Grant, Giant Tree, King's Canyon National Park (centre)

No living creature on earth has ever been larger, not even the mightiest whales or the giant dinosaurs, nor older: the giant trees of California can grow to a height of 135 metres over 4000 years – unimaginable Methuselahs. Several remarkable specimens stand in King's Canyon National Park in the mountains of the Sierra Nevada east of Fresno. It was established in 1890, only a quarter of a century after the end of the American Civil War, whose victors were honoured by having the largest trees named after them. One was naturally dedicated to General Grant, who was president between 1869–1877 and therefore was entitled to a particularly beautiful tree: 81.5 metres tall with a circumference of 32.5 metres at the base, it towers over several 'teenagers' that still have several centuries on the clock.

Yosemite National Park (bottom left)

In the heart of the Sierra Nevada in Central California, the Yosemite Valley and the 800 metre deep canyon of the Merced River were recognised by nature lovers as far back as 1890 as treasures urgently in need of protection. The national Park established at that time was extended several times to over 3,000 square kilometres, at altitudes of 670 to almost 4,000 metres. It is hard to imagine a more varied landscape: massive, erosion-smoothed granite cliffs alternate with forests of giant sequoias, waterfalls (e.g. the Bridal Veil) roar, cliffs and walls fall into the bottomless deep, and in the highest places the glaciers shine. 1,400 species of plants, 230 of birds and 74 of mammals live here. UNESCO World Heritage Site since 1984.

Sequoia National Park (bottom right)

Sequoia National Park directly adjoins King's Canyon National Park in the Sierra Nevada mountains of California. As the name indicates, it is particularly designed to protect the giant sequoias or Sierra redwoods that for long were logged pitilessly. However, it also concerns saving the high mountain world of Mount Whitney, at 4,419 metres the USA's highest mountain outside Alaska. In addition to nature conservation, the park also does something for culture: since 1978 it has incorporated the old mining town of Mineral King, which has been under threat of decline and decay with the closing of the no longer productive mining works and the migration of its inhabitants. Its fabric has now been saved.

Hearst Castle, San Simeon (far top)

On the outside a bit of St Peter's Square with a colonnaded walk, the facade a neo-Baroque nod to the Cathedral of Santiago de Compostela, the interior decorated à la Versailles and Tuileries – and that's the 'Ranch', as the newspaper tycoon William Randolph Hearst (1863–1951) liked to call his palace at San Simeon in California, with just a touch of understatement. For European eyes a bold (where not tasteless) conglomeration of the wholesale-purchased and the cribbed, the over-the-top estate is a happy marriage of Disneyland and Neuschwanstein. And even critical souls cannot fail to admire the boldness of the combinations and the atmosphere of nouveau riche maharajas.

Santa Barbara Mission, Los Angeles
(top left)

While in the east of the continent, with their Declaration of Independence, the New England states were embarking on the formation of the United States, at its other end Franciscan monks under Spanish command were creating the 'King's Way', Camino Real, and establishing a series of mission stations along the Californian coast. One of them, built in 1781, has now become Los Angeles ('The Angels'). Another one further northwest was Santa Barbara. The old Spanish-Mexican mission has long since been surrounded by the city. And yet the building, with its plain and virtually unadorned but massive church, still sets a tone in the frenzy of the fast-living present that stops many people in their tracks: time is not only money, but an opportunity to realise that more than human endeavour was part of making one country out of the East and the West – God's own country.

Salt Lake City (top centre and right)

Even saltier than the Dead Sea in the Holy Land, though at 1,350 metres above sea level at a considerably higher altitude, the Great Salt Lake in Utah is only a shadow of its former self, sometimes more and sometime less. In earlier times it covered 50,000 square kilometres and reached far into Idaho, whilst now it has shrunk to about one tenth of that on average, depending on precipitation. In rainy years its level rises such that 6,000 square kilometres may be flooded, but in times of drought it contracts to half of that. This inconstancy has not bothered the religious community of the Mormons, or the Church of Jesus Christ of Latter Day Saints, and here in this salty land they established their capital and that of Utah, Salt Lake City. Their centre includes the six-turreted temple (see picture), the Tabernacle and the surrounding temple district.

Bryce Canyon, Utah (bottom)

The painter Monet should have been here to create a counterpart to 'Impression, Sunrise', the work after which the Impressionist school is named. In this case, it would be 'Impression, Moonrise'. The sun paints the tall cliffs of Bryce Canyon in Utah with its last rays, while the full moon rises above the high horizon and takes up its nocturnal guard duties. In its light, the crevasses and gorges of this wild rocky landscape will cast even more mysterious and sharp shadows, through which the bats and owls will silently glide while the rocks crack and recover from the day's heat.

Arches National Park, Utah *(top)*

The sculptor Henry Moore might have called such a piece created in his workshop One Big Form, perhaps as a starting point for the Two Big Forms standing in front of the former Chancellery in Bonn. However, the British artist was not the one who was at work here and created this Delicate Arch, but rather an even more significant force by far, namely erosion. This occasional tendency to come up not only with bizarre creations but also with graceful ones is something that visitors to Arches National Park can see at many other places, since apparently the local stone is just right for the tools of weathering: wind, frost, water and heat, which shimmers at sunset on the high arches.

Grand Canyon National Park *(centre)*

"So unearthly that it might have been found on another, extinct planet", said once the Scottish writer John Muir about the Grand Canyon in northern Arizona. This is true for the rocky outcome of millions of years of non-stop chiselling, but not for the chisel itself, the Colorado River, that has cut its channel almost 1,500 metres deep into the rocks and exposed layer upon layer of earth history. It keeps on working indefatigably along the 447 kilometre long gorge, flowing at speeds of almost 20 kph, cutting away at some banks and depositing material at others and forming 160 rapids. And even this rocky desert is not dead. Firs, aspens, junipers and 1,500 other plant species cling to rock crevices and find nourishment in them, and 300 bird and 76 species of mammal are at home in this UNESCO World Heritage Site (1979).

Lake Powell, Arizona *(bottom)*

Water is a rare commodity in the arid regions that make up wide tracts of Arizona. One should not let it simply flow away unused as the Colorado River was doing at Glen Canyon until a few decades ago. Then the gorge was spanned by a dam and the water forced to stop. Now it can be utilised not only for energy generation and for irrigation, but also humidifies the hot air above the rocky desert and flows around the mountains so picturesquely that the tourists come along in their droves and leave their dollars in the region's cash tills.

Native Village (Pueblo), Taos *(top)*

For 300 years people lived here in their traditional native culture, until in 1615 the Spanish came and brought so-called advances such as firearms and firewater, as well as Christianity. The inhabitants of the pueblo of Taos, northeast of Santa Fé in New Mexico, wanted neither the one nor the other, rebelled and thus were coerced to accept the religion of brotherly love. In 1846, after 200 Spanish years, it was the United States that came and claimed mastery over the region. Again the Natives resisted, this time against the American Way of Life, and again the new government imposed its rule by force. Amazingly, the tribe did survive and even hung on to a large part of its traditions. Its village still consists of rectangular clay houses on five levels, and is the subject of Taos research and a UNESCO World Heritage Site since 1992.

Meteor Crater, Arizona *(top centre)*

In the age of space travel it is not only UFOs, little green men and other extraterrestrials that engage human fantasy. We have also become aware of quite real cosmic perils that earlier we might not have known about, or perhaps ignored as an inevitable part of existence: the earth is constantly exposed to bombardment by meteorites, much to the delight of shooting star enthusiasts. But although 99.9% of those fragments are harmless, they don't always have to be: around 20,000 years ago, i.e. only yesterday in geological terms, a huge rock hit central Arizona, vaporised completely as a result of the energy released through the impact and left behind the 167 metre deep and 1,186 metre wide Meteor Crater, also known as Barringer Crater and Canyon Diablo – in an urban area this would be a horror scenario.

Mesa Verde National Park *(bottom centre)*

Until 1888 nobody had the slightest idea that as far back as the 8th century, i.e. in early Pre-Columbian times, Pueblo Indians lived on the Colorado plateau in the states of Arizona, New Mexico and Colorado. After the first discovery by two farmers, hundreds of their fortress-like 'cliff dwellings' gradually came to light in ravines and caves, under mountain overhangs and up rock faces. The most impressive ones have been protected since 1906 in the Mesa Verde National Park in southern Colorado and since 1979 have also been a UNESCO World Heritage Site. The inhabitants were well protected behind massive walls – but not against drought; apparently, in the 13th century it forced the inhabitants to abandon their dwellings and migrate elsewhere.

Montezuma Castle *(bottom)*

No wonder that it took so long to discover that humans had settled in Colorado and Arizona even before the Native Americans of modern times: at one time, the numerous inhabitants of the craggy mountain regions only existed in the myths of the Navajos, who spoke of so-called 'Anasazi' or 'the ancient ones'. Towards the end of the 19th century, local farmers discovered that this was more than just a myth. In almost inaccessible gorges they found entire abandoned rock cities, even 'fortresses' as one soon started calling them, since the houses of these Pueblo Indians, built in caves and up rock faces, could only be reached through roof openings by way of ladders. One of the most ancient of these complexes is Montezuma Castle, named after the last ruler of the Aztecs: of course, he lived much further south in the 16th century.

Gateway Arch, St. Louis *(top)*

'Westward ho!' was the slogan of trekking settlers in 19th century USA. But the West was Wild, and many of them sought a place to stop. One of those places was Saint Louis on the Mississippi River, today the largest city in Missouri. Here the adventurers could consider one last time whether they really wanted to venture further into the unknown. Many preferred to stay, whilst for others the city became the gateway to the West and thus the starting point for opening up the huge landmass beyond the great river. In the 1950s, the city fathers wanted to commemorate this pioneering achievement — the Native Americans see this somewhat differently — with a monument, and appointed the architect Eero Saarinen (1910–1961) to build it. In 1959 he designed a 191 metre tall steel arc, the Gateway Arch, completed in 1965.

Chaco Culture National Historical Park *(top centre)*

Evidence for the culture of the 'Anasazi' (a Navajo word meaning 'the ancient ones') can also be found in northwestern New Mexico, in the 15 kilometres long and two to three kilometres wide Chaco Canyon. It gave its name to the culture that flourished here between 500 and 1200 AD, and its centre is also known as Chaco. This was a small town of almost 6,000 inhabitants during its best periods, whose everyday life and culture we can discover from abandoned tools and from the partly very large, multi-storey buildings. This centre was connected to 75 smaller settlements through a network of trails. The total area occupied by the Chaco culture, which died out due to drought, was 65,000 square kilometres. The park has been a UNESCO World Heritage Site since 1987.

Great Smoky Mountains National Park *(bottom centre)*

The Appalachians in eastern North America climb towards the south, where they cross the 2,000 metre line in the Great Smoky Mountains. Here they almost achieve high mountain status, with 16 peaks above 1,800 metres. That is why the primeval forest straddling Tennessee and North Carolina has remained nearly untouched, and has been under protection since 1926. In the meantime (1983), UNESCO has declared these 2,000 square kilometres a World Heritage Site, even further enhancing the protection afforded to the 3500 indigenous plant species. The animals benefit too, of course. Special mention goes to the salamanders of which there are thirty different species here, more than anywhere else.

Mammoth Cave National Park *(bottom)*

Visitors to the Mammoth Cave National Park in Kentucky can dive into an underworld of caves, grottoes and corridors over 550 kilometres long, covering five storeys going down over 100 metres. Its name derives from the immense dimensions of this cave system, the world's largest. However, it may just as well be called Prehistoric National Park for the countless prehistoric finds discovered here, evidence of earlier human use of parts of these natural catacombs. And it can also be regarded as a very special kind of zoo, being home to many animals (in particular those completely adapted to darkness), including a dozen bat species and several of cave fish. UNESCO World Heritage Site since 1981.

French Quarter, New Orleans *(top left)*

At first, the people of Louisiana were glad to be rid of the French when the USA bought it in 1803. Today they congratulate each other on the French past of their largest city, New Orleans. A breeze of Parisian elegance blows through the subtropical streets of the 'Vieux Carr' or French Quarter in the city on the Mississippi delta. The trellises on some of the balconies are so light and airy that they appear to float. The walls glow red behind them, and the green of the hanging plants completes the colour symphony – architectural Impressionism.

Everglades National Park *(top right)*

1,000 plant species, including two dozen orchids and scores of tree species, 40 of mammals, 60 of reptiles and amphibians and 350 bird species – such a paradise must be placed under protection, as was done in 1947 in the Everglades at the southern tip of the Florida peninsula. Part of this unique wetland was already lost, having been drained for agricultural purposes, and it was vital to save the remaining 6,000 square kilometres. UNESCO got involved in 1979 and declared the Everglades a World Heritage Site. This also serves to protect numerous archaeological sites and the Seminole Indians, who have a reservation here.

Cape Canaveral, Florida *(centre)*

Three – two – one – ignition! When a countdown proceeds smoothly like this, the rocket engines roar to life at Cape Canaveral US Air Force Station and a gigantic projectile lifts into the sky. The cape on the east coast of southern Florida is familiar to children worldwide, being the place where Kennedy Space Center launches its manned missions into space. There have been triumphs, as in 1969 when Apollo 11 left for the moon and took the first humans to the earth's natural satellite. The name also denotes disasters, such as the explosion of the Challenger space shuttle on 28 January 1986. Cape Canaveral has survived the shock and is, as it was before, a bustling space terminus. At the same time it is a museum of space travel so far.

Bridge Cavern, San Antonio *(bottom)*

It's always so difficult to remember: is it stalagmites or stalactites that hang down from the ceiling in limestone caves? A mnemonic might help: stalaGmites rise from the Ground, stalaCtites hang from the Ceiling ... Thus also at the Bridge Cavern near the Texan city of San Antonio, where the solidified limestone cones occur in multitudes like organ pipes and in places even form proper bridges, spanning underground brooks. Elsewhere the caves widen into entire halls or lead to corridor systems, where an expert guide is needed.

Mexico

Archaeological sites at Paquimé, Casas Grandes *(top)*

Did Pueblo Indians, migrating from the Colorado plateau in the 13th century, settle here? There is a lot of evidence to support this, since the ruined city of clay buildings discovered in northwest Mexico forms a kind of link between the culture of the hunter-gatherers in the north and the high civilisation of Central Mexico. The site of Paquimé lies at the edge of the town of Casas Grandes and displays signs of settlement dating to the 8th century. However, most of the finds, including the best-preserved ones, are from the 13th century. The town was abandoned after a fire in 1340 AD. UNESCO World Heritage Site since 1998.

Lagoons, El Vizcaíno *(centre)*

Although most of the interior of the Mexican peninsula of Baja California (Lower California) is arid, the water is lively enough. This is particularly true at several lagoons along the coast of the El Vizcaíno desert, about halfway up the 1,200 kilometre gulf separating the peninsula from the Mexican mainland. 3,700 square kilometres are designated as a reserve to protect the wildlife surviving in the sparse vegetation, but even more so in order to safeguard the local whale breeding grounds. Grey whales come from afar in order to give birth in the protected bays, and give their calves their first swimming lessons. Marine turtles also breed in this region, a UNESCO World Heritage Site since 1993.

Rock Drawings, Sierra de San Francisco *(bottom)*

The El Vizcaíno desert stretches north-west of Santa Rosalía, around the midpoint of the 1,200 kilometre Mexican peninsula of Baja California (Lower California). The prevailing climate may have been more hospitable several thousand years ago, given the black and red rock drawings found in San Pablo Canyon in the Sierra de San Francisco. They are up to 3,000 years old and mostly represent larger than life people and fleeing animals, thus probably used for hunting magic purposes. A UNESCO World Heritage Site since 1993.

Historic Centre, Guanajuato *(top)*

Northwest of Querétaro in Mexico's Sierra Madre Oriental, at an altitude of over 2,000 metres, Spanish soldiers of fortune came across a silver bonanza that proved to be so productive that soon a whole town grew around it: Guanajuato. Wealth makes beautiful, and thus many impressive buildings sprang up over next few centuries. Those worth visiting include Baroque churches such as La Compañia, La Valenciana and the Basilica of the Madonna, but also public buildings such as the Alhóndiga de Granaditas, built around 1800, and the university founded in 1732 (see picture). During the so-called War of the Reform in 1857–1860, Guanajuato was even briefly the capital of Mexico. Today the historic centre is a UNESCO World Heritage Site (1988).

Toltec Capital, Tula *(bottom left)*

For around 250 years, from 920 to 1160 AD, what is today a ruin was the centre of a flourishing culture: Tula (Tollan) in the Mexican highlands is the place that the Toltec nation, migrating from the north and named after the city, chosen to be the residence of its rulers. They could not live off the barren land alone, and accordingly developed excellent craft and trading skills. These brought with them prosperity and the means necessary for building elaborate pyramids such as the Temple of the Morning Star (see picture for figures) and other public buildings. But also for weapons: the Toltecs extended their domain up to today's Guatemala and Yucatan. However, in the 12th century they themselves became victims of warlike tribes from the north.

Old City, Zacatecas *(bottom right)*

They didn't find gold, but silver there was plenty: in 1546 AD, Spanish adventurers who liked styling themselves 'conquistadors' started criss-crossing the Sierra Madre Oriental northwest of today's León in Mexico. Two years later, at the place 'where the Zacate grass grows' (i.e. Zacatecas), they found a rich vein, and 32 silver mines were in operation barely two years after that. The Spanish king Philip II, during his 1558 journey to his kingdom of New Spain, insisted on visiting the silver city and helped to dedicate the newly established Franciscan monastery (in the picture: keystone with Franciscan emblem). The colonial city, melding with the terrain, is well preserved and has been a UNESCO World Heritage Site since 1993.

Old City, Morelia *(top)*

In 1541, fifty Spanish families laid the foundation stone of today's Morelia, capital of the state of Michoacán northwest of Mexico City. The centre is dominated by numerous ecclesiastical buildings in the Mexican Baroque style, including the cathedral with its two huge bell towers (dedicated in 1744) and the Palacio de Gobierno (1770), originally a seminary. Another typical feature is the tradition of painting the houses, made of brownish trachyte stone, a light pink colour. Until 1828 the city was named after its Spanish sister Valladolid, and then was renamed to honour José María Morelos (1765–1815), the priest and hero of the War of Independence. UNESCO World Heritage Site since 1991.

Silver Mines, Guanajuato *(Centre)*

The Mexican town of Guanajuato, 2,000 metres up in the Sierra Madre Oriental, is the place to visit for amazing industrial history. The miners in this silver city founded in the 16th century, in digging deep for the sought-after noble metal, did a thorough job and created a whole underground world, the so-called Subterranea. At Boca del Infierno ('Infernal Maw') they reached a depth of 600 metres. The wealth brought up to daylight created an attractive Old City, which together with the mining works has been a UNESCO World Heritage Site since 1988.

Querétaro *(bottom left)*

Before the Spanish arrived in 1531 there already existed here a Native American settlement, and Querétaro northwest of Mexico City still bears features of native architecture. Overall, though, it is dominated by the planned, checkerboard-like Spanish colonial town with beautiful Baroque churches and a cathedral dedicated in 1805, an ensemble that has been a UNESCO World Heritage Site since 1996. This is where, in 1810, the victorious war of Mexican independence began with the 'Grito de Dolores' (Cry of Pain). Liberty was at risk once more when the French emperor Napoleon III attempted to set up a Mexican puppet kingdom. However, this venture ended with the shooting of his straw man Maximilian in Querétaro. on 19th June 1867 (Picture: 'The Shooting of the Emperor Maximilian of Mexico' by Edouard Manet, 1867)

Pre-Columbian Town, El Tajin *(bottom right)*

Before or after the arrival of the discoverer Columbus – in American history, 1492 has almost the quality of Year 0. We talk about Pre- or Post-Columbian events or cultures, because the Spanish fairly thoroughly destroyed the cultures they encountered in the New World. That is why historians eagerly investigate any trace of Pre-Columbian remains, and at El Tajin north-west of Veracruz they have a whole ruined city to explore. One eye-catching ancient monument is the 25 metre tall Pyramid of Niches, whose 365 stucco-decorated steps may have served as a calendar for the Totonacs who lived here until around 1100 AD. UNESCO World Heritage Site since 1992.

Archaeological Site, Xochicalco
(bottom left)

The ruins of Xochicalco, which means 'in the place of the flower house', lie in the Mexican state of Morelos south of Cuernavaca. This is a fortified Aztec centre of worship, a crossroads of several ancient American civilisations. The site's golden age was the 'Period of Confusion' between 650 and 900 AD, when political powers such as Teotihuacán were in decline. The preserved part of the main pyramid on the hill and the remains of the district's surrounding walls display advanced building technology and rich decorations in reliefs. UNESCO World Heritage Site since 1999.

Historic Centre, Mexico City *(bottom right)*

'Noche triste' – 'Night of Sadness', that is how the conquistador Hernán Cortés called 30 June 1520, when rebellion by Tenochtitlán's population forced him to flee from the Aztec capital. But his return on 13 August 1521 was much sadder still, signifying as it did the end of the once magical lagoon city. The Spanish were thorough in building on top of the former centre of the Indian kingdom, and it was not until 1900 that its remains saw daylight again during Mexico City's canalisation works. More ruins have been excavated since then, and together with the Spanish Old City and its beautiful and thus somewhat placatory churches (in the picture: churches on Plaza Morelos) they form the historic core of this metropolis of almost 10 million souls. UNESCO World Heritage Site since 1987.

Ruins, Teotihuacán *(for bottom left and right)*

There is so much to see at the 'Place where the Gods were created', as Teotihuacán northeast of Mexico City would be called in English. Still, we know relatively little about the nation whose civilisation gave rise to the ruins lying here in heaps. It did maintain distinct religious practices, as shown by the parade called the 'Street of the Dead' and the buildings lining it, such as the Pyramid of the Sun (picture, left) and the Pyramid of the Moon (picture, right), the Citadel and the Temple of the Feathered Serpent. The beginnings of Teotihuacán go back to the 2nd century BC, and it reached its greatest power in the 3rd century AD. By the 7th century, the mysterious and fabulous culture had come to an end. Its ruins have been a UNESCO World Heritage Site since 1987.

Xochimilco, Mexico City *(bottom left)*

When the Spanish conquerors reached Tenochtitlán, the capital of the Aztec kingdom, in 1519, they found a lagoon paradise with floating gardens, the so-called Chinampas. When they destroyed the city two years later with the help of Indian allies, they also brought to an end an exemplary system of agriculture, or at least nearly: outside Mexico City, which was built on the drained ruins of Tenochtitlán, an example of this type of land management continued to exist at Xochimilco, south of the city. Canals surround large vegetable and flower plots that are still profitably cultivated today, although the canals are also increasingly being used for boating. Xochimilco is part of the 'Old City of Mexico City' UNESCO World Heritage Site (1987).

Plaza of the Three Cultures, Mexico City *(bottom right)*

The Aztec kingdom's destroyer, Hernán Cortés (1485–1547), has not been given a memorial in the Mexican capital, and had the Spanish left one behind there is no doubt it would long since have been razed. The country harks back deliberately to its great Aztec past, if nothing else then in order to integrate the Native American population. This does not mean that the dominating Spanish cultural components are ignored, but only that they no longer enjoy predominance and are placed on the same footing as the Pre-Columbian ones and those of modern Mexico. This is symbolised by the ensemble at the Plaza of the Three Cultures built in 1964, where excavated buildings from the late Aztec period stand alongside modern highrises and the Baroque church of Santiago de Tlatelolco.

Monasteries on the slopes of Popocatépetl *(far bottom right)*

One cannot deny the trust in God displayed by the monks who established their monasteries southeast of the capital immediately after the arrival of the Spanish in Mexico. They showed a marked preference for the slopes of the 5,452 metre volcano Popocatépetl, by no means extinct. Whether this was supposed to indicate an attitude of Closer My God to Thee or simply a sign of devout Christian faith, must remain an open question. At any rate, the result was several Dominican, Franciscan and Augustin monasteries in a marvellous landscape, of which 14 are still well preserved and in use to this day. They have been a UNESCO World Heritage Site since 1994.

Historic Centre, Puebla (top)

The million-plus metropolis Puebla, southeast of Mexico City, may be called the City of Facades, since sometimes the old buildings from the Spanish colonial period are almost overloaded with the finest stucco ornaments, tiles and convoluted balconies. The Baroque cathedral (1575–1649, see picture) does not need such decorations, since its sculptures, bell towers and domes are all the ornaments it requires. Founded in 1531 and a bishopric since 1545, Puebla was richly provided with ecclesiastical buildings, among which we can also mention the Jesuit church, brightened up with a dome of blue faïence, the Baroque Church of San Augustín and the Rosary Chapel at the Church of Santo Domingo. The Old City has been a UNESCO World Heritage Site since 1987.

Old City, Oaxaca (bottom left)

Oaxaca, capital of the equally named state and centre of a fertile high plain, lies southeast of Mexico City. The Spanish, advancing in 1521, quickly noticed the productive local agriculture and founded the city on a checkerboard ground plan. The cathedral (see picture), begun in 1544, is well worth seeing, albeit no longer in its original form but in an 18th century Baroque version, having fallen victim to an earthquake in 1714 and rebuilt between then and 1733. The same happened to other buildings, which together form the Old City and since 1987 have been a UNESCO World Heritage Site as a memorial to colonial times.

Nuestra Señora de Los Remedios, Cholula (bottom right)

In front of the smoking pyramid of Popocatépetl, at Cholula south of Mexico City, the people of Teotihuacán placed one of the world's largest pyramids, with a base area of 16 hectares. The Mixtecs took over the huge shrine around 800 AD, and in the 15th century it fell into the Aztecs' hands. Then came the Spaniards and destroyed the structure apart from a large foundation that they crowned with a church, Nuestra Señora de los Remedios. Its Baroque charm offers some consolation for the regret due to the decay of such an informative Pre-Columbian religious site. The caption to this panorama might be 'Celestial building before a hellish maw'.

Ruins, Monte Alban (top)

West of Oaxaca, which in turn lies southeast of the capital Mexico City, the Spanish came across ancient Native American settlements on their arrival in 1521. This sealed their fate, and it was only very recently that archaeologists have undertaken thorough investigations here at Monte Alban. They found remains going back to the 8th century BC, and exposed monumental religious buildings from the Zapotec period (until around 1250 AD). There are also later ruins from the subsequent Mixtec rule, in part destroyed before the Spanish period by the Aztecs who conquered the place in 1458. Together with the Old City of Oaxaca, this Pre-Columbian annexe has been a UNESCO World Heritage Site since 1987.

Ruins and National Park, Palenque
(centre)

The ruins of Palenque constitute the strongest evidence that one centre of Maya culture existed in southernmost Mexico, in the state of Chiapas. Settled by the 3rd century BC, this city flourished mainly between 600 and 750 AD and at that time covered an area of eight square kilometres, which provides archaeologists with almost literally an endless site to explore. Today this is a national park, and since 1987 also a UNESCO World Heritage Site. Numerous religious buildings such as the Temple of the Inscriptions with the sarcophagus of a Mayan ruler in the crypt, provide interesting clues about the life and beliefs of the Native American nation.

Santa Maria del Tule Cedar, Oaxaca
(bottom left)

With a 45 metre girth, this 2,000 year old cedar at Oaxaca, southeast of Mexico City, is thicker than all known giant sequoias in the Redwood forests of North America and one of the oldest living beings on earth. Of course, in height it cannot compete with the sequoias, but the latter rarely reach such an age precisely because of their size and often fall down before reaching their full growth limit, since their roots cannot support the tree's weight and the pressure of the wind. The cedar is proof against this hazard, and with its thick base it can stand up even to hurricanes.

Ruins, Chichén Itzá (bottom right)

No millipede has 1,000 feet, only a great many. Just the same is true for the thousand-pillar complex of Chichén Itzá, the ruins of a Mayan religious site in the north of the Mexican peninsula of Yucatan. The remnants of 600 pillars surround the Temple of the Warriors, approached by way of a wide open air staircase. The Sacred Well, as the site's name may be translated, also includes an observatory where the priests calculated the calendar from the angle of the incident sunlight. The complex also includes the Platform of Eagles and Jaguars, the Temple of the Bearded Man, the 30 metre tall Pyramid of Kukulkan and other religious buildings. After the Mayas, Chichén Itzá was used by the Toltecs from the end of the 10th century onward. UNESCO World Heritage Site since 1988.

Mayan Ceremonial Centre and City, Uxmal *(top left)*

Between the 7th and 10th centuries, the Mayas on the Mexican Yucatan Peninsula south of Mérida developed their city Uxmal into a religious centre. Among the ruins, the visitor's eyes first alight on the Magician's House pyramid (see picture), due to its oval ground plan that contrasts with the usual angular customs of Mayan builders; in addition, it rises steeply to a temple 38 metres tall. Other buildings, such as the Governor's Palace, the Dovecote and the Convent, are characterised by fantastic ornamentation and are decorated with mosaics, masks and snake motifs. UNESCO World Heritage Site since 1996.

Sian Ka'an Bio Reserve *(top right)*

The name sounds like Chinese but is even harder to understand, being in the Mayan language and meaning 'Beginning of the Sky'. For many living creatures, it really does begin here at the Sian Ka'an Biosphere Reserve, a 4,000 square kilometre area on the east coast of the Yucatan Peninsula, which together with 1200 square kilometres of sea is under protection and since 1987 has also been a UNESCO World Heritage Site. Almost 1000 plant species, 103 mammals, 339 birds and 42 reptiles and amphibians have been identified by the biologists in this subtropical paradise.

Historic City and Fortress, Campeche *(centre)*

The Yucatan Peninsula was an obvious landing site for the Spanish Conquistadors in their push towards the American mainland. In Campeche, today capital of the same-named Mexican state on the west coast, they built a harbour and fortified it against attacks from the sea, whether by British rivals or by the Caribbean's ubiquitous pirates. Like many of their other planned settlements, the Spaniards laid out the city in a checkerboard pattern and surrounded it with walls. Campeche outgrew them soon enough, but the encircling fortifications still exist today; together with the Old City they have been a UNESCO World Heritage Site since 1999.

Mayan Palace, Sayil *(bottom)*

Monumental buildings were a speciality of the Maya architects in the Yucatan lowlands of modern Mexico, and the great palace at Sayil is one of the most important examples. The powerful impact of its dimensions is further enhanced by the massive foundations and by the ornamented facade. The decorations include geometric patterns, plants and snakes that intertwine along the walls, and masks of the rain god Chac are evidence of the Pre-Columbian builders' fertility cult. In a landscape pampered but often also tortured by the sun, rain is far more significant for the populace than at more temperate latitudes. That is why Chac played such a dominant role in the Mayan pantheon.

Belize

Barrier Reef *(left)*

Seven conservation areas along the coast of the Central American state of Belize, in the eastern part of the Yucatan Peninsula, form a national park with a total area of around 1,000 square kilometres. It serves to protect the coral reef, parts of which stretch very close to the shore. It is 250 kilometres long, which makes it the second largest in the world after Australia's Great Barrier Reef and a huge sanctuary for numerous amphibians, fish, molluscs and seabirds. The lagoons and mangrove forests are particularly important as a breeding ground for turtles, but it is also because of the corals themselves that the reef enjoys international protection as a UNESCO World Heritage Site since 1996.

Coastal Islands *(right)*

Where such extensive coral reefs are to be found as along the east coast of Yucatan in the Central American country of Belize, atolls and lagoons will follow. The coastal lowlands merge directly into this shallow-water zone and break up into islands, which like the atolls are tailor-made breeding areas for seabirds and crocodiles. They live on the large numbers of indigenous worms, crabs, mussels and fish. The coastal islands of Belize are therefore ringed by several conservation areas, although they are often disturbed by diving and sailing enthusiasts – not a trivial matter for animals with a large flight distance. Being listed as a UNESCO World Heritage Site (1996) has focused more international attention on the region and improved its protection.

Guatemala

Tikal National Park *(top)*

Both culture and nature are protected in the 567 square kilometres of Tikal National Park in north-eastern Guatemala. The former only accounts for three percent, but what three percent! If this were not comparing apples with oranges, one could almost say that they are more significant than the other 97 percent: they consist of a whole Mayan city with the remains of 4,000 buildings, including temples (in the picture: Temple of the Jaguar) and fantastic pyramids. Open-air staircases climb up to the shrines at their summits, at tree canopy height. As far as nature is concerned, we are talking about the largest continuous tropical rainforest in Central America, sanctuary for numerous species and together with the culture monument a UNESCO World Heritage Site since 1979.

Antigua Guatemala *(bottom left)*

It is regrettable enough that Central American buildings from the Pre-Columbian period can only be viewed as ruins. But to have whole Spanish cities fall into decay is an exception. Southwest of Guatemala City, the capital of Guatemala, there is such an exception: Antigua Guatemala, one of the most beautiful colonial Spanish Baroque cities of the 18th century, was laid waste by earthquakes so often that in the end it was no longer rebuilt. Some of it has been restored, at any rate, so that for example the admirable cathedral, begun in 1545, can be appreciated. UNESCO World Heritage Site since 1979.

Quiriguá Archaeological Park and Mayan Ruins *(bottom right)*

In 1840, the ruins of a Mayan centre of worship were found at Quiriguá (eastern Guatemala) on the Río Motagua, north of the Honduran city of Copán. Among the most impressive finds are numerous steles, some over 18 metres tall, and animals and fabulous creatures chiselled out of stone blocks. The remains of the sculptures and temples, with writing that has not yet been completely deciphered, are from the golden age of the Mayan culture between 500 and 800 AD. The latest traces date from 900 AD, after which apparently the complex was abandoned and became submerged for almost 1,000 years in the primeval forest. UNESCO World Heritage Site since 1981.

El Salvador

Ruins, Joya de Cerén (top)

Due to their massive construction, temples and palaces are often the only remains of vanished cultures, while we know little about the houses and lives of ordinary people. One counterexample does exist at Joya de Cerén in south-western El Salvador, northwest of the capital San Salvador. Here, a Mayan community was buried in 600 AD by the Loma Caldera volcano and only rediscovered in 1976. The excavated remains include huts made of clay bricks and timber, animal skeletons, fossilised food — in short, an informative snapshot of everyday village life many centuries ago. In 1993 UNESCO declared Joya de Cerén a World Heritage Site.

Honduras

Mayan Ruins, Copán (centre)

The inscriptions on the Mayan temples of Copán in western Honduras, near the Guatemalan border, permit quite precise dating. Although complete decipherment of the script has to wait a little longer, several dates have already been worked out with the help of this site. Thus we know that a ruler called Yax Pak ('First Dawn') ascended the throne on 2.7.763 AD. He had the city, lying in a 24 square kilometre valley, developed and expanded, and the two-storey temple decorated with rich sculptural ornaments. A total of 6,000 figures can be seen here, which in turn wear fantastic finery. The location was abandoned after 800 AD, and since 1980 has been protected as a UNESCO World Heritage Site.

Biosphere Reserve, Río Plátano
(bottom)

The core section of Río Plátano National Park, located in north-eastern Honduras, covers 1,300 square kilometres; another 3,700 square kilometres are a buffer zone with less strict conditions. In addition to a whole series of archaeological sites belonging to the Mayan civilisation, the protection primarily applies to the species living in this rainforest region. It offers a sanctuary to reptiles and amphibians and hundreds of bird species, including toucans and curassows, as well as to a whole range of increasingly rare mammals such as spotted jaguars, jaguarundis and manatees. UNESCO World Heritage Site since 1982.

Costa Rica

Talamanca Nature Reserve and La Amistad National Park *(top)*

From Costa Rica south of Limón, a mountain range covered in primeval forest stretches all the way into Panama. Here, several reserves and national parks were united into one UNESCO World Heritage Site in 1983. It covers a total of 5,700 square kilometres, and reaches an altitude of 3,820 metres at Cerro Chirripó. Four percent of all terrestrial animal species and 9,000 plant species, including as many as 1,000 ferns and 900 lichens, occur in this park, since the region rises across a short distance through many climatic zones, from tropical rainforest to sparse mountain forest. This diversity, and a few traces of settlements going back 12,000 years, make the national park into a natural and cultural monument.

Guanacaste Nature Reserve *(right)*

In north-western Costa Rica, the Cordillera Guanacaste mountains rise from the Pacific coast to an altitude of 1,580 metres. Due to its wealth of species, part of this range was placed under protection and was declared a UNESCO World Heritage Site in 1999. It contains the region's largest continuous tropical dry forest. With its intact ecosystems, from the coral reefs along the coast to the spectacular broadleaf paradise of the central mountains (in the picture: Yellow Trumpet or Pui tree), it provides sanctuary to animals and plants which elsewhere had to give way to encroaching human habitation.

Panama

Historic Quarter, Panama City *(top)*

At first Columbus believed that Cuba was India, later the Central American mainland was thought to be the beginning of Asia, and only on 25 September 1513 did the conquistador Núñez de Balboa manage to prove that a New World had been discovered. From the mountains of Panama, "Silent, upon a peak in Darien" as the poet Keats described it, he saw the Pacific, which he called the South Sea. Panama City, the first European settlement on the coast of this far from pacific ocean, was founded in 1519 on a rocky peninsula. Among the first large buildings were the cathedral, boasting five naves and two white bell towers, and several monasteries. Later they were joined by French and eventually genuine American buildings (see picture), all of them together declared a UNESCO World Heritage Site in 1997.

La Amistad National Park *(bottom right)*

The role played by Chirripó on the Costa Rican side is paralleled by Chiriqui on the Panamanian side. At 3430 metres in altitude, it is only marginally lower than the summit to its northwest. They are separated by the border, but only those travelling along the Pan-American Highway notice it, whilst the animals in the primeval mountain forest of La Amistad National Park pay no attention to it whatsoever. They benefit from protection across an area of 5700 square kilometres, where jaguars and ocelots, pumas and eagles can continue hunting undisturbed by human predators and find rich nourishment in the cloud forests. The park's listing as a UNESCO World Heritage Site (1983) is designed to ensure this situation.

Darién National Park *(bottom left)*

Southeast of Santa Fé and the Gulf of San Miguel in Panama, a tropical rainforest stretches across the mountains of Darién and other mountain ranges. It begins with mangrove at the coast, and gradually merges into highland rainforest. A total of 6000 square kilometres have been protected since 1972, and since 1981 have enjoyed international status as a UNESCO World Heritage Site. Located on the border with Colombia, the national park with its 50 metre high canopy forms a natural bridge to South America. The numerous mammals in the forest include jaguars, giant anteaters, ocelots, various monkeys and tapirs, and among the reptiles — caimans and American crocodiles.

Cuba

Old City, Havana *(far top left)*

Even 40 years of Communism have not been able to shake the Cubans' Catholic faith. This became evident during the Mass that Pope John Paul II held in Havana in January 1998 in front of 800,000 people, just where in 1519 the first open-air prayer meeting marked the foundation of to-day's teeming metropolis and capital of the island republic. More evidence of deep piety can be seen at the colonial Baroque Cathedral of San Cristóbal (dedicated 1724) and at several monasteries in the heart of the Old City. Thanks to these cultural monuments and the simple but inviting complex of arcades around the Plaza de la Catedral, it was made a UNESCO World Heritage Site in 1982. The picture shows the old presidential palace, today housing the Museum of the Revolution.

Fortifications, Havana *(far top right)*

After his first landing in the islands of the New World in 1492, it took Columbus another two weeks to reach Cuba. By 1511 it had been conquered by the Spanish, who comprehensively fortified the harbour of Havana prior to it becoming the springboard for the mainland's conquest. Some parts of the imposing military architecture are still in place, even though the city wall was pulled down in 1863. The main fortresses, Castillo de la Fuerza and Fort El Morro (picture top right), still guard the harbour entrance, only 200 metres wide. In 1982, together with the Old City behind the Calzada de Malecón shore-side promenade, they were declared a UNESCO World Heritage Site.

Viñales Valley *(top left)*

With a boycott being imposed by the USA, the Cuban econ-omists had to come up with an idea for sourcing foreign currency and opened the country to tourism. True, because of the prosperity gap between the holidaymakers and the local population this has the potential to cause unrest, but tourism was easy to promote: the island has such beautiful beaches and such attractive prices that the tourism boom simply had to happen. For some, this devalued the secret of Cuba, but not for those who do more than merely roast themselves on the beach. In the island's interior there are wonderful destinations such as the Viñales Valley north of Pinar del Río: beautiful forested karstic limestone hillocks, the so-called mogotes, lend it a fascinating charm.

San Pedro de la Roca Fortress, Santiago de Cuba *(top Centre)*

Cuba's first capital (until 1556) lies at the foot of the Sierra Maestra: Santiago de Cuba was founded in 1514, five years before Havana. After the Armada's heavy defeat in 1588, when the Spanish lost their hegemony on the seas, they had to fear British attacks on their bases in the Caribbean and massively fortified the most important ones. In order to safeguard the bay, Santiago was provided with the fort of San Pedro de la Roca. Built between 1590 and 1610, it kept suffering earthquake damage but each time was rebuilt and extended, most recently in the 18th cen-tury. It was restored in 1978, made a national monument in 1979 and a UNESCO World Heritage Site in 1997.

Sugar Factories at Valle de los Ingenios, Trinidad *(top right)*

The sugar factories at Valle de los Ingenios, northwest of Trinidad, are reminders of Cuba's currently isolated position in the world's economy. 56 of these factories were in operation in 1830, a sign that the Spanish colony was well on its way to becoming an agricultural monoculture. At that time it brought wealth to a small entrepreneurial class and to the district, as Trinidad's beautiful urban fabric demonstrates (in the picture: Church of San Francisco). Due to the trade problems it is at risk, and both the town and the industrial monuments need care and maintenance. UNESCO World Heritage Site since 1988.

Haiti

Palace of Sans Souci, Cape Haïtien
(top)

Versailles was the inspiration, when the self-proclaimed King Henri I of Haiti decided to build himself a palace in 1811 and gave it the French name Sans Souci ('Carefree'). The fact that the potentate did have plenty of cares is still evident today when observing the ruins of Ramiers south of Cape Haïtien, whose massive walls had something of the quality of fortifications. The magnificent double open-air staircase and the floors above are now covered by moss and grass. The empty window openings are reminiscent of Shelley's poem about the transience of power and glory: "Nothing beside remains. Round the decay of that colossal wreck, boundless and bare, the lone and level sands stretch far away". A UNESCO World Heritage Site since 1982.

Historic National Park and Citadel
(bottom)

In 1804, Haiti threw off the yoke of French rule, in 1807 Henri Christophe became president of the country's northern part, and in 1811 he declared himself king as Henri I. In constant fear of the return of the French, he had an immense citadel built on a jutting rock at Pic Laferrière, south of Cap Haïtien. It covers an area of 10,000 square metres, and is also his last place of rest (picture: bottom centre). The citadel was never needed, but the coloured population saw in it a symbol of liberation.

South America

Nature and culture in harmony

The culture of the Inca had reached its 'old peak' (the meaning of the name Machu Picchu) in the 16th century, when the Spanish catastrophe fell upon them and turned the New World's southern half-continent into part of the Old one. South America has been radically Europeanised, and strangely fascinating traces such as the Nazca Lines or the ruins of the terraced mountain-city Machu Picchu are all that remains of the native Pre-Columbian world. Churches and cathedrals have displaced the temples and pyramids. We only realise with hindsight that they had – and have – the same aim: to link the human here-and-now to the heavens. The wonders of the Andes and the Amazon, the surrounding oceans and the wide vistas of the Pampas in the interior make it evident that the opulent South American natural world imprints itself on human culture. Anyone who has looked up towards the snowy summit of Aconcagua or across the silent mirror of Lake Titicaca, anyone who has heard the thunder of the mighty Iguaçu waterfalls or the breakers at Cape Horn, grasps how small human endeavours are compared with the forces of nature. Native American sacred sites and Christian houses of God are one and the same expression of this insight. The fact that humans can give it concrete form is also one of the wonders in this part of the world, so well endowed with wonders. They teach us that culture can only succeed in harmony with nature. South America exhibits many fine examples of this principle.

South America

Caribbean Ocean

JAMAICA
Kingston
Port au Prince
HAITI
Santo Domingo
DOMINICAN
REP.
San Juan
Puerto Rico
(USA)
Anquilla
ANTIGUA
& BARBUDA
ST. KITTS
& NEVIS
Guadeloupe
DOMINICA
National Park
Martinique
ST. VINCENT
& GRENADINES
ST. LUCIA
BARBADOS
GRENADA

Neth. Antilles
Willemstad

Barranquilla
Cartagena
Maracaibo
Coro National Park
Barquisimeto
Caracas
Port of Spain
TRINIDAD
& TOBAGO

PANAMÁ

Medellín

Bogotá

Cali

COLOMBIA

Popayán
San Agustín

Ciudad
Bolívar

VENEZUELA

Salto Angel

Canaima
National Park

GUYANA

Georgetown

Paramaribo

SURINAM

Cayenne

Fr.
Guyana

Galapagos Is.
National Park

Quito

ECUADOR

Guayaquil

Sangay
National Park

Cuenca

Amazon

Iquitos

Manaus

Santarém

Belém

Forta

Teresina

Chan Chan
Trujillo
Huascarán
National Park
Chavín
de Huantár

Río Branco

Porto Velho

P E R U

Manú
National Park

Callao
Lima
Sacsayhuamán
Machu Picchu
Cuzco

Nazca
Colca Canyon
Lake Titicaca
La Paz
Arequipa
Copacabana
Cochabamba

B O L I V I A

B R A Z I L

Rondonópolis

Brasília

Goiânia

Salvador d

Iquique
Sucre

Potosí

Jesuit missions
of the Chiquitos

Guairá

Campo
Grande

Congonhas
Belo Horizonte
Ouro Prêto
Vitória

P A C I F I C

Antofagasta

PARAGUAY

Concepción

São Paulo

Santos

Nova
Iguacu
Rio de Janeiro

Curitiba

O C E A N

Tucumán

Asunción

L.S. Trinidad

Corrientes

Iguaçu
National Park

Jesuit missions
of the Guaraní

Pôrto Alegre

Rapa Nui National Park
(Easter Island)

Valparaíso

Santiago

Mendoza

Aconcagua

Córdoba

Rosario

URUGUAY

Buenos Aires

Montevideo

Maldonado

La Plata

Concepción

Auca Mahuida (volcano)

Bahia Blanca

Mar del Plata

Valdivia

Osorno
(volcano)

A R G E N T I N A

C H I L E

Valdés
Patagonia

C. Rivadavia

Falkland
Islands

Los Glaciares
National Park

Río Gallegos

Punta Arenas

Ushuaia

0   250   500   750
km

Dominican Republic

Colonial-era Quarter, Santo Domingo *(top)*

The city of Santo Domingo, on the southern coast of the island of Hispaniola, was founded in 1496 by Bartholomew, brother of America's discoverer Columbus. Thus, today's metropolis of two million inhabitants and the capital of the Dominican Republic is one of the oldest Spanish settlements in the New World, and has become a model for many later ones. The heart of the Old City is made up of religious buildings such as the Basilica Menor de la Virgen de la Anunciación with the hotly-disputed tomb of the city's founder and several monasteries, and secular ones including the Ozama fortress and a number of palaces, all dating from the early 16ᵗʰ century. Since 1990 this has been a UNESCO World Heritage Site.

Dominica

Morne Trois Pitons National Park *(bottom)*

On a Sunday in the year 1493 Columbus landed at an island that he therefore named Dominica. Although only 750 square kilometres in size, almost ten percent of the interior is protected. This is active volcanic terrain with tropical rainforest, which forms the Morne Trois Pitons (Three-Peak Mountain) National Park. Fumaroles hiss, a 'boiling lake' bubbles, hot springs reach the surface and fall down to the valley in cascades. And roundabout grows a marvellous primeval forest that provides to numerous plants and animals a living space almost inaccessible to humans. UNESCO World Heritage Site since 1997.

Puerto Rico (USA)

Fort San Felipe del Morro, San Juan
(top)

Even 300 years and more after its construction, that part of the fortifications of La Fortaleza called El Morro in San Juan, the capital of Puerto Rico, caused problems for the USA navy. During the 1898 Spanish-American war, a Spanish complement was barricaded here and only surrendered when the overall situation became hopeless. If they hadn't, the navy is certain to have had to contend with the walls of El Morro for much longer. As it turned out, they took over the fortress relatively undamaged and in 1942 installed in it an underground bunker complex. The rest has been restored since 1992 as a protected monument, and today once again it looms with its old menacing might.

Old City, San Juan *(bottom)*

The southernmost part of the USA is the island of Puerto Rico in the Caribbean, at about the same latitude as Honduras. The Spaniards settled here in 1521 and held fast until 1898, when the USA laid its hand on the land and its capital. This capital, the beautiful San Juan, bears unmistakably Spanish features: due to British naval competition, immediately upon arrival the European rulers built the military fortress La Fortaleza (1533–1540) and the Catholic Faith citadel, the Gothic San Juan Cathedral (built 1540; see picture). Around those grew up the present colonial Old City, which together with the military architecture was declared a UNESCO 1983 World Heritage Site in 1983.

Colombia

Harbour and Monuments from the Colonial Era, Cartagena (top)

Amerigo Vespucci landed here in 1499 and gave his name to the entire New World. He also named this land after the New World's discoverer, Columbus. Cartagena, in north-western Colombia north of the capital Bogotá, was the first Spanish establishment in South America and gained a reputation as the Pearl of the Caribbean. It owes this reputation to the effervescent joie de vivre of the Old City, adorned with wonderful Baroque buildings, among which the cathedral (built 1575–1612), the convent church of San Pedro Claver and the fortress of San Felipe de Barajas (see picture) set a more serious tone. The harbour, fortress and Old City of the colonial jewel have been a UNESCO World Heritage Site since 1984.

Plaza Bolívar and Cathedral, Bogotá (bottom left)

Liberation from the Spanish colonial power succeeded, the sought-after unification of the liberated South American countries did not: that is why the historical assessment of Simon Bolívar (1783–1830) is somewhat shaky. His statue however, in the square named after him in the Colombian capital Bogotá, stands solid in front of the Classicist-Baroque cathedral (see picture). The latter has not always displayed the memorial's stability, occasionally being severely damaged by earthquakes as the repairs demonstrate. But this only makes the original parts, the domes and towers, appear even more splendid.

San Agustín Archaeological Park (bottom right)

Deep in Colombia's interior, where the Río Magdalena rises, are ruins of whose builders we don't know much more than can be seen at San Agustín. There are sculptures everywhere, often mixed figures, half human and half jaguar. In total there are 350 such stocky figures, guarding the entrances to the grave complexes or lying in ambush. They are up to 2,500 years old, and even the most recent ones have been around for 1,200 years. They are evidence of a warlike disposition and great creative imagination. Neither of these has managed to hold up their decay, and it is important to preserve what is left: which is what the archaeological park being chosen as a UNESCO World Heritage Site (1995) is designed to support.

Curaçao *(Holland)*

Harbour and Town Centre, Willemstad

Dutch style in the Subtropics: the Old City and harbour of Willemstad, the capital of the Dutch Antilles on the Caribbean island of Curaçao, exhibit clear West European features. However, the colonial note cannot be ignored either. Willemstad was founded in 1634 by Dutch seafarers, who developed it in a planned fashion over the following centuries. The modern town at the picturesque natural harbour, by now boasting 70,000 inhabitants and large industrial installations, remains architecturally characterised by earlier buildings from the founders' era. As a typical example of the Colonial style, Willemstad has been a UNESCO World Heritage Site since 1997.

Venezuela

Coro National Park *(top)*

It is not only towards the end of the 19th century and at the beginning of the 20th that Germans played a brief part in colonial history. As far back as the 16th century, in return for granting substantial credit to the king of Spain, the Welser trading house of Augsburg received exploitation rights in today's Venezuela, especially in the vicinity of Coro west of Caracas. The Welsers left hardly any traces, or they have long since gone with the wind in this dry region in the foothills of the Cordillera del Norte. The national park established there is dominated across wide tracts by wonderfully curved dunes, in whose valleys some modest vegetation has established itself.

Canaima National Park *(bottom)*

The whites have mercilessly plundered the New World's native population, persecuted them and in cases of resistance even deliberately exterminated them. It took a long time before understanding of the human status of the supposedly primitive natives sank in. Reservations were created, but rarely as successfully as at the Canaima National Park in Venezuela, on the border with Brazil and Guyana. 30,000 square kilometres are under protection here, and the ca. 10,000-strong Pémon people can live undisturbed and according to its old customs in this paradise. The park spreads from the rainforest in the east to the rock formations of the Gran Sabana, and has been a UNESCO World Heritage Site since 1994.

Angel Falls *(centre)*

Towards the east, the primeval forest of the Venezuelan Canaima National Park opens up and merges into the Gran Sabana limestone plateau that features table mountains, steep cliffs and innumerable waterfalls. One branch of the Carrao River, near the border with Brazil and Guyana, drops about one kilometre into the abyss: a world record for waterfalls. When back-lit, the long veil of water shimmers in all colours of the rainbow, or it lights up as a white ribbon and looks almost unreal in front of rock and forest. At the bottom, the wet element falling from the sky is captured in a deep channel and flows gently away.

Ecuador

Galapagos Islands National Park *(top)*

Everyone has seen these enormous lizards on television programmes. Had conservation measures not been taken, then this biological Garden of Eden would probably have ceased to exist by now, since the ecosystems on the 13 large and 17 small Galapagos Islands (Spanish for Tortoise Islands) are highly fragile. That is why almost their entire area of 7,812 square kilometres – excluding only a few inhabited locations – has been a national park since 1959, and since 1978 also a UNESCO World Heritage Site. 70,000 square kilometres of the sea around the islands are also under protection. Hence it is still possible to experience here the scenes that Charles Darwin saw during his 1835 visit, scenes that gave the impetus to his revolutionary theory of evolution.

Sangay National Park *(centre left)*

This national park stretches from the treeless plains of the Ecuadorian lowlands, all the way to the altitude of the three 5,000 metre volcanoes Sangay, El Altar and Tungurahua, covering an area of almost 5,200 square kilometres of which 2,700 have been recognised as a UNESCO World Heritage Site since 1983. Up to an altitude of 3,000 metres the mountain slopes are covered by impenetrable and therefore untouched primeval forest, with an animal world whose variety can hardly be found anywhere else. Special attention is reserved for the large cats such as puma, ocelot and jaguar, as well as for the increasingly rare mountain tapir, the spectacled bear and the Andean condor, at 3.25 metres wingspan the world's largest flying bird.

Old City, Quito *(centre right)*

When the Spanish came in 1533, they destroyed this capital of the northern Inca kingdom and during the following year started building their own settlement, nowadays a teeming metropolis and the capital of Ecuador. The original heart of the city, with its numerous monasteries and churches that have given Quito the nickname Baroque Jewel of the Andes, is well preserved to this day. Quito lies at an altitude of 2,850 metres, and thus almost 2,000 metres lower than the nearby peak of Pichincha (4,776 metres). The mountain looks down on a sea of houses, whose old centre was declared by UNESCO in 1978 as a World Heritage Site. In the picture: Plaza Independencia with cathedral, Presidential Palace and the Independence Fighters' Memorial.

Cathedral, Cuenca *(bottom)*

If the Native Americans regarded the Europeans who descended on them out of the blue in the early 16th century as demigods, the newcomers were quick to assert that an even greater power, indeed an omnipotent one, loomed behind them. Churches, monasteries and cathedrals were among the conquerors' first great buildings. Thus also in Santa Ana de Cuenca, the capital of the Ecuadorian province of Azuay. By 1590 there was already a cathedral at its centre, which since the end of the 19th century has had a modern sister (see picture) standing across from it, the 105 metres long and 43.5 metres wide symbol of the city.

Peru

Amazon *(top)*

The catchment area of the world's water-richest river system, with its source in Peru, is seven million square kilometres in extent, reaching almost the size of Europe. The Amazon is formed by the three rivers Marañón, Huallaga and Ucayali. After about 6500 kilometres it reaches the Atlantic in Brazil, flowing into the sea in a gigantic delta up to 250 kilometres wide. Its banks and those of its tributaries are fringed by extensive tropical rainforests, effectively the lungs of the whole earth. As a result of economic exploitation, road building and slash-and-burn clearance, it — and thus the world's climate — is increasingly at risk. Therefore, and in order to preserve the disappearing Indio cultures, protective measures are urgently needed.

Cathedral, Lima *(centre left)*

An earthquake in 1746 destroyed the first cathedral in the Peruvian capital Lima. Its replacement was lent a Baroque character by way of domes, ornamental spires and facade decorations. This contrasts somewhat with the address, since the cathedral stands on the Plaza de Armas (Place of the Poor) whose name is not a reference to the church's arms. Churches and castles fulfilled similar functions in the early days of Spanish conquest in the New World: a demonstration of strength, where a bit of ecclesiastic muscle could do no harm. This dark side was somewhat brightened up in 1985 by a coat of yellow festive paint on the occasion of Pope John Paul II's visit.

Ruins of Chan Chan *(centre right)*

The Spanish conquerors found only a partially destroyed city in 1535 when they came to Chan Chan, north of Lima and Trujillo in Peru. In 1470, the Incas conquered the Chimú capital that had flourished for over half a millennium; the Spaniards completed the destruction. The ruins are scattered across 18 square kilometres, which tells us something about national wealth in the Chimú period. Nine citadels or palaces have been identified by archaeologists, as well as a variety of shrines on platforms, so-called Huacas. The fortifications still standing include a wall one kilometre long and up to seven metres tall. UNESCO World Heritage Site since 1988.

Huascarán National Park *(bottom)*

This Peruvian national park in the Cordillera Blanca in the Andes, lies between an altitude of 2500 metres and the double summit of the Huascarán at 6768 metres. In purely numerical terms it is hard to beat, with 27 snow-covered mountains over 6000 metres high, over 650 glaciers, almost 300 lakes and 40 rivers. The plants growing below the tree line include, among others, the world's largest bromeliads and 798 other plant species. The animal world is represented, for example, by spectacled bears, pumas, vicuñas as well as Andean condors and hummingbirds. The tropical mountain rainforest and the high mountain region have been a UNESCO World Heritage Site since 1985.

Ruins of Machu Picchu (top left)

The conquistadors did not destroy Machu Picchu directly, since they were quite ignorant of its existence. The Inca fortress-city north-west of Cuzco, at an altitude of 2450 metres in the Peruvian Andes, was built around 1450. The site fell into decay because the empire it served was destroyed by the Spaniards. It was only in 1911 that news of this place went round the world, and since then it has exerted a magical pull on scientists and tourists alike. The ruins of the city stand on a rock outcrop, laid out in a U-shape on terraces, with artisan, agricultural and religious districts. The 'Old peak', as the name might be translated, with its Temple of the Sun, Sacred Plaza and Royal Mausoleum, joined the list of UNESCO World Heritage Sites in 1983.

Old City with Franciscan Monastery, Lima (top right)

The Old City of Peru's eight million inhabitant capital Lima, the Ciudad de los Reyes (City of the Kings), stretches along both banks of the Río Rimac. Founded by Pizarro on 18ᵗʰ January 1535, it was beautified with a cathedral and several palaces, including the famous Palacio de Torre Tagle. As a result of earthquake damage some of the first buildings were replaced by Baroque ones in the 18ᵗʰ century. This has helped to enliven the appearance of the old city, since 1988 a UNESCO World Heritage Site.

Manú National Park (centre right)

The largest Peruvian national park, covering over 15,000 square kilometres, is in the country's south-eastern reaches in the Amazon basin along the flanks of the Cordillera de Carabaya. It stretches along the Río Manú and Río Alto Madre de Díos, and is home to probably the world's richest variety of both lowland and montane rainforest plants. One quarter of all South American bird species occur here, as well as 13 species of monkey, 12 reptile and 77 amphibian species. The mammals include giant armadillos, ocelots, spectacled bears and short-eared foxes. This conservation effort is supported by UNESCO, the park having been a World Heritage Site since 1987.

Ruins of Chavín de Huantár (bottom)

This impressive witness to the earliest Pre-Columbian culture of South America is located in the northern Peruvian highland of the Cordillera Blanca, in the Río Mozna valley. Chavín de Huantár was a place of worship, 5400 square metres in size. Created during the golden age of the Chavín culture between 700–300 BC, it was built out of stacked granite blocks that formed a three storey main temple up to 9 metres in height, decorated with ornaments. One of the most remarkable finds is a sculpture called El Lanzón, a deity fashioned out of a single stone with jaguar face and claw hands. UNESCO World Heritage Site since 1985.

Cuzco *(far top)*

Kingnapping, Hidalgo style: during his assault on the Inca kingdom in today's Peru, the Spanish conquistador Pizarro managed to get his hands on King Atahualpa. To pay his ransom, the Incas scraped together all the gold hoarded in their capital Cuzco and handed it over to the attackers. They took it happily, had the king strangled and in 1533 invaded the city, where they assumed they would find a great deal more gold. This proved to be a misapprehension, for which the inhabitants had to carry the can. All that remained of their city were the huge granite blocks of the temples and fortifications, which the victors were unable to move. These ruins make Cuzco the 'archaeological capital of the Americas', while the Baroque buildings erected by the new rulers on top of the Inca walls add colonial magnificence. This mixture is the reason why the metropolis in the Andes, 3,400 metres up, was made a UNESCO World Heritage Site in 1983.

Inca Fortress, Sacsayhuamán *(top left)*

The ruins of the old Inca fortress of Sacsayhuamán, which presumably was also a place of worship, are 200 metres higher up than even the sky-high location of Cuzco. Visitors from around the world come here to admire the walls joined together without mortar, ranged in three rows of blocks of which several are nine metres tall and weigh 350 tonnes. Here, during state and religious ceremonies, the ruler and 'Sun Prince' sat on a high throne hewn out of the rock and looked down on his capital just to the south, which together with the fortress has been a UNESCO World Heritage Site since 1983.

Colca Canyon *(top centre)*

The Río Colca cuts deep into the Andean highlands in southern Peru, in fact twice as deep as the Grand Canyon in Arizona. It flows at an altitude of 1,400 metres, passing between the 6,288 metre peak of Nevado de Ampato and the 6,614 metres of Nudo Coropuna, 100 kilometres north of Arequipa. Eventually it joins the Río de Majes, which flows into the Pacific. The actual gorge, i.e. the direct steep drop from the surrounding highlands into the river valley, is 3,233 metres deep, which is a world record. Nowhere else can the mountain-building folding force of the earth's crust be studied better than here, where the traveller on foot or on whitewater rafts feels tiny before the gigantic walls all round.

Nazca Lines and Pampas de Jumana *(top right)*

One hundred years ago it would not have occurred to anyone to regard the mysterious drawings of Nazca and Pampas de Jumana in Peru as landing pads for spacecraft. But ever since humans themselves have started venturing into the earth's cosmic front yard, terrestrial explanations have become just too simple. There must be aliens involved, even though the gigantic drawings south-east of Lima turn out to be remarkably accurate depictions of earthly scenery when observed from a bird's perspective: distributed across 350 square kilometres you can find a 'tulip tree' (see picture), a 46 metre spider, a 188 metre reptile and gigantic animals such a hummingbirds, monkeys and dogs. Most likely there were religious motives behind the early Native American art of the 6th century. In 1994 the region was declared a UNESCO World Heritage Site, where further research can be conducted.

Brazil

Teatro Amazonas, Manaus

The locals had a monopoly: if you wanted rubber you had to go to Brazil, or more precisely to Manaus, the capital of the state of Amazonas, standing just upstream of where the Río Negro joins the continent's largest river. Until 1913 there was no competition, and the city and the state wallowed in prosperity. These heavenly times are long gone, but a literally fabulous monument still remains: the Teatro Amazonas, the town's opera house built in 1896 in Neo-Renaissance style. Arcades and balconies, borne aloft by tall, slender columns, cover the facade in Art Nouveau elegance. Curved, relief-ornamented gables crown the house of the muses.

Jesuit Church and Convent of Saint Francis, Olinda *(top left)*

Architecture can benefit from nature, and this certainly is the case in Olinda, lying on the Atlantic coast in the Brazilian state of Pernambuco. Its marvellous setting impressed the new Portuguese arrivals in 1535, and the priests and monks who followed them. They built their churches and monasteries in the palm groves on the hills by the sea, thus giving the place the reputation of a 'Baroque Pearl'. In fact the buildings are comparatively plain, as exemplified by the Jesuit church or the Convent of Saint Francis. Their idyllic surroundings turn them into jewels.

Historic Centre, Salvador de Bahia *(top right)*

Church builders have not always made it easy for priests to keep their flock (and themselves) on the straight and narrow. Sinful fantasies were sometimes impossible to suppress when confronted by the naked cherubs in the Baroque houses of worship. This must have been especially difficult for visitors and preachers at the Franciscan church in Brazil's Salvador de Bahia. Here everything sparkles golden, the buttocks and cheeks of the cherubs and the skin of the breastfeeding Mother of God. The other 169 local churches are no less splendid (in the picture: Church of the Way of the Cross). The town, founded in 1548, consists of two distinctly separate parts: the upper town on a long rocky ridge, the lower town immediately on the shore. They are connected by an elevator called the 'Lacerda'. UNESCO World Heritage Site since 1985.

Old City and Carmelite Church, Olinda *(bottom)*

The centre of the Brazilian town of Olinda, north of Recife in the state of Pernambuco, forms an ecclesiastical ensemble: the Cathedral of São Salvador, the Convent of Saint Francis, the Church of Nossa Senhora do Monte, all founded in the 16th century and in parts refurbished after being pillaged by the Dutch in 1630/31. Only the Church of São Bento is a good century younger, and accordingly built in Baroque style. In contrast, the earlier buildings tend to be plainer, especially those of the Carmelite order whose rules require them to observe humility. The Old City of Olinda (in the picture: typical district) has been a UNESCO World Heritage Site since 1982.

National Congress, Brasilia (far top)
Between 1958 and 1970, the architect Oscar Niemeyer built the two office blocks of the parliament (National Congress) on the Plaza of Three Powers in the capital Brasilia. Their adjacency is supposed to symbolise the separation of powers in a democracy, though one is bound to ask what has happened to the third one. Furthermore, in view of the political and social circumstances in this country, many a visitor may feel uncomfortable at the sight of such exuberant symbols cast in concrete and of the emptiness of the wide spaces all around. In 1987, UNESCO declared the synthetic city a World Heritage Site worthy of preservation.

Iguaçu National Park (above left)
Just before the confluence of the Iguaçu and the Paraná rivers, the two neighbouring countries of Brazil and Argentina have established nature reserves. This is a region of species-rich rainforest, where the river – four kilometres wide – leaps down 70 metres from the Brazilian plateau. The national park on the Brazilian side extends across 700 square kilometres, and like its Argentinean 'partner' offers shelter to threatened plants and animals. Yew pine, philodendron and ilex grow in the forest, patrolled by giant otters, ocelots and jaguars. The reserve's inhabitants are at risk from the Salto de Caixas dam that became operational in 1998. UNESCO World Heritage Site since 1986.

Old City, Ouro Prêto (above right)
South-east of Belo Horizonte, in the state of Minas Gerais, the traveller finds a little town that unlike most others has hardly grown since the 18th century. That is why it has retained all its Baroque beauty, which as a gold mining town it could well afford at the time. Among the sites worth seeing on the Praça Tiradentes, named after Joaquim Xavier (nicknamed 'Tooth-puller') who was executed in 1792 for encouraging Brazilian independence and is today revered as a national hero, are the governor's palace and the churches of São Francisco de Assis and Nossa Senhora do Pilar, decorated with masterpieces by Antônio Francisco Lisboa (1730–1814, known as Aleijadinho or 'Little Cripple') and extravagantly gilded. The radiant Old City has been a UNESCO World Heritage Site since 1980.

Good Jesus Pilgrimage Church, Congonhas (top left)

By the time he reached old age he could only crawl on his knees, which is why he was known as Aleijadinho ('Little Cripple'). Even so, the artist born Antônio Francisco Lisboa (1730–1814) continued working on his masterpiece: between 1796 and 1805 he sculpted groups with 66 plaster-covered wooden figures recounting the Story of the Passion, for the six chapels that line the road to the pilgrimage Church of Bom Jesus de Matozinhos in the Brazilian town of Congonhas (Minas Gerais). The scenes prepare the pilgrims for their encounter with a Baroque building of movingly simple beauty. The statue of the artist stands in front of the brown-trimmed, ochre-coloured facade of the Sanctuary, which has been a UNESCO World Heritage Site since 1985.

Sugarloaf Mountain, Rio de Janeiro (top right)

Travellers arriving by air or by sea are greeted from afar by the famous emblem of Rio de Janeiro: Sugarloaf Mountain, or Pao de Açúcar to the locals. 395 metres tall, it captivates by its perfect bell-like form. Behind it to the west rises Corcovado, nearly twice as high. From this peak, a 38 metre tall statue of Christ looks in benediction across the city and the Sugarloaf, whose summit can be reached by cable car. At the visitors' feet lay the bays of the Atlantic, among them the most famous beach, the Copacabana.

Cathedral, Brasilia (bottom)

Circus tent, upside-down vase or broad-legged eggcup? There is probably nothing more difficult in architecture than ecclesiastic buildings, and a kind of ambiguity emanates from this prickly cathedral, built by Oscar Niemeyer between 1960 and 1969 in the Brazilian drawing board capital. One's resistance to this synthetic architecture only dissolves slowly inside, where the sky itself seems to be captured and its light floods the high interior space. But would the Brazilian people's piety feel at home here?

Bolivia

Lake Titicaca *(top)*

The border between Bolivia and Peru runs right through the world's highest navigable lake: at 3812 metres above sea level, Lake Titicaca is at three times the altitude of Ben Nevis. Its area of 8300 square kilometres is almost 140 times that of Loch Lomond. The bottom tilts sharply toward the Bolivian shore, near which it reaches its greatest recorded depth of 281 metres. Numerous islands and peninsulas dot the lake, located north-west of the Bolivian capital in the Andean highlands.

Jesuit Missions of the Chiquitos
(bottom left)

The work of the Jesuits in South America was regarded with growing misgivings by the Spanish authorities. For some in power, the care they provided to the Native Americans went too far. The Jesuits believed in 'civilising' through intensive missionary work, established safe villages for the local population around their missions and also assisted in material improvements. Suspected of encouraging rebelliousness through excessive liberality, the Jesuits were eventually expelled in 1767. In the Chiquitos savannah, north of the Bolivian town of Santa Cruz, seven of their missions are preserved almost intact and have been a UNESCO World Heritage Site since 1990. The picture shows a crucifix dating from the 17th century, made in the Chiquitos tribal areas.

Church of the Virgin, Copacabana
(bottom right)

In the southern reaches of Lake Titicaca, a T-shaped peninsula projects far towards the northeast. On its north-western shore, just inside the Bolivian border, lies the town of Copacabana. Any similarity to Rio's extravagant beach is limited to its name, and if anything it is the exact opposite, its multi-nave Baroque church being a popular pilgrimage destination. At this altitude of 3812 metres, its white walls shine against the deep blue sky. Its lovely recessed gates invite believers to enter, whilst its fortress-like walls deter sinners.

City and Silver Mines, Potosí *(top)*

'The Gate of Hell' was the name given by a priest, as far back as the 16th century, to the silver mines ravine in the 4850 metre high Cerro Rico near Potosí, southwest of Sucre. He was referring to the inhuman working conditions of the Native American slaves, who risked their lives here and in many cases also lost them while the Spanish bosses lived in luxury. The earthly Mammon ensured that the silver city was adorned with grand ecclesiastical buildings and magnificent secular ones. After the end of the boom, these buildings saved a little of the splendour of the colonial era for the dreary new times. As monuments of an early capitalist economy, Potosí and the mountain perforated with shafts have been a UNESCO World Heritage Site since 1987.

Monastery of Philippe Neri, Sucre *(bottom left)*

The ecclesiastical buildings epitomising the old university town of Sucre, Bolivia's official capital, include the monastery named after the popular saint of Rome, Philippe (Filippo in Italian) Neri (1515–1595). He founded the Oratorian order, which in the main looks after pilgrims. Anyone who comes to Sucre searching for faith and visits the beautiful old houses of God, will find at the monastery advice and also accommodation. The attractive inner courtyard is made for a stroll, the tower – just right for gazing across the city over the tiled roofs and for planning a sightseeing tour.

Old City, Sucre *(bottom right)*

In 1538, the Spanish conquistador Pizarro founded the town of Villa de la Plata on the site of a native settlement in the Bolivian mountains. Since 1825 it has borne the name of Antonio José Sucre (1795–1830), hero of the War of Independence. Proximity to productive silver deposits bestowed wealth on the city, thus generating diligent Baroque building activity and an unusually charming townscape. These features are preserved almost unchanged, and give the country's constitutional capital – which long since has been eclipsed by the seat of government La Paz – an ambience of the colonial era. Both ecclesiastical and secular buildings (in the picture: government palace) contribute to this atmosphere, and in 1991 caused UNESCO to honour the Old City of Sucre as a World Heritage Site.

Uruguay

Paraguay

Calle Emilio Reus, Montevideo *(top left)*

Montevideo is quite young among the Spanish settlements in South America: it was only founded in 1724 and has been Uruguay's capital since its independence in 1830, following the end of Spanish-Argentinean-British-Brazilian hostilities. It is almost the only city in the country worth mentioning, since close to half the population live in this 1.4 million strong metropolis. Many parts are attractively designed, for example around the Calle Emilio Reus, a splendid street in every sense of the word. The colourful houses march on in cheerful variety, as though a high-spirited painter wanted to try out his palette. The rows of arched windows and the garlanded balconies seem like the incarnation of Spanish guitar music.

Cathedral, Maldonado *(top right)*

The bell tower roofs of the Cathedral of Maldonado seem to have fetched down their blue from the sky, and the sun is kind to its facade. It glows against the background of the beautiful dome on the palm-fringed square, a busy communication centre as in all Spanish-South American towns. The only quiet times are during Mass and in the midday heat, when everyone has found a shady corner for the siesta. But in the mild evenings, the scene becomes lively again in front of the cathedral's ecclesiastical backdrop, which looks down tolerantly on the colourful hustle and bustle in this coastal town in Uruguay's south-eastern corner.

Cathedral, Asunción *(centre)*

The Cathedral of Asunción, Paraguay's capital and largest city with 500,000 inhabitants, seems almost small. But a century ago this was a town of only 20,000 people, and then it was quite a magnificent cathedral. It was built soon after Asunción's foundation in 1537, and was so impressively designed because this was the starting point for the Spanish colonisation of the South American interior, and because the new rulers wanted to display their status as God's emissaries. The fortress-like nature of the walls also served to demonstrate strength.

Jesuit Missions of La Santísima Trinidad de Paraná and Jesús de Tavarangue *(bottom)*

During the early period of Spanish colonial exploration in the New World, the central authority's arm did not reach particularly far. Just as the ever-present marauding adventurers had to be left alone, so the governors hardly managed to control the missionaries either, at least to begin with. It was mainly the Jesuits who concerned themselves with the subjugated population's 'spiritual salvation'. But they also defended their protégés against exploiters and other riff-raff, as shown by the so-called 'reductions' or Indian colonies in which the missionaries organised Amerindian community life. Two such facilities, with their beautiful Baroque churches, are preserved in Trinidad de Paraná and in Tavarangue, northeast of the Paraguayan town of Encarnación near the Argentinian border. They have been a UNESCO World Heritage Site since 1993.

Argentina

Mount Aconcagua *(top left)*

Mount Everest of the southern hemisphere cannot quite compete with its northern counterpart, but in terms of most countries it does reach almost Himalayan proportions: at 6,959 metres, Aconcagua in the Argentinian Andes is the loftiest summit in the Americas and the highest mountain outside Asia. The 'stone guardian', as its name could be translated, stands in a nature reserve over 700 square kilometres in size, established for one thing because the mighty mountain attracts climbers from all over the world, a Swiss having been the first to climb it in 1897. But only practised Alpinists should try to emulate him: the icy desert on the upper slopes demands top form.

San Ignacio Miní *(top right)*

The largest of the so-called Indian 'reductions', or Jesuit colonies, in northern Argentina on the Paraná was San Ignacio Miní. The ruins of the 74 metre long and 24 metre wide Baroque church, with its Native relief decorations, still permit the settlement's structure to be recognised: the most important facilities – workshops, community house, classrooms, cemetery, gaol – were grouped around a large square. Today, a very well equipped museum tells the story of the Jesuits' activities and their care of the Guaraní. 4,000 of them lived for a while in the safe village founded in the 17th century, soon abandoned by its inhabitants after the Jesuits' expulsion in 1767.

Jesuit Missions of the Guaraní *(centre)*

The centre of the Jesuit missions in the 17th and 18th centuries was in Paraguay, but in the south they reached all the way to today's Argentina. There, east of Posadas, the remains of four so-called Indian 'reductions' or Jesuit colonies are preserved, Guaraní communities under Jesuit management and Jesuit protection: San Ignacio Miní, Santa Ana, Nuestra Señora de Loreto and Santa María la Mayor. Visitors to the ruins can see that the Jesuits by no means imposed their own European culture to the exclusion of everything else. They left the Natives plenty of cultural freedom, so that we may speak of Guaraní Baroque. Unfortunately, after the missionaries' expulsion in 1767 the reductions rapidly fell into disrepair. Their remains are preserved as a UNESCO World Heritage Site (1983). The picture on the right shows a 17th century scorch drawing on parchment, on which the creed developed by the Jesuits can be read in pictorial writing.

Valdés *(bottom)*

On the San Matias Gulf, about 300 kilometres south of the town of Bahia Blanca in eastern Argentina, the 3,250 square kilometre Valdés peninsula projects eastward into the Atlantic. This is a nature reserve, protecting its fauna against disturbance as far as possible: sea birds fly above the shore, seals rest on it and whales swim along it – a zoological Garden of Eden, although its botanical component is rather light on the ground since like elsewhere in Patagonia, the land can only offer sparse vegetation. In contrast, the sea contains a jewel: the Isla de los Pájaros, where many of the birds breed. With a good pair of binoculars it is possible to observe their colonies, but only handpicked ornithologists may set foot on the rocky island.

Patagonia *(top)*

Big country: in Argentina's south, the plains never want to end. Patagonia begins beyond the Río Colorado, stretches all the way down to Tierra del Fuego and covers an area of 650,000 square kilometres. The only variety in the landscape takes place east to west, a direction in which the land rises first into hills and moderate mountains and finally into the high mountains of the southern Andes, at an altitude of up to 4,000 metres. As a result, the Argentinian plateau lies in the rain shadow of this mountain range and only sparse bush and grass vegetation can survive. Huge herds of sheep graze here, occasionally right next to drilling towers, since the only natural resource of Patagonia is the oil around Comodoro Rivadavia and Plaza Huincul.

Auca Mahuida Volcano, Patagonia
(centre left)

When we think 'eggs', we mostly imagine something nicely smooth and oval. The Dinosaurs saw this quite differently, since the eggs of these 'terrible lizards' appear rather sacklike and trapezoid. Nor can there be any talk of smoothness, since the young monsters' packaging prior to hatching was as knobbly and deeply grooved as the skin of the adults. We know all this from finds such as these at the volcano Auca Mahuida at the northernmost tip of the Argentinian region of Patagonia, between the rivers Negro and Colorado. The conical peak rises to 2,253 metres, and we can imagine with a slight shudder how millions of years ago the dinosaurs, with their long necks, peeped out between the treetops and the boulders.

Ushuaia, Tierra del Fuego *(centre right)*

The 'End of the World', as the inhabitants of the capital of the Argentinian part of Tierra del Fuego (Land of Fire) themselves call their higgledy-piggledy collection of houses at Ushuaia, does not look exactly homely. Several concrete castles, a few huts but also a row of smarter colonial buildings make up the assemblage on a bay in the Beagle Channel. This windy corner of the world has always been notorious among seafarers, and the Museo del Fin del Mundo in Ushuaia shows why: there is flotsam and jetsam of all sorts from foundered ships, as well as photographs of picturesque wrecks. Tierra del Fuego National Park, 20 kilometres further west on the Chilean border, is also worth a visit.

Los Glaciares National Park *(bottom)*

Climate researchers almost everywhere look on anxiously as glaciers shrink and the ice caps become thinner. They may feel better after a visit to the Los Glaciares National Park in Argentinian Patagonia, lying between Lake Viedma and Lake Argentino on the Chilean border in the Andes. Here they can admire the largest ice field outside the Polar regions, with a total glacier area of 22,000 square kilometres of which 6,000 square kilometres are under - protection in the park. For example, the Moreno glacier sticks out its icy tongue, 60 kilometres long and five kilometres wide and constantly growing. Will the greenhouse effect give Los Glaciares a wide berth? The condors, majestically circling over the huge expanses of ice, don't seem too bothered.

Chile

Rapa Nui National Park *(top)*

When the Dutch captain Jacob Roggeveen saw the island on Easter Sunday 1722, being the first European to arrive here, he must have had quite a fright: from the high shores of Easter Island (Isla de Pascua in Spanish), he was stared at threateningly by giants, the so-called Moai. To this day it has not proved possible to interpret conclusively what these tuff figures, some over ten metres tall and up to 240 tonnes in weight, really mean. The predominant opinion is that they are an expression of ancestor worship by the Polynesian inhabitants, who settled down at the 'Navel of the World' or the 'Big Place' (Rapa Nui) around 350 AD. Their artistic creativity is also displayed in several thousand carved rock drawings, which as part of the national park have belonged to the UNESCO World Heritage Site since 1995.

Volcano, Osorno *(bottom)*

For over 100 years this perfect volcano, southeast of the Chilean port of Valdivia, has shown itself only from its nice, snow-white side. But is it really extinct? There are countless examples of craters that had remained quiet for very much longer, and nevertheless started again spewing fire and destruction. Be that as it may, the cooled lava layer at the foot of the 2660 metre high mountain has produced fertile soil and flourishing forests.

Australia
and Oceania

Multi-faceted far south

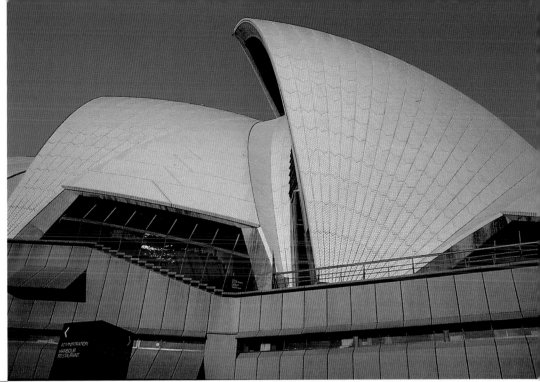

'Terra australis incognita' — unknown southern land. That is what the European seafarers of the early 16th century called the fifth continent before it was recognised as such. And even today we can barely talk about knowing it. Why has this land on the opposite side of the globe developed so differently from the other continents, with its marsupials and eucalyptus forests? When exactly did it separate from the Eurasian giant? And what was its human prehistory like? We know all this only in outline at best. Of course, rock drawings from ancient times and the customs and myths of today's Aborigines tell us a certain amount about the pre-European past, but this is a far cry from a full understanding of this alien world, if such cross-cultural comprehension in the true sense of the word is even possible. The magnitude

and beauty of the task may be symbolised by the rock that the Aborigines call Uluru and we know in English as Ayers Rock. Just as it changes in the shifting light, so does the only inhabited continent lying entirely in the Southern Hemisphere, with its Oceanic-Polynesian island world, vary its appearance to the visitor. Worlds separate the tropical regions on the Gulf of Carpentaria from the Antarctic wilderness around Admiralty Mountains, and equally remote from each other are the unending outback and the vibrant cities founded after the arrival of the First Fleet in 1788. Sydney, host to the first Olympic summer games of the third millennium, is one of them. Its opera house is both a memorial to the historic landing at the historic site, and a banner for the future: Full sail ahead!

CHINA

JAPAN

Bonin-Is.
(Jap.)

Ryukyu Is.

Vulcan-Is.
(Jap.)

CHINA

Okino-tori-Is.
(Jap.)

Wake (USA

M a r i a n a I s.

(USA)

Saipan○

Luzon

P H I L I P P I N E S

MARSHALL-ISLA

Philippine

Sea

Guam
(USA)

FEDER. STATES

Kolonia○

Dalap-Ulig

Mindanao

Palau Is.○
Koror

OF MICRONESIA

Talaud

PALAU

Morota

Borneo

Yaren○
Coral structures

Biak

Celebes

Sula

New
Guinea

PAPUA

Bismarck
Archipelago

NAURU

INDONESIA

NEW GUINEA

Bougainville

Kai Besar

Coral atoll

SOLOMON
ISLANDS

Honiara○

Tanimbar

Port
Moresby

Timor

●
Christmas Is.

Melville

Darwin●

Kakadu
National Park

Coral

VANUATU

Sea

Kimberley Plateau●

Cairns○

Broome●

Townsville○

New
Kaledonia
(Fr.)

○Por

●Great Barrier Reef

Norfolk
(Austr

Devil's Marbles●

Nouméa

Shark Bay
Marine Park●

Uluru ●
National Park

○Alice Springs

●Fraser Is.

A U S T R A L I A

Glasshouse Mountains●
●Brisbane

Geraldton
○

●Rainforest Parks

Nambung
National Park●

Kalgoorlie
○

Bourke○

○Perth

●Wave Rock

Port Augusta○

Newcastle
●

Albany○

○Adelaide

Blue Mountains●
Canberra●

●Sydney
●Wollongong

Kangaroo Is.●

●Mount Kosciusko

S O U T H E R N

Melbourne●

Port Campbell●

●Wilson's Promontory
National Park

O C E A N

King Is.

South

South-West
National Park●

Tasmania

C
Mount Coo

●Port Arthur

Fjordland
National Park●

○Inver

Snares Is.●

Admiralty Mountains,
Ross Dependency (NZ)

Auckland Is. ● ●Campbel

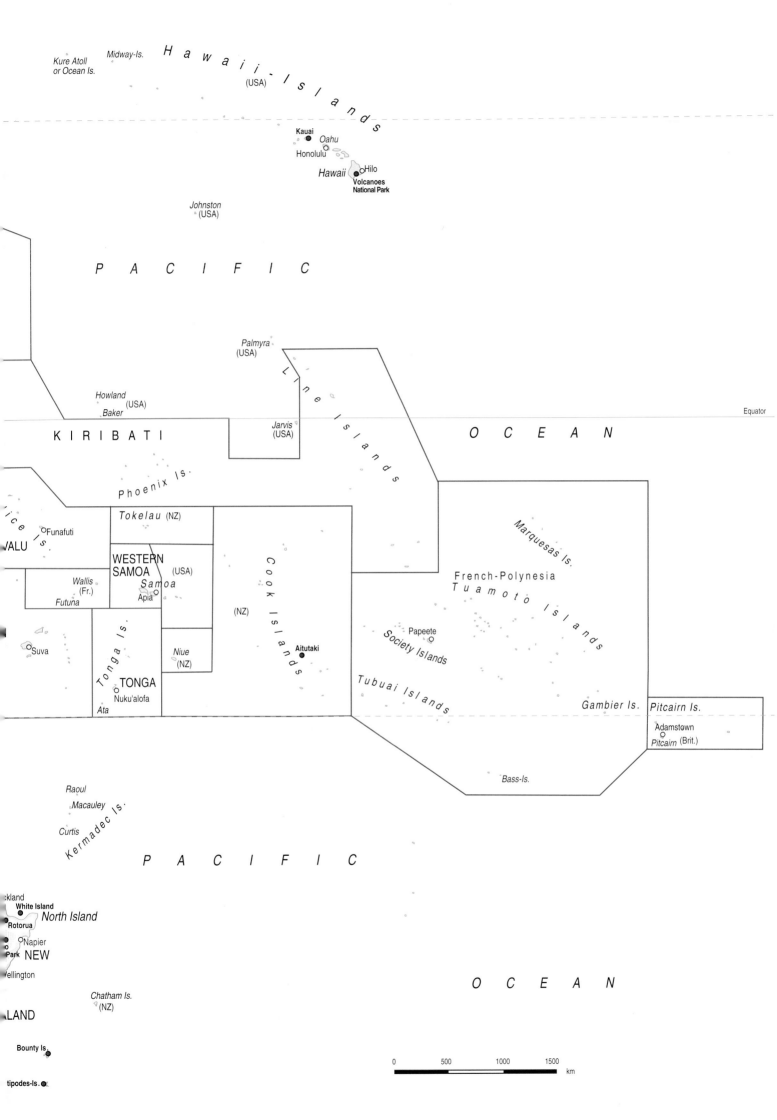

Kure Atoll
or Ocean Is.

Midway-Is.

H a w a i i - I s l a n d s

(USA)

Kauai
●
Oahu
○
Honolulu
Hawaii ●
○ Hilo
**Volcanoes
National Park**

Johnston
(USA)

P   A   C   I   F   I   C

Palmyra
(USA)

Howland
(USA)
Baker

L i n e   I s l a n d s

Equator

Jarvis
(USA)

K   I   R   I   B   A   T   I

O   C   E   A   N

Phoenix Is.

Tokelau (NZ)

ice Is.

○Funafuti

ALU

**WESTERN
SAMOA**

(USA)
Samoa
○
Apia

Marquesas Is.

French-Polynesia

T u a m o t o   I s l a n d s

Wallis
(Fr.)
Futuna

C o o k   I s l a n d s

(NZ)

○Suva

Tonga Is.

Niue
(NZ)

Aitutaki
●

Papeete
○
Society Islands

Tubuai Islands

○
TONGA
Nuku'alofa

Ata

Gambier Is.

Pitcairn Is.

Adamstown
○
Pitcairn (Brit.)

Bass-Is.

Raoul

Macauley

Kermadec Is.

Curtis

P   A   C   I   F   I   C

ckland

White Island
●
North Island
●
Rotorua
●
○Napier
○
Park NEW

ellington

Chatham Is.
(NZ)

O   C   E   A   N

LAND

Bounty Is.
●

0   500   1000   1500

tipodes-Is. ●

km

Hawaii *(USA)*

Waimea Canyon, Kauai *(bottom)*

Hell's jaws seem to open up right next to the Garden of Eden on the island of Kauai in the Hawaii chain: the yawning chasm of the Waimea Canyon that opened up during the island's volcanic formation. Unlike on the windward side, here in the lee (the mountains' wind shadow) there predominates a relatively dry climate, and yet defiant shrubs and trees have established a foothold in the rock cracks. They make the bizarre faults and folds of the rocks appear milder, and the adventurous wanderers who are not stopped by any inhospitable terrain find a little shade: from here they can enjoy a great view of this stony world.

Volcanoes National Park, Hawaii *(top)*

A total of 930 square kilometres on the islands of Maui and Hawaii in the Hawaiian archipelago have been under protection since 1916, since they offer a peerless volcanic hell right by the sea and in the tropical paradise of the islands. Mauna Loa spews fire at an altitude of 4,169 metres, and glowing lava flows from the neighbouring crater Kilauea down to the valley during eruptions. There it cools down and becomes fertile soil for a forest of giant ferns. In the volcanically formed landscape live many plants that are indigenous nowhere else, while the fauna is rather sparse apart from a few bird species. UNESCO World Heritage Site since 1987.

Australia

Christmas Island (top)

Of all times in the year, it is the Christmas period when the otherwise lively Australian tourist flow to Christmas Island dies down. The ones who do come are quite different: they are travellers who are interested in marine biology, rather than the usual surfers and divers. This is because every December the island is overrun by an invasion of crabs, and anyone who thus far never knew what the expression 'red as a lobster' means certainly will know after witnessing a host of these animals. They do not walk as far as the hotels in Flying Fish, the main town on the 135 square kilometre Christmas Island, located almost 1,000 miles northwest of the Australian mainland, south of Java in the Indian Ocean; or at most turn up there as a tasty Christmas dinner.

Kakadu National Park (bottom right)

Nature needs space. This was taken into consideration by the Australian authorities when they established Kakadu National Park in Arnhemland, southeast of Darwin on Van Diemen Gulf: nearly 20,000 square kilometres of nature conservation and protection. Many mammals live in this land of open eucalyptus forest and water, including dugongs and the increasingly rare Australian ghost bat. The rivers and the mud flats swarm with over 100 reptilian species, among them death adders, green sea turtles and estuarine crocodiles. The air is ruled by almost 300 bird species, including the white-bellied sea eagle. UNESCO World Heritage Site since 1981.

Aborigine Art,
Kakadu National Park (bottom left)

Nature conservation in the enormous North Australian Kakadu National Park (about half the size of Switzerland) also benefits cultural concerns: in the south, across more than 500 kilometres, spreads the Arnhem Escarpment, a rugged rocky landscape created by erosion. Humans lived here over 50,000 years ago, and immortalised their world and culture in numerous rock drawings of great artistic brilliance. The drawings represent people, animals and their interaction. Some figures dance, others are in discussion, fantastic fish swim about, game animals jump and run away. A fascinating gallery of prehistoric art, and since 1981 a UNESCO World Heritage Site.

Great Barrier Reef *(bottom left)*

For over 2,000 kilometres, from the Tropic of Capricorn all the way to Cape York, in fact even beyond it towards New Guinea, the coral reefs march on against the East Australian coast and together form the Great Barrier Reef. It is the largest living reef system on earth and covers around 200,000 square kilometres. Almost the entire area is under protection, and has been a UNESCO World Heritage Site since 1981. Whether this will succeed in saving it from unrestricted tourism in the long term, is something only the future can tell. At any rate, it provides a home for 4,000 species of molluscs, 450 of corals, 1,500 of fish, six of turtles and 24 species of sea birds. It is worth mentioning, in particular, that the reef protects a 'delivery room' of the humpback whales.

Rock Drawings, Kimberley Plateau *(bottom right)*

The Australian Aborigines have been practising the art of rock drawings for many thousands of years. The earliest are characterised by realistic representation, later ones exhibit a symbolist and even later an ornamental or decorative phase. The common feature to all, including nowadays, is their magical character and an intensive dialogue of forms and colours with nature and metaphysical forces. Very well preserved drawings, up to 75,000 years old, are found on the walls of the nearly 1,000 metre high Kimberley Plateau in north-western Australia. Scientists take measurements and safeguard them.

Shark Bay Marine Park *(far bottom)*

Between Carnarvon in the north and Geraldton in the south, where Australia projects furthest westward into the Indian Ocean, the sea is full of frolicking dolphins and humpback whales, dugongs laze about on the beach, hare kangaroos spar on land while ospreys circle overhead. They can all do so quite unmolested since ca. 10,000 square kilometres around Shark Bay are a conservation area. Many small facilities have been unified into one nature park, to which one may also be grateful for valuable palaeontological finds, including traces of the earliest life forms which scientists estimate are over three billion years old. UNESCO World Heritage Site since 1991.

Nambung National Park (bottom)

North of the West Australian city of Perth one encounters dry bush country, with a whole series of dunes. But before the traveller can become bored, it presents startling surprises: from the yellow sandy soil grow thousands of columns and rock chunks, some up to four metres tall, sticking up like carious teeth from an underground mouth. This came about because the local chalk-rich sand layers were forested here after the Ice Age, and eventually the trees used up the available chalk. Where no trees grew it solidified and remained standing stubbornly when the wind blew away the soil from under the former forest. Hence the stumps, known as The Pinnacles.

Wave Rock Wheatlands (far bottom left)

An imaginative artist has been at work here, drawing water into solid shapes on a massive scale. It is doubtful whether any human mind could have created this: but north of Albany and southeast of Perth in the farthest Australian southwest, the poet Nature has made a wave solidify into rock such that no artist could have painted. You stare at it in the expectation that any second now, the 15 metre tall granite formation will turn into a breaker with a crown of stony foam. However, the wave stands rigidly spellbound in the landscape of the Wheatlands, forever frozen in its motion.

Uluru-Kata Tjuta National Park
(far bottom right)

The name Kata Tjuta means 'many heads' in the Aborigine language. This is a rocky landscape in Uluru National Park, named after the famous red monolith also known in English as Ayers Rock in honour of a former Australian prime minister. Kata Tjuta, with its highest peak Mount Olga, lies about 30 kilometres further southwest and is almost the exact opposite of Uluru: whatever is round and soft in the latter, is rugged and angular at Kata Tjuta. This is because the rocky massif, at 1,052 metres considerably higher than Uluru, consists not of sandstone but of conglomerate rocks fused together. Only the domes of those 36 rocks are eroded and round, and below them the walls fall down steeply into fields of sharp boulders.

Ayers Rock, Uluru, Uluru – Kata Tjuta National Park *(top)*

Uluru (Ayers Rock) is not exactly imposing in its dimensions: its summit reaches only 863 metres above sea level and 343 metres above the surrounding terrain; it measures only nine kilometres in circumference. The rock stands lonely as an island in the empty landscape. During the day it shimmers in red, and glows when the rising or setting sun add to its colour. No wonder that the Aborigines regard it as a sacred object that plays a central part in their myths. Now its magic is threatened by the modern tourist hustle and bustle, despite the national park established in 1977 and the sandstone monument's listing as a UNESCO World Heritage Site (1987).

Devil's Marbles *(centre)*

Anyone travelling on the Stuart Highway from Alice Springs in the heart of Australia towards the north in the direction of Tennant Creek, and having passed Wauchope, should allow themselves a break. After well over 300 kilometres this is more than deserved. But a fiendish surprise awaits the unprepared not far from the road: the Devil's Marbles stare grimly at the traveller. These are head-like round rocks, scattered across the terrain like marbles, gazing into the wilderness out of deep, weathered eye sockets. Those not up to this shock should grab their mobile phone and alert the Flying Doctors, who will save them free of charge from the devil's spell.

Fraser Island *(bottom)*

Off the East Australian coast, 250 kilometres north of Brisbane, stretches the world's largest sand island: 125 kilometres long and up to 22 kilometres wide. One should not imagine it as merely a large dune, although there are dunes aplenty; one even rising 230 metres high. But in addition, the island supports a rainforest, which is not seen anywhere else growing on sand. After sitting on the endless white beach, you can dive straight into the shady green or the blue of the sea. Mangroves and various eucalyptus species have also established themselves in several places. The timber of the Satinay palms has long been particularly sought-after for ship building, and had a nature conservation area not been established in 1972, and a UNESCO World Heritage Site in 1992, this forest and bird paradise would probably not exist today.

Glasshouse Mountains *(top left)*

North of Brisbane in eastern Australia, the lovely landscape suddenly grows mounds: island-mountains rise up sharply like tents. In profile they look like the fronts of greenhouses, hence their name, Glasshouse Mountains. From their peaks one has a wide view out to sea, where further north Fraser Island comes into view, a sandy beauty in the Ocean. No less enchanting is the view across the land, pampered by summer rain, a lush green that provides plentiful food for well nourished livestock. Forests flourish between the 'Glasshouses', a favourite leisure destination for towndwellers.

Mountain Landscapes around Mount Kosciusko *(top right)*

In den Snowy Mountains of the Great Dividing Range in southern New South Wales, the continent reaches its highest point of 2,230 metres at Mount Kosciusko. Both here and along the rest of the east Australian mountains, ranging from Cape York all the way to the southern tip of Tasmania, the scenery is quite reminiscent of the Black Forest and other European forests. The highest elevation in Australia is named after the Polish hero, who in 1794 rebelled against Russia and Prussia and despite ultimate defeat became a hero to all Polish patriots. Many of them went into exile, and not a few to the Southern Land (which is what Australia means). A ski resort was developed around the small giant, kept in check by the establishment of a national park of 5,300 square kilometres in size.

Blue Mountains *(centre)*

The view from Sydney in eastern Australia towards the west conjures up a holiday atmosphere: the Blue Mountains, reached via Parramatta, shimmer from afar like an azure ribbon. Once there, this range turns out to be a high sandstone plateau with deeply cut gorges, steep drops, roaring waterfalls and sharp rock needles such as the famous Three Sisters at Katoomba. In the Australian spring between September and December, wild flowers bloom and turn the mountains to a rock garden. Forest and thickets turn green and the air is full of eucalyptus aroma.

Conservation Areas of the Temperate and Subtropical Rainforest *(bottom)*

Over 50 conservation areas for the shrinking rainforest in central-eastern Australia were joined together by the country's environmental authorities into one national park. It covers both temperate and subtropical rainforest, and extends from the coast on the border between the states of Queensland and New South Wales into the interior. It is designed to protect the typical Australian flora and fauna. Among the animals this involves mainly a whole range of marsupials, including various kangaroo species, flying fox bats as well as numerous bird species such as Wonga pigeons, barn owls and scrub birds. UNESCO World Heritage Site since 1986.

Harbour Bridge, Sydney *(top left)*

Eight car lanes and two railway tracks lead across Harbour Bridge from the north, 50 metres above the water, into the harbour district of the largest city on the fifth continent. This is a steel arch structure built in 1932, spanning 503 metres, affectionately known by Sydney's residents as the Coat Hanger. It groans under the weight of traffic and would have collapsed long ago, since the travel bug has infected this city of four million too, and only a tunnel managed to save the veteran bridge. A small museum in one of the towers teaches the story of its construction, and a beautiful view across the city can be had from the Coat Hanger's viewing platform, reached via 200 steps.

Melbourne *(top right)*

The most southerly metropolis in Australia is also regarded as the most English on the smallest continent. The capital of the Australian state of Victoria, which between 1901–1927 was even the seat of government, was founded in 1835 and named after the then British prime minister Lord Melbourne. It is full of buildings in the Neo-Gothic and — as here — Neo-Renaissance style. But it has not rested on its old laurels, instead opting for rapid modernisation that was further accelerated when the Olympic summer games were held here in 1956. Thus, a fascinating mix of the old and the new characterises the cityscape of this industrial metropolis, the headquarters of many business conglomerates.

Opera House, Sydney *(centre)*

Sydney Opera House stands today where the first settlers landed over 200 years ago. Its roof is a concrete construction weighing 21,000 tonnes, emulating the shape of sails and harking back to the landing of the First Fleet in 1788. The 100 million dollar wonder, designed in 1957 by the Danish architect Jörn Utzon (born 1918) and opened in 1973, is 67 metres high, 183 long and 118 wide. In the concert hall it has 2,700 seats, in the opera 1,500 and in the theatre 500. Once hotly argued about, today it is the pride and the emblem of the greatest city on the smallest continent.

Dunes at Wilson's Promontory *(bottom)*

The Australian mainland reaches its most southerly point at Cape Wilson in the state of Victoria, at the foothills known as Wilson's Promontory or Prom for short, on a bay across which the foothills of the Australian Alps come into view and form a sweeping skyline. Its counterpart is the swell of the sea in the 210 kilometre wide Bass Strait that connects the Southern Ocean to the Tasman Sea. The gentle dunes on the peninsula merge into wide sandy beaches, and just like the mountains in the interior, invite the visitor to long, leisurely walks.

Remarkable Rocks, Kangaroo Island
(top left)

100 kilometres south-west of Adelaide in South Australia, at the eastern end of the Great Australian Bight off Encounter Bay, lies the continent's third largest island: the wildly romantic Kangaroo Island, where the kangaroos are so tame that they beg for food from visitors. The wilder side is found mainly along the shore at Cape du Couedic where the breakers have shaped the rocks into Admiral's Arch, and a little way further back on the beach where the wind and spray have also been busy sculpting. To them we owe the Remarkable Rocks, hollowed out, rounded or worked into giant hand axes. A truly remarkable sculpture park.

Twelve Apostles, Port Campbell
(top right)

Imperturbable in the thundering surf, these rocks jut up near Port Campbell in the western part of the Australian state of Victoria. They are probably called the Twelve Apostles because of the equanimity with which they stand up to terrestrial storms. Mind you, as regards imperturbability, this is only true for today's visitors who can enjoy the unchanging yet manifold shapes of these rocky saints: their bizarre forms are due to obstinate sculpting by weather, wind and water. It took them many millennia to create this grandiose, wave-enveloped landscape of arches, gorges, caves and in particular upright Apostles, and still they continue working on it.

Church of Port Arthur, Tasmania *(centre)*

100 kilometres east of Hobart, the capital of the Australian state of Tasmania, you reach the Tasman Peninsula, and there you stand amazed in front of ruins. The 65 000 square kilometre island, 'hanging' under the continent's south-eastern corner, was discovered in 1642; it has only been known as Tasmania, after its discoverer, since 1856. Its name was changed around the time that the deportation of convicts to the island as slave labour, ongoing since 1803, was discontinued. They also built the Neo-Gothic church, where today the sea wind howls so romantically through the empty window frames.

South-West National Park, Tasmania *(bottom)*

The whites that came to Tasmania at the end of the 18th century made sure that none of the native inhabitants survived. They also plundered the island's natural resources pitilessly for a long time, until those with a less blinkered view realised that continued overexploitation would cut off the very branch on which they were sitting. That is why a whole series of conservation areas was set up in the south-western part of the island, where nature has managed to recover and rejuvenate itself. Eucalyptus trees up to 90 metres tall grow here; and in the forest, bush and mountains, animals such as the Tasmanian devil, the brush-tail possum, skinks, swift parrots and many others have found sanctuary. UNESCO World Heritage Site since 1982.

Nauru

Solomon Islands

Corals along the Coast, Nauru *(top)*

Where there are corals, there are fish. Nowhere else do the swimming flashes of colour find such good hiding places as in the branched and pronged system of the reefs (in the picture: Yellow Emperor Fish). The tiny, 20 square kilometre state of Nauru on a South Sea island is fringed by countless reefs that afford the inhabitants a little extra income. For decades they did not have to rely on it, since the phosphates accumulated in huge deposits of bird dung (guano) provided the country with unimagined wealth. But the end of the boom is on the cards, therefore the local population concentrates on the undersea natural treasures, promotes tourism and hopes for an upturn in the fishing industry.

Coral Atoll, East Rennell *(bottom)*

The island group of the Solomon Islands east of New Guinea includes numerous coral islands. One of them is the raised coral atoll of East Rennell, where this photograph was taken. It shows the stunning beauty of reefs (in the picture: horn corals), sadly threatened by increasing sea pollution. In many places, the island-building coelenterates have already died and become bleached. But here in the expanses of the Pacific, corals still flourish magnificently. They form shrub-like, branched or cup-shaped limestone skeletons that can appear black, white or red. The skeletons are used by the inhabitants of the South Sea islands to make imaginative ornaments and jewellery.

New Zealand

Cook Islands, Aitutaki (top)

Anyone whose heart does not beat faster must have the soul of a filing cabinet: palms, beach, sea, sky – you can virtually hear the tunes 'Bali Hai' and 'Some Enchanted Evening' from South Pacific playing in the breeze. This atmospheric image certainly applies to Cook Islands, or more accurately in this case to one of the most southerly among them, Aitutaki, lying in the south-westerly reaches of Polynesia and belonging to New Zealand, several thousand kilometres away. Countless such fairytale beaches surrounding quiet lagoons are scattered here in the Pacific, and some can even be bought from island vendors. Mind you, getting in supplies across the vast expanses of the ocean can turn out to be problematic, and anything but dreamlike.

Whakarri Volcano, White Island
(bottom left)

New Zealand has a whole series of Volcanoes, the most active of which, Whakarri, is on White Island off the northern coast of North Island. In November 1999 (see picture) it spewed gas and clouds of steam once again into the South Pacific sky, attracting hordes of sometimes rash visitors. Time and time again, the volcanologists and seismologists working here must intervene and draw attention to the dangers that threaten excessively bold climbing expeditions: eruptions can disgorge a lot of material from the depths of the earth. Then it may rain ash or even stones to a distance that is difficult to judge.

Tongariro National Park (bottom right)

As far back as 1884, New Zealand's authorities placed the heart of North Island, the Tongariro region with its three active and three extinct volcanoes, under protection. At Ruapehu the mountain massif reaches an altitude of 2,800 metres. On its flanks in the national park grow orchids, ferns, myrtles and inaka, the South Sea variety of our heathers. The local animal world is safe, at least to a certain extent, from the domestic and wild animals brought along by Europeans, such as cats and martens, against the attacks of which flightless birds like kiwis are helpless. Even with this protection there are recurring losses, mainly to feral dogs. The glacier-crowned park has been a UNESCO World Heritage Site since 1990.

Whakarewarewa Thermal Region near Rotorua *(top)*

East of the town of Rotorua, the north coast of New Zealand's North Island rises steadily to an altitude of 1700 metres. The forested slopes of the Whakarewarewa region are a restless tectonic terrain, where volcanic and geothermal activities take place ceaselessly. Fumaroles, geysers and hot springs send up clouds from underground towards those floating high up in the sky, and give the scene something of the character of stage productions where mist swirls around the actors' feet. Wandering about in the mist from the depth is not recommended, or at least only with an expert guide.

Fjordland National Park *(bottom left)*

New Zealand's south-western coast looks like a slightly smaller version of the Norwegian one: a whole series of fjords divides it up and cuts just as powerfully into the land, which in the south reaches an altitude of 1700 metres and in the north – over 2700 metres. The 12 250 square kilometres of this region make up a large proportion of the national park, to which the area around Mount Cook also belongs. The wild terrain, with its waterfalls and quiet bays, was placed under protection as far back as 1904, allowing a large colony of Australian fur seals to arise and rare New Zealand birds like the kakapo and tahake to survive. In 1990 UNESCO added the Fjordland to its list of World Heritage Sites.

Mount Cook *(bottom right)*

The mountain range known as the New Zealand Alps stretches along the south-western part of South Island. They really do deserve their name: even restricting ourselves to just the 26 000 square kilometres of the national park around Mount Cook, or Aoraki the Cloud Piercer (at 3764 metres, the country's highest mountain), we can find 28 peaks above 3000 metres rising into the South Sea sky. In places one feels vividly reminded of the landscape around the Matterhorn and other Alpine summits. Just like there, New Zealand's high mountains support ski tourism. And here too there are glaciers, such as the 29 kilometre long Tasman glacier. Many threatened animal species find sanctuary in the national park. As a UNESCO World Heritage Site since 1990, it also enjoys international protection.

Antarctica

Antarctica

Endless tracts: this almost completely ice-covered continent is larger than either Australia or Europe, and almost as large as both put together. The interior is inhospitable and menacing. That is why you would not find it in an ordinary travel brochure. In any event, a cruise along the coast with its gigantic icebergs is well worthwhile, with boat excursions to the offshore islands that are only inhabited by penguins, seals and birds. The morning and evening sun conjures up fabulous colours on the icebergs and ice floes, and with a bit of luck you can see the polar lights flickering in the sky above the South Pole.

Index

Picture sources